PRAISE FOR
PLANET INDIA

"This book is an absolute *must*-read. It's by far the best book on India and globalization to date and on top of that it's a fun read."
—Clyde Prestowitz, author of *Rogue Nation* and
Three Billion New Capitalists

"A brisk and conversation-filled ride through India's corporate offices, film studios, farms, and slums. Kamdar is an engaging writer."
—Ramachandra Guha, *Financial Times*

"This briskly written, vivid account shows how that subcontinental country's films, technology, and service industries have made India an ever-growing presence on the American scene."
—*The Atlantic Monthly*

"*Planet India* is a worthy addition to the burgeoning shelf of serious books about twenty-first-century India."
—Shashi Tharoor, *The Times of India*

ALSO BY MIRA KAMDAR

Motiba's Tattoos

Planet
INDIA

*The Turbulent Rise of the Largest
Democracy and the Future of Our World*

M IRA K AMDAR

S CRIBNER

N EW Y ORK   L ONDON   T ORONTO   S YDNEY

SCRIBNER
A Division of Simon & Schuster, Inc.
1230 Avenue of the Americas
New York, NY 10020

First Scribner trade paperback edition February 2008

SCRIBNER and design are trademarks of
Macmillan Library Reference USA, Inc., used under license
by Simon & Schuster, the publisher of this work.

For information about special discounts for bulk purchases,
please contact Simon & Schuster Special Sales at
1-800-456-6798 or business@simonandschuster.com.

Designed by Kyoko Watanabe
Text set in Sabon

Manufactured in the United States of America

1 3 5 7 9 10 8 6 4 2

Library of Congress Control Number: 2006052300

ISBN-13: 978-0-7432-9685-4
ISBN-10:   0-7432-9685-0
ISBN-13: 978-0-7432-9686-1 (Pbk)
ISBN-10:   0-7432-9686-9 (Pbk)

In loving memory of my grandfathers,
Prabhudas Bhagwanji Kamdar and Ejner Peter Christiansen.
Each lived his life to the end according to the
principles in which he believed.
Both followed Gandhi's teachings; one knowingly,
one by intuition.

And for my children, Alexander and Anjali,
who will have to make their lives on this one good earth.

And to the great precept of the Jains: ahimsa.
Above all, do no harm.

Contents

The city burns—
its guard sleeps contentedly,
He says,
My home's safe—
the town may burn,
but my things are unharmed.

—Kabir

In finding the solution to our problem, we shall have helped
to solve the world problem as well. . . . If India can offer to
the world her solution, it will be a contribution to humanity.

—Rabindrinath Tagore, Nobel Laureate,
On Nationalism, 1917

Author's Note

Many of India's anglicized city names have been re-Indianized over the past decade or so. For example, Bombay is now officially Mumbai; Calcutta, Kolkata; Madras, Chennai; Benares, Varanasi. Bangalore has officially become Bengaluru, closer to the local Kannada-language name for the city, Benda Kaal Ooru. India's information-technology capital's new name means "town of boiled beans." The name changes are not without controversy among Indians. In several instances, the name change represents a struggle between a cosmopolitan elite and a local, regional-language populace over defining the city in ways that go far beyond a simple change of name.

I have chosen for this book, destined for English-language readers who will not all know India well, to call some cities by their old name, some by their new name, depending on the most common current usage among English-speaking Indians. I use Bombay and Calcutta but also Chennai, as the old name for this city, Madras, has almost completely fallen out of use. This may seem idiosyncratic but it feels to me to be the most natural way to handle India's city-name issue in this book.

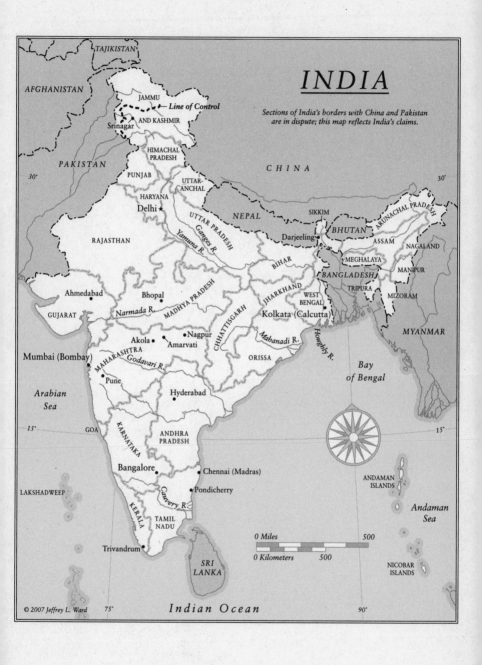

INDIA

Sections of India's borders with China and Pakistan
are in dispute; this map reflects India's claims.

TAJIKISTAN

AFGHANISTAN

JAMMU

Line of Control

Srinagar

AND KASHMIR

PAKISTAN

HIMACHAL
PRADESH

CHINA

30°

PUNJAB

UTTAR-
ANCHAL

HARYANA

NEPAL

SIKKIM

ARUNACHAL PRADESH

Delhi

UTTAR PRADESH

Darjeeling

BHUTAN

RAJASTHAN

Ganges R.

Yamuna R.

ASSAM

NAGALAND

BIHAR

MEGHALAYA

MANIPUR

Ahmedabad

Bhopal

MADHYA PRADESH

JHARKHAND

BANGLADESH

TRIPURA

MIZORAM

GUJARAT

Narmada R.

CHHATTISGARH

WEST
BENGAL

Kolkata (Calcutta)

MYANMAR

Akola

Nagpur

Amarvati

Mahanadi R.

Godavari R.

ORISSA

Hooghly R.

Mumbai (Bombay)

MAHARASHTRA

Pune

Hyderabad

Bay
of Bengal

Arabian
Sea

15°

GOA

KARNATAKA

ANDHRA
PRADESH

LAKSHADWEEP

Bangalore

Cauvery R.

Chennai (Madras)

Pondicherry

ANDAMAN
ISLANDS

Andaman
Sea

KERALA

TAMIL
NADU

Trivandrum

SRI
LANKA

0 Miles   500

0 Kilometers   500

NICOBAR
ISLANDS

© 2007 Jeffrey L. Ward

75°

Indian Ocean

90°

30°

15°

Life on Planet India

I REMEMBER THE LAST TIME THE WORLD WAS TALKING ABOUT India. It was a fleeting fashion moment following the Beatles' trip to Rishikesh. Nehru collars and beads came into fashion, along with paisley motifs in psychedelic colors. Transcendental Meditation became the latest fad for stress relief. *Laugh-In* replaced *Leave It to Beaver* as the iconic American show. India was suddenly cool. Countercultural types embraced India as the antithesis of the West, lost to the empty materialism of the famous "plastics" scene in the movie *The Graduate*. India wasn't backward; it was wise and spiritual. But then the West moved on. Plastics prevailed, and India faded into the background.

My Indian father's family lived in Bombay. Every few years, we prepared for the incredible journey to the other side of the world. We collected precious supplies for our relatives in India: jeans and sneakers for our growing cousins, huge jars of Tang, later giant bottles of Tylenol, plastic bags of California-grown almonds and pistachios. Our family mailed us lists, and we stuffed whatever we could into our suitcases.

Living in Bombay in 1967 and 1968, I felt like I had been exiled from the real world. My grandparents' flat in Juhu, though surrounded by the homes of Bollywood stars, had no television. Across the main road near the apartment building was a reeking slum. The only relief from the paralyzing heat was to sit under a crazily beating fan. Everything was different: the food, the language, the climate, the rules of what could and couldn't be worn, what could and couldn't be said. There was no privacy. From early morning until late at night, I could hear neighboring housewives banging pots, parents screaming at children, Hindi film songs blasting, and bicyclists ringing their little bells.

In the morning the milkman came around with his cow. My grandmother or one of my aunts brought a brass pot down to him and he squatted next to the cow and sent warm streams of milk into the pot. I learned to keep a keen eye on the milkman to make sure he didn't, via a well-concealed tube, water down the milk. We took the milk upstairs and boiled it. While I sipped hot milk mixed with Ovaltine, I dreamed of dragging my fingers through the condensation on the outside of a tall glass of cold milk.

My aunt and uncle live in Gurgaon now, a booming suburb south of New Delhi. They have two refrigerators and buy pasteurized milk in sealed plastic bags. A huge, flat-screen television with cable brings hundreds of Indian and foreign channels into their living room. They keep in touch with family dispersed around the world via e-mail and telephone. Air conditioners in the bedrooms keep the apartment pleasantly cool. A late-model Honda four-door sedan is parked downstairs.

From the rooftop terrace of my aunt and uncle's flat, I can see buildings going up everywhere, the little tarps of the migrant construction workers dotting vacant lots. Women in full gathered skirts and flowing half-saris, arms covered with bangles up to their shoulders, carry loads of freshly mixed cement in baskets on their heads to the men who transfer the burden onto their own heads before scrambling barefoot up rickety scaffolding to deliver the wet mass. Near the tarps, a child runs crazily next to an old tire he urges forward with a stick. Beyond him, a Citibank office tower rises into view.

On a recent trip to India, I sat in the new Bombay domestic airport waiting for a flight on Kingfisher Airlines, whose slogan is "Fly the Good Times," my laptop propped on my knees. I typed in the code from the card I had just bought from a Tata Indicom kiosk and immediately got a strong wireless connection. On the way to the airport from the old family flat in Juhu, I had passed forlorn groups of destitute families, huddled under an unfinished highway overpass on thin mats of filthy cotton, the little babies naked and snot-nosed. It was the kind of scene that profoundly shocks first-time visitors to India and to which I have never become immune.

As I checked my e-mail in the gleaming terminal among the Indian and foreign businessmen and families waiting for one of the many flights departing for every part of the country, I thought about the India I lived in forty years ago and India today, and I wondered where India would be forty years from now.

"'Where are we headed with our billions?' That is the question India is asking itself," a friend told me in New Delhi over a drink. It is a question the entire world should be asking.

Half my family is Indian. During most of my lifetime, India changed, but did so almost imperceptibly. Then, suddenly, the changes began to come with dizzying speed. With each arrival, I felt I was watching time-lapse photography. No democracy in history has undergone a transformation of India's magnitude or velocity.

Traveling the length and breadth of the country, I witnessed the churning of India's incredible metamorphosis. I interviewed hundreds of people who shared their visions of India's future, most utopian, some grim, with me. I talked to the people in the culture industries who are reimagining India's ancient stories for a new global audience. I met businessmen who are dedicated to including the poor in India's booming economy, even as they take their companies global. I listened to household servants, taxi drivers, farmers, and street vendors talk about their daily struggles, their frustrations, their faith that their children's lives would be better. Everywhere, I was stunned by the pride, the bullishness, the sense that this moment belongs to India. I caught a glimpse of India's future, its possibilities and its perils, and in that future I saw our own, for as goes India, so goes the world.

The World in Microcosm

No other country matters more to the future of our planet than India. There is no challenge we face, no opportunity we covet where India does not have critical relevance. From combating global terror to finding cures for dangerous pandemics, from dealing with the energy crisis to averting the worst scenarios of global warming, from rebalancing stark global inequalities to spurring the vital innovation needed to create jobs and improve lives—India is now a pivotal player. The world is undergoing a process of profound recalibration in which the rise of Asia is the most important factor. India holds the key to this new world.

India is at once an ancient Asian civilization, a modern nation grounded in Enlightenment values and democratic institutions, and a rising twenty-first-century power. With a population of 1.2 billion, India is the world's largest democracy. It is an open, vibrant society. India's diverse population includes Hindus, Muslims, Sikhs, Christians, Buddhists, Jains, Zoroastrians, Jews, and animists. There are twenty-two official languages in India. Three hundred fifty million Indians speak English.

India is the world in microcosm. Its geography encompasses every climate, from the snowcapped Himalayas to palm-fringed beaches to deserts where nomads and camels roam. A developing country, India is divided among a tiny affluent minority, a rising middle class, and 800 million people who live on less than $2 per day. India faces all the critical problems of our time—extreme social inequality, employment insecurity, a growing energy crisis, severe water shortages, a degraded environment, global warming, a galloping HIV/AIDS epidemic, terrorist attacks—on a scale that defies the imagination.

India's goal is breathtaking in scope: transform a developing country of more than 1 billion people into a developed nation and global leader by 2020, and do this as a democracy in an era of resource scarcity and environmental degradation. The world has to cheer India on. If India fails, there is a real risk that our world will become hostage to political chaos, war over dwindling resources, a poisoned environment, and galloping disease. Wealthy enclaves will employ private companies to supply their needs and private militias to protect them from the poor massing at their gates. But, if India succeeds, it will demonstrate that it is possible to lift hundreds of millions of people out of poverty. It will prove that multiethnic, multireligious democracy is not a luxury for rich societies. It will show us how to save our environment, and how to manage in a fractious, multipolar world. India's gambit is truly the venture of the century.

In Search of a New Paradigm

"Our biggest challenge is the challenge nobody has solved in the world: how to grow equity," Mukesh Ambani, chairman of Reliance Industry, India's biggest company, told me. Can liberal democracies forge a global market economy that is environmentally sustainable and reduces inequality? The United States has failed to achieve this. While it has proven its capacity to generate vast wealth, the so-called Washington consensus has advanced corporate interests over the welfare of average citizens and small businesses, exacerbated gaps between the affluent and the poor, and operated with stunning disregard for the environment. America's prosperity is dependent on overconsumption of the world's resources—with just 6 percent of the world's population, the United States consumes 30 percent of the earth's resources. And it produces a disproportionate share—25 percent—of dangerous greenhouse gases.

American technological, economic, and strategic dominance is being challenged for the first time since the fall of the Soviet Union. Ironically, the communication and information technologies that propelled America to the forefront during the 1990s are now contributing to the erosion of American dominance. These technologies have created a world where time and space are compressed as never before, where ideas, money, services, and people are constantly in motion, freed from the constraints of national boundaries.

The process of globalization spurred by these technological innovations has created what the economist Amartya Sen calls "an age of great affluence," where billions of dollars are amassed by a few while billions of people barely get by. With China's rapid rise, on the one hand, and new terrorist threats on the other, one of the truly pressing questions of our time is whether liberal democracies can deliver to all citizens, including the poor, the freedom to realize their human potential.

The irrepressible optimism of America, its conviction that life can only get better, has dimmed beneath the grim shadow of its war on terror, the debacle in Iraq, and a shifting global economy. According to the Pew Global Attitudes survey, world opinion of the United States is at a historical low. Even in India, where the United States continued to be held in dizzyingly high regard long after it had tumbled elsewhere, positive opinion dropped dramatically from 71 percent approval in 2003 to 56 percent in 2006.[1] Americans themselves feel less secure and less confident about their future.

India and China realize they cannot blindly imitate the American model: the earth simply cannot sustain billions of people consuming finite resources at American levels, nor churning out pollutants at the rate Americans do. The vast majority of the world's people cannot afford to pay the prices Americans are asked to pay for the foundation of a decent life: quality health care and education. Already beset by extreme inequality and dire environmental and health crises, neither India nor China can allow a small portion of their populations to live an American lifestyle.

Europe has achieved a better balance between affluence and equity, committing important resources to universal health care, affordable housing, unemployment, and other benefits for average citizens. The European Union has emerged as the world's first supranational political and economic entity, putting centuries of national enmity and the terrible legacy of two world wars in the twentieth century firmly behind it. But Europe is also struggling with high unemployment and the challenge of integrating growing populations of Muslim immigrants.

Under the regime of Vladimir Putin, Russia has squashed opposition voices and moved away from the open society it embraced after the breakup of the Soviet Union. Japan is much too culturally homogeneous to serve as a model for the rest of the world, and it has recently moved toward the far-right end of the political spectrum with calls for a renewed full-fledged military and national education that glosses over Japan's wartime behavior. China's sheer size ensures that it will have a great impact on the world order as its economy grows, but China's system sits uncomfortably with those nations that value democracy, freedom of expression, and a vibrant press.

India, with its open society, dynamic economy, its commitment to democratizing the institutions of world order and to creating wealth in a way that is inclusive and sustainable, is forging a compelling alternative paradigm.

The Asian Century

"India and China can together reshape the world order," said Prime Minister Singh to Chinese premier Wen Jiabao when he visited New Delhi in 2005. Between them, India and China account for 2.4 billion people—one-third of humanity. India is the second-fastest-growing economy after China, posting an annual growth rate of 8 percent in 2006, with the ambition to sustain growth of 9 to 10 percent during the next five years and beyond. India, like China, has embraced a market economy and moved to reap the benefits of globalization. Both India and China see this moment as a historic turning point where the future is gravitating toward Asia. They see the twenty-first century as the Asian century, a time when the institutions that established the global order after World War II will give way to a new framework based on new alignments and a new balance of power.

India and China are working to resolve a border dispute that has festered since the two countries went to war in 1962. India has long distrusted China's close relationship with Pakistan, especially with regard to nuclear weapons' technologies, but India has put that wariness aside to move its relationship with China forward. Trade between China and India is growing more than 40 percent per year. In 2007, China will unseat the United States as India's biggest single-country trading partner. India and China realize they face common challenges of widespread poverty, a growing urban-rural divide, environmental degradation, and galloping energy needs for billions of people. Both know that any one of these problems could derail their impressive momentum, and mire their countries in domestic unrest or regional conflict.

At the same time, India and China are aware that in the race to secure essential natural resources, especially oil and natural gas, and to assert influence over a neighborhood they largely share, they are competitors. But even if China forever eclipses India in sheer economic might and military power, it will never be able to match India's immense advantage as a democracy.

India's democracy is a tremendous soft-power asset and a natural safety valve for its citizens' frustrations. India goes forth in this fragile and rapidly changing world as a friend to superpowers as well as to developing nations, as a global source of cultural creativity and technological innovation, and as an open society.

Young India

India is the world's youngest country. Fifty percent of India's people are under the age of twenty-five. By 2015, there will be 550 million teenagers in India. Long after the populations of Europe, the United States, and even China have grown old, India will still be a young country, with no labor shortages and no lack of customers. India's information-technology industry and its role as a global services provider have given the country a boost. Manufacturing is booming in India, while its real economic engine, retail spending, is just beginning to warm up. Buoyed by strong economic growth and a new smorgasbord of consumer goods and entertainment options, India's youth is filled with fresh confidence, fueled by high expectations. They believe the future belongs to them.

The nation has been swept by a can-do spirit that has set India's imagination on fire. A slogan from low-cost Air Deccan, one of several new private airlines in India, certainly fits the mood: "Every time we take off, the whole economy looks up."

Gopal is a forty-eight-year-old taxi driver in Bangalore. He is very proud of his daughter, seventeen, who is a star student. He wants her to get a job in Bangalore's information-technology industry. He's been driving for a living for more than twenty years. He owns the car, which he drives six days a week, up to twelve hours per day to make a living. "What do you think about India's future?" I ask him on our third day together. "Very fine. India is going to be number one." He turns his head, breaking into a broad smile and scaring the hell out of me because he's no longer looking at the crowded road.

Durgavati Upadhyay, a nineteen-year-old college student in Bombay, tells me, "You see, America is coming down whereas India is moving up. You people will not like it. But it is there," she says, cocking her head in a move that is at once demure and defiant. She lives in one of Bombay's slums. Her father, a taxi driver, supported her desire to go to college over her mother's objections.

Bhavesh Bavishi sells auto parts in Akola, Maharashtra. The thirty-five-year-old husband and father says, "India is coming up. You can see it. We feel very proud. We have done very well. My son, he will do even better." His extended family all around nod their heads.

Nandan Nilekani, the CEO of leading Indian information-technology company Infosys, tells me in his office in Bangalore, "People are seeing light at the end of the tunnel. Finally, we are going to break out of this trap. There's a sense that our future can be better for our children than for us. That has put us into problem-solving mode."

Nilekani is a legendary figure in India's technology boom and an international celebrity thanks to his acknowledged role in giving Tom Friedman the idea for his blockbuster book *The World Is Flat*. Nilekani positively lights up when he begins talking about his company: "Infosys is symbolic of this moment of possibility for India. We have sixty-six thousand employees and the average age is twenty-seven. It's about building a global brand. It's about achieving on merit. It's a company about the future, and not about the past."

Striding onto the World Stage

"A company full of Indians" paying in "monkey money," is how former Arcelor chief executive Frenchman Guy Dollé described the bid by Indian-owned Mittal Steel for Europe's steel giant. In June 2006, after months of high-profile wrangling—and after the government of India oddly stepped in to defend a native son who lives in London, owns a Luxembourg-registered company, and had, at that point, never invested in his home country—Mittal Steel succeeded in taking over Arcelor. Indians around the world were jubilant.

For Indians, Mittal's takeover of Arcelor symbolized the coming-of-age of Indian business and the end of a Western commercial imperium. Until Mittal came along, French fears about globalization were emblematized by the Polish plumber willing to work for wages far below French levels. The Indian corporate raider proved a much scarier avatar. Despite Mittal's assurances that there would be no mass layoffs of workers at Arcelor, whose generous wage-and-benefits packages are everything the French fear losing, many French couldn't shake the impression they'd let the fox into the henhouse.

Shortly after the Mittal Steel coup, Vijay Mallya of India's United Breweries went after Taittinger champagne. The French said, *"Assez."* Unspecified "local interests" upped competitive offers, and Mallya withdrew his offer. Steel is one thing, champagne is another!

Indian companies have been quietly acquiring companies around the world, including in Europe and in the United States. Bharat Forge owns companies in Sweden, Germany, the United Kingdom, the United States, and China. Infosys is expanding its operations in China, the United States, and Europe. Indian wind-power giant Suzlon has snapped up companies in Europe and the United States and invested in wind farms in Minnesota. In 2005, Indian information technology leader Wipro acquired New Logic, a microchip company involved in mobile communications based in the French high-tech center of Sophia-Antipolis.

Mere months after the Mittal takeover of Arcelor, Indian steel giant Tata smoothly sealed a deal to buy the Anglo-Dutch steel concern Corus for a cool $8.1 billion in cash. Tata's beverage company, Tata Tea, now earns more than two-thirds of its revenues from first-world markets. Tata Tea has been systematically acquiring European and American beverage companies, beginning with UK-based Tetley in 2000, continuing with the American tea company Good Earth in 2005. In 2006, Tata bought the American classic Eight O'Clock Coffee; JEMCA, a Czech company; and took a 30 percent stake in American Glacéau flavored waters.

Indian companies expanding overseas are hiring local managers and employees. Tata Consultancy alone has ninety-five hundred employees in the United States. In 2006, they announced plans to hire one thousand more U.S. employees. Mahindra & Mahindra has been manufacturing tractors in Tomball, Texas, under its U.S. subsidiary Mahindra U.S.A. since 1994, and in 2003 it opened a new factory near Atlanta, Georgia. Ranbaxy Laboratories, a leading Indian pharmaceutical company, has nine thousand employees in seventeen countries.

Last year, I gave a presentation on India to my daughter's sixth-grade class. I told them that when they grow up there is a good chance they will work for a Chinese or an Indian company. This didn't seem to bother them at all. Americans who once feared their job being off-shored to India may find new job opportunities working for Indian companies. Europeans will increasingly find themselves in the same situation.

In his living room on the Worli seafront in Bombay, Tata Consultancy Services (TCS) chairman T. C. Ramadorai told me, "Asia had a global leadership role for thousands of years, then it shifted to Europe, then to America. Now it is shifting back to Asia. It is going to be difficult for the United States and Europe to accept the fact that Asia, including India and China, but also Malaysia, Singapore, and others, will be the center of wealth-creation."

The Third Industrial Revolution

"Any business that does not require physical presence can be cosourced," Azim Premji, CEO of Wipro, one of India's largest companies engaged in offshore outsourcing, told me at his company's headquarters in Bangalore. India has become a major source of skilled, low-cost labor, with a corps of English-speaking, highly skilled workers who can compete with the best, especially in technology and science, for a fraction of what a comparable worker is paid in the United States or Europe.

Kiran Mazumdar Shaw, CEO of Biocon, the pioneering Indian biotechnology firm, and one of India's most prominent woman executives, told me: "India has the potential to be the laboratory of the world. We have bright minds and a cost advantage. We're addressing the medical needs of the world and we're saying, 'You have to develop drugs that are affordable. Two-point-five-billion dollars in development costs for a single drug is not sustainable.'"

India is becoming an important center for research and development for scores of major multinational companies. IBM has invested nearly $2 billion in India over the past four years. It plans to triple that to a total of $6 billion over the next two years. IBM now has 43,000 employees in India out of 330,000 worldwide. Intel will invest $1 billion in India over the next five years; Cisco, another $1.1 billion. Microsoft will invest $1.7 billion and hire 3,000 more employees.[2]

The proportion of jobs in finance, technology, life sciences, human resources administration, and business management outsourced from Europe and the United States to the developing world is expected to increase from its current level of less than 5 percent to 30 percent by 2015.[3] By the same year, an estimated 3.5 million white-collar U.S. jobs along with $151 billion in wages will be outsourced, with India the top outsourcing destination.[4]

The world economy is undergoing a major reorganization that is rebalancing jobs and capital investment toward Asia. Information and communications technologies have created an environment where the only jobs that have to remain local are those that require face-to-face interaction. All others can be outsourced to a remote location leveraging digital technologies. Alan S. Blinder, a professor of economics at Princeton University, calls this the third industrial revolution. The first was the shift of labor from farms to factories. The second was the shift from manufacturing to services. The third is a shift made possible by the information age.

Blinder believes that the ultimate dimensions of the third industrial revolution "may be staggering." Though it is neither possible nor desirable to reverse a revolution, I share Blinder's conviction that "the governments and societies of the developed world must face up to the massive, complex, and multifaceted challenges that offshoring will bring."[5] At this point, they are not. In the United States, workers whose jobs have been lost due to offshoring are left largely to their own devices.

With more and more highly skilled jobs in India, brain drain—the flow of talent toward the developed countries of the West, especially the United States, that characterized the second half of the last century—has developed a countercurrent in this century: brain recirculation. My Indian father, an aeronautical engineer, had hoped to return to India after college in America, but there were no opportunities to match what he could get in the United States. Today, as Indian businesses expand in Europe, and European and American companies move into India, the demand for foreign-educated Indians and Indians with experience in the world of international business is growing. High-paying jobs and private communities offering American-style amenities are flourishing in India, and more and more Indians are deciding it is time to go home. Indians returning from the United States and the United Kingdom are a powerful modernizing influence on their mother country, demanding more efficient services, complaining about corruption, voicing their dissatisfaction with poor infrastructure.

In 2003, The Indus Entrepreneur group (TIE) estimated that fifteen thousand to twenty thousand Indians had left Silicon Valley to return home. Amar Babu of Intel India told me that about 15 percent of Intel's employees in Bangalore are Indians who have returned from the United States. Many people who return from the United States have imbibed a good dose of entrepreneurial spirit. They are using their entrepreneurship and their money to create new businesses in India. Some are basing themselves in India, some are starting new companies in India while remaining based in the United States. Others are in an airplane so often, they don't know where they live anymore.

The Indian Renaissance

India's 1.2 billion people and 20-million-strong diaspora are beginning to flex their cultural and economic muscles. "Who needs the American audience?" film producer Smriti Mundhra told me over lunch in New York. "There are only three hundred million people here." This statement absolutely floored me. I doubt the American audience, with its bottomless appetite for entertainment, is going to cease to matter any time soon. But Smriti has a point: everything is on a different scale in Bombay or Beijing than it is in New York or Los Angeles.

"The great comic heroes we know and love," Sharad Devarajan, the man who took *Spider-Man* to India, and is part of the new Virgin Comics and Virgin Animation venture, told me, "have fifty years of history. But in India we have superheroes with five thousand years of history." India's rich cultural heritage provides a deep well of creative material from which to craft art and entertainment for the world's first truly global audience.

As Sharad and his partner Gotham Chopra see it—drawing inspiration from their mentors filmmaker Shekhar Kapur and spiritual guru Deepak Chopra—they are involved in nothing less than the creation of an Indian Renaissance. Much as the finest achievements of Western art and philosophy were forgotten during the Middle Ages to be rediscovered to dazzling new effect in the Italian Renaissance, Indians believe that Indian art and philosophy have too long slumbered under the darkness of Western imperial domination and its aftermath. "The world needs a new mythology," Deepak Chopra told me. Indian culture has all the elements to create one.

"It's so exciting," Sharad and Gotham told me separately. "You feel like you are one of the Medicis when you are in the studio in India."

Evidence of India's renaissance is everywhere. Once again, the world thrills to Indian fashion, Indian music, and Indian-inspired clothes. Indian actors are on television and movie screens across the United States and around the world. Forty years after the Beatles put India on the map of Western consciousness, Indians are situating the West on a new global topography. Indian movie directors and producers are tying up deals with Hollywood heavies. Indian animation companies are not only producing content for the world's biggest media conglomerates, they are building their own intellectual property. Indian audiences and Indian consumers have the numbers and are beginning to have the money to command the attention of media companies around the world, while Indian entertainment companies are taking their talent and vision global. Last November, the Virgin Comics team signed up Hollywood megastar Nicolas Cage to play the lead role in a feature film version of their comic book saga *The Sadhu*.

Daunting Challenges

An astonishing 40 percent of the world's poor live in India, including one-third of the world's malnourished children. A report to the United Nations General Assembly in September 2006 by special rapporteur Jean Ziegler, *The Extent of Chronic Hunger and Malnutrition in India*, indicated that hunger and malnutrition are bigger problems now in India than they were in the 1990s, and that the gap between those who eat well and those who can't get enough to eat has widened.[6] In a country that prides itself on its information-technology leadership and strong economic growth, a shocking number of Indians live in conditions no better, and in some cases worse, than in sub-Saharan Africa.

According to a report last year from UNAIDS, India has the world's single largest population of people with HIV/AIDS, more than 5.7 million people, though the actual number may be much higher—there are simply no reliable mechanisms for getting accurate numbers. A host of private foundations are working with UN agencies and the World Bank to bolster the efforts of the Indian government to stem the tide of this dangerous epidemic, and provide care and low-cost treatment for victims. Generic drugs produced by Indian pharmaceutical companies have driven down the costs of treatment dramatically, in India and in other parts of the developing world. Whether India will be able to conquer the spread of this terrible disease in time to prevent serious damage to its economy is an open question. A 2006 report from the National Council of Applied Economic Research (NCAER) put the cost of an unchecked HIV/AIDS epidemic at .86 percent of India's annual economic growth for the next decade.[7]

When I met him for coffee in Bombay recently, Ajit Balakrishnan, the founder of Rediff.com, India's largest Internet portal and a media company that owns the newspaper *India Abroad* among other publications, sketched for me his worst nightmare: "Do you want me to tell you what keeps me up at night? I'll tell you. I may not have these figures exactly right, but I'm not far off. When we got our independence, eighty percent of our GDP came from agriculture and seventy-five percent of our people lived in rural areas. Today, only thirty percent of GDP comes from agriculture, yet nearly seventy percent of our people still live in rural areas. We probably only need about ten percent of the population engaged in agriculture. So you tell me how the hell we are going to create five hundred million jobs for the people who are going to come off agriculture and will need employment, plus the tens of millions of jobs we need for the under- and unemployed already in the cities, plus the new generations coming up as the population continues to grow? That," he said, leaning back in his chair and fixing me with his eyes, "is what keeps me up at night."

India's IT sector has attracted international attention and created a shift in the mind-set of a new generation of Indian youth, who see that merit and hard work can lead to recognition and success. However, for all the visibility of high-tech Bangalore, India's information-technology businesses have only directly generated 1.3 million jobs with another 3 million jobs created indirectly. This does not remotely approach the scale of job creation India's growing population requires. Manufacturing will create some of the jobs India's youth so badly need. New credit products, especially in microfinance, will allow others to launch small-scale businesses. The development of rural India, where 850 million Indians live, has the potential to improve farmers' lives and to create new opportunities in the country's small and mid-size cities. India will need all of this, and more, to meet the basic needs and newly kindled aspirations of its many people.

Nandan Nilekani agrees that job creation is one of India's biggest challenges. Speaking of the information-technology sector alone, he told me, "We need to really improve our economic growth because we need to create ten to twelve million new jobs. There is also a great deal of regional disparity: Goa's per capita income is four times Bihar's. Globalization is in our favor. Innovation is not a problem. We have no shortage of ideas but the challenge is scaling it up."

The challenge is also to act quickly and to deal with multiple crises all at once. In addition to hunger, HIV/AIDS, and mass unemployment, India is facing a severe water crisis. With 17 percent of the world's population but only 4 percent of the world's freshwater, India's water resources are already stretched beyond capacity. Its aquifers are being drained faster than they are being recharged, causing dangerous chemicals including arsenic and fluoride to leach into remaining underground water stocks. India's water is also highly polluted with raw sewage, untreated industrial waste, and pesticide runoff. China is threatening to dam the Brahmaputra River before it reaches the Indian border, a move that would have devastating consequences for millions of Indians.

Global warming is shrinking glaciers in the Himalayas and may be altering the rainfall patterns on which much of Indian agriculture depends. A process that will affect the tropical South much more negatively than the temperate North, global warming has the potential to drown India's Andaman and Nicobar islands and submerge coastal areas that are home to hundreds of millions. In West Bengal and neighboring Bangladesh alone, as many as 60 million people could be displaced by predicted rises in sea levels if nothing is done to dramatically curb greenhouse gases.

India's rush to develop its steel industry and manufacturing base is pushing mining interests into areas traditionally home to Tribals, or Adivasis as they are now known. There have been bloody conflicts in mineral-rich areas in the states of Chhattisgarh and Orissa between powerful steel companies and indigenous people being expelled from their ancestral lands. Extreme economic deprivation and cruel social divisions have fueled the growth of a Maoist rebel movement called the Naxalites, after the town of Naxalbari in West Bengal where a splinter group from the Communist Party of India staged a militant peasant uprising in 1967. The Naxalites have now spread far beyond West Bengal. The movement boasts an army of some 20,000[8] and an unknown number of sympathizers whose ranks are being swelled by brutal social and economic injustices. Villagers where the Naxalites are active are caught in the cross fire between rebels and security forces. A senior Indian analyst confided to me in New Delhi last year that some fear the Naxalites' so-called Red Corridor has the potential to stretch the full length of India and link Maoist rebels in Nepal with guerrillas in Sri Lanka.

Clearly, India faces daunting challenges that must be overcome—and fast—or the incredible momentum of India's resurgence will suffer.

Innovating to Survive

One top Indian executive told me, "We have a window of between five and seven years." India does not have the luxury of time. It must immediately address a host of problems in ways that are scalable and sustainable. It must leverage new technologies to minimize environmental damage while maximizing scarce resources to bring badly needed benefits to a huge population. India will have to use its proven talent for technological innovation to create the solutions it needs.

India's new cars, power plants, and factories risk adding millions of pounds of carbon to an already overloaded atmosphere unless the country moves to power its growth with clean, alternative energies. India is the only country with a Ministry of Non-Conventional Energy. It has the potential to become a leader in new technologies for clean energy production. The Indian company Suzlon is an example of how India can scale up alternative energy, and take it global. In just a few years, Suzlon has become one of the world's leading wind power companies, selling power to utilities in the state of California and other foreign markets. As oil prices rise, alternative technologies are becoming increasingly more attractive. India has the technological acumen and the pressing need to find clean energy solutions.

India is using digital technologies to bring health and education services to the poor in remote rural areas. It is developing generic drugs and low-cost therapies for pandemic disease. It is creating new paradigms for delivering quality health care, including state-of-the-art surgeries, to the poor. "We are trying to dissociate health care from affluence," Dr. Devi Shetty, the founder of Narayana Hrudayalaya heart hospital and one of the most extraordinary people I met in India, told me. "People may continue to be poor, but they will have access to high-tech health care with dignity." India has also become an attractive destination for medical outsourcing: Americans who cannot afford expensive procedures in the United States can travel to India and have them performed for a fraction of the cost.

India is using technology to drive down the cost of basic goods, making them affordable to more and more people. India is producing $20 mobile phones and designing $2,000 cars. It is making low-cost computers that resist high temperatures and repeated power interruptions. It is setting up test models of small-scale power plants run on crop waste, where farmers can sell excess electricity back to the grid. Most people in the world cannot afford the prices charged for goods and services in the West. India has the potential to make those goods and services available at prices the whole world can afford.

India's Way

In his famous speech, broadcast on the radio at the midnight hour of India's birth as an independent nation on August 15, 1947, Jawaharlal Nehru, the country's first prime minister, articulated the new nation's promise to its people:

> The future beckons to us. Whither do we go and what shall be our endeavor? To bring freedom and opportunity to the common man, to the peasants and workers of India; to fight and end poverty and ignorance and disease; to build up a prosperous, democratic, and progressive nation; and to create social, economic, and political institutions which will ensure justice and fullness of life to every man and woman.[9]

These goals remain as inspiring as they have been elusive. India's poor still wait for opportunity and justice; too many of their lives are still fraught with poverty, ignorance, and disease. No doubt, some of the worst exploitation of human beings occurs in India—indentured servitude, sexual trafficking of women and children, child labor, female feticide and infanticide—and the less dramatic but just as debilitating daily violence of poverty, disease, and hopelessness.

Faced with crisis situations it must solve or risk squandering the incredible promise of this moment, India is undertaking the Herculean task of fulfilling the pledges Nehru made at the hour of India's independence. It has taken the country sixty years to reach this point, not a long time in the career of nations; no time at all on India's ancient civilizational time line.

India realizes that it must invent its own way in the world. Over and over, I have heard some version of the following radical strategy for India's success. The starting premise is counterintuitive: treat every problem as an opportunity. In a nation of more than 1 billion people, begin with the assertion that, in a knowledge economy, every untapped brain is an asset waiting to be realized. Bring the proven power of entrepreneurship to bear on the most intractable problems but don't assume that private investment alone can do the job on the scale and at the speed required. Forge partnerships among business, government, and NGOs. Nurture networks and mentor relationships between those who have the know-how and those who want to learn; between those who have the capital and those who need seed money. Relentlessly drive down costs in order to drive down prices. Listen to the poor; they know what they need. Empower them by giving them a good education and the means to earn a livelihood. Figure out how to meet their needs, and you will do well.

"By design," Shiv Sivakumar, who is the creator of ITC's innovative e-Choupal program that links farmers to markets in rural India, told me, "our models fuse the belief that we can only do well if we do good, and we only do good when we do well."

Narayana Murthy, the recently retired cofounder of Infosys, has a theory of "compassionate capitalism." He told me how he sees it: "The primary role of a corporation is to create wealth, legally and ethically. That is our primary responsibility. In the context of a developing country like India, however, the corporation's responsibility goes beyond that. You must create goodwill in the society. That doesn't mean business should take over the government's responsibilities. The major contribution where a company can create a public good is in private-public partnerships."

In the United States, to paraphrase Charles Erwin Wilson, former chairman of General Motors, in testimony he gave to the Senate

Armed Services Committee after being named secretary of defense by President Eisenhower, "What's good for GM is good for the country." Since this sentiment was uttered in 1952, GM has fallen on hard times, laying off thirty thousand people in the United States in 2006. Still, the notion that whatever favors corporate America is good for the American people remains a core concept for U.S. foreign and domestic policy.

Most Indian corporate leaders I have met turn the formula on its head. They truly believe that their businesses will ultimately succeed to the extent they contribute to addressing the pressing problems of their country. Mukesh Ambani put it succinctly, "What's good for India is good for Reliance."

Inclusive Capitalism

Y. C. Deveshwar, chairman of ITC, one of India's largest corporations, delivered a rousing speech last year to his shareholders. While he was pleased to announce to investors that annual returns were 30 percent, he was truly proud to tell them these results had been achieved "even as your company is creating new benchmarks in Triple Bottom Line performance." As the head of a company whose traditional business is tobacco, Deveshwar has special incentive to turn ITC into a good corporate citizen. Still, the company's corporate responsibility profile is impressive. ITC, which was already "water positive," became "carbon positive" in 2006 and is well on its way to achieving "zero solid waste status."

The Triple Bottom Line takes into account financial, social, and environmental returns. Mr. Deveshwar attributed ITC's success across all three of these bottom lines to the company's values, deeply rooted in a distinctly Indian ethos. This ethos, Deveshwar maintained, "determines choice of corporate strategy, orients such strategy in favor of Indian value chains wherever feasible, and engages the organization willingly in confronting the larger societal challenges of inclusive and sustainable growth."[10]

Increasingly, some of India's most visionary leaders are coming around to this new capitalist paradigm that creates wealth and promotes social inclusion and environmental sustainability. India's government has made a politics of inclusion the centerpiece of its domestic policies, emphasizing improved education for all and enacting a National Rural Employment Guarantee Act to provide a minimum social safety net to India's rural poor. The reason is simple: there is no other way.

The Power of Imagination

From Anand Mahindra to Mallika Dutt, from Gotham Chopra to Rohini Nilekani, I have heard so many Indians say that the only thing that can hold their country back at this critical historical moment is a failure of imagination. The same is certainly true for the rest of us. Our planet teeters on the edge of so many terrifying crises, from global warming to lethal pandemics to the anarchy of terrorism and war. To believe that economic growth and development are possible only by sacrificing the life potential of billions of human beings or by inflicting colossal damage to our shared environment is to suffer from an acute failure of imagination. If India can create a knowledge economy that is an economy attuned to the challenges it faces, if it can change the information age into an age of wisdom, it will save itself— and the rest of us as well.

In the best of all possible worlds, India's politics of inclusion will temper the economic divisiveness of American capitalism, while American-style entrepreneurship will spur India's economy. India's commitment to a multipolar world and to the democratization of the emerging world order will curb America's overt unilateralism. India's focus on innovation in developing alternative energy sources and in extending educational opportunities, medical care, and livelihoods to the poorest citizens will catapult India into leadership positions in a host of new areas, forcing the United States to reconsider its policies and priorities. The commitment of Indian companies to doing well by doing good will set the example of an inclusive capitalism that will be a model for the world. The tired old argument that the United States would like to do the right thing—for example, reign in the production of greenhouse gases—but just can't afford to do so will be put to bed as India shows the world no one can afford not to address these problems. By daring to imagine a different world, India will surge forward on a wave of economic growth fueled by innovative solutions to the problems that threaten our collective future.

As Goes India, So Goes the World

No matter which pressing problem we contemplate—from global warming to pandemic disease to the energy crisis to yawning gaps between the rich and the poor—time is of the essence. With its large population and rapid economic growth, India faces all of these challenges with much more urgency than people in the industrialized world. We must pay attention to where India is heading: we are all likely to end up there, sooner or later.

India encompasses all the promise and peril of this critical moment in human history. The Indians I have had the privilege of meeting and who shared their vision and dedication with me marry incredible ambition to problems so terrifying many of us are tempted to pretend they don't exist. Indians don't have the luxury of pretending. Ultimately, neither do we.

India is already touching our lives in more ways than most of us realize. In a very real sense, we already live on planet India. This book is about what kind of planet that can be.

CHAPTER ONE

Indians and Americans

T HIS EXPERIENCE WILL CHANGE YOUR LIFE," SAID VICTOR Menezes, a member of the board of directors of the American India Foundation (AIF). A group of recent college graduates and young professionals stood absorbing Menezes's words. New AIF Service Corps Fellows, they had all made it through a rigorous selection process and were now gathered at a reception in their honor at AIF's New York headquarters. With wine glasses and small plates of Indian appetizers in hand, some shifted nervously on their feet, others beamed confidently. A few had been to India before. Some were Indian Americans who spoke an Indian language. Many had no connection to India at all, aside from a desire to gain practical experience in areas as diverse as improving livelihoods, women's health, and primary education.

Connecticut native Margorie Schulman, a petite blond woman in her early twenties, wanted to learn more about microenterprise so she could better serve poor communities in the United States. Vimala Palaniswamy, raised in Augusta, Georgia, was headed to South India. She confessed, "My Tamil's not fantastic, but I can get along." The daughter of immigrants from India, Vimala looks unmistakably South Asian but she sounds every bit like the American she is. She told me that a stay in India a couple of years earlier made her realize how American she really was. "They all referred to me as the American girl," she told me still a little amazed, having been the Indian girl growing up in Georgia. All the fellows I spoke with invariably intended to take their experience in India and apply it in careers they hoped to pursue in banking, medicine, or public service.

I cornered Victor Menezes, dressed in an elegantly understated business suit and a red silk tie, and asked him what, beyond the skills and education these young Americans were taking to India, the value of the program was to AIF. "These young Americans become ambassadors for India and Indian causes when they get back," he explained. "Look, there is far more in common between India and the United States than there are differences. India is a wonderful laboratory for a lot of issues. It is a microcosm of every important policy question the world faces."

AIF was awarded a major grant from the Ford Foundation last year to encourage philanthropy in the Indian-American community. The Indian-American trend toward giving back will likely be spurred to new levels by this effort, enhancing a virtuous cycle that benefits both India and the United States.

The United States and India: People to People

Until this century, the India-U.S. relationship was almost exclusively a people-to-people affair. Business and political relationships were negligible, not the least because for a considerable time the government of India was that of Great Britain. Under British rule, Indians identified with the United States as a fellow British colony and admired it for having achieved what India so desired: independence. Strong philosophical currents flowed back and forth between the two countries, currents that significantly affected the political futures of both nations. Indian philosophy and theology were sources of profound inspiration to the American transcendentalists. Ralph Waldo Emerson and Henry David Thoreau read Indian sacred texts, including the *Vishnu Puranas* and the *Mahabharata*. Both wrote poems and essays inspired by their Indian readings.

My parents' wedding invitation cited the following lines from Walt

Whitman's poem "Passage to India" from his famous 1855 collection *Leaves of Grass:*

> *Passage to India!*
> *Lo, soul, seest thou not God's purpose from the first?*
> *The earth to be spann'd, connected by network,*
> *The races, neighbors, to marry and be given in marriage,*
> *The oceans to be cross'd, the distant brought near,*
> *The lands to be welded together.*

Their Indian-American union was unusual in 1957. Quoting Whitman helped ground it in a recognizable American tradition. This did not prevent the dean of women students, however, from summoning my mother to her office to try to dissuade her from making a terrible mistake: while she might not be doing anything illegal in the state of Oregon, she would be breaking antimiscegenation laws in the American South.

Mahatma Gandhi, like thousands of other Indians of his generation, including my own grandfather, read Emerson and Thoreau. Gandhi was inspired by Thoreau's notion of civil disobedience and integrated it into his political tactics of nonviolent resistance. Gandhi was also haunted early on by a chance encounter, the day after the famous incident when he was thrown out of a whites-only compartment on a train, with "an American negro" as dispossessed as himself in apartheid South Africa. Gandhi and his followers identified the plight of subjugated Indians, especially of untouchables, with that of African-Americans in Jim Crow America.

During the 1920s and 1930s, African-Americans closely followed the progress of Gandhi and India's freedom movement in such widely read publications as *The Crisis.* In 1936, Howard Thurman led a Negro Delegation of Friendship to South Asia and met Gandhi. They discussed the similarity of the oppression of India's untouchables with that of African-Americans. Martin Luther King came to know about Gandhi and his philosophy via Thurman's *Jesus and the Disinherited.*[1] In the footage of Martin Luther King delivering his famous "I Have a Dream" speech on the steps of the Lincoln Memorial, the followers flanking him are wearing white Nehru caps. King said of Gandhi's contribution to his movement, "Christ furnished the spirit and motivation, while Gandhi furnished the method."[2]

Sympathies between the Indian struggle for independence and the African-American struggle for equal rights ran deep. Historically black colleges encouraged Indian students to come to study at their institutions. Writer Marina Budhos told me that her father, an ethnic Indian from Guyana, attended Howard University in the 1950s along with a group of students from India.

On the West Coast, Punjabi Sikhs and other immigrants from India came to Seattle and California's Central Valley around 1900 to work as laborers in logging and agriculture. Acutely aware of their unprotected status as colonial subjects of Great Britain, they started a revolutionary movement for India's independence from British rule called the Ghadar movement. The Ghadars were headquartered in San Francisco, where they published a newspaper. These Indian Americans raised money for their homeland's freedom, organizing a boat (which sank) loaded with guns and ammunition for freedom fighters in India. Other Punjabi immigrants to California saved enough money to buy land and start their own farms. A thriving Punjabi community still exists in and around Yuba City, California. Allowed into the United States as single men, many married Mexican-American women. When their farms were threatened with confiscation under the terms of the 1913 Alien Land Exclusion Act, many put their properties into the names of their wives to save them.[3]

While the peoples of India and America drew inspiration from each other's struggles for freedom and social justice, the governments of the two countries pursued a very different tack. After a brief warming following India's independence in 1947, the United States and India drifted into wary estrangement, each aligned with the other's archenemy: India with the Soviet Union, and the United States during the Afghan war with Pakistan. Ironically, the Cold War imperative to beat the Soviets opened the doors of the United States to immigration from India. Racing for technological and military dominance, the United States sought to harness the skills of the best and brightest, even if they had to come from Africa and Asia. In 1965, the United

States moved to open its borders to highly skilled workers from non-European countries whose immigration had previously been severely limited.

When my father came to the United States in 1949 on a student visa, there were only ten thousand persons of Indian origin in the entire country, the same number as in 1900. After 1965, Indian engineers, doctors, scientists, and other college-educated individuals or people seeking an education in these fields began arriving in increasingly large numbers. The Indian engineering student stereotype was born (my own father, though he came earlier, became an aeronautical engineer), to be replaced a couple of decades later by the Indian information-technology whiz.

The numbers of Indians studying, living, and working in the United States increased steadily during the 1970s, 1980s, and 1990s. For the last several years, India has consistently sent more students to study in the United States than any other country. In 2005, over eighty thousand students from India came to the United States for higher education. That's nearly 30 percent more than the sixty-two thousand who came from China. Not every Indian who comes to study or work in the United States stays. Many return to India. This used to be true only of members of the upper class where the opportunity to take over a family business or to scale the heights of government service was attractive. An impressive number of India's top business and political leaders have studied, lived, or worked in the United States. Many more have children or other close family members who have. The number of Indians in senior positions I have met who have MBAs from prestigious American institutions such as Stanford, Harvard, Wharton, or Kellogg—where many of the top professors are Indian as well—is amazing. These experiences create powerful links to the United States, and a natural affinity for an American approach to policy and business.

By 2000, 1.2 million persons of Indian origin were living in the United States. There are now approximately 2.2 million. Fueled by ongoing immigration and by the natural growth of the resident population, that number is expected to double every decade, making Indian Americans the fastest-growing Asian immigrant group.

Indian Americans

Indian Americans are one of the most prosperous and well-educated immigrant groups in America. Fifty-eight percent of Indian Americans have a college degree, whereas only 27 percent of the general population do. Their median household income is $64,000, as compared with the national average of $50,000. Indian Americans command a whopping $76 billion in disposable personal income.[4] Many of these impressive numbers derive from U.S. immigration laws, which favored highly skilled and highly educated immigrants from India, who had the opportunity to get high-paying jobs.

Indian Americans command a disproportionate presence in certain fields, such as medicine, the hospitality industry, information technology, research science, and business management. Americans have become used to entrusting their medical care to Indian doctors. According to the American Association of Physicians of Indian Origin, there are forty-two thousand physicians and fifteen thousand medical students of Indian origin in the United States.[5] CNN's Dr. Sanjay Gupta is the media-icon version of the trusted American family physician from India.

The market value of the properties in the United States owned by members of the Asian American Hotel Owners Association, an organization founded by immigrants from India and dominated by Patels originally from the Indian state of Gujarat, is estimated to be $29.9 billion in franchised properties and $8.1 billion in independent properties. The association explains on its Web site the origin of the name Patel: "In ancient India, rulers appointed a record keeper to keep track of annual crops on each parcel of land, or 'pat.' That person became known as a 'patel.'"[6] This group's success in the American hotel and motel business has given rise to the expression *Patel motel*.

Prominent Indian-American senior managers include Indra Nooyi, CEO of PepsiCo; Rajat Gupta, worldwide managing partner and former CEO of McKinsey and Co.; Vikram Pandit, former president and COO of the Institutional Securities and Investment Banking Group at Morgan Stanley; Shailesh Mehta, former CEO of Providian Financial

Corporation; and Victor Menezes, senior vice chairman, Citigroup. One factor in this phenomenon is the highly competitive Indian Institutes of Technology (IIT) and Indian Institutes of Management (IIM), which admit only one out of sixty applicants and give those who make the cut an outstanding education. Graduates of these schools are snapped up by leading companies around the world.

The contribution of Indians in Silicon Valley to the United States' technological leadership and to India's economic take-off has been tremendous. Veteran journalist Michael Lewis wrote in his comprehensive study of the Silicon Valley phenomenon in *The New New Thing: A Silicon Valley Story* back in 2000, the "definitive smell inside a Silicon Valley start-up was curry."[7] Many IIT and other technical graduates gravitated to Silicon Valley, contributing to the tech boom there in the 1980s and 1990s. Others ended up in business or scientific research. Of Indians who went to Silicon Valley, a significant number started their own companies. By 2000, Indian Americans either owned or were in top management positions at 40 percent of all Silicon Valley start-ups and had a collective net worth of $62 billion.[8] Some of the better known Indians who made huge fortunes during the tech boom include Vinod Dham, the creator of the Pentium processor; Vinod Khosla, one of the founders of Sun Microsystems; Sabir Bhatia, who created Hotmail.com; Suhas Patil, the founder of Cirrus Logic; and Kanwal Rekhi, the founder of Excelan.

One day in 1992, a group of Indian Silicon Valley entrepreneurs was waiting at the airport to meet a visiting Indian government official. They got to talking, and decided to start something that could help aspiring entrepreneurs benefit from their experience. TIE, The Indus Entrepreneur, was born. TIE began with one hundred members. It now counts ten thousand members in forty-five chapters and nine countries. India is the country with the most chapters after the United States. TIE has become one of the most powerful networks of entrepreneurs in the world and is expanding at a dizzying pace. Since 1992, individuals associated with TIE have created businesses with a combined market capitalization of $200 billion.[9] Born in Silicon Valley, TIE was very much a product of the unique set of circumstances that gave rise to the information technology revolution: the proximity of

Stanford University with Xerox's Palo Alto Research Center, and the success of the original techie garage tinkerers, Bill Hewlett and Dave Packard, the founders of Hewlett-Packard.

TIE, however, introduced something uniquely Indian to this environment: the ancient learning relationship of *guru-shishya,* or teacher-disciple. TIE mentors (*gurus*) help budding entrepreneurs, professionals, and students (*shishyas*) learn the ropes by sharing their experience and knowledge. TIE also fosters the principle of doing well by doing good. When asked about the role of social entrepreneurship and TIE, Vish Mishra, senior venture partner with Clearstone Venture Partners and a charter member of TIE, explained, "Social entrepreneurship caters to the needs of the poor. Bottom-tier markets have thus far been neglected."[10]

The commitment on the part of successful Indian Americans both to give something back to their country of origin and to help others succeed has grown into an important engine driving the U.S.-India relationship. Private investment capital is pouring into India, much of it flowing from successful Indian Americans who are familiar with both countries. "At Clearstone," Vish Mishra told me, "we're very familiar with India as a talent source and as a market. We really believe that India has achieved ignition. An educated population is the fuel. The oxygen is a stable sociopolitical environment. The spark is the young, upwardly mobile population that wants to consume." Clearstone now has an office in Bombay.

During the twelve-month period ending in August 2006, venture capital (VC) firms invested $2 billion in early- and late-stage companies, and several new India-focused VC funds were being raised totaling $3 billion.[11] Last year, Matrix Partners announced a $150 million India fund. Sequoia Capital India was created by Sequoia Capital's acquisition of Westbridge Capital, a five-year-old fund focused on India. Other VC firms investing in India include Kleiner, Perkins, Caufield & Byers, New Enterprise Associates (NEA), Norwest, Battery, Sierra, and Canaan Partners.

Especially exciting is the focus of many of these private investments on microfinance, improving the environment, and tackling pandemic disease. Silicon Valley–based venture capital focused on India is reinventing the concept of "green" to mean both environmentally friendly and profitable. Vinod Khosla was cofounder of Sun Microsystems and a longtime general partner at Silicon Valley VC giant Kleiner Perkins, Caufield & Byers, which has funded Google, Genentech, and Sun. Having made his billion dollars and helped many other companies and individual make theirs, Khosla has left Kleiner Perkins. He is now doing his own investing, picking and choosing socially relevant investments such as biofuels, fuel cells, and solar cells. His new benchmark is "maximum social impact rather than maximum profit."[12] This doesn't mean Khosla is looking to lose money. It means that he is taking a wholistic approach when he does cost-benefit analysis on a prospective investment that includes environmental and social factors. Khosla is bringing together the best of California and India. Efforts such as these are changing the paradigm for Indian philanthropy away from a traditional concept of charitable giving, toward a paradigm of socially responsible investment.

Perhaps the largest philanthropic organization focused on India, AIF was born from the rubble of the catastrophic earthquake that hit India's Gujarat state in 2001. At the urging of President Bill Clinton, a number of high-achieving Indian Americans from across the United States were brought together under the leadership of Rajat Gupta and Victor Menezes to respond to the disaster. Working with carefully selected local NGOs, AIF has since extended its mission to address key areas of need in India, including internal stress migration, women's empowerment, HIV/AIDS prevention and care for HIV/AIDS victims, and water scarcity. In just five years, AIF has raised more than $35 million. Clinton remains honorary chair of AIF.

Rajat Gupta is also the chairman and one of the founders of the Indian School of Business (ISB) in Hyderabad. ISB is an associate school of the Kellogg School of Management, Wharton, at the University of Pennsylvania and the London Business School. Its executive board is as much a Who's Who of Indian business as its governing board is of international business. From building a school in their home village to million-dollar donations to an alma mater, Indian Americans are dedicated to improving their country of origin. The creation of an institution of the caliber of ISB, closely tied to American and British business schools and to prominent members of the Indian diaspora, will help forge strong linkages between India's future business leadership and the international business elite.

In the spring of 2006 in Bangalore, the big news was the salaries garnered by graduates from the local Indian Institute of Management. On average, IIM Bangalore graduates were offered starting salaries of $90,000. The highest offer, a record-breaker, was for $193,000 offered by Barclays Bank in London. That record fell a short time later when ISB produced a graduate who received a starting offer of $233,000—from an Indian company. It would have been unimaginable just a few short years ago that Indian graduates would command starting salaries such as these—from an Indian company no less.

Indian talent is peppered across the American business-school landscape, where some of the most celebrated professors hail from India. Many have explicitly made a philosophy of doing well while doing good a cornerstone of their intellectual legacy. The most famous of these is undoubtedly University of Michigan's C. K. Prahalad, the author of *The Fortune at the Bottom of the Pyramid,* who argues that capitalism and poverty eradication can go hand in hand. Harvard Business School's Rakesh Khunara is working on reforming an American culture of greed into one of equity. Dipak Jain, dean of the Kellogg School of Business, has invited author and spiritual guru Deepak Chopra to give courses to executives searching for ways to be better businessmen and better people, and has made courses on ethics and social responsibility a part of the curriculum.

A Powerful New Political Force

With growing economic clout and sheer numbers, Indian Americans are coming of age politically. First-generation Indian immigrants' confidence in their ability to participate in the American political process has grown in tandem with their economic success. Second-generation, native-born Indian Americans have grown up comfortable with asserting themselves publicly. Many have been nurtured in ethnic organizations through the Indian and South Asian clubs that have proliferated on college campuses across the country. Indian Americans, such as Louisiana Republican congressman Bobby Jindal, San Francisco district attorney Kamala Harris, Maryland legislative majority leader Kumar P. Barve, and New Jersey state legislator Upendra Chivukula, have been elected to public office. Others work for prominent elected officials or closely advise the current administration. Neera Tanden is a senior policy adviser to Senator Hillary Clinton, and was her legislative director before joining the Center for American Progress where she now works. Bombay native Ashley Tellis, now a senior fellow at the Carnegie Endowment for International Peace, worked closely with former ambassador Robert Blackwill during his tenure as U.S. ambassador to India during the first term of the George W. Bush administration.

Tellis, one of the main proponents of the nuclear deal signed by President Bush and Prime Minister Singh last year, took a leave of absence from Carnegie in 2006 to advise the Bush administration on securing passage of the deal by both houses of Congress. While Tellis was advising senior members of the Bush administration, his former boss Robert Blackwill was working for the Indian government on the same issue. Blackwill now leads Barbour, Griffiths & Rogers, a powerful lobbying group on Capitol Hill. His company was paid $700,000 by the government of India to help push through congressional approval of the deal. India also paid $600,000 to Venable, a lobbying outfit staffed by, among others, former Democratic senator Birch Bayh.[13]

In their quest to get Congress to approve the nuclear deal, the government of India and the Bush administration tapped a formidable ally: Indian-American lobbying groups. Though relatively new actors in Washington, Indian Americans are flexing strong political muscles. The U.S. India Political Action Committee, USINPAC, created in 2002 by Sanjay Puri, is the most active Indian-American political action group on the Hill. Other groups include the Indian American Center for Political Awareness (IACPA), the Association of Indians in America (AIA), the National Federation of Indian Associations (NFIA), the National Association of Americans of Asian Indian Descent (NAAAID), and the Indian American Forum for Political Education (IAFPE).

These are all dwarfed in terms of influence, however, by USINPAC, an organization with more than twenty-seven thousand members.[14] As a member of USINPAC's e-mail alert list, I regularly get messages exhorting me to write or call my senator or congressman every time something is coming up on the congressional agenda that affects U.S. policy toward India or Indian Americans. The stated mission of USIN-PAC is to advance the interests of the Indian-American community by providing "bipartisan support to candidates for federal, state and local office who support the issues that are important to the Indian American community."[15] The organization has pinpointed five areas of particular importance: U.S.-India relations, immigration, anti-hate-crime measures, equal opportunity and civil rights, and entrepreneurship and business. The last, rather vague category is explained by USINPAC on their Web site as "advocacy for issues such as small business."

From its inception, USINPAC has worked closely with pro-Israel lobbying groups. The organization got its start under the tutelage of AIPAC, the American Israel Public Affairs Committee. On the AIPAC model, USINPAC has placed young Indian-American interns in congressional offices, building a corps of former insiders who know the ropes and have connections with members of Congress.[16] "It's pointless to reinvent the wheel," USINPAC founder Sanjay Puri has pragmatically declared.[17] As Kumar Barve told the *Washington Post* in 2003, "Indian Americans see the American Jewish community as a yardstick against which to compare themselves. It's seen as the gold standard in terms of political activism."[18]

Another pro-Israel group USINPAC works closely with is the American Jewish Committee (AJC). The AJC features USINPAC on its Web site under its "advancing interethnic and interreligious partnerships" heading.[19] The real glue between these two organizations is around strategic and defense-related issues, particularly those aimed at combating terror, especially by Islamic groups. USINPAC lobbies specifically to support a U.S.-India strategic alliance and defense cooperation between the two countries under the rubric "terrorism and homeland security." In particular, the group seeks to insure "India's inclusion in National Missile Defense."[20] Many Americans believe that supporting Israel is in the best interest of the United States; USIN-PAC and other Indian lobbying groups are working hard to convince Americans the same is true of India.

The efforts of these lobbying groups were critical for passage of the nuclear deal, which required changes in U.S. law and the transformation of decades of U.S. nuclear nonproliferation policy. Efforts to fuse the notion of U.S. security with selling nuclear technology to India took inventive routes. Last year, Jack Bonner of Bonner & Associates created yet another lobbying group: the Indian American Security Leadership Council. The purpose of the group, according to *PRWeek* magazine, was to "mobilize military veteran groups in favor of legislative changes to enable nuclear power technology to be sold to India even though it is not a signatory to the Non-Proliferation Treaty." The group had its work cut out for it: India was not top-of-mind among U.S. veterans. "Quite frankly," Bonner confessed, "the veterans' groups weren't very aware of the issue when we first talked to them about it, so we had to work with them in order for them to be comfortable with it." Why target U.S. veterans' groups when it is U.S. representatives who will vote on the nuclear deal? "The issue is not just the message," Bonner explained, "but the messenger—who is credible on this."[21] This is a strategy of training the mouse to kill the cat: What congressman or senator can resist an issue pushed by U.S. veterans as crucial to America's security? According to *PRWeek*, the Indian American Security Leadership Council effort was paid for by affluent Indian Americans from both parties, including Ramesh Kapur, a trustee of the Democratic National Committee, and Krishna Srinivasa, a campaign supporter of Bush in 2000 and 2004.

The Congressional Caucus on India and Indian Americans was created in 1994. It counts 173 members of the 109th Congress, including 105 Democrats and 68 Republicans. "The objective of the Congressional Caucus on India & Indian Americans is to push the Indian American community's agenda on the Hill."[22] Robert M. Hathaway, who served for twelve years on the staff of the House Foreign Affairs Committee and is now the director of the Asia Program at the Woodrow Wilson International Center for Scholars, under-lined the power of the India Caucus, saying it "is to an important extent—certainly not exclusively, but to an important extent—responsible for that sea change and it genuinely is a sea change in the attitude of members of Congress about India and about the importance of the U.S.-India relationship."[23] In 2004, the U.S. Senate followed suit and established the Friends of India. The group is cochaired by the Republican freshman senator from Texas, John Cornyn, and Democratic freshman senator Hillary Clinton. It is the first-ever group of its kind in the U.S. Senate focused on a single country. Then Indian ambassador to the United States Lalit Mansingh was reportedly delighted: "I have to commend all the Indian leaders of the Indian-American community that finally made this happen."[24]

India "may one day be second only to Israel among international interests able to influence Washington policy makers," stated Robert Hoffman, a lobbyist for Oracle, for an article in the *International Herald Tribune* in July 2006.[25] The U.S.-India Business Council (USIBC), part of the U.S. Chamber of Commerce, channeled a huge lobbying effort on behalf of the two hundred U.S. companies it represents, including General Electric, Boeing, J. P. Morgan Chase, American International Group, Ford, Dow Chemical, Lockheed Martin, and the Bechtel Group. The U.S. Chamber of Commerce also weighed in, hiring Patton Boggs, Washington's biggest lobbying firm, to help push through approval of the deal.

The nuclear deal is all about profits for American companies: the U.S. Chamber of Commerce estimates $100 billion in energy sales to companies such as GE and Bechtel. GE has raised its forecast for 2010 sales in India from $5 billion to $8 billion. Supporters of the deal estimate that India could spend $27 billion on nuclear plants through 2020. American companies are hopeful they would build at least one of India's new plants. According to a senior adviser to the U.S.-India Business Council, Raymond Vickery, if the deal is approved, Lockheed would have "a reasonable chance to get a $4 billion to $9 billion contract to supply 126 combat fighter planes to India's navy, a contract that India would have been unlikely to approve while sanctions were in place." Vickery further estimated that U.S. companies could get "a considerable portion of the $20 to $40 billion in acquisition that the Indians plan to make by 2020."[26]

Indian companies were no less focused on the potential profits to be reaped. The Confederation of Indian Industry (CII) has worked tirelessly if discreetly to woo members of Congress, paying out more than $538,000 in travel expenses to India for nineteen Congress members, eleven spouses, and fifty-eight congressional staffers between 2000 and 2005—and that was before CII registered as a lobbying group. In April 2005, after registering to lobby for the first time, CII paid Barbour, Griffiths & Rogers $500,000 to lobby various U.S. government agencies "including Congress, the White House, the State Department, and the Department of Defense."[27] As Illinois senator Barack Obama, who has expressed strong views supporting nuclear nonproliferation, quipped, "There appears to be a very coordinated effort to have every Indian-American person that I know contact me." He also said he'd received calls from "prominent investment bankers."[28]

On July 26, 2006, the U.S. House of Representatives gave overwhelming approval to the U.S.-India nuclear deal. Days after midterm elections gave back to Democrats control of both houses of Congress, the Senate approved the U.S.-India nuclear deal by a substantial margin of 85 to 12 votes on November 16, 2006.

Growing India-U.S. Trade

Commercial links between India and the United States are growing rapidly. Both Indian and American companies have a bigger and bigger stake in major foreign policy decisions affecting the relationship between the two countries. Between 1990 and 2006, through a series of different governments led by different political parties, trade between the United States and India grew a whopping 400 percent to over $26 billion. Bilateral trade between the two countries was set to grow by 21 percent last year alone. At a meeting of the U.S.-India Trade Policy Forum in New Delhi last May, the two governments pledged to double this to approximately $60 billion within three years. While this still remains far lower than U.S. trade with China, pegged at $280 billion in 2005, everyone expects that India-U.S. trade will continue to increase dramatically. The Indian government is anxious to increase U.S. investment, without which there is little hope of obtaining the $150 billion it says it needs over the next decade to upgrade its severely underdeveloped infrastructure. In a startling acceleration of the tearing down of barriers to foreign companies doing business in India, Minister for Commerce and Industry Kamal Nath last year announced rises in the foreign direct-investment ceiling to 100 percent in a range of sectors, including airport construction, oil and gas infrastructure, and cash-and-carry wholesale trading. This is all the more radical when one considers that the first two of these areas were nationalized for decades.

The United States continues to press hard for remaining limitations on investment to come down. Multibrand retail, for example, is a sector in which foreign companies are not allowed to operate in India, but Wal-Mart has already set up an office there, and press reports of its plans for the Indian market were proliferating as this book went to print. Last fall, the Bush administration organized the biggest delegation of U.S. businesses to India ever. The trip was pitched as a rare profit-making opportunity. According to the U.S. Department of Commerce's Export.gov Web site about the then planned delegation, "India, the world's fastest growing free-market democracy, presents lucrative opportunities for all types of businesses—especially U.S. companies. In 2005, U.S. merchandise exports to India were almost $8 billion, double what they were in 2002."[29]

Level Playing Field

As Amartya Sen has pointed out, democracy is legitimate when it is fully participatory, at the ballot box and in terms of economic opportunity and social justice. India's burgeoning economy is growing unevenly, with significant disparities between regions and social classes. The United States, though far richer, faces similar challenges. Both democracies need to harness growth to the purpose of creating jobs and economically enfranchising all citizens. The challenge is clearly greater for India, but it is a challenge neither country can afford to ignore. The examples of South Korea, of postwar Japan and

Germany, show that when the right kind of government policies are married to economic growth, with a premium placed on high literacy, agricultural reform, and basic social security, miracles can happen. Brazil, on the other hand, was blessed with extremely high growth in the 1980s, but because it failed to make the investments in its people required to reduce social inequalities, it has remained a country of economic extremes. India is working hard to avoid this fate. The United States is not.

In 2006, *The Economist* magazine did a special report on inequality in America. The magazine cited a widely discussed study by Emmanuel Saez of the University of California and Thomas Piketty of the École Normale Supérieure on just how startlingly wealth is being concentrated toward the very top of the American socioeconomic ladder. According to Saez and Piketty's study, the share of aggregate income going to the highest-earning 1 percent of Americans doubled from 8 percent in 1980 to over 16 percent in 2004. The top one-hundredth of 1 percent—14,000 taxpayers—quadrupled between 1980 and 2004.[30]

The Economist predicted that this trend was not likely to be temporary because it was due to structural changes in the U.S. job market caused by global economic integration, especially of India and China. "The integration of China's low-skilled millions and the increased offshoring of services to India and other countries has expanded the global supply of workers. This has reduced the relative price of labour and raised the returns on capital. That reinforces the income concentration at the top."[31] The trend toward extreme inequality is so pronounced that Ben Bernanke, the chairman of the Federal Reserve, cautioned in August 2006 that steps needed to be taken "to ensure that the benefits of global economic integration are sufficiently widely shared."[32]

India's role as a source of relatively low-cost, highly skilled labor is increasing rapidly as corporations race to gain competitive advantage and maximize profits. Pleading that a shortage of skilled workers, particularly in information technology, impairs their ability to grow, U.S. companies have pressed to increase the cap on H-1B visas—visas that admit highly skilled workers for up to six years when sponsored by an employer. The H-1B visa and offshore outsourcing are two sides of the same coin: connecting highly skilled workers from foreign countries, particularly from India, to American jobs, either by bringing the worker to the United States or by taking the job to the worker overseas. Last year, Microsoft and others pressed hard to get Congress to raise the cap from 65,000 to 115,000 and to allow some foreign students to bypass the visa program and move directly from completion of their degree to a sponsored green card.

Meanwhile, before the Committee on Small Business of the U.S. House of Representatives, Ron Hira, a professor of public policy at Rochester Institute of Technology and chair of the R&D Policy Committee of the Institute of Electrical and Electronics Engineers—USA (IEEE-USA), testified "on the offshoring of high-skilled jobs" in October 2003. Professor Hira told the committee, "According to the most recent data from the Bureau of Labor Statistics, electrical, electronics, and computer hardware engineers continue to face a higher unemployment rate than the general population, and over double the rate for other managers and professionals. The news for engineering managers is even worse, with an unemployment rate of 8 percent."[33] Hira attributes this directly to the growth of offshoring and of H-1B visas given to foreign technical workers.

Moreover, he identifies Indian Americans (he is himself of Indian origin) as a prime factor in this process. "There's a clear connection between the Indian diaspora in the United States, the use of H-1B, and offshore outsourcing," he says. Indian nationals account for 37 percent of H-1B recipients. The Programmers Guild, an advocacy group for computer-industry workers, is concerned that H-1B body shops are exploiting foreign workers while driving down U.S. wages, paying wages of less than $45,820 to computer professionals when the Department of Labor puts the median wage for computer occupations at over $62,000.[34]

Ron Hira is not opposed to bringing in needed technical workers with H-1B visas. He is opposed to the body shops that bring in workers at salaries far below American industry levels, driving down wages, and contributing to high unemployment among American computer professionals. The flip side of the H-1B visa question is offshoring. An estimated one million American jobs have already been offshored. By 2015, it is estimated that 3.4 million white-collar U.S. jobs will be off-shored. In all, a staggering 14 million U.S. white-collar jobs, or one in nine, are at risk of being offshored, with India being the top outsourcing destination.[35] The U.S. government must acknowledge how the third industrial revolution, including offshoring and H-1B visas, is affecting U.S. workers, and come up with policies that will help American workers survive these sweeping structural adjustments.

The Indian Side of Offshoring

I recently had a problem with my laptop that required me to contact customer service at IBM, Microsoft, and Linksys. All three companies routed my call to India. I spoke to a young woman in Bangalore with IBM, a young man in Gurgaon with Microsoft, and another young man in Pune with Linksys. These young Indians were unfailingly polite and surprised to have someone on the line who knew something about their country. But when I repeated the tagline *Koi desh perfect nehi hai* (No country is perfect) from *Rang De Basanti,* a recent movie hugely popular with college-age kids in India (and which they had all seen), one of them replied, sounding a bit frightened, "Actually, ma'am, we're not allowed. We have to speak English only."

Call centers are magnets for urban Indian youth, providing them with income sometimes greater than their parents', and a chance to work in an environment filled with young people their age. Their job is hard, no doubt. They work the night shift, when it is daytime in the United States, and are frequently subject to abuse from irate customers. A whole call-center culture has sprouted up, with restaurants, coffee shops, and nightclubs catering to a pool of young people with disposable incomes who are, to a large extent, free from parental overview (most young Indians live at home). Last year, Chetan Bhagat published a novel that became a best-selling sensation in India called *One Night @ the Call Center.* A cast of characters set adrift in the barren night of the Delhi satellite city Gurgaon wrestle with a host of problems unique to their generation. The group's boss is a conniving, greedy guy who sucks up to his American bosses. All of the young people I spoke with during my computer-problem tour of India told me they had heard of this book, and one had read it. When I asked him if it portrayed his experience accurately, he replied, "Ma'am, it depends a lot on your boss." And then I remembered that "this call may be recorded for quality-assurance purposes."

Before India's technological revolution, social mobility was almost nonexistent. A young person's prospects were largely determined by his family's status, connections, and wealth. India's information technology companies have changed this. They have proven that it is possible to be hired and to succeed purely on merit. Narayana Murthy, chairman and cofounder of Infosys, told me the meritocratic paradigm introduced by Infosys was "the most revolutionary thing that has happened in this country." For India, offshoring provides a vital and growing stream of new jobs for a young population hungry for opportunity. It has been a major factor in the growth of India's information technology sector, which is projected to increase from 1.4 percent of India's GDP in 2001 to 8–10 percent by 2008.[36]

Infosys, the blue-chip, Bangalore-based company that is the poster child for India's potential in BPO or business process outsourcing, is growing at the astonishing rate of 50 percent per year. From its beginnings a mere twenty-five years ago as a start-up launched by a group of friends who possessed nothing more than a passion to create a business, Infosys now has sixty-six thousand employees in twenty different countries. The average age of its employees is twenty-seven. Wipro and Tata Consultancy Services are the two other Indian IT giants, and there are hundreds of smaller companies. All of these companies are fast expanding the range of services they provide, moving from systems maintenance into software development, systems redesign, consulting services, and other areas. Jobs are shifting away from middle-aged Americans with expensive health care and benefits to Indians in their twenties eager to get a job. The starting salary for a software engineer in India is about $5,000. That same job in the United States goes for $60,000.[37]

By 2009, 20 percent of IBM's worldwide workforce of approximately three hundred thousand employees will be in India. Intel,

Cisco, Microsoft, and HP are just some of the other U.S.-based companies with facilities in India. These companies are looking at India as a two-pronged opportunity: one, as a way to significantly reduce labor costs and access high-quality research, and two, as a market with the potential to outstrip markets in the United States, Europe, and developed East Asia. As Amar Babu, managing director of Intel India, told me, "Intel views India as a critical research and development site for Intel worldwide. At the same time, India is a consumption market for IT. A lot of future growth will come from emerging markets. Intel's India business is growing at thirty percent."

Americans in India

For many years, the only Americans I saw in India were tourists at the airport. Now, the new restaurants and bars are filled with young American and European expats who are in India partly for the adventure, and partly because they see India as an opportunity destination. According to an article in *BusinessWeek* last year, thirty thousand expats work for tech and outsourcing companies in India, an increase of 300 percent in just three years.[38] *TimeOut Mumbai,* the Bombay edition of *TimeOut* magazine, estimates the number of Americans working and living in Bombay at four thousand.[39] This is not a huge number compared to, say, the fifty thousand Americans who live in Paris or the hundreds of thousands of expatriates from around the world who make their home in New York, but it is a lot more Americans than ever used to live in Bombay.

Aside from the Indian Americans or Indian nationals who were U.S. residents that are returning to India in droves, there are recent college grads like Nathan Linkon, a native of Milwaukee, Wisconsin, and Peter Norlander, a graduate of Cornell University. Both in their early twenties, they work for Infosys at the company's posh complex in Bangalore. When I visited Infosys early last year, their boss, Nandan Nilekani, set me up in a conference room overlooking the company's entrance so I could chat with them.

Peter was the more savvy of the two. He had visited India with his family and had also lived in Bombay on his own for a while during college as an intern writing for the *Financial Express*. Nathan had never been to India before taking the job with Infosys. When I asked him how a boy from Wisconsin ended up in Bangalore, he told me, "I was doing my job search, just like everyone else, and I stumbled on the Infosys listing. I didn't even realize it was for a job in India. When I spoke with my father about it, he basically said he'd disown me if I didn't go for this. So, then I got the offer, and I'm like okay, this will never happen to me again." They told me there were seven American employees at the company. They live in an apartment complex owned by Infosys. While it is only seventeen kilometers, a little over ten miles, from the Infosys campus, it takes them between one and two hours to make their way through the terrible Bangalore traffic between home and work.

"We don't cook," explained Nathan. "We order in. There are a couple of Chinese places. Pizza Hut. Domino's. Or we go across the street to a place where we can get a whole South Indian meal for twenty rupees [about forty cents]." They told me about Bangalore's nightlife, and the difficulties dating Indian girls. Either girls don't go out, or, as Linkon told me, "the girls are, like, way richer than you are, you know? Like really rich. They are so snobby. If they talk to you, it's because they've been abroad and they know it's okay to talk to guys."

After I met with Nathan and Peter, Infosys dramatically expanded its U.S. hires, picking up three hundred new employees, many with technical backgrounds from top schools such as MIT. Most of these new recruits will spend a couple of months training at the company's facility in Mysore, India, then move out to company locations around the world, including back in the United States. The trend is clear: companies from any country will seek the best talent they can get, wherever they can find it, and that includes Indian companies hiring Americans and Europeans.

Infosys isn't the only Indian company hiring Americans. Anand Mahindra, a graduate of Harvard College (magna cum laude) and the Harvard Business School, started hiring Ivy League graduates in 2003 when a Yale graduate, Ryan Floyd, e-mailed him asking about opportunities. In November 2004, after a year with the company, Ryan made the rounds for Mahindra & Mahindra, hitting Harvard, Tufts, Yale, Princeton, Penn, and Columbia for recruits. Anand Mahindra's strategy is straightforward: "These guys might stay two years but they become ambassadors for the country and the company. A person like that is going to have a drive and intelligence beyond the usual. I pay them what I pay an Indian MBA. We get the value."

When I asked him how he knew which young people would be up to an India experience and which ones just wouldn't, he replied, "I use the *Matrix* pill question. I ask them, 'Are you a person who takes the red pill or the blue pill? Certainly, if you come, your life will be changed.'"

I was chatting with Anand in the foyer to the private dining room in Mahindra's corporate headquarters in the Worli neighborhood of Bombay. Off the main road, in the middle of the old mill area, the angular redbrick building was broken up by open spaces, landscaped areas, and different levels going off in different directions. Anand called David Aranow, a Harvard graduate who was working for him, to come and talk to me.

A clean-cut, tall twenty-three-year-old with blue eyes that matched his tie, David Aranow had never been to India before. "I wanted to work in Latin America," he told me. "I hadn't really heard about India's boom. But I was intrigued by the opportunity to work on auto exports to Latin America by an Indian company." He paused. "You know, most of the companies that come to recruit are consulting firms. There is almost nothing international. This seemed like an unusual opportunity."

I asked him if he liked his job.

"You get more responsibility here and you can get a lot more done than you could ever do in consulting. I'm learning so much," he replied.

I wondered what it was like for these young Americans to live in Bombay. "The first two months were really difficult. I had to relearn everything. I had to relearn how to walk down the street," David said.

Two other Americans were working for Mahindra when I was there last year. "The three of them share an apartment in Bandra," explained Anand Mahindra. Bandra, Bombay's first suburb, where old bungalows and modest apartment buildings are scattered along tree-lined streets and some of the newest restaurants and clubs have opened, is a popular spot with young people, less expensive and more happening than south Bombay. Anand smiled and said, "They're known as the Mahindra boys." Glancing at David with a glint in his eyes, he said to me, "I heard about the Christmas party where they were dressed as elves."

David looked up surprised and exclaimed, "You know more than we know you know!"

Anand laughed.

CHAPTER TWO

India Imagines the Future

On an unseasonably warm evening last November, the cultural cream of Indian society in New York gathered in the Crystal Pavilion at Tavern on the Green in Central Park following a private screening of Mira Nair's haunting new film interpretation of Jhumpa Lahiri's novel *The Namesake*. The screening kicked off the sixth IAAC Film Festival sponsored by the Indo-American Arts Council (IAAC), and preceded a gala dinner and auction. Under one of the many wonderfully mismatched chandeliers that are part of the room's charm, authors Salman Rushdie, who, with his stunning wife, model Padma Lakshmi, chaired the gala; Kiran Desai, who had just been awarded the Booker Prize for her novel *The Inheritance of Loss*; Shashi Tharoor, who had come in second in the voting to be the next secretary-general of the United Nations; and Orhan Pamuk, who had just won the Nobel Prize for Literature and happened to be in the neighborhood as he was teaching at Columbia University, were deep in conversation. Around them, guests in fancy Indian dress, little cocktail numbers, business suits, and artist-casual outfits milled around, drinks in hand, calling out greetings and bussing newcomers on the cheek.

At the cocktail party preceding the screening, the Who's Who list of the Indian diaspora cultural elite went on endlessly. I did catch celebrated actress and author Madhur Jaffrey, just out with her memoir *Climbing the Mango Trees*, and her husband, accomplished violinist Sanford Allen. Filmmaker Jagmohan Mundhra—his movie *Back-*

waters was capping off the festival a few days later—and his wife, Chandra, and their film producer daughter, Smriti Mundhra, were there. I saw Sarita Choudhury, who starred in Mira Nair's film *Mississippi Masala*. Kal Penn, who performs his first serious dramatic role in *The Namesake,* was there, and shared the podium with Mira Nair for the Q&A after the movie. Sreenath Sreenivasan, dean at the Columbia School of Journalism and the founder of the South Asian Journalists Association (SAJA), was talking with Neelam Deo, consul general of India in New York. I said hello to Sundaram Tagore, who runs Tagore Gallery, and Vishaka Desai, president of the Asia Society. Anand and Anuradha Mahindra had come over from Bombay. Mahindra was the lead sponsor of the evening, and the festival program's back cover featured the message: "Mahindra: Bringing You India Through Cinema." Anand majored in filmmaking and photography as an undergraduate at Harvard, and has clearly never lost his interest in movies. Making it all come together, Aroon Shivdasani, executive director of the IAAC, and one of the driving forces in fostering Indian and Indian-inspired arts in New York, seemed everywhere at once.

The Namesake is an inspired interpretation of a deft novel about the Indian immigrant experience in the United States, charting an Indian Bengali couple as they make a life in America's cold Northeast and raise two children who are inevitably caught between the culture of their parents and the American culture into which they are born. Indian Americans find the story deeply moving because it is a variation, told superbly, of our own stories.

The film is a profoundly affectionate portrait of two cities dear to Mira Nair, Calcutta and New York (Boston in the book), and two cultures, Indian and American. Sooni Taraporevala, who has worked with Nair since her 1988 film *Salaam Bombay!,* wrote the beautiful screenplay.

The Namesake is a landmark film in the evolution of international Indian cinema, based on rich subject matter, with superb acting by a cast that includes Indian actors Irfan Khan and Tabu in performances that break your heart (there wasn't a dry eye in the packed theater), as well as Indian-American rising star Kal Penn, London-born Zuleikha Robinson, and Americans Glenne Headly and Brooke

Smith. Mira Nair emotionally identified with the novel, as she told me when I interviewed her last winter. "I'm from Calcutta, and I'm from New York too. I remember what it felt like when I first came to this country. I still don't like to wear shoes," she said. Sitting in the darkened theater surrounded by members of the community whose story was unfolding on the screen was a profoundly moving experience.

The picture, destined for a worldwide audience, is a coproduction of American movie company Fox Searchlight Pictures and Indian entertainment company UTV Motion Pictures, with additional financing from Japanese producer Entertainment Farm. UTV will distribute the film in India; Fox in other markets. Both hope this will be the film, following the success of Nair's 2004 movie *Monsoon Wedding*, that confirms the coming-of-age of Indian cinema in the global market.

UTV is run by Ronnie Screwvala. A self-made man in his forties who started his company at the dawn of India's television boom, Ronnie is affable, more comfortable in jeans than in a business suit. Despite the casual demeanor, Ronnie is serious about taking Indian entertainment, and his company, global. His 2005 hit release *Rang De Basanti*, which featured British actress Alice Patten speaking fluent Hindi, didn't play in New York at the "Indian" movie houses in Queens or Edison, New Jersey. It ran in a mainstream house in Manhattan; the same for UTV's 2006 gangster-pic *Don*, starring Shahrukh Khan. Combining with Fox Searchlight Pictures to do *The Namesake* makes perfect sense for the global direction Ronnie is taking UTV.

A prime audience abroad for Indian television and Bollywood films is the Indian diaspora. In the United States and the United Kingdom, the diaspora has emerged as a powerful bridge between India and the rest of the world.

A Bridge Between India and America

Like waves of immigrants before them, Indian-Americans are slowly but surely adding their own flavors to the American stew. Everywhere Americans turn these days, they run into something from India. Yoga is the fastest-growing leisure activity in the country. Indian restaurants have proliferated from coast to coast, from fast-food joints such as Naan Stop on California's coast to temples of the latest nouvelle cuisine such as Suvir Saran's Devi in New York, the only Indian restaurant to make it into the Michelin Guide to New York's best restaurants. Frozen packs of premade Indian food are available in supermarkets everywhere.

Indian Americans and Indians who live in the United States are giving an Indian inflection to the world of art and letters beyond cinema. Abstract painter Natvar Bhavsar has lived and worked out of his loft in New York's SoHo for forty years. His paintings, where intense pigments trace a poetics of color, hang in leading museums and private collections around the world, and his shows in New York regularly sell out. Zubin Mehta was the first Indian to take the world of American classical music by storm. Born in Bombay, Mr. Mehta was musical director of the Los Angeles Philharmonic Orchestra for sixteen years before assuming the directorship of the New York Philharmonic Orchestra, a post he held until 1991. In New York, Rekha Malhotra, better known as DJ Rekha, regales a mixed crowd at S.O.B.'s with her monthly Basement Bhangra, a veritable *mela* or festival of remixed music set to flashing visuals.

Literature was the first cultural area where Indian artists burst onto the contemporary American scene. Salman Rushdie, who now lives in New York, marked the founding moment of India's literary explosion in the English language with *Midnight's Children*. Canadian authors Rohinton Mistry (*A Fine Balance*), Shauna Singh Baldwin (*What the Body Remembers*), and M. G. Vassanji (*The In-Between Life of Vikram Lall*) are all well known in the United States. Amitav Ghosh, author of a series of critically acclaimed books, including his latest, *The Hungry Tide,* lives in Brooklyn, as does Jhumpa Lahiri.

Twenty-four-hour cable and satellite stations provide an umbilical cord to the mother country for overseas Indians. The diaspora's purchasing power is transforming the distribution and the content of Bollywood movies. Indian media companies are buying themselves a foothold in Hollywood, while Indians with experience in the American media environment are taking their skills and knowledge back to India. The big American media conglomerates seek Indians comfortable in both the United States and in India to facilitate their entry into a booming market. With one foot in America and one foot in India, this group of people is igniting a paradigm shift in the production and content of global media.

India is poised to become not just a huge market for entertainment products or an important cheap labor pool for animation and other labor-intensive processes, but a fount of original content created by Indians for a global audience. The day India unseats America as the media and entertainment superpower may be coming sooner than we think.

Tellywood

Television is playing a uniquely powerful role in India's transformation. The growth of television in India over the last couple of decades has been breathtaking. Until 1991, there was a single state broadcaster, DoorDarshan. With support from UNESCO, television was introduced to India by its government in 1959. Originally lodged in the DRDO (Defence Research and Development Organisation), its primary purpose was to uplift and unify a diverse nation. This remained the national broadcaster's mission throughout the 1980s, when color television arrived in India and the Indian government encouraged the purchase of sets by lowering import duties. In 1983, television signals were available to just 28 percent of the population, doubling to 56 percent by 1986, and reaching over 90 percent by 1990. Rechristened the DD group of channels, DoorDarshan still reaches over 90 percent of the Indian population and carries a variety of programs in English and in eleven regional languages on twenty different channels.[1]

CNN and MTV came to India in 1991, riding on STAR's satellite waves. A mere sixteen years later, Indians can choose from as many as 350 channels, and now every major media conglomerate, from Disney to Time Warner to Viacom to the BBC, has channels broadcasting in India.[2] India's opening to the rest of the world in 1991 precipitated an explosion in media. Whereas most Americans have experienced the advent of each of these media as different waves, one breaking over the other and advancing communications and enter-tainment incrementally, many Indians are being exposed to them all at once. India is experiencing rapid growth in television, both in the number of households that have television and the number of chan-nels and programs available. Set in motion by the arrival of new pri-vate Indian channels, such as Zee TV, the number of Indian-owned networks and Indian-created programs is growing by leaps and bounds, as is the number of foreign networks and programs. Whole segments of the population that used to be isolated from the rest of society and from the world are now plugged in. Lower-income house-wives, farmers, and small shopkeepers are today watching television, using cell phones, and beginning to use the Internet.

It is hard to imagine how quickly India is changing and the extent to which media and entertainment are driving this transformation. Such fast change naturally throws notions of national and personal identity into question. The media are not only the spaces where many of these issues of identity are explored, they are also where images of the new India—a fast-modernizing country on the move—are created and disseminated, both to Indian audiences and to audiences around the world. At the same time, the so-called digital divide that plagues the planet, starkly separating those who have access to these power-ful technologies and those who don't, exists within India itself. One of the core challenges facing the country is how to bring India's poor into the media and communications revolution.

The explosion of television has coincided with—and been a goad to—accelerated economic growth, the penetration of the Indian mar-ket by transnational brands, and the rise of a new consumer class. Along with new Indian soap operas, game shows, talk shows, music shows, and news shows, television has served up a smorgasbord of slick advertisements for a growing array of products and services. Television has made the world outside India newly visible to an expanding number of Indians. It has introduced urban India to rural villagers. It parades the lifestyles of the rich before the eyes of the poor. It has opened up enticing new worlds of possibility to a range of Indian viewers, even as it reinforces the gap between those citizens who are a part of the new India and those who are not.

Television in India has been a force for the democratization of aspiration. A host of new "Tellywood" stars have cropped up to challenge the demigods and goddesses of Bollywood. Ordinary citizens have made instant fortunes and achieved overnight fame on such shows as *Kaun Banega Crorepati*—the Indian version of *Who Wants to Be a Millionaire*—and *Indian Idol*. Along with a multitude of channels in Hindi, the national language, regional-language channels are proliferating, spreading the television experience well beyond the English-language elite and Hindi-speaking urban and northern populations. India is a highly segmented society—divided by language, region, religion, class, and caste—where 53 percent of women and 30 percent of men are illiterate, as are 26 percent of youths ages fifteen to twenty-four.[3] Many women in India do not work outside the home, and access to television is connecting them, and other citizens, to the life of the nation and the larger world.

India's growth since the 1980s has been meteoric but also uneven. The sudden embrace of liberalization, American-style capitalism and consumerism by India's governing and business elite is passionately contested in this vibrant, often chaotic democracy. There is a backlash against the quick opening up of the country. There is anxiety about the rapid influx of foreign goods, companies, and lifestyles. The power and prevalence of television advertising and the spectacle of foreign or foreign-inspired programming have caused television to be blamed for a turn India has taken toward consumer capitalism that not all Indians agree with and that has, in any case, left many behind.

Television's ascendance in India has also coincided with a fragmentation of Indian politics, an increase in caste-based and regional-based parties and leaders, a series of national coalition governments—some more fragile than others—and the rise of Hindu nationalism.[4] In fact, the televised serialization of the *Ramayana* epic from January 1987 to August 1989, which saw record viewership across India, coincided with the rise of the Ram Janmabhoomi movement, which eventually propelled the Hindu nationalist Bharatiya Janata Party or BJP into power. India's recent history has been fraught with political violence. The country has repeatedly been riven by terrorist attacks, violent clashes between religious groups, particularly Hindus and Muslims, as well as between forest-dwelling Tribals, or Adivasis as they are called in India, and powerful mining interests, not to mention the growth of the Naxalites and other Maoist-inspired rebel movements.

Mallika Chopra was the point person in India for MTV in 1995. She had always wanted to work in media, and the opportunity to go to India with MTV was exciting. She was put up in the splendid Taj Hotel, overlooking the Gateway to India on the waterfront in Bombay. However, after a while, she began to question what she was doing. "Sitting in a car going through the slums of Bombay and watching twenty kids shoeless in a store watching MTV, I felt like 'Oh my God, I'm spreading this in India.' That's when I decided to leave MTV."

I can see those twenty shoeless kids, dusty feet and splayed toes, mouths agape, watching TV. Just past Dadar, on the way into South Bombay to have dinner, or to go to a party, I have passed the long row of one-room shanties, many with a second-story addition reached by a ladder. The shanties are squeezed between the road and a wall along the railroad tracks. Families spill onto the street, cooking, sleeping, washing from a bucket, sitting and chatting with neighbors as my car whizzes by. Dogs trot along, wending their way among the people, some already asleep, curled into grateful oblivion on a thin pallet. Goats nibble at bits of trash. Doors are open. There are no windows, or sometimes a small opening with iron bars is set high in the wall to let in a little air, a little light. The only running water is from a single tap some distance away. There are no toilets. Near an open garbage area, a small child squats and defecates. You can see into the interiors: stacks of trunks, clothes hanging on hooks, a bed shared by the entire family, and in every other tiny dwelling, people crouched in rapt attention before the flickering blue glow of a television.

Despite jarring economic inequities, television has provided a diverse population with a sense of national community during a period of intense economic, political, and social transformation. It is a medium in which millions of citizens can share the experience of new aspirations and new anxieties.[5] Cricket matches, particularly against neighboring nemesis Pakistan or former imperial Britain, bring together Indians from every part of the country, indeed every corner of the planet, and every walk of life in a powerful, shared national experience. Game shows have become wildly popular with hometowns and states rooting for their participants, and millions of viewers sending in their votes via SMS text messages from their cell phones. On the soap operas, generations collide over diverging values on such shows as the hugely popular *Kyunki Saas Bhi Kabhi Bahu Thi* (Because the Mother-in-Law Was Once Herself a Daughter-in-Law), or one of my aunt's personal favorites, *Millie*.

Because I often stay with them, I have watched *Millie* several times at my aunt and uncle's home in Gurgaon, the fast-developing southern suburb of New Delhi. At first, the high-camp antics, exaggerated camera moves, and sound track that emits an earsplitting screech every time some dramatic truth is revealed or backstabbing remark is made led me to believe the show was absurdly superficial. The female servants in the show's wealthy family sport pink-and-white, French-maid miniskirt outfits with white sneakers, false eyelashes, and visible Pan-Cake makeup. But once I understood the story line, I realized *Millie* was a poignant tale of class conflict in a changing India. Millie, the title character, a young woman who is one of the maids, turns out to be the illegitimate daughter of the privileged son in the family. Beneath the camp, *Millie* confronts uncomfortable questions of class and sexual exploitation in the heart of India's most sacred institution, the family.

Television advertisements are also playing an important role in transforming India. During the commercial breaks from *Millie* or the latest news from NDTV, young, attractive Indians in tight jeans and fashionable haircuts strut their stuff across the small screen, race off in new cars, flirt as they swig from ice-cold bottles of soda, all to a catchy pop-music sound track. Housewives in saris debate the merits of new products and brands that reduce the daily drudgery of cooking or demonstrate their loving care of families lucky to have mothers who know how to make wise consumer choices. A man in Western casual clothes helps his father, dressed in a traditional *kurta*—a long tunic—off a train. This modern son knows that the right life insurance policy is the key to helping his parents live with dignity in their old age.[6]

No matter the product, ads for Pepsi or Coke or Bajaj motorcycles or Satya Paul saris are encouraging a consumerism that, until recently, was foreign to Indians. The potential for television advertising growth in India is impressive. A report from PricewaterhouseCoopers suggests that electronic-media revenues, including television, could nearly triple from $4.6 billion in 2005 to $12.8 billion by 2010.[7] India is expected to have 180 million television households by 2008. Compare that to a little over 100 million American television households today. With some 600 million viewers, India is already the largest television market in the world.[8] Sixty percent of Indian households, approximately 119 million, have a television, and 42 percent of these have cable service.[9]

There are thirty news channels in India, with the highest viewership going to the non-English-language channels, which broadcast in different languages, including Hindi, Marathi, Gujarati, Punjabi, Bengali, Kannada, Tamil, Oriya, Malayalam, and Telugu.[10] In India, twenty-two languages are spoken by more than 1 million people, and most states have their own distinct official language. The total number of languages spoken every day in India is an astounding 850. Most regions not only have a thriving television industry in their regional language, they also have their own film industry with their own stars. They have their own music and their own radio, as well as rich literary traditions, daily newspapers, and a variety of magazines. India's linguistic diversity makes for an incredibly kaleidoscopic media environment.

When I was invited to give live commentary last year on Headlines Today, one of the main English-language news channels, during President Bush's visit to India, my host was excited to discover I spoke Hindi and immediately wanted to put me on Aaj Tak, their Hindi-language news channel. "Ma'am, you don't understand. We are getting very high viewership today. That means about fifteen million people are watching Headlines Today," anchor Rahul Kanwal explained. "But there are at least sixty million people watching Aaj Tak. They never get to hear a foreign analyst. They would be so happy." I protested, quite petrified at the thought of playing the expert in a language I speak proficiently but not at all perfectly.

"Don't worry. If you don't know the Hindi word, just use the English one. Anyway, we all do it," was the quick reply, referring to the Indian tendency to mix Hindi and English into "Hinglish," a trend that has been reinforced by television and has created what is another distinct Indian dialect, much to the dismay of the cultured, Hindi-speaking elite. Hinglish is one more way for a younger generation to announce their connection with the rest of the world and to differentiate themselves from an older, more dogmatic generation.

When I asked Tom Freston, the former CEO of Viacom, about the potential of television in India, he said, "India has a dynamic you don't see in many other markets. India has more homes, and many of these don't yet have televisions. So, you've got more people and also more people who don't have TVs but want them and are getting the means to buy them: that means a lot of growth potential." In fact, revenues from subscriptions to television-cable and other broadcast services are forecast to grow from an estimated $1.67 billion in 2004 to $4.2 billion in 2009.[11]

Viacom's MTV was one of the first foreign channels to come to India. Since then, it has launched VH1 and Nickelodeon. I asked Freston, who at the time was CEO of Viacom, if he had any other plans to expand Viacom's television presence in India.

"I'd like to launch an Indian comedy channel," Freston replied. "That's something that doesn't travel very well. It's a challenge in the Indian market. In the United States, we are a multitelevision audience. People buy a new TV, and the old one goes into one of the kids' bedrooms. In India, it is a single-television market. When people buy a new TV, they trade in their old one and someone who doesn't have a TV and can't afford to buy a new one buys that old one. The old ones end up in the villages. So, you have the whole family in front of one TV. We've traditionally programmed to specific audiences, you know, MTV for youth, Nickelodeon for kids. India is still a general market, so that's a challenge for us."

The challenge of India's general television market hasn't stopped U.S. giants in niche entertainment from going into the country. When I was in India last May, there were gigantic posters all over Bombay for the hit Disney kid and tween show *That's So Raven* with lead actress Raven Symoné looking amazingly Indian in the foreground and a couple of way-too-cute Indian kids in the background of each billboard.

Disney has three channels in India, two of which, Toon Disney and Hungama, a children's station they purchased last year from Indian media conglomerate UTV, broadcast in Hindi. Of the purchase of an established Indian children's television station, Walt Disney International president Andy Bird said, "India is a long-term strategic priority. It is very important that we grow our business locally as well as through exporting U.S.-originated content."[12] In terms of U.S. content, the company's target ten-to-fifteen-year-old Indian audience can watch *Lizzie McGuire, JoJo's Circus,* and *Kim Possible* along with movies and other Disney shows and cartoons. Disney is also planning to produce a Bollywood movie version of its immensely popular *High School Musical* television series and movie.[13]

Of course, Disney is introducing much more than a set of characters and television shows to Indian children. Before launching television channels in India, Disney already had fifty-five-plus franchisees and tie-ups with retailers all over the country to do what it does so well in the United States: sell a range of consumer products tied in to various Disney properties.[14] The current generation of Indian children is the first to grow up with a set of characters on television and in movies specially created for them, and then to translate that into a desire to buy affiliated products. The impact on the future growth of India's already superheated consumer market of this type of experience will be phenomenal.

In the fiscal year ending in 2005, advertisers spent some $26 million pushing products on Indian children's television, an increase of 16 percent over the year before.[15] In *Born to Buy,* Juliet B. Schor links the advent of children's television channels and the subsequent growth of advertising specifically targeted at children in the United States with the transformation of American children in the 1980s into "the epicenter of American consumer culture."[16] That epicenter may be about to shift to the other side of the planet.

The quintessential American children's program was added to India's television pantheon in 2006. With support from USAID (United States Agency for International Development) and in partnership with Turner's Cartoon Network and POGO, *Sesame Street India,* aka *Galli Galli Sim Sim,* was born.[17] The program boasts a local set of characters specially created for the Indian market, including humans Basha and Dawa, and Muppets Chamki, a tomboyish-girl character, Boombah, a lovable big lion, Aanchoo, who is transported to another space and time when she sneezes, and the bookish Googli.[18] The show includes locally produced animation and cameos with beloved American *Sesame Street* characters such as Elmo. It aims to reach 157 million Indian children under the age of six and will use radio and other platforms to do so. *Sesame Street* worked closely with Indian educators to make sure its content was adapted to the needs of a very young Indian audience.[19] The show will be created in Hindi, with Tamil as a possible second-language version down the line. Adjunct materials in other media, including print and the Internet, may be created in other Indian languages as well.

Only 65 percent of India's preschool-age children in rural areas and 52 percent in urban slums can access existing early-childhood-education resources.[20] Ironically, *Sesame Street,* a consummate American show, aims at fulfilling one of the original purposes of television in India as conceived by the early leaders of the nation: education. It will be interesting to see what the actual impact of *Sesame Street India* is in a country where 47 percent of the children are malnourished.[21] Still, launching *Sesame Street* in India is an ambitious project, pulling in private-sector media, nonprofit educational television, and the support of the governments of India and of the United States.

India is hardly *Sesame Street*'s first foray in front of foreign audiences. The program is aired in more than 120 countries. Country-specific versions include *Vila Sesamo,* Brazil; *Semamstrasse,* Germany; *1, rue de Sesame,* France; *Ulitsa Sezam,* Russia; *Rechov Sumsum Shara's Simsim,* Israel and Palestinian Territories; and *Takalani Sesame,* South Africa. From 1998 to 2001, a Chinese version, *Zhina Jie,* was broadcast nationally in China. Since 2000, there has been an Egyptian version of *Sesame Street,* and versions are planned for Bangladesh and Afghanistan. While U.S. government officials in the White House and at USAID have lauded the usefulness of *Sesame Street* in promoting "American values" and building goodwill toward the United States overseas, especially in Muslim countries, the Children's Television Workshop, which has long produced *Sesame Street,* firmly denies that it pushes American or Western values.[22] In any case, the arrival of *Sesame Street* in India is a dramatic example of how much the Indian government has shed its wariness of foreign influence or interference, especially of the United States.

In 1991, when the Indian government began to open up India's television market to private broadcasters, foreign conglomerates weren't the only companies to seize the opportunity. Indian companies such as Zee TV (which has since partnered with Turner Broadcasting), UTV, NDTV, TV Eighteen, and Sahara staked their claims. Most have tied up with the big transnational conglomerates to one extent or another and are expanding into overseas distribution to survive in a fast-evolving international market. Much of their overseas ambition is aimed at the Indian diaspora, with the Dish Network in the United States offering South Asian satellite-TV packages in English and Hindi as well as in Punjabi, Gujarati, Telugu, Malayalam, Bengali, and Tamil. NDTV received licenses to broadcast a 24-7 channel in Canada in 2005.

Despite these new forays, Indian media companies still have a way to go before they can compete in size or cash with the established transnational media conglomerates based in the United States, Europe, Australia, or Japan. There is no Indian media company, including the print media titan Bennett, Coleman, India's largest, that is yet on par with a Sony, a Viacom, a Disney, or a Time Warner. But as India continues to develop, Indian media companies will be more and more able to compete internationally, beyond the India diaspora.

Taking on the American Media Machine

Until recently, there was nowhere Indian-Americans could see themselves portrayed realistically, if at all, on television. MTV Desi is changing that. Nusrat Durrani is the general manager of MTV World, a suite of MTV music channels that cater to bicultural audiences in the United States. MTV Desi, launched in July 2005 and aimed at South Asian Americans, was the first of three channels. The second, MTV Chi, aimed at Chinese-Americans, was running in December

2005, and MTV K, for a Korean-American audience, premiered in June 2006.[23] When I asked Nusrat what content they show on MTV Desi, he told me, "Our programming is hybrid. An example is our show called *Video Kichdi,* where everything is mixed up. We might run a clip by Green Day, then an old Bollywood film clip, then a Missy Elliott clip, and then one by Karmacy, the San Francisco–based Gujarati hip-hop band, reflecting the tastes of the audience.

"The Bollywood phenomenon is being given a twist," he continued. "What's interesting to young U.S. audiences is programming that appeals to their dual identity. There is a lot of experimentation going on. Missy Elliott has a tune with Indian music. When Alanis Morissette was in India, she used a lot of Indian influences. Nelly Furtado just taped something with a Bollywood producer."

A native of Lucknow, Nusrat quit his job as a marketing director for Honda in Dubai to follow his dream of working at MTV. He started at the company's headquarters in New York as an intern at the age of thirty-five. With his faintly punk hairstyle, black jeans, and Converse sneakers, he still looks like a member of the MTV generation. "The basic question of identity, of 'Who am I?' is the motivator for what we are all about," he tells me. "Research showed us that Asian-Americans don't see themselves on mainstream TV. There is nothing out there that speaks to your biculturalness." That's why, Nusrat says, "Rabbi Shergill launched MTV Desi's transcultural theme: young, old, being from the U.S., being from India." Rabbi Shergill shot to the top of the Indian pop charts with his contemporary musical rendition of eighteenth-century Sufi poet Bulleh Shah's *Bulla ki jana main kaun,* meaning "I know not who I am." Twenty-first-century Indian youth and South Asian American youth can relate to being so mixed up, they're not sure who they are anymore.

Nusrat Durrani is convinced that the moment for the breakout of a major Asian artist in the United States is imminent. "It will only take one big act to break into the mainstream in the way Ricky Martin did for the Hispanic-American audience." Bally Sagoo, Karsh Kale, MC Punjabi, and the London group Cornershop have all attained a level of international popularity just below superstardom. MTV World is seeking the Asian star who will catapult into the international spotlight.

Indian content is already traveling outside the diaspora Indian market, finding its way into the mainstream of New York, Hollywood, and Burbank. This is being driven in part by an emerging generation of young Indian immigrants and American-born children of Indian immigrants that is coming into its own in every single area of media and entertainment. One sign is more Indian faces on television news broadcasts, such as PBS's *Wide Angle*'s Daljit Dhaliwal or CNN's Dr. Sanjay Gupta, and in serials, such as Naveen Andrews in the popular reality show *Lost*. Another is the presence of Indians in powerful positions in the media business, such as Sonia Nikore, former vice president for casting at NBC Studios. Sonia was a factor in successfully casting Indian-origin actors, such as Parminder Nagra— who costarred with Keira Knightley in *Bend It Like Beckham*—in *E.R.* Sonia helped bring out an American sitcom called *Nevermind Nirvana,* featuring an Indian-American family of doctors. She cast Kal Penn (*Harold and Kumar Go to White Castle, The Namesake*) as the son. Ultimately, like so many new network shows that are floated, the program was not picked up. Sonia is convinced, however, that the moment when television networks start producing programs for the ethnic-Indian niche market is fast approaching.

Mira Nair and M. Night Shyamalan, the two biggest Indian-origin directors of Hollywood movies based in the United States, Gurinder Chadha (*Bride and Prejudice*) and Shekhar Kapur (*Elizabeth*) in England, and Deepa Mehta (*Water*) in Canada are the top international Indian directors. While Shyamalan limits the Indian content of his movies to cameo appearances of himself or the country of his birth (aliens turning up in India during a brief TV moment in *Signs*), the others are deeply engaged with exploring the themes of India and its diaspora.

Bollywood Comes to Hollywood

Mira Nair came to the United States from India in 1976 to study at Harvard. Her first feature film—*Salaam Bombay!*—launched her to fame in 1988. Her 2001 crossover movie *Monsoon Wedding* was an international hit and set the stage for the worldwide currency of movies far from the Bollywood formula that depict the reality of contemporary Indian life. Her most recent film, *The Namesake,* confirms this.

In 2005, Nair signed a deal with Twentieth Century–Fox to do a remake of the hit Bollywood comedy *Munnabhai.* To find out more about this venture, I met her at a studio in midtown Manhattan, where she was busy dubbing sound for *The Namesake.* Dressed in one of her trademark color-drenched silk *kurti* and black slacks, Nair left instructions for her team before we left for lunch. Mira Nair is the kind of individual whose creative passion hits you like a force of nature, filling a space much larger than the person herself. She suggested a nearby Afghan restaurant. It was clear the staff knew her well, though not that they knew who she was. I asked her, "Why *Munnabhai?*"

"It was my son Zohran's favorite film. You know there's so much junk out there for kids, and I wanted, as a mother," she told me, "to make a movie for my son's age group that was better than that. Zohran is very involved with the project.

"I saw *Munnabhai* at a mall in Juhu, in Bombay, and as I was walking out, I just had a vision of doing the film with African-Americans and Indians in the U.S. Vinod Chopra," who produced the movie, "is a childhood friend. So, I called him up and told him I wanted to buy the rights. He gave them to me for a buck. You know, we Indians do things like that," Nair said, smiling.

She promptly did a deal for the movie with Twentieth Century–Fox. "I'm calling the new movie *Gangsta MD,*" she said. "I chose Jason Filardi, the guy who wrote *Bringing Down the House,* to write it. He's on the third draft. Basically, the main character is an African-American guy who falls in love with an Indian-American doctor. I'll cast a Bollywood star for the love interest. For the main character, I want Chris Tucker. He costs twenty-five million dollars but I'm hoping to get him. It will be the first big-budget Hollywood remake of a Bollywood film."

For years, Bollywood has been remaking Hollywood films, invariably without buying the rights first, even for a dollar. While still in development (Nair said recently she may produce rather than direct the movie), *Gangsta MD* will be an important milestone in the flow of Indian content into the American mainstream.

I was told by several people in the business that other Hollywood motion picture companies are trolling Bollywood buying up rights as well as signing deals with Indian directors. Hollywood star Will Smith has caught the Bollywood bug. His company Overbrook Entertainment signed a $30 million deal with India's UTV in 2006. Smith announced plans to produce two movies, a $10 million live-action film and a $20 million computer-graphics animated picture. Sony Pictures will distribute them internationally. Hollywood has clearly recognized the global appeal of Bollywood properties and the largely untapped talents of seasoned Bollywood producers and directors.

Bombay: Movie Capital of the World

No other city in India is more associated with cleavage, bare midriffs, muscled biceps, smoldering leading men, and primping, pouting starlets than Bombay. Bombay is the capital of Bollywood, India's movie and television industry. The city is also the financial capital of the country, home to the Bombay Stock Exchange, and to every major foreign bank and investment house in the world, from Goldman Sachs to HSBC to Deutsche Bank. Bombay is to India what New York plus Los Angeles would be to the United States. Well before India's recent economic takeoff, Bombay was a mecca for every ambitious Indian looking to make a fortune or make his mark.

The beachfront, palm-studded curve of Bombay's Marine Drive, with its classic art deco buildings overlooking the gentle waves of the Arabian Sea, resembles a shabbier version of the Croisette in Cannes, where each year an ever larger delegation of Indian film stars and filmmakers go to strut their stuff and sell their wares. Indian movie star Aishwarya Rai, an official model for L'Oréal in India, has become a predictable sensation in Cannes, with both the Indian and the French press stalking her every move and detailing her sumptuous outfits. But whereas in Cannes the gleaming white yachts of the azure Mediterranean attract speculation about which princes of Arabia or Silicon

Valley have dropped anchor, in Bombay small wooden fishing boats bob offshore in a leaden sea. Indian women in saris and *salwar kameez,* their drapes of silk and sheer cotton billowing upon the breeze, walk along the curve of the bay, a world away from the top-less sunbathers of the French Riviera. On Chowpatty Beach, vendors serve fresh coconut water and creamy *kulfi* flavored with pistachios, almonds, and saffron. Bombay is not Cannes, nor is it California.

Contrary to what the name suggests, India's film industry has actu-ally been around a lot longer than Hollywood's. One of the Lumière brothers' silent pictures was screened in Bombay in 1896, and India's first director, Harishchandra Bhatvadekar, made his first movie in the city in 1899. The actual Bollywood studios are located in the north-ern suburbs of Bombay, far from Marine Drive and the legendary old movie palaces: the Eros, the Regal, and the now sadly demolished Metro, where my father spent days watching Hollywood movies before emigrating to America in 1949. The stars live in between, the wealthier ones in concrete bungalows smothered in bougainvillea off Juhu Beach (think Malibu), others in ocean-view flats in Bandra (Santa Monica). The lavish mansions of Bombay's movie stars are part of the charm of what could be one of the most beautiful cities in the world if more than 60 percent of its residents did not live in slums or on the streets.[24]

When I was a child, I lived for a while in Juhu, where my Indian grandparents had their apartment. Every evening, we'd go out into the neighborhood looking for film shoots in the homes of the stars. India was then much poorer than it is now. Movies with opulent-interior scenes were often shot in private homes. We would try to get a peek at the stars on their way in or out. They almost never failed to stop and smile at us, or to give us an autograph, though I remember one actress becoming a little testy before hurrying off in a ten-year-old American station wagon with fake-wood paneling on its side. This was well before the days when BMWs, Mercedes, or, as of last year, Rolls-Royces could be purchased in India.

Today, I'd as likely see a Bollywood film being shot on the streets of New York as in Bombay. Bollywood directors are going global. Sixty percent of Bollywood's profits now come from overseas markets, and Indian movies are catering more and more to international audiences, both in the Indian diaspora and in the industry's huge traditional distribution footprint, ranging from East Asia to the Gulf and beyond. Movie producer Yash Chopra, the king of the classic Bollywood movie, has been turning out hit after hit for decades. A few of his more recent successes include *Dilwale Dulhania Le Jayenge, Dil to Pagal Hai, Neal 'N' Niki,* and *Fanaa.* His company Yash Raj Films distributes Indian movies, not only in India but abroad through Yash Raj Films USA Inc. and other foreign-registered companies.

Karan Johar has excelled in making movies featuring Indian-American characters or Indian characters living in the United States. *Kabhi Alvida Naa Kehna,* which was released last year, tackled the shocking possibility of divorce among Indian couples. Certainly, the film's setting in the United States made this sensitive issue easier for Indian audiences to deal with even as it spoke to the stresses of modern life both in India and in America.

One of the most ambitious gambits is India's Adlabs Films Ltd.'s tie-up with Hollywood-based Ashok Amitraj's Hyde Park Entertainment to take on Hollywood. Adlabs has offices now in the United States and England. Adlabs Films was set to distribute eighteen to twenty Indian movies abroad in 2006. Conversely, Hyde Park Entertainment is moving into the Indian market. These examples are just the tip of the iceberg. Everyone wants to get into the Indian entertainment boom.

Vin Bhat and Neal Shenoy, two Indian Americans in their thirties, launched a company called [212]Media in 2003 to put Bollywood content in front of American television audiences. They formed BODVOD—Bollywood On Demand, Video on Demand—in 2004. They partnered with Time Warner to put Bollywood on Demand on their cable network. Neither Vin nor Neal had ever watched a Bollywood movie growing up in the United States. In fact, it wasn't until they went to India to work on a celebrity charity event to raise money for Richard Gere's foundation's efforts to stop the spread of HIV/AIDS that they became aware of a possible opportunity. They met a lot of Indian producers in Bombay who groused about getting their content distributed in the United States without getting fleeced by middle men.

BODVOD was born. Their biggest triumph so far was getting the rights to UTV content, and putting the 2005 hit *Rang De Basanti* on Time Warner. They advertised "cross-cable," pulling in viewers from markets beyond the dependable Indian diaspora.

Vin and Neal just signed a deal to distribute UTV movies with Google Video. "Bollywood is poised to change the distribution paradigm. Hollywood would never endanger theatrical revenue, but UTV is such an innovative company, they've allowed us to experiment and see what we can do with mobile communications, with Google Video," Vin explained to me. "At UTV, there's one guy. We can call him up, and he'll take our call, and we can talk to him. It works like a family. There's a certain level of trust. In Hollywood, there are so many big egos, you just can't do that."

Animating India

One of the fastest-growing businesses in the world of Indian entertainment is animation, an area that seems tailor-made for India in the information age. Digital animation using industrywide 2-D and 3-D software such as Maya and Softimage and the communications revolution of the Internet have fostered a loose global confederation of independent animation production studios. The big studios—DreamWorks, Disney, Pixar—under pressure from ambitious animation upstarts and looking to drive down costs are increasingly producing their movies using a network of less expensive, skilled digital animators in various international locations. The big studios can assemble and dissolve these networks according to the needs of each project. As Larry Kasanoff of Hollywood's Threshold Entertainment put it, "What do we care if the guy is in Van Nuys or India?"[25]

Even with computer graphics, animation remains a highly labor-intensive process. A full-length animated feature demands thousands of man-hours, taking months of work by teams of animators. The same cheap labor that has fed the call-center and the BPO (business process outsourcing) booms in India has supported an increase in high-volume, low-price animation work. However, that model is changing as ambitious Indian animation houses are moving up the value chain with an eye on becoming owner-producers of international-quality animated entertainment properties.

Digitally animated movies are extremely profitable, reaping $225 million per film at the U.S. box office in 2005 as compared to $33 million for a live-action feature.[26] The global digital animation industry is anticipated to reach $75 billion in 2009. The Indian component of the industry is registering 35 percent annual growth and is expected to hit $950 million by the same year.[27] Innovations in animation software, which can cost as little as $5,000 and can be run on a PC, make a production facility with banks of computer workstations relatively inexpensive to set up.

Several major studios in India are reaping big contracts from international entertainment conglomerates, as well as coproducing and creating original productions. These include Toonz Animation in Kerala, and Crest Animation Studios, UTV Toons, Prana Animation, and Maya Entertainment in Bombay. These companies employ hundreds of animators and work with the world's largest entertainment companies. Some of these companies are aggressively moving from a work-for-hire shop on the BPO model toward coproductions or even building up their own intellectual property libraries.

Maya Entertainment, founded by award-winning Indian filmmaker Ketan Mehta and actress Deepa Sahi, has benefited from investment from Intel Capital India Technology Fund to upgrade their computing systems with the latest Xeon-processor-based workstations. Maya also teamed up with Intel, a company committed to improving educational opportunities in the information-technology area, to found MAAC or Maya Academy of Advanced Cinematics. MAAC provides education in 3-D animation, visual effects, and postproduction.

UTV Toons has moved entirely into high-tech 3-D and Flash animation. According to UTV CEO Ronnie Screwvala, the animation company "will not rest until we achieve a leadership position, and for this we have given ourselves a time frame of twenty-four months."[28] This is the trajectory Indian animation must follow if it is to move beyond the BPO model and create world-class companies that produce Indian-inspired content as opposed to American or European content executed by inexpensive Indian animators.

Ronnie Screwvala of UTV is convinced that the BPO model is not a long-term competitive model for India. Someone, somewhere, will always come along to do the job for less. He has faith in the potential of Indian artists to make sure "the high-yielding intellect side of the animation business remains within the shores. This could fuel another round of growth in animation in India. Moreover, in Flash and 3-D animation services, no country worldwide has been able to obtain a clear lead as yet. India is still in the forefront and will substantially grow in this arena."[29]

The turning point will be when an Indian animation studio produces a full-length original feature film with global-market appeal, an Indian *Toy Story*. Or perhaps a *Hanuman*? Produced by Sahara One Media and Entertainment and animated by Silvertoons, *Hanuman* was the first full-length-feature animated film produced in India with Indian characters and story line. Released in October 2005, the movie got good reviews on content but was found lacking on technical panache. As Sukanya Verma put it in one review, "To expect *The Little Mermaid* or *Tarzan* kind of finesse in the computer graphics department will be unreasonable. For beginners, the animation is a fairly decent effort. One does notice a few blotches here and there, but the overall content is powerful enough to hook. Hopefully, in another five or six years, things will look even more promising."[30] With India's industry leaders already focused on the goal of competing head-to-head with Pixar, Disney, and DreamWorks in an exploding market tilting toward Asia, it may happen sooner than that.

On my home computer in New York last summer, I watched an animated short called *Maharaja Cowboy*, laughing hysterically until tears came out of my eyes. Atul Rao, vice president for creative affairs at Toonz Animation India, sent this to me to give me an idea of the kind of work he does. A writer, producer, and performer in theater, television, and film for many years, Atul—a Canadian of Indian origin—moved to Trivandrum, India, four years ago to join Toonz after stints at Fox, Nickelodeon, and Warner Brothers. He's having the time of his life.

"In India, we are, eight years into the game, where Korea and Japan were after twenty-five years," he tells me a little breathlessly. "A lot of it is timing: the software now is just amazing compared to even a couple of years ago. But more than that, it's the drive and the creative energy here. When I came to visit from Canada, I thought this place was incredible. There were problems, sure, but there was such a push to learn and to do whatever they needed to do to become the best. I just thought this would be a special opportunity."

I asked Atul about what I'd heard from so many people: that the creativity had been trained out of Indians by a regimented educational system that stressed mathematics, engineering, and learning by rote, and that it would take time to get a corps of good Indian script writers up to Hollywood levels of storytelling. He laughed. "Yeah, I've heard that lack of creativity argument so many times. It's manufactured. The Indian people I've met are incredibly creative, incredibly imaginative. It's all pent up, so when they get into a situation where they can express themselves, they just explode. And it's not the educational system's fault, it's the industry's fault. Bollywood has put no value on script writing. With them, it's been, 'Never mind the story. Let's bank on the songs and the stars.' It's not creativity that's lacking; it's the discipline of scriptwriting and the will within the industry to support an infrastructure conducive to creativity, using traditional models of development. Now that's starting to change. Look out!"

One of the reasons G. A. Menon, the now deceased founder of Toonz, set up the company was to create jobs. Animation is highly labor intensive, and Menon felt it was a good industry for India. He established a training school, Toonz Academy. "The only people who can truly animate 3-D are the people who learn traditional animation first," explained Atul. Toonz Academy graduates can work anywhere they like, and have no trouble finding jobs in India's booming animation industry.

I asked Atul about the potential for an Indian animated feature film to go global. "For a full-length feature film to go around the world," he told me, "you need the right script. Even Hollywood doesn't always get it right, you know. *The Ant Bully* wasn't a bad movie, but it flopped. For India, it's just a matter of time. Part of the problem is the shyness in the United States about taking in foreign movies. The Hollywood infrastructure can be so insecure. Part of it is breaking the distribution scene, but that will happen sooner or later because all the new media will force them to open up."

A Communications Revolution

India is emerging as a major factor in the proliferation of new media, especially media that is portable. I consider my cell phone to be nothing more than a portable phone. I want it to work reliably as a phone, anytime I want to use it, anywhere in the world. I have had screaming matches with twentysomething salespeople who want to sell me a cell phone loaded up with bells and whistles I think of as distractions. "Listen," I try to tell them, "I don't want a toy. I want a phone." They don't get it. Clearly, as someone in my forties, I am not part of the target market for broadband communications. My fifteen-year-old son, on the other hand, treats his cell phone as a handheld multimedia device. He takes still and moving pictures, text-messages his friends constantly, plays games, listens to music, downloads ringtones. He is part of the new-media target market of twelve-to-twenty-four-year-olds, a demographic segment with enormous potential in India.[31]

When I talked to Tom Freston, at the time CEO of Viacom, he told me, "In terms of the potential for content on cell phones, we're talking to Reliance. Their business is exploding. We're talking to Airtel too." Reliance and Airtel are two of India's biggest cellular-phone-service providers. No one in television can afford to ignore mobile communications, especially not in India, where the latest television trend is interactive TV using cell phones. Shows that ask their audiences to SMS or text-message their votes or opinions as the show is broadcast live have zoomed in popularity in India. Indian citizens may feel their sentiments may be ignored when they vote for politicians, but when they vote for their favorite veejay on MTV or their favorite performer on *Fame Gurukul*, they get instant results. This translates into huge profits for both the network, which charges a healthy fee for access to the program, and the mobile phone company, which charges the customer for each SMS.

The Indian mobile phone market is adding more than 3 million new subscribers per month, for a total that was expected to reach 78.5 million in June 2006 (up from 38.6 million in January 2005).[32] India's youth mobile subscription base is growing at more than 300 percent per year.[33] India is also the top mobile gaming market of the so-called BRICs, the fast-growing emerging markets of Brazil, Russia, India, and China, likely to grow more than 700 percent by 2010. Experts predict that 220 million people will be playing games online by 2009, of which the Indian market is poised to capture a share worth $336 million.[34]

Indian Internet usage is soaring. According to 2006 estimates, India counted over 50 million Internet users, up from 35 million in 2005 and just 5 million in 2000. The United Nations pegs its growth at a whopping 89 percent annually.[35] Fifty million sounds like a large number, but it is only 4.5 percent of India's total population. In comparison, in the United States, there were 205 million Internet users in 2005,[36] while China counted 110 million users. Connecting India via landlines is simply not feasible. Instead, the country is leveraging the success it had with mobile communications to expand Internet connectivity via high-speed wireless. In 2006, Reliance Infocomm, the largest wireless-service provider in India, announced a plan to join LG Electronics to push rapid expansion of wireless broadband connectivity across the country.[37]

The Indian Institute of Technology—Madras (of the city now called Chennai) has led a project to bring Internet connectivity via wireless kiosks to the more than 700 million Indians who live in villages. These kiosks are booths featuring a computer that usually uses touch-screen technology with simple icons suitable for illiterate users. Eighty percent of these kiosks are being run by women.[38]

A report released in 2006 by Juxt Consult, a Delhi-based information-technology consulting firm, asserted that an astounding 51 percent of Indian Internet users come from India's lower-middle class, with incomes of less than ten thousand rupees (about $250) per month, while 24 percent earn between ten thousand and twenty thousand rupees per month. Many of these are accessing the Internet in India's popular Internet cafés.[39]

While keen to accelerate the connectivity of the country and bring millions more Indians online, the government is also wary of the negative aspects of the Internet. Last summer, a hue and cry went up among Indian Internet users when they found they could no longer access their favorite blogs, including the popular blogspot.com. The government first made no comment, then admitted it had ordered the sites sponsoring the blogs blocked, then announced that it had never intended to block all the blogs but had simply wanted to block access to one blog where inflammatory postings had gone up following the terrorist bombings in Bombay. The government said it had had to act in the interest of preventing Hindu-Muslim violence. Then it further stated that it didn't have the technology to block just one and so the servers had had to block all access. As of this writing, the situation has still not been resolved.

National, state, and local governments have also tried to crack down on the use of the Internet by terrorists intent on hitting Indian targets, as well as on Internet pornography, a booming illegal activity in India.[40] One of the real annoyances of using a computer in a cyber-café in India is the steady stream of pornographic pop-ups one is subjected to. Indian society is sexually conservative—last year, an Israeli couple paid a fine in lieu of serving a ten-day jail sentence in Rajasthan for kissing each other during their wedding ceremony, and the state is warning foreign tourists that contact between men and women in public is not acceptable.[41] In 2005, the Tamil film star Khushboo had to tearfully apologize to her public after making a statement that premarital sex existed in her state. Protesters rampaged in the streets.[42]

The traditional Indian family living arrangement is known as the joint family, where brothers and their wives and children live together in the same house. It is extremely unusual in India for people to live alone, and it is hard to find privacy. India is a crowded country. Internet cafés are one of the few places where people, most frequently men, can access pornographic material anonymously. Many Internet cafés enjoy informal reputations as "porn houses." More than once I walked into an Internet café in India to check my e-mail and realized, too late, by the quality of expression on the all-male clientele, that I had picked the wrong establishment. Far more popular than pornography are marriage sites. Shaadi.com, BharatMatrimony.com, and Jivansathi.com are three of the biggest.

The Internet is one of the main ways the Indian diaspora keeps in touch with the mother country. Rediff.com is the number one Web portal in India and has revenue three times greater than its closest competitor, Sify.com.[43] I read Indian newspapers and magazines online to keep up with news in the country, as do most of the Indians I know abroad. A study by Paul C. Adams and Emily Skop of the University of Texas in 2004–5 indicated that Indian-Americans who identified themselves as using Indian-oriented Web sites were more likely to perceive cultural preservation as a goal and to believe that Indians have contributed more to world civilization than Europeans.[44] Indians can be biased about the superiority of their culture and the evidence of their technological acumen, especially highly skilled technical immigrants to the United States who are homesick, worried about their children losing their Indian identity, and anxious not to be confused with less economically and educationally successful minorities.[45] The Internet has made it possible for the far-flung members of the Indian diaspora to keep in touch with each other and with the mother country even as it is connecting Indians from every region and every walk of life in India.

Movies for Download: Beating Pirates in the World's Biggest Market

The Internet is just beginning to function as a medium for film distribution: pay a fee, download a copy of the movie, and do so for less than buying a DVD or a theater ticket. Hollywood has been reluctant to embrace this technology because it saw how CD sales plummeted when people started to download music. But Hollywood faces declining ticket sales in theaters as well as DVD sales. It also has a major problem with piracy. The *Wall Street Journal* reported last year that the results of a study on piracy were so much worse than expected, the industry wanted to suppress it. According to the article, "U.S. movie studios are losing about $6.1 billion annually in global whole-sale revenue to piracy. On top of that, losses are coming not only from lost ticket sales, but from DVD sales that have been Hollywood's cash cow in recent years."[46] In India, potentially the biggest media market on the planet, it is estimated that only 30 percent of the market is reached by legitimate product. A whopping 70 percent is reached via pirated videos and DVDs.[47]

Ben Rekhi and Smriti Mundhra, two young Indian-American film-makers, decided last year to use the Internet to try to avoid piracy losses while maximizing distribution for their independent movie *Waterborne*. They turned down a six-figure traditional distribution deal that would have opened *Waterborne* in theaters across the United States. It was a brave move for a couple of budding filmmakers. Ben and Smriti opted instead to let Google cofounder Larry Page use *Waterborne* to launch Google Video. On Google Video, the movie was made available for download, worldwide, 24–7, for $4. Ben, the son of one of Silicon Valley's most successful pioneering IT entrepreneurs, Kanwal Rekhi, told me the deal happened "because, like, I grew up in Silicon Valley, my cousin Manu Rekhi works for Google, and we did a screening on the Google campus." Smriti went into more detail: "We had a screening at the Google campus in Mountain View, California. We told the people at Google, 'Look, we want to explore a whole new way of distributing movies.' They totally loved it. You know it costs me nothing to put my movie on Google Video, so I can charge four dollars for a clean copy someone can download legally and not expose their computer to viruses. People will pay four dollars for that. Plus, anyone in the world can see our movie, anytime they want."

Smriti is the daughter of veteran Hollywood and Bollywood film-maker Jagmohan Mundhra, whose 2006 crossover film *Provoked* starred Aishwarya Rai, Miranda Richardson, Robbie Coltrane, and Naveen Andrews. Smriti grew up in the movie business. While teach-ing marketing at California State University at Northridge in Los Angeles' San Fernando Valley, her father dreamed about how to get into the business. Mundhra's first move was to buy a dilapidated single-screen theater in Culver City in the 1970s, where he began showing Bollywood movies to a small but growing Indian immigrant community starved—in the days before video, DVDs, the Internet, or satellite television—for entertainment from their homeland. His sister, Madhushree, manned the snack bar, where she served homemade samosas. As an Indian, he had a tough time breaking into the movie business in Los Angeles, eventually finding an entry point in the direct-to-video market for Ashok Amitraj, Roger Corman, and other independent producers.

"I knew I could write a better script, and I didn't have many options out there. I had to break the catch-22 of people saying to me, 'You've never made an American movie so how can you make one?'" he told me when I met him last year in London, where he was finishing up *Provoked*.

By the time Smriti was a teenager, her father had a score of movies under his belt made both in Hollywood and in Bollywood, and not all for the video market. His 2001 film *Bawander*, or *Sandstorm*, starring Nandita Das was a critically acclaimed indictment of caste and gender oppression in rural India. Kanwal Rekhi, Ben's father, was a former classmate of Mundhra's from IIT Bombay, one of India's highly competitive Indian Institute of Technology campuses. His son Ben was obsessed with making movies. Was there anything Jag could do for him? It just so happened that eighteen-year-old Smriti had gone off to Alabama to intern on the set of the Coen brothers' movie *O Brother, Where Art Thou?* Would Ben be interested in joining Smriti on location? That's how the now inseparable friends and business partners met, hanging out with George Clooney in the swamps of the American South.

As a child, Ben had access to cutting-edge digital-imaging equipment before it hit the market. He told me, "I had Apple digital-effects and processing equipment that cost like thousands of dollars. I got it from my friend Peter Wu, whose uncle worked for Apple. I was just fascinated by the movies and went around with a camera in my hand all the time like from the age of nine. By the time I was eighteen, I'd made my first feature with some friends of mine in the neighborhood. I think it was when my dad was taking tickets at the door to our local movie theater in Los Gatos where my buddies and

I screened the movie that he first thought, 'Ben might be able to do this for a living.'"

Ben didn't embrace his Indian heritage until he'd grown up. "I didn't know I was Indian, I mean, I just didn't connect with my Indian side at all. Then I went to India and I had an incredible sense of familiarity. Now I'm really into being Punjabi and Sikh." In fact, his film *Waterborne* features a Sikh family that comes under threat when tensions run high following a terrorist attack with a biological agent on Los Angeles' water supply. Veteran Indian actress Shabana Azmi plays the tough family matriarch. There are moving scenes of Sikh religious ceremonies, with explanatory commentary by the family's son to the white, Jewish girlfriend he's brought home.

Waterborne is the kind of film Americans will be seeing more of. It doesn't trumpet its Indian connection. It's about American characters in an American setting, only some of those characters, like more and more people in real American life, including the filmmakers, happen to be Asian Indians.

Smriti is clear on where the future of the movie business is. When we met in New York, she made this startling statement: "Who needs the American audience? There are only three hundred million people here."

She explained how she sees the business between India and the United States unfolding: "Hollywood will try to take over Bollywood, because they know that's where the market is. But they will fail. Bollywood has been self-sufficient for a long time. Those guys, like Yash Chopra, they really know their audience and they are very good at what they do. In the last decade, India has had a big ego boost. We have to tailor our products to meet the needs of Indian audiences. They aren't in awe of things here anymore. Actually, I'm in awe of what is going on there."

Smriti is banking on the Internet to help her get her movies to audiences around the planet, including India, while making sure she doesn't get ripped off in the process. Hollywood is following her lead. MGM, Paramount, Twentieth Century–Fox, Universal, Warner Bros., and Sony are some of the joint owners of a digital distribution company called Movielink that was launched in 2006. CinemaNow is another service that has begun offering movies, from Sony Pictures Home Entertainment, MGM, and Lionsgate, for download at the same time they come out on DVD. Sony Pictures Home Entertainment has also signed a deal with online video distributor GUBA, which will get access to Sony's extensive movie catalog.[48] None of these deals take the more radical step Smriti and Ben did with *Waterborne* to release on the Internet instead of or at the same time as the theatrical release. According to a story in 2006 in *Tech News World*, the young filmmaking duo is about five years ahead of the rest of the industry. When it catches up, there will be "a major change in the way movies are distributed."[49]

The New Medicis

The Chopra family—celebrity spiritual-guru father Deepak, former investigative-journalist son Gotham, and author daughter Mallika, the former MTV point person in India—along with Sharad Devarajan of Gotham Entertainment, who owns the India rights to Marvel and DC Comics, and filmmaker Shekhar Kapur have a new venture. This group signed a deal with Richard Branson last year to form Virgin Comics and Virgin Animation. Using the Virgin store chain as outlets for their product, not to mention the powerful Virgin brand itself, the company will bring top-quality Indian content to a diverse, integrated global media market. The group's ambitious goal is to create a new mythology for our time, a mythology grounded in the legends of India and the spiritual forces of Asia, based on a new cast of superheroes for a troubled era and an audience increasingly located outside the West.[50]

Originally named Gautama, like the Buddha, Gotham Chopra changed his name a few years ago because, well, given the way the name is written in Sanskrit, Gotham actually is another way the name could be spelled. The new spelling also made the name a lot more cool and turned out to be uncannily prescient: Gotham's name is what got him involved in the comics business.

"I met Sharad Devarajan [now his principal business partner] because he had a company called the Gotham Entertainment Group.

I thought this was either a total coincidence, or it was destiny," Gotham confided.

I asked him, "Why comics?" It seemed a lightweight medium for such an ambitious project.

"My father," Gotham explains, "has always said, 'I'm just a translator bringing Indian philosophy to the world,' and I feel like I'm doing the same thing. Shekhar Kapur, the movie director, was also a tremendous influence. To me, he's the very embodiment of taking India to the world. I grew up with Shekhar, along with my dad of course, and I had these two strong role models who believed in bringing stories from India to the rest of the world. When I met Sharad, I immediately put what he was doing together with what my dad and Shekhar had been trying to do. I also brought a lot of my own experience putting together stories as a journalist." Gotham worked as an investigative television journalist for seven years for the private, in-school Channel One station.

Sharad Devarajan's personal style is very different from Gotham's. A Jersey boy, born and raised, he is a tall, dark, polished man who wears well-tailored, well-pressed clothing: crisp shirts, nicely draped slacks. He is much more formal than Gotham, who carries a backpack slung over his shoulder and dresses in jeans. Sharad lives on Manhattan's Upper East Side. Gotham lives in Santa Monica, California.

Sharad Devarajan talks fast and is extremely articulate about what he does. He seems in a hurry to do a million things, but these things so inspire him, he is willing to take a little time to share them with you. I had a hard time tracking Sharad down: the man lives in an airplane, as far as I can tell, constantly jetting between New York and Bangalore, with forays to Los Angeles and London, and side trips to the rest of Asia and Europe.

"I grew up in a media household," he tells me right away. "My dad became president of Warner Music Media and BMG Direct in the United States. He had no prior experience in the media business. He was an Indian Institute of Management graduate." An artist by inclination, Sharad headed to art school after high school. A series of odd jobs finally led him to DC Comics.

"In 1997, DC let me have the Indian publishing rights. I asked

Marvel and got the Indian publishing rights from them too. That's like having both Coke and Pepsi. It's pretty amazing. India was just totally off the radar back then, and they didn't understand the potential." Sharad did understand it.

"Look," said Sharad, "there are two hundred movies in development based on comic books right now, like *V for Vendetta*. The general public has no idea these movies are based on comic books. *The Incredible Hulk,* sure. *Superman,* okay, but the others? No way."

Sharad grasped that he could not only use what he calls "the truly free medium" of comics to Indianize well-known DC and Marvel characters such as *Spider-Man* for an untapped Indian market, but he could also take original Indian comics and animated content to the rest of the world. The precedent was Japanese anime and manga, which have taken the planet by storm. "What happened with Japan is a paradigm for what can happen with India. Korea has done an even better job with *manhwa,* which has taken all of Korean culture with it, including the pop star Rain, who is now an international talent. So, what we feel is that comics have to be part of a whole cultural package with movies, music, fashion, everything."

Sharad sees his company as working "on the frontier of the new global India." He is acutely aware of the elements at play at this historic moment of India emerging onto the global stage. Issues of identity are perennially at the core of what matters to youth, as each generation seeks to define its time.

"So, what are the themes of India's youth?" Sharad asks rhetorically. "There is a lot of anxiety about globalization. Part of our themology is the exploration of identity. When we took *Spider-Man* to India, we wanted to show the conflict between the traditional and the modern, the kid from the village who has to cope in Bombay, the 'dual time zones' in India today when changes are happening extremely fast and not always on the same track."

The character created for the Indian version of *Spider-Man,* Pavitr Prabhakar, is a village kid so backward he wears a dhoti, the traditional Indian male garment wrapped around the waist and legs that Gandhi used to wear. He arrives in the big city of Bombay to go to school. Like legions of country-bumpkin heroes before him, he finds himself the laughingstock of the more sophisticated urban dwellers, only this is twenty-first-century India. The kids at the school he attends are completely westernized and out of touch with their Indian roots. The girls, who sport skintight jeans and bared midriffs with pierced navels, are particularly cruel, except for one, of course, who senses the hero's true worth.

"Comics have always been a great medium to address social issues. You can't talk about them in the present time, so you do it in the future through science fiction," Sharad tells me. "Take the *X-Men,* they were talking about racism and exclusion with mutants. They were the blacks of the sixties, the gays of today. Science and the metaphysical are seamlessly linked in India. Science fiction is a natural. That all comes together in comics.

"In terms of the Indian market, MTV and Cartoon Network came in through television, but no one was going into print. In publishing, there was no one building a magazine distribution program for our audience." Sharad dove in. "I got the distribution network going in India, then expanded it into Singapore, Malaysia, this year Indonesia."

Sharad's ambitions go far beyond Southeast Asia. "Now we're going to reverse the funnel and bring classic, timeless Indian stories and fables, such as the *Ramayana, Mahabharata, Jataka Tales,* the *Panchatantra,* out to the world. But now these myths will have to be reimagined for a world with the Pokémons and the Harry Potters. Our heroes are grounded in a very different ethos and way of thinking from that of the West, whose heroes are defined by a Judeo-Christian philosophical view. So what happens in a country of a billion people that aren't coming out of that tradition? What does that mean? Our stories will be rooted in Indian tradition, but they have to be unique versus the Western stories that still dominate the scene."

Gotham shares Sharad's vision about how Indian content, through the media of animation and comics, could take off in the West. He told me, "Sharad and I were looking around at Japanese anime, at Pokémon, at the success of *Crouching Tiger, Hidden Dragon,* and thinking if this East Asian content could be so successful in America,

then why not Indian content? My dad and Shekhar were also convinced that the time had come to create Indian content not just for
India but for the West as well."

Gotham and Sharad got together and formed Gotham Studios
with the plan to produce characters for books and animation. They
wanted to do the creative work in India, and their third partner,
Suresh Seetharaman, had an extensive background in media and actually knew how to set up a studio in India and make it work.

I asked Gotham how often he goes to India.

"I go pretty much every two months or so for a week to ten days,
and once a year I go for a couple of months straight," he replied. "I feel
like I need to go regularly to reinvigorate myself. There's nothing like
being in the studio. It's so exciting. You feel like one of the Medicis."

Sharad used this same analogy when I talked to him a few weeks
later: "It's like a Medici laboratory we have going in Bangalore. You
feel like you are there with people creating, drawing."

The Medici analogy is interesting because Gotham and Sharad,
like many other Indians and people of Indian origin, truly believe that
one of the defining aspects of our time is India's renaissance as a
major cultural and political presence. Their mission in this renaissance
is not only to create vehicles for Indian mythology and iconography
but also to nurture Indian talent that is waiting to blossom. Along
with vision, money is the necessary lubricant to rev up the creative
engine that will drive India's renaissance.

"Why is India creatively depressed?" Sharad asked me rhetorically.
"Economics. You have to pay high wages to get and retain good talent, and to pay high wages you need to sell beyond India. We have top
illustrators we are paying lakhs [a lakh is one hundred thousand
rupees, about $2,500]. We identify and pay for talent. We also want
to bring up the next generation. We're trying to work with the
National Institute of Design. Suresh is talking to a lot of these schools
to address the dearth of creativity. Indian schools turn out technicians,
not artists. They kill creativity. What we want is for young people to
know that they can send a message that will change the world."
Sharad admits they do outsourcing work but tells me they do it
"because it also trains our guys." He knows that sooner or later,

someone, somewhere, will be able to do the work cheaper and that, ultimately, outsourcing is a dead end.

Sharad and Gotham's ambition is awesome: "We don't want to be the best stuff out of Asia," Gotham announced. "We want to be the best in the world. We will pull in the best talent out there, whether established headliners or first-timers." For that, they needed to raise some serious money.

"We started to explore the VC route [venture capital]," Gotham explained. "We looked at the friends-and-family route. Then one day, Sharad and I sat down and said, 'Look, what is our dream team? If we could involve anyone in the world in this, who would it be? And the name that kept coming up at the top of the list was Richard Branson. So, I just picked up the phone, and using a combination of my skills as a journalist and also strategically dropping a few names like my dad's and Shekhar's, I got Branson's assistant to admit that we had something the man might be interested in. Two days later, Branson called. He said, 'I loved *Elizabeth*,'" the film Shekhar Kapur directed starring Cate Blanchett, "'I love your dad's books.' That was it. Richard is a real innovator. He sees the future of the Virgin brand in Asia given that is where the growth is."

Just eight months after the deal was signed, the company began to roll out its first products, three comic books with a lineup of new characters, *Sadhu, Devi,* and *Snake Woman,* followed by another comic series, *Ramayan Reborn.* The venture will rapidly branch out into animation, games, and movies.

Gotham is fully conscious of the reality of today's integrated media environment. "More people are going to see our product on their cell phones than in paper books or in a theater," he predicts. The focus is to create memorable characters who can function in different media, characters inspired by the rich legacy of Indian culture. "Sure," he admits, "the great comic heroes we all know and love have fifty years of history. But in India, we have superheroes with five thousand years of history."

He points out that the most successful mass cultural content is fundamentally mythology, "all about destiny, about the chosen one." He cites *The Matrix, Lord of the Rings,* and *Harry Potter.* "Look at the first act of the new *Batman* movie where the whole thing opens with him getting his powers in Tibet. This is all made-to-order for Indian stories."

I ask him about *Star Wars,* which always struck me as the ultimate Joseph Campbell experiment in mythmaking. Gotham agrees completely: "You know, I was lucky enough to be close to George Lucas. He was always very explicit about Luke Skywalker being a budding yogi. Yoda, he's just like Maharishi."

Sounding a lot like his father, Gotham concludes, "These are basic archetypes. These are things that are deep in our psyches. That's why what we're tapping into is going to work."

After listening to Gotham and Sharad talk about the company, I wanted to get the elder Chopra's perspective. I wondered why a medical doctor who had built his career on the mind-body connection and bringing spiritual values to the West was involved in a comics and animation venture.

Deepak Chopra agreed to meet me at the Chopra Center & Spa near Times Square. The entrance was filled with Dr. Chopra's bestselling books. A spiral staircase led down to the spa area, where the calming music, soft lighting, and scent of incense made me wish I had time for a massage or an ayurvedic treatment. I recognized Deepak Chopra immediately. After greeting me warmly, he invited me into a small but pleasant office furnished with an Indian antique reproduction desk and chairs.

Deepak Chopra surprised me. He was completely clear-eyed about the hype surrounding the "India rising" story. That is precisely why he is involved with Virgin Comics and Virgin Animation.

"Yeah, Bollywood has become popular. So what?" he snorted. "India is about to have huge numbers of billionaires. So what? How does that help? There's no clarity in this whole renaissance of India. Something is happening for sure, but India is a country of extreme contradictions. Nehru had the vision to create a number of educational institutions. We are now reaping the results. Some of the graduates came to the West because they were affluent, and they became more affluent. But economic disparities have increased in India. Food rots in godowns, while at the same time thirty percent of the food is being exported to the Middle East. Really, what do we have to feel good about?"

I was, frankly, stunned by this critical assessment. Amid the celebratory din surrounding the emergence of India, it is rare to find a dissenting voice, especially from a supersuccessful Indian sitting in New York. Chopra then framed what was happening in India within the larger global picture.

"Look, the world is a mess. If we survive—and I think that may be a long shot—if you see *An Inconvenient Truth*," Al Gore's film on global warming, which had just been released in theaters, "coastal Bangladesh and Florida are finished—so, if we survive, we have to look at the bigger things. Nationalism is a disease. Krishnamurti called nationalism 'tribalism.' Einstein likened nationalism to measles.

"Society is in a large part its mythology. The reason I am excited about Virgin and the kids, and why Shekhar and I are supporting them, is that we need to create a new mythology. We need new imagination, new creativity. I support it wholeheartedly, not out of nationalism but because we need new raw materials for our imagination, materials that are transnational. Shekhar says, 'If one day the mask of Spider-Man is ripped away and it is revealed that he is Chinese, it will be a good thing.'"

Sharad Devarajan is much more anchored in the idea of what Indian culture in particular will contribute to creating this new mythology. On the one hand, the Virgin team will draw their mythology from a cultural inheritance that is five thousand years old; on the other, Sharad says, "The Indian cultural explosion is going to happen much faster than any other we've seen. It's going to be driven by Indian youth and the vehicles they have that are all tied to the Internet. Shekhar, Deepak, and Gotham are building new, multilayered characters in *Ramayan Reborn*. India has traditionally been a culture that asks questions. What are Hinduism and the religions and philosophies of the East? They are the quest of the seeker. They are a launching pad for you to think."

Thinking, ultimately, is what the Virgin team would like to inspire their audience to do. Deepak Chopra sees this as an urgent and critical mission: "The response to the attacks on 9/11 has been a colossal failure of imagination. We need contextual understanding. Technology with no context is very dangerous. I recently had the opportunity to give a talk at the Pentagon. I told them, 'In ten years, a little device like this'—I held up my Treo—'will have the power to destroy the United States.'" This scares me. He concludes, "We can't afford for imagination to fail us again."

An Indian Entertainment Empire

One area in which America has incontestably led the world is popular culture. Whether in movies, music, television, or the Internet, the United States has been the global trendsetter. American dominance in global media and entertainment is something Americans—and others around the world—have taken for granted for decades. It is one of the reasons the United States has wielded considerable influence over generations of enemies and allies alike.

Two factors are pushing the pole of global influence away from the United States and toward Asia. America's reputation as an open society, of its social and cultural icons, has become severely devalued by the debacle in Iraq, allegations and images of torture, and the appalling aftermath of Hurricane Katrina—images of which have been broadcast around the world. At the same time, the incredible dynamism of Asia's economies and the rise of the world's biggest giants, India and China, is igniting creative imaginations and pulling investment toward what are emerging as the biggest markets for entertainment and media the world has ever seen. Moreover, India's stature as a multicultural democracy and a leader of the developing world give it moral authority to match its cultural currency. Indians are eager to assert these basic elements of what Joseph Nye calls soft power, the power to persuade, the power to get others to want to do what you want them to do.

The global entertainment industry is expected to grow to $1.8 trillion by 2009, increasing by more than 6 percent every year. Meanwhile, the rise of India and China, with their gigantic youth populations and rapidly expanding middle classes, is causing a tectonic shift of the global economy toward Asia. American media and entertainment companies are scrambling to get into these markets. By 2015, 70 percent of the world's media and entertainment revenues will come from Asia. India, with an economy fired by a boom in consumption and the world's youngest population, will account for half of this, more than one-third of the global total.[51]

"Indians have an incredible advantage over Western media because everything comes there and the youth audience loves everything," argues Amitav Kaul, a filmmaker based in Manhattan who has worked in India and has raised more than a million dollars to produce a movie version of Jhumpa Lahiri's Pulitzer Prize–winning collection of short stories, *The Interpreter of Maladies*. "It could be Chinese or Middle Eastern or whatever, they don't care, they love it. It's an incredible openness. In the West, the old is dissolved to make way for the new. In India, the new grafts onto the old. Bill Roedy," the vice chairman of MTV and head of MTV International, "used to say, 'Indian youth culture is the future of pop culture.' He should know. And I think it's for that reason, that openness of Indian youth and how they can layer on different stuff from different places."

India is much more than a lucrative market for American content. It is a nation on the move, uniquely focused on media and entertainment in the digital age, endowed with one of the richest cultural heritages in the world and connected to a prosperous diaspora population. I asked Tom Freston if he thought Indian entertainment could have the same kind of international impact American entertainment has enjoyed.

"You haven't had creative content really go global from anywhere else than the U.S.," he replied. "But it will happen in India. Language has a lot to do with it. English is a language that sort of travels. Anything else is going to remain 'art house.' Indian producers are getting more savvy and they're making more money. Soon, they'll have the money to import actors, which I think they will do. So, you'll see American actors in Indian movies. That will get attention."

I imagine Scarlett Johansson or Brad Pitt starring opposite Shahrukh Khan or Preity Zinta in an Indian movie. It's not such a far-fetched notion. The 2005 hit *Rang De Basanti* costarred the very blond, very British actress Alice Patten, the daughter of the former governor of Hong Kong Chris Patten. Alice learned Hindi for her role, which she spoke fluently in the film, surprising and charming Indian audiences. After years of having Indian interlocutors react with surprise when I addressed them in Hindi and asking me, "Madam diplomat *hai*?" I had the novel experience last year of taxi drivers and street vendors in India smilingly tell me (in Hindi), "Oh, I feel like I'm in *Rang De Basanti* listening to you!"

Electronic media is a powerful force for creating imagined communities. If there is such a thing as a global community, surely it is a global youth community. India's youth are eager to realize their own and their country's potential. They are coming online with tremendous ambition and confidence. As Amitav Kaul told me, "Indians now, they want to be leading the whole thing. I can remember a director with MTV India in my face when I was working on a video for her telling me that what Cyrus Oshidar, then the creative director of MTV India, was looking for was 'cut-ting edge, Amitav, we need more cut-ting edge,' and every time she said it, her hand would come down in a chopping motion. 'Make it cut-ting edge.' I'm telling you, that's where 'cut-ting edge' is going to come from. It's going to come from India and the rest of Asia."

Branding India

Advertising in India is evolving as quickly as the media in which it appears. Transnational corporations swiftly learned that to sell their products to Indian consumers they would have to Indianize them. Conversely, Indian companies work on associating their products with Western quality standards and either with what is commonly called the global Indian—a well-educated, cosmopolitan person as comfortable in Bombay as in New York or London—or with traditional Indian values. In either case, the product is pitched as providing the consumer with an experience that at once affirms his cultural integrity as an Indian and celebrates his arrival in the world of Western affluence and sophistication. Advertisements for products as diverse as Nescafé instant coffee and Raymond-brand men's clothing achieve this mix, often with a suave male voice-over in a flawless upper-class Indian accent, ever so British but with just the right touch of lilt.

The traditional concept of *swadeshi* celebrated Indian self-sufficiency obtained through the sacrifice of Western consumption. Under the leadership of Mahatma Gandhi, thousands of Indians threw out their imported clothing, destroying it in bonfires that echoed the fire of nationalism sweeping the country. Hand-loomed cotton called khadi became the preferred material of Indian dress. Foreign technology in the form of power looms and foreign products in the form of manufactured cloth were to be resoundingly rejected. The spinning wheel, on which Gandhi daily produced hand-spun thread, was so powerfully associated with India's independence that it was placed in the center of the flag of the new nation, where it was replaced at the last minute by Ashoka's wheel.

Today, everything has changed. India now sees itself as coming into its own precisely through the embrace and mastery of foreign technology and products, much the way the legions of past invaders who came to conquer the country instead fell under its spell. India's acumen in information technology and scientific innovation, which has propelled it to the forefront of research and development, is a good example of this. Indians are tremendously proud that they can not only meet but even, in some cases, exceed international standards. Because so much has been achieved in so little time, India's people have a new faith in their country's limitless potential and note with satisfaction that the world is finally giving India the kind of attention it deserves. These sentiments are reflected and reinforced by what Indian viewers see on television. The media and entertainment industries, including their sidekicks advertising and marketing, have seized on India's new bullishness: they celebrate and encourage it.

Print journalism in India has also jumped on the feel-good bandwagon, in some cases tossing a stellar history of hard-bitten investigative reporting and independent analysis to the wind to chase advertising revenue. No print media group has been more guilty of this than Bennett, Coleman, which publishes the *Times of India*. Indu Jain, the matriarch of this extremely profitable family-held group run principally by her two sons, is now a member of *Forbes* magazine's exclusive billionaire list. She has a declared net worth of $1.7 billion.

She has amassed no small part of her enormous wealth by transforming her publications into efficient vehicles for advertising.

Naresh Fernandes, the editor of the Bombay edition of *TimeOut* magazine, who used to work at the *Times of India,* told me, "The *Times of India* is really responsible for the dumbing down of this city. You know, the Page 3 kind of thing." There has been such a cancerous growth in Indian newspapers of the "Page 3" society section that it is hard to get any news about India, much less the world, from reading these papers, which concentrate on parties, movies, media stars, and society types.

Feel-good journalism about India has not been limited to Indian publications. In 2006, magazine covers around the world trumpeted "The Rise of India," "India Inc.," "The New India." The new India became, well, news.

To a degree, however, this new India of an empowered consuming class seizing its sunlit moment in history via the information-technology revolution is an India invented by the media. India's new ability to project a positive image of itself beyond its borders, onto the screens and into the consciousnesses of people around the planet, has been achieved not a little by design. It is done by taking part of the story—the story of a richer, smarter, and more powerful India becoming more like the West—and turning it into the whole story. The result is a cosmetically enhanced image of India where the less attractive realities of endemic poverty, a raging HIV/AIDs epidemic, environmental catastrophe, and collapsing urban infrastructure are conveniently glossed over, if not completely ignored.

The point isn't that the new India does not exist. It does, and it is genuinely exciting and brimming with potential. However, the old India is hardly dead and gone. Indians freely talk about what they call the two Indias, often referring to the new India by its English name, India, and the old India by its Indian name, Bharat. India is what gets celebrated in the media, while the uncomfortably persistent realities of Bharat are pushed offscreen and out of the headlines, effectively rendering invisible a host of serious problems and the suffering of hundreds of millions of India's people. Images of illiterate Indians with a standard of living no better than in sub-Saharan Africa do not attract foreign direct investment. Pictures of clean-shaven young professionals on California-style information-technology campuses do. New highways with a few shiny sedans whizzing along render India recognizable to Western investors and readers. Choked city roads where way too many cars and trucks compete with pedestrians, bicyclists, and wooden carts pulled by bullocks, camels, horses, or people belie this progressive vision.

The new India is most adeptly branded and marketed to an international audience by the India Brand Equity Foundation. According to its literature, IBEF "is a public-private partnership between the Ministry of Commerce and Industry, Government of India, and the Confederation of Indian Industry. The Foundation's primary objective is to build positive economic perceptions of India globally." India's government and business leadership is fully aware that, especially in a heavily mediatized knowledge economy, perceptions matter, and IBEF's purpose is to accentuate the positive when it comes to global perceptions of India. IBEF's most remarkable success to date was surely the contribution it made to India's huge splash at the annual gathering of the superrich and powerful members of the World Economic Forum at Davos, Switzerland, last year. Attendees were blitzed with billboards proclaiming INDIA: THE WORLD'S FASTEST-GROWING FREE-MARKET DEMOCRACY. When they arrived in their hotel rooms, they were treated to an iPod loaded with Indian popular music and a complimentary pashmina shawl. A Bollywood-style stage extravaganza was the entertainment highlight of the gathering. India's rise was trumpeted to the world's elite, which was, by all accounts, charmed.

Bharat bit right back. A few days later, a strike by workers at India's major airports brought air travel in and out of the country to a grinding halt and treated travelers to overflowing, stinking restrooms and long waits. As Anand Mahindra put it to me, "People land in Bombay for the very first time, clutching the copy of *The World Is Flat* they've read to prepare for their trip to India, and before they're even off the plane, they see the slums stretching out beneath them and think, 'Whoa, what page was that on? I missed that part.' I tell visiting businessmen it's the mind-set above all which has changed in India. The rest will follow." Anand knows that he is exaggerating when he relates this anecdote. Clearly, more than the mind-set is changing. There is reality behind the hype. But he and other top Indian business leaders also know how much more work there is to do to bridge the gap between India's reality and its new image.

After decades of bearing the burden and the shame of being from a poor country, many members of the Indian elite and their counterparts in the Indian diaspora are relieved to have a good story to tell about India. They are euphoric at the prospect of India becoming a rich and powerful global player to rival the United States and China. They are impatient with the poor.

Many feel that it is about time that India, one of the world's great civilizations, recover from the terrible injury of colonization and reclaim its rightful place among the great nations of the world. Indians are among the most patriotic people I have encountered in a lifetime of travel, making even flag-waving Americans look like nationalist lightweights. The word in Hindi for patriotism is *desh-prem*, love of country, and Indians react emotionally both to their country's successes and to any perceived insult or humiliation. India's poverty is felt by many Indians to be the ultimate humiliation, stealing from the nation its rightful status as a global power, a lingering reminder of the colonial injustice that looted the country during the British Raj. Indians have a profound belief that, given a level playing field, they can beat the West at its own game.

This was fundamentally the message of the 2002 Academy Award–nominated film *Lagaan*, which told the tale of a ramshackle group of poor Indian villagers who literally beat their British masters at their own game: cricket. The Indian captain, played by Aamir Khan, not only wins the game but also the heart of a beautiful young Englishwoman who secretly instructs him in the rules. But he spurns her for a lovely Indian girl from the village.

Trying to Control the Press

This does not mean that hard-hitting investigative journalism does not exist in India. In March 2001, the weekly *Tehelka* rocked the nation when it released tapes secretly made by two of its reporters, Aniruddha Bahal and Mathew Samuel, showing bribes being taken in the ministry of defense at the highest level of the Indian government. Then minister of defense George Fernandes resigned as a result of "Operation West End," or what became known simply as the *Tehelka* tapes." Such impertinence by an uppity news rag was not to be tolerated. The newspaper was hounded by the government until it had to shut down, its staff reduced from 120 to just 4 people. Two investors, Shankar Sharma and Devina Mehra, were targeted, though they had only a minority financial interest in the paper and were not involved at all in its editorial direction.

Tarun Tejpal, the founding editor of *Tehelka,* simply would not give up. He and a skeleton crew never lost faith that *Tehelka* would live again, even though, as he told me at a dinner party in Delhi a couple of years ago, "Gitan [his wife] and I were stripped of everything. We had some hard years." A group of founder subscribers was enlisted to give material support to get the paper back on its feet. Almost 14,000 Indians took advance subscriptions. Among these are some of the most celebrated names in Indian media and entertainment, including Mira Nair, Shabana Azmi, and Mahesh Bhatt, not to mention Bollywood superstar Shahrukh Khan, as well as leading Indian industrialists, socialites, and intellectuals. In January 2004, *Tehelka* appeared again. The print edition of the paper hit a circulation of one hundred thousand. The online edition reaches readers around the world. The paper continues to conduct sting operations, exposing corruption at every turn, from pilot licenses that can be obtained without ever flying an aircraft to political parties paying off witnesses in criminal cases to prevent them from testifying. Its example has catalyzed investigative journalism in print and broadcast media. Tarun wrote to me, "Today, every news channel carries out sting operations and there is a constant feistiness in the air." *Tehelka*'s resurrection is testimony to the feisty spirit of Indian journalists who will not be silenced.

Another indomitable figure in Indian media and culture is Mallika Sarabhai, who sent television crews into the streets in 2002 to film the carnage in her home town of Ahmedabad, Gujarat, during a government-sanctioned pogrom against the state's Muslims. She subsequently participated in filing a public interest litigation complaint (PIL) against Narendra Modi, chief minister of the state of Gujarat. After this, she faced continuous harassment, including charges that she was using her dance academy, Darpana, to cloak a smuggling ring getting people illegally into the United States. An internationally celebrated actress, dancer, choreographer, and media personality who has long fought for human rights including women's rights, Mallika had to take her case to the Supreme Court of India before the Gujarat police dropped the ridiculous charges made against her.

Last year, she received a green light from India's Planning Commission for an ambitious television series designed to bring critical social and development issues to a mass audience via an engaging soap opera format. After receiving a Memorandum of Understanding formalizing the support, Sarabhai commenced production. The funds never materialized. *The Pioneer* newspaper ran an inflammatory story accusing the government of giving Sarabhai money for "Gujarat bashing." She told me, when I called her up to find out what was going on, simply that she was finally told, "Your CM [chief minister] was not happy."

In 2006, India was ranked 105th by Reporters Without Borders (the United States came in 53rd). Its press was deemed "partly free" by Freedom House. While India has a vigorous, even a tumultuous press—especially compared to almost any other country in its region, and certainly compared to China—critics of national, state, and local governments can face severe harassment if their reporting upsets the status quo, exposes endemic corruption, or projects what is considered the wrong image.

Print circulation in India is booming. Literacy is increasing. New magazines and newspapers are being introduced at a dizzying rate, both Indian versions of well-known American and European publications and Indian start-ups. There are Indian versions of *Elle, Cosmopolitan,* and even a toned-down *Maxim.* These have joined established Indian magazines such as *Femina, Outlook,* the issue-focused *Seminar,* and India's own lusciously glossy bimonthly devoted to "bling," *Verve,* published by Bombay socialite Anuradha Mahindra.

The print-media boom in India is attracting star journalists back home from abroad. Raju Narisetti, the former editor of the *Wall Street Journal Europe*, quit his job last year to return to India to launch an Indian edition of the *Journal* with the *Hindustan Times* group. This will be the first single-country foreign edition of the *Journal*. *TimeOut*'s Fernandes moved back to India in 2001 after five years with the *Wall Street Journal* in New York. Gautam Adhikari, who spent years in the United States and also at the *Times of India*, started a serious newspaper in 2005 called the *Daily News & Analysis*, known by its acronym, *DNA*.

Less than two decades ago, India was a country in which the state directed change from above in an environment protected from global capital. Aside from a more or less free press in print, the media environment was controlled. People had limited opportunities to witness the world outside their immediate environment. They had even less opportunity to participate in that world. The reigning ethos was one of austerity and asceticism. India today is rapidly becoming a nation dominated by consumer-citizens, who see globalization and their own consumption as the dual engines that will propel the country to fulfill its destiny as a global power. Indians both in India and in the diaspora are diving into the media and entertainment businesses. Their ambition is limitless and their vision is radical.

As India, a rising civilizational giant, gains economic and political power, its cultural clout will increase as well. One day soon, when a critical mass of the talent, the money, and the market is in Asia, a tipping point will be reached, and India will move from joining the game, or even winning the game, to inventing new rules for new games. Then things will get interesting.

CHAPTER THREE

Retailing India

L AST YEAR, DURING MY FREQUENT TRIPS TO GURGAON, THE bustling New Delhi satellite city that is one of the hubs of the new India, I counted no less than six shopping malls. There is construction everywhere these days: apartment blocks, office towers, roads. In between the new buildings going up are the little huts of the construction workers and their families. Stray dogs and wandering cows share the roads with new cars. Billboards blast offers from mobile phone companies, banks, and clothing stores at every turn. Trucks rumble by on the main road from Delhi to Jaipur. Little Maruti and Tata Indica sedans zip in and out of traffic, honking their horns. Many companies, both Indian and foreign, have offices here—Tata Consulting, Nestlé, Citibank, Ranbaxy, to name a few—their sleek glass surfaces mirroring the dusty trees and vacant lots around them. Call centers abound, as do the cafés, fast-food restaurants, and malls that cater to their young employees.

None of the malls I saw in Gurgaon was more than a few years old. Five more were under construction. All shelter a mix of international and Indian brands. Some are specialized: Gold Souk houses jewelry stores. MGF Plaza specializes in electronics, featuring such brands as Sony, Panasonic, Phillips, LG, Samsung, and India's own Videocon. Malls dedicated to one-stop shopping for weddings are enormously popular in India. There is one on Sohna Road, beyond the DLF golf course.

The Metropolitan Mall, anchored by the popular Indian department store Shopper's Stop, houses a variety of shops including Sam-sonite, Adidas, Swatch, Rolex, and Marks & Spencer. There is also a Raymond's—the longtime Indian, upscale men's clothing store, and a Wills Lifestyle shop. Wills' slogan is "Enjoy the change." Associated with ITC's Wills brand cigarettes, Wills is meant to appeal to young, urban Indians. The brand's Web site proclaims, "Wills Lifestyle is a chain of exclusive specialty stores providing a truly international shopping experience through world-class ambience."

Across the street from the Metropolitan Mall, at DT City Center, a seven-screen multiplex theater anchors a collection of stores and restaurants. The multiplex cinema is another relative novelty in India, where the old art deco single-screen houses outlasted their American and European counterparts by at least two decades. Last year, in the theater lobby, there were posters for *Harry Potter and the Goblet of Fire*. I could have been in a multiplex theater in an upscale mall in the United States.

My aunt and uncle and I were there to see *Taj Mahal*, a historical film set during the seventeenth-century reign of Mogul emperor Shah Jahan, who ordered the famous monument built as a tomb for his beloved wife, Mumtaz. Touted as the most expensive film in Bollywood history, *Taj Mahal* lavished its reported $18 million budget on elaborate costumes and opulent sets. The movie's stilted dialogue in Persianized Urdu to evoke the Mogul era was as incomprehensible to my Indian aunt and uncle, who live in Gurgaon and speak fluent Hindi, as it was to me. When the film was over, it was a jolt to step out of Mogul India into the air-conditioned hush of the mall, with its polished marble floors, eternally climbing escalator, and some of the cleanest public restrooms I have seen anywhere in the world.

Afterward, we went for a stroll. There were home-decor shops, a couple of sari and *salwar kameez* stores, and several shoe stores. Anchoring one end of the open central area of the mall was a Barista coffee shop offering a selection of sandwiches and cakes along with cappuccino, espresso, and other hot and iced coffee drinks. A Chinese restaurant, a tandoori joint, and a Ruby Tuesday restaurant were available for heartier appetites. DT City Center also features a modern supermarket called Crossroads filled with packaged and processed foods from India and around the world.

Moving in pairs and small groups throughout the mall were all kinds of shoppers—families with children in tow, groups of young people in their late teens or early twenties, couples of various ages. Almost all the twentysomething crowd, male and female, were dressed in jeans and T-shirts or jeans and *kurtis,* the popular women's short Indian tunic. Many of the mothers and middle-aged women wore the traditional *salwar kameez.* Few women were in saris. No men wore traditional Indian clothing. I didn't notice people carrying a lot of shopping bags, and when I asked my aunt about this, she told me, "Not many can afford to buy here. People come to look, see what they like, then they go to Karol Bagh or Lajpat Nagar market where the prices are better."

Karol Bagh and Lajpat Nagar are commercial strips of stores strung along busy avenues near the residential neighborhoods of South Delhi. They are much more like the traditional Indian bazaar, with different vendors hawking their wares along the thoroughfares, all color and noise, and hard bargaining. This is where we shopped when I lived in India as a child.

Despite the recent frenzy of mall construction, most Indians still shop in traditional bazaars and strips of small shops along roadways or the twisting lanes of old city neighborhoods. Shop owners know their customers by name, always offer to give a discount, and often extend credit. The ceremonial procedures of shopping for a new sari in a traditional shop involve first removing one's shoes at the threshold, then finding a comfortable spot on the floor covered by immaculate white cotton sheets over thin mattresses. A cup of tea or a cold drink is served. The store owner's assistants have already begun to unfurl yards upon yards of silk, some intricately woven, some delicately embroidered, one from Kanjeevaram, another from Patan. Expert weavers have spent months producing a single length of shimmering fabric, which is accepted or approved with a nod of the head, or a wave of the hand.

The malls are giving India's traditional markets a lot of competition. "Coming Soon: India's Biggest Mall. One KM of Shopping,"

trumpeted a huge billboard where yet another mall was going up. I
wondered if *KM* meant one square kilometer or one linear kilometer;
either way, the thing was going to be huge. "The Goddess of All
Sales!" boasted a billboard near a mall in Bombay. "The League of
Global Indians," bragged a large sign in the window of a Shopper's
Stop in Calcutta.

Organized retail is just taking off in India. Shopping malls and big
stores account for 80 percent of the retail business in the United
States, and 20 percent in China. They account for just 3 percent in
India. India is truly a nation of shopkeepers. Some 12 million *kiranas,*
small mom-and-pop shops, tiny kiosks, and roadside stands, provide
India's billion-plus people with their retail shopping needs. *Kiranas*
can be found everywhere. In cities, they may be narrow shops, walls
lined with shelves all the way up to the ceiling, the shopkeeper behind
a glass display counter, fielding requests for packages of biscuits or
bidis, tiny hand-rolled cigarettes, tooth powder, or tinned Amul-brand
cheese. In villages, they may be little more than a roadside shack with
a few popular essentials. This is about to change. Within the next
couple of years, the government of India is expected to relax rules bar-
ring multibrand retail chains, such as Wal-Mart and French mega-
chain Carrefour, from operating in India. Indian companies are
scrambling to establish a strong retail presence and capture market
share before that happens.

Kishore Biyani's Pantaloon Retail Ltd. is India's largest retailer. His
company has three main retail store chains: a department store called
Pantaloons, a mixed-retail discount chain called Big Bazaar, and a
grocery-store chain called Food Bazaar. Trent Ltd., a division of the
Tata company, followed the successful launch of its department-store
chain Westside a few years ago with a discount retail chain called
Trent's Star India Bazaar. Real estate giant K. Raheja group launched its
popular Shopper's Stop department store back in 1991. Godrej Agrovet
Ltd., a division of Godrej Group, long involved in agriculture, has gotten into the grocery business with Nature's Basket, an upscale supermarket. At its flagship store on Warden Road in Bombay, there is a juice
bar and a nutrition consultant. The store offers home delivery to the
nearby posh neighborhoods of Malabar Hill and Nepean Sea Road.

Whether they cater to India's most affluent or to its striving middle class, these store chains have been enormously successful. The chaotic colors of India's traditional bazaars, the unique local specialties of each town, each neighborhood, and even each vendor, the cacophony of cries of merchants and their touts competing for the customers' attention are giving way to uniformity, predictability, and the omnipresence of Musak. Indian producers may well gain markets, and Indian consumers consistency, but India will also have lost part of its magic.

A Retail Revolution

According to a 2006 AC Nielsen Consumer Survey, India is the most financially optimistic country in the world. More than 66 percent of Indians think that now is the time to buy what they want or feel they need. This is a higher percentage than in any of the other forty-one countries surveyed.[1] India's shopping mall boom is in direct response to this optimism. There are expected to be 343 shopping malls built in India by the end of 2007.[2] In addition to restaurants and multiplex cinemas, malls offer children's play areas, video game parlors, even bowling alleys and discotheques. As Aroon Purie, editor in chief of *India Today*, observed, "You don't buy a product in a mall, you buy an experience."[3]

Malls are a way for affluent Indians and India's aspiring middle class to experience a luxurious environment free from the discomforts of the typical Indian street. Upscale shopping malls provide a space cocooned away from the poor, stray cows, pariah dogs, and the little piles of garbage and drifting plastic bags that one finds on the street right outside. For as long as you are in the mall, you can enjoy a bubble of air-conditioned, first-world pleasure in a country where most people can't even afford a slice of pizza from one of the fast-food restaurants. The terms *global* and *world-class* are in advertisements for both the products sold in malls and for the malls themselves. All Indians need to do is shop in a mall surrounded by these brands to feel as if they are part of the rich, developed world—and, at that moment, they are.

The notion that purchasing power is the way to connect to the world beyond India is something advertisers use to tap Indians' perceptions about globalization. A full-page ad in the home-decorating magazine *Inside Outside* for American-made Glodecor-brand wall panels tells potential Indian customers, "Bring American Interiors to India (No Visa Required)."[4] At the airport in Calcutta, while waiting several hours for a delayed flight, I had ample opportunity to study a rotating, backlit, three-sided advertising poster for Compton Greaves, a large Indian company. The three messages were "Buy a Compton Greaves product, get global technology at no extra cost"; "While international brands flood the market, one Indian brand is making waves in the Indian market"; "Most Indian companies compete only against each other. Compton Greaves competes against the world's best."

Morgan Stanley chief economist Stephen Roach asserts that the Indian consumer may be about to give the American consumer—longtime king of the global consumption realm—a run for his money. He notes that private consumption in India accounts for an astounding 64 percent of GDP, only slightly less than top spender the United States at 70 percent and higher than Japan (57 percent), Europe (54 percent), or China (38 percent).[5] He warns that the global economic engine of U.S. consumption will weaken as the housing bubble bursts. With emerging economies dependent on exports, "the world needs a new consumer," says Roach.[6] Indians appear more than happy to step into the breach.

Couple Indians' penchant for spending with the young demographic of the country's population—300 million people between the high-spending ages of eighteen and thirty-five—and you have the makings of the biggest consumer market the world has ever seen. The New Delhi–based National Council for Applied Economic Research breaks down India's burgeoning middle class as follows: 90 million people earning between $4,400 and $21,800 per year, plus 287 million with a household income of between $2,000 and $4,000 per year who aspire to join the middle class.[7] By 2010, this group of Indian consumers will number a whopping 561 million people. Add to that an estimated 37.2 million upper-middle-class urban households, and you've got a consumer market roughly equal to the combined population of the United States and the European Union.

The numbers of Indian consumers are eye-popping, but they represent a minority of India's total population. Eight hundred million Indians do not have the purchasing power to participate in the country's retail explosion. The gap between those who can buy and those who can't is widening. As it grows, the risk of serious social friction grows apace.

The growth of India's consumer class is being driven to a large degree by India's youthful population. Urban, affluent Indian youth is coming of age in a new world where shopping malls are a popular hangout for young people in India. For them, the shopping experience their parents find so revolutionary is just the way things are. India's retail sector will continue to grow as subsequent generations become consumers—assuming they find adequate employment. Many millions of Indian youth do not have good jobs or affluent parents. They cannot afford the goods that dance so tantalizingly in front of their eyes on television. One of India's biggest challenges is to create employment opportunities for its burgeoning youth population that will allow more of them to participate in the country's retail revolution.

While affluent youth are buying clothing, accessories, and personal entertainment products, a lot of the new spending in India is on household goods. Sales of microwave ovens, air conditioners, washing machines, VCD/DVD players, color TVs, and refrigerators are up impressively.[8] Korean home appliance giant LG Electronics, which makes many of these products, is aiming to boost revenue five times between now and 2010, when it expects to hit $10 billion in revenue from India.[9] Most Indians live in traditional "joint families," where brothers bring their wives home to live under their parents' roof. While each family works out its own arrangement of shared versus private income, generally each earning member of an Indian family contributes to household expenses. With more people living under one roof, incomes are pooled, expenses reduced, and purchasing power is magnified. Home appliances are acquisitions the entire family can enjoy. In many middle-class Indian homes, the refrigerator sits proudly displayed in the living-cum-dining room, whether or not there is space for one in the kitchen. Accumulating home appliances and electronics is a tangible indicator of families' economic progress.

One of the most disturbing faces of the new consumerism is reflected in the sharp increase in consumer products as part of a bride's dowry. Traditionally, an Indian bride came with a collection of jewelry, clothing, some household items, and some cash. Dowry is illegal in India, but that hasn't made the practice disappear. Today, grooms' families demand televisions, washing machines, motorcycles, and even automobiles. There are many tragic tales, especially in North India where the practice of dowry is more widespread, of brides hounded to the point of suicide or even murdered by their in-laws—known as dowry deaths—because the poor girl's parents could not deliver the full list of goods demanded by her new husband's family.

In the United States, we think of home appliances as releasing housewives from the drudgery of homemaking. In India, this is not necessarily the case. The great divide between rich and poor, and the large numbers of very poor, mean that household help is readily available even in lower-middle-class households. Even modest households boast servants who do the washing up. Women's work in homes that can afford new consumer goods is often limited to cooking. This can easily be a full-time job, as most Indian food is prepared fresh every day, so kitchen appliances are very popular. Mixers and food processors have long been fixtures in middle-class Indian kitchens.

Microwave ovens are a real boon. Food preparation can be finished in the morning, and the dishes heated up when the meal is served later in the day. In this case, the housewife or even the working wife does save time and effort. In the homes of my own family and friends, it is a convenience for the servants, who simply heat and serve the family their meal, prepared earlier by the women in the household or the family cook. Typically, the servants eat their meals after the family has finished eating. This is usually done on the kitchen floor. The household servants gather around the serving dishes and eat together. I have barged into the kitchen during what is understood to be a private break for the servants, surprising animated mealtime banter before hastily excusing myself. Then, while the women of the house take their afternoon nap—a good way to get through the hottest part of the day, and necessary when people have gotten up early to take advantage of the morning cool and stayed up late to enjoy the evening hours—the servants wash all the dishes and clean up the kitchen.

Home appliances such as washing machines put people out of work. Clothes washing is a specialized occupation in India. Professional clothes washers, called dhobis, are famed for their ability to collect laundry from many different households and never lose or confuse a single item. Many households have someone come in every day whose job it is to wash the clothes. The family's dirty clothes are collected and put to soak in buckets of water after everyone's morning bath. The dhobi then comes, washes everything, and hangs it up to dry on a balcony or rooftop terrace. Many Indians I know who are buying washing machines do so because they feel their clothes get clean with less wear and tear. Modern clothes, especially synthetic ones, do not do well when washed using the traditional Indian method of whacking them with a wooden bat on a large, flat stone.

Ironing is also commonly sent out to a neighborhood clothes presser. Where my aunt and uncle live in Gurgaon, on a quiet, tree-lined suburban street of comfortable bungalows, there is a traditional clothes presser on the corner. He has built a simple, little one-room shack where he does all the neighborhood ironing and also lives with his family. He uses great, heavy cast-iron irons that have a hollow cavity for hot coals. Items given to him for pressing in the morning are returned perfectly pressed that evening. He is paid by the piece. My aunt and uncle have an electric iron and ironing board at home, but this is used mostly for touch-ups or last-minute ironing needs. It's just too convenient to give things to the local clothes presser, just as many urban Americans find it convenient to have their shirts pressed at a laundry rather than iron them at home.

Every economic revolution in human history has taken a toll on the modes of life and livelihood that it unseated. India's retail revolution will be no different. Labor-saving devices will certainly put people out of jobs. Small shops and local specialities will disappear. One hopes that the millions of young people lured by an urban consumer culture will find the employment they will need, that the millions of rural poor, mostly farmers, will find new markets for their produce. This is India's true retail challenge.

Going Mobile

In India, using the telephone used to be a hellish undertaking. It took my grandparents years to get a phone installed in their pleasant suburban Bombay apartment because they refused, on principle, to pay the bribe that would have expedited the process. Their telephone, like all the others I saw in India in the late 1960s and 1970s, was a heavy, black rotary-dial affair from the 1930s. You had to yell into the mouthpiece to be heard across town and over the cross-communications of other people's conversations audible on the line. To make a call to another Indian city, much less abroad, you had to book what was mysteriously called a trunk call, then wait in a queue until the operator called and put you through. This could take hours.

Now, several mobile telecommunications companies, including Reliance, Bharti Airtel, and Hutch, vie for customers. The success of mobile communications has created serious competition for the government landline provider, resulting in dramatic improvement in landline connections as well.

Mobile communications are changing India's retail landscape all the way up the value chain, from producer to consumer. Fishermen and farmers can track wholesale prices on the Internet or via their cell phone. Retailers, even very small ones, can better communicate with customers. My aunt and uncle's clothes presser, for example, may live in a one-room shack, but he has a cell phone. It has become a key part of his business. Whenever my aunt and uncle have clothing they need pressed, they call him and he comes and picks it up. When the clothes are ready, he calls and asks when he can deliver them. Fishermen from tiny fishing villages along India's coast call shore when they are ready to bring in their catch to find out in which nearby coastal market the fish they've caught are selling for the highest price. Fruit and vegetable sellers, tailors, household servants, chauffeurs (quite common in

India), all use cell phones in their daily working lives to keep in touch with suppliers, customers, and employers.

The small vendor or domestic employee who has a phone has a competitive advantage over his or her competitors who don't. Many people who own cars in India employ drivers since wages are low and choked roads and limited parking make driving a nightmare. Most employers now get their drivers a mobile phone if they don't already have one, the better to reach them whenever they are needed. Everywhere you turn in India, people are talking or busy sending SMS text messages on their cell phones. The per-minute charges have been driven down by intense competition among the major providers, with Reliance slashing charges when I was in India in 2006 to one rupee—less than two cents—per minute for a call anywhere in India. Billboards across the country trumpeted, *Ek rupee, ek desh,* or "One rupee, one country."

I can attest to the powerful draw of mobile phones. At a large party for my cousin's fortieth birthday at her house in Alibagh, the beach resort that is the equivalent of the Hamptons for Bombay's superwealthy, my phone disappeared off a coffee table. Much frantic searching ensued, but the consensus was that the unguarded phone was simply too tempting for one of the boys in the small army of waiters hired for the evening—all teenagers earning in a month less than most of the guests spend in a typical minute—to resist. When I recounted the story to a friend in Delhi, she simply replied, "That is normal. It happens to everyone."

In 2006, Nokia built a new plant in India, and before the plant was even finished the company had commitments for 1 million phones. Motorola's CEO, Edward J. Zander, underlined the importance of the Indian market to his company when he declared, "Motorola is the first multinational to make India its global headquarters for the High Growth Markets [HGMs] initiative. We chose India as the headquarters because of the country's strategic importance to Motorola's global operations and because of the highest growth rate and potential within the identified HGMs and the geographic advantage." Motorola has invested $150 million in a new plant in India. The company plans to expand India's mobile phone market by pushing down handset prices. Initially, phones made in its Indian factory will retail for $40 with a goal of rapidly bringing that down below $30.[10] Sunil Bharti Mittal, chairman of Bharti Enterprises, which includes Bharti Telecom, says, "It's my dream that handset prices will fall to twenty dollars [Rs 900] or less."[11] Low production costs are attracting mobile phone manufacturers to set up plants in India for export markets. LG is investing $60 million by 2010 in a plant that will produce 20 million phones per year, of which half will be destined for export.[12]

The expansion of mobile communications in India is also driving growth in personal computing, with notebook sales beginning to take off as prices have come down. According to Vinnie Mehta, executive director of the Indian industry group MAIT, Manufacturers' Association for Information Technology, "The progression [of notebook sales] actually came from mobile phones, where people in India started to engage in mobility as a part of their business."[13] The increase over two years is dizzying: while computer sales in general rose 30 percent in the year ended May 2006, notebook sales climbed a gigantic 168 percent.[14] Competition has been fierce, with international brands Acer, HP, and IBM slashing prices to gain market share.[15] Michael Dell has announced that his company will double its workforce in India to twenty thousand employees, and that it is actively looking for a site to set up a factory there. With annual computer sales in India expected to rise from 5 million in 2006 to 20 million by 2010, the potential of the Indian market is simply too big to ignore.[16]

India's cheapest desktop costs about ten thousand rupees ($220). The low prices are sending sales up in smaller cities and rural areas where incomes are lower. The second four largest cities saw sales of PCs increase 50 percent in 2006 over the previous fiscal year. In 2007, PC sales in India were expected to reach 6 million units.[17] The competition for India's booming PC market is intense. Chinese giant Lenovo, which bought out IBM's PC business in 2005, designated India as its fifth geographic region effective on January 1, 2006. According to Adrian Koch, a senior vice president with HP, the company is "evaluating to what degree and how fast to expand." Meanwhile, Dell has ambitions to become "No. 1 in the overall Indian market." The fastest-growing PC company in India last year was the Indian company HCL, which plans to expand annual production to 1.4 million units by 2007.[18]

Turning Adversity into Opportunity

India's rural areas lag well behind its major cities in personal computing and Internet connectivity. The country is making a concerted effort to push IT into rural areas, where the majority of the population still lives. A lack of reliable electricity, extremely hot temperatures, dust, and excessive humidity all conspire to make computer use all but impossible in many places where home consists of a one-room wattle and daub cottage with a thatched roof, or an uninsulated concrete block with window frames filled only with iron bars.

However, as Anand Mahindra explained to me, "India is a weird place for all sorts of applications to work. In a low-cost, cost-sensitive economy, many options that never get explored in richer countries become viable here." A good example of this phenomenon is Intel's collaboration with Wipro and HCL to produce low-cost, sturdy PCs. "The systems are designed to withstand the rigors of daily life in rural India: temperatures hot enough to fry an egg, dust and intermittent power outages." While they will cost slightly more than standard PCs, "customers will save money because they will not need to install airconditioning, extra power generators, or other equipment just to keep the machines working."[19]

This is an excellent example of precisely the kind of innovation that India's adverse environment is fostering. India's lack of infrastructure hampers the expansion of the Indian market for goods designed for rich consumers. So, instead of waiting for reliable electrical service and air-conditioning to reach all the far-flung areas of the country, Indian companies are making new devices that simply require less energy and can operate in a hot climate—which happen to be the conditions in which billions of people in the developing world live.

In 1994, Tulsi Tanti set up two windmills in a desperate bid to provide enough electrical power to his family's textile mill in Gujarat state.

The fix was so successful, he realized he'd stumbled onto a gold mine. Suzlon Energy, the company that Tanti created out of his experience with energy adversity, makes and installs wind turbines. It is now the fifth-largest wind energy company in the world.[20] Suzlon has quickly established itself as a major global player, acquiring in 2006 Hansen Transmissions, a major wind-turbine gearbox manufacturer based in Belgium.

In addition to the largest wind park in Asia with capacity of five hundred megawatts, near India's southern tip where trade winds constantly blow, Suzlon has a large wind park in southern Minnesota. "With orders worth $600 million in hand from U.S., Chinese, and Australian customers, Suzlon has invested in a service support facility and a workshop in Pipestone, Minnesota, to manufacture rotor blades,"[21] reported Naazneen Karmali in *Forbes* magazine.

India has committed itself to energy independence by 2020. By 2030, India will need to generate four hundred thousand megawatts of power to meet its projected development needs. President of India Abdul Kalam has vowed that this will be achieved through "three different sources, namely hydel capacity, nuclear power, and nonconventional energy sources."[22] He argues that India must increase the proportion of renewable energy in its total energy consumption from the current level of 5 percent to 25 percent. For energy for transportation, India is developing carbon-neutral biofuels, promoting hydrogen-based fuels and electric automobiles. In 2000, India mandated that passenger vehicles meet norms set by the European Union and, in 2001, required vehicles in four major cities—Bombay, Delhi, Calcutta, and Chennai—to meet the EU's stricter Euro II norms. India's Ministry of Non-Conventional Energy has directly aided the expansion of wind power by Suzlon and other wind companies by creating a wind atlas for picking the best sites in the country to set up wind farms. The government of India has also offered the industry tax breaks, allowing Indian investors in wind power to claim 80 percent depreciation from the first year.[23]

The result of India's forward-looking energy policy is that Suzlon and other Indian energy companies are becoming global leaders in the cutting-edge technologies and products that can mitigate India's own

carbon footprint as well as reduce the world's production of greenhouse gases. "The difference" between India and the developed
world, argues Anand Mahindra, "is that we will create an IPR [intel-
lectual property rights] that deploys these new technologies, and we
will become leaders."

Wireless technologies are playing a similar role. Personal computing without Internet connectivity is almost useless in today's world.
Vast areas of India remain without reliable phone lines and electricity,
much less broadband cable. Wireless is obviously the way to connect
India's far-flung rural population. Microsoft has signed up with Intel,
HCL, and the telecom company Bharti Sangam Nigam to expand wireless, broadband PC penetration. Microsoft is investing another $2 bil-
lion to set up fifty thousand Internet cafés over the next four years.[24]
The combination of multiplying PC sales in small towns and rural
areas with expanded broadband penetration in an environment of
falling prices means that many more Indians across a much broader
social and geographic range are going to be connecting to the Internet.

This will literally open up a world of new possibilities for education, entertainment, news, and social interaction to a whole host of
Indians across the country. Their lives will be changed, and they are
in turn bound to change India's economic, social, and political climate
in ways that are hard to predict. It took several generations for Americans to go from an operator-assisted call on a multiple-party phone
line more than a century ago to wireless, broadband communications
today. Many of India's citizens today are moving from the era before
that single shared line directly to wireless remote computing virtually
overnight. They are like time travelers who start in the nineteenth century and end up in the twenty-first century. The social and economic
impact of rural India's 700 million people entering the Information
Age will be revolutionary.

Detroit Hits the Deccan

I remember as a child bumping along a curve of Indian road, careening
around bullock carts and women with huge bundles on their heads,

while crammed along with several of my siblings, aunts, and cousins into the backseat of an Ambassador, every strong steel spring in the sturdy, upholstered seat palpable beneath my skinny bottom.

For decades in India, there were only two models of automobile to choose from: the boxy, unbreakable Ambassador, a copy of the 1948 Morris Oxford sedan, usually painted plain white, and the smaller, more feminine 1958-vintage Premier Padmini, modeled on the Fiat 1100. If you wanted to buy one of these stalwarts of the Indian pot-holed road, you paid cash up front at the time you placed a "book-ing," putting yourself into a queue for a car scheduled to roll off the assembly line at some future date. You never "traded up" for a new model: there weren't any. You repaired the car forever and felt lucky to have one at all.

India is now Asia's fourth-largest automobile market, and grow-ing fast. Every major automobile manufacturer has set up factories in India. In 2005, India surpassed the 1-million mark in passenger-vehicle sales. Honda is busy expanding its operations there in antici-pation of strong growth. Ford Motor Company had sold twenty-five thousand cars in India by June of 2006, as many as during the entire year of 2005. "We feel that going by this rate, we will end 2006 with a near one hundred percent growth in year-on-year sales," Ford India president and managing director Arvind Mathew declared last year.[25] General Motors' sales in India of its Aveo, Tavera, and Optra models increased 37 percent in July 2006 over July of the previous year. The company is investing $300 million in a second manufacturing plant in the state of Maharashtra that will be able to produce 140,000 units per year, more than doubling GM's current capacity in India to a total of 225,000 units per year.[26]

A number of factors are driving India's booming automobile mar-ket. Roads are improving, and customers can actually put higher-performing cars through their paces on the country's new highways. The old social ethos, represented by Gandhi's ascetic lifestyle, that discouraged displays of wealth in a poor country has evaporated. Status-conscious Indians show off their affluence by driving luxury cars. Large families who can afford it are trading up from smaller, economical models to new minivans and SUVs. Members of affluent joint families heading off in different directions during the day each need a vehicle. But most people are still looking for the best value. Ninety percent of cars in India sell for less than $15,000. This is still a fortune in a country where the average annual income is only $500.

For this reason, despite the onslaught on the Indian market of the U.S., European, and East Asian auto giants, the dominant passenger-vehicle company in India remains Maruti Udyog. In 1983, the Maruti 800, the brainchild of Sanjay Gandhi, Indira Gandhi's elder son, was launched in India as an inexpensive "people's car." It is widely credited with jump-starting India's automobile revolution and remains the most popular brand of passenger automobile in India. The company has ceded a controlling stake to Suzuki, the original foreign collaborator on the project. Priced at around 250,000 rupees or $5,500, the Maruti 800 remains a popular, affordable car.

In terms of what the Indians call lifestyle vehicles, SUVs have become enormously popular with those who can afford them. Mahindra & Mahindra, a diversified conglomerate that started life in the 1950s making Willys Jeeps in India before branching out into the tractor business, decided to return to its roots in 2002 with a new SUV. This time, however, the aim was at India's status-conscious luxury market. Anand Mahindra, the dynamic, Harvard-educated third-generation leader of the firm, took a phenomenal risk, making the single largest investment in the company's history, $120 million, in developing and manufacturing in record time a vehicle that would push the company into a new market. The Scorpio was an instant hit. Costing just 20 percent of what a similar effort would have in the United States, the vehicle became profitable after just fifty thousand units. Anand Mahindra, who believes in driving his company forward with relentless innovation, has vowed that 20 percent of the company's manufacturing sales must henceforth come from new products.

Following the success of the Scorpio project, Mahindra & Mahindra partnered with French automaker Renault to manufacture the Logan, a low-priced car that currently sells in Romania for six thousand euros or about $7,500. Logans will start rolling off the assembly line in India this year. The deal includes the use of Renault's distribution network to help the expansion of Mahindra vehicles into foreign markets, including Malaysia, Russia, South Africa, and Indonesia.[27] Anand Mahindra is convinced that going global is the only way his company will survive. Mahindra & Mahindra, which has manufactured and sold tractors in the United States since 1994, is now preparing to become the first Indian automobile manufacturer to tackle the American market with a planned launch of its SUV.

The Indian automobile industry is expected to be able to produce more than 2 million units by 2008. That will put India ahead of the United Kingdom and Canada in terms of production capacity, and in a tie with Brazil for eighth-largest auto producer in the world. More than one-third, 37 percent, of Indian car buyers are first-time buyers. In China, however, first-time buyers account for 81 percent of automobile purchases. The potential for growth in the Indian market is enormous, assuming India can continue to expand the circle of its citizens who have enough purchasing power to buy a car.[28]

Those Indian consumers who can't afford to buy cars, buy motorcycles. They can choose from models named Avenger, Pulsar, Discover, Ambition, Splendour, or Passion. Hero Honda was running both a print and a television campaign when I was in India last year for a model aimed exclusively at women. The model's name: Pleasure. The tagline from the advertisements, which featured comely young women turning down offers of rides from guys in cars in order to straddle their hot two-wheelers, was "Why should boys have all the fun?" Young Indian women are increasingly working before getting married and even after marriage. They have money to spend, a need to be mobile, and a desire to be independent. In India, a motorcycle is the family car for many people who just can't afford an automobile. It is common to see whole families, including babies in arms, lined up on a motorcycle, weaving through traffic.

Waiting for more Indians to be able to afford to upgrade the family two-wheeler to a four-wheeler is one way to expand the automobile market. Driving down cost is another. Tata Motors Ltd. has announced plans to manufacture a new five-passenger family vehicle that will retail for one lakh rupees, or about $2,200.[29] The company has not released a lot of details as of this writing, but using adhesives instead of welding parts together is one strategy that has been broached. Making the cars modular for assembly on demand at Tata's extensive network of dealerships and repair shops is another. If Tata is successful, it will bring that ultimate symbol of freedom, mobility, and individualism—the private car—within reach of whole sections of Indian society that hardly dare dream of owning such a thing now.

India's automobile industry is also pushing to lower emissions and increase gasoline efficiency. While some can afford gas-guzzling SUVs, most Indian car buyers are as interested in fuel efficiency as they are in purchase price. Several municipalities have given the auto industry a good nudge by requiring public vehicles, such as buses and taxis, to run on compressed natural gas (CNG). Mahindra & Mahindra has hired Dr. Arun Jaura, who ran Ford's Escape SUV hybrid project, for their own hybrid car project. India is also poised to get into flex-fuel cars, which use up to 80 percent ethanol, produced from plant sources such as corn, mixed with diesel. Flex-fuel cars now account for 75 percent of the Brazilian new-car market. Feeling the pinch of increasing demand and rising oil prices, India is aggressively looking into developing biofuels such as ethanol.

One of the most exciting automobile companies in India is tiny Reva. Based in Bangalore, Reva manufactures completely electric cars. It currently offers a two-passenger hatchback. Founded in 1995 to develop environmentally friendly vehicles, Reva is getting ready to market its car aggressively in Europe. Its model has EEC (European Economic Community) certification and is already being exported to the UK and Malta and test-marketed in the United States, Norway, Switzerland, Cyprus, Japan, and Sri Lanka. India has far more incentive to pursue innovative manufacturing strategies that drive down retail cost as well as innovative technologies that enhance fuel efficiency and reduce emissions than the United States, where American automobile manufacturers have been content to coast on easy money and lax government fuel-efficiency requirements for far too long. Necessity is driving India toward a global leadership role in low-cost, highly efficient, and low-polluting vehicles.

Easy Money

While salaries for some, along with purchasing power, are rising in India—up an average 13.5 percent in 2005—one of the most important factors in India's consumer boom is the explosion of new credit opportunities for Indian consumers. The days when families scrimped and saved until they had the cash to plunk down for a new refrigerator, motorcycle, car, or even home are fading. Eighty percent of passenger automobiles are sold now with financing. In Gurgaon, a brand-new auto mall is being constructed. There will be showrooms for different brands of passenger cars, as well as financing facilities, all under one roof. In 1995, only 2.6 million Indian households could afford a mortgage. By 2003, that number had increased to 20.5 million. That's still a tiny portion of the country's total 1.2 billion population. Still, India's mortgage market is expected to grow by a galloping 30–45 percent annually, reaching a total value of $77 billion by 2008.[30]

When I talked to him in Bombay in 2006, Credit Suisse Boston's India head, Mihir Doshi, told me, "The consumer lending environment is totally different in India now as compared to the early 1990s. Then, rates were north of 20 percent. Now, they are south of 10 percent. The quarter-billion middle class are taking advantage of lower rates and borrowing to spend."

Everywhere you go in India there are billboards and advertisements for consumer loans, with banks competing furiously with each other to catch the attention of an Indian consumer newly open to borrowing. Morgan Stanley's Stephen Roach confirms that banks in India are "focused on consumer-oriented growth strategies, especially in the mortgage finance and credit and debit card business."[31] These banks include Citibank, HSBC, and GE Money, along with a raft of Indian banks including ICICI, Dena Bank, and HDFC, to name only a few.

While consumer lending has no doubt helped propel India's consumer boom, there are worries that a credit bubble could be forming. Housing values are climbing fast, banks are aggressively pushing to get a piece of the consumer lending market, and customers have little experience managing credit. In December 2005, over a cup of coffee off the lobby of the Oberoi Hotel in Bombay, Ajit Balakrishnan, the CEO of Rediff.com, explained his wariness about this trend. "Consumer lending opened up about five years ago, with low-cost lending and low down payments. It is now reaching proportions which are quite scary. Retail lending is driving up the cost of consumption in India, and the government has been saying, 'Don't create a bubble.'" It seems like his concerns are well-founded: in April 2006, the Reserve Bank of India put into place a series of measures designed to protect banks from bad loans. According to a 2006 report in the *Banker,* banks in India were "pausing to assess the risks of lending to millions of small borrowers that have a scrappy credit history. The panic is not yet on, but the banks and the regulators are uneasy about how a rise in interest rates, sky-high property prices, or a sharp downturn in the equity markets could affect banks' balance sheets."[32] Retail lending has become an important part of the banking business in India, comprising about one-fourth of bank credit.

To recoup bad loans, banks have resorted to more and more drastic measures, from hiring bands to bang drums outside defaulters' homes to hiring thugs to intimidate them. An Indian graduate student in New York I interviewed for a research position told me she knew lots of Indian students who, convinced banks wouldn't be able to catch up with them abroad, had left a trail of credit-card debt behind them before leaving for the United States. One student she knew got a panicked call from his parents in India telling him, "They sent some guys to smash up the car who told us they'll smash us up next if you don't pay up." He promptly did.

Education loans have proliferated in India as ambitious parents scramble to pull together the enormous sums required to send their children to the best schools. Many of the beneficiaries of these loans use the money to study overseas, where tuition costs can far exceed an Indian family's budget. In a bid to find defaulters who've skipped the country, the Indian banking industry is considering using bar codes on borrowers' passports to make it easier to track them down.[33] This drastic measure, which violates borrowers' privacy, is an indication of how desperate Indian banks are to catch up with defaulters and avoid bad loans.

Lending to the Poor

"If you draw a line at, say, three to four dollars per day in income," explained Dr. Nachiket Mor, deputy managing director of India's ICICI Bank, "a very large proportion of India's people will fall below that line." He explained that ICICI Bank originally began looking at helping India's poor majority with a classic social-responsibility model: the bank set aside some money, and used it to support health, education, and microfinance initiatives. While it still pursues health and education as a part of its social responsibility effort, it realized that microfinance could be taken to scale as a business opportunity, and after some false starts, ICICI seems to have hit on a formula for giving the poor something middle-class and wealthy people take for granted: access to affordable credit and other financial services.

"The only real collateral a poor person has is the quality of life he or she has led," Dr. Mor explained. "I got up in the morning. I worked hard. I took care of my family. The fact that someone has been disciplined over a lifetime is enormously valuable." He pointed out that a used car is not worth very much as collateral, yet banks persist in thinking of tangible collateral as the only asset worthy of consideration. Very poor people don't have tangible assets, but the reputation that they have built as upright citizens could be a lot more valuable. "ICICI Bank asked, why not make this reputation itself the collateral through the famous Grameen-style group model of lending? Our one assumption is that everyone can do something. A woman with nothing, no education, nothing, can do something. If she can get a small loan, she can buy a buffalo and sell the milk. She can start a kitchen garden and sell the vegetables," Dr. Mor argued.

This is precisely the philosophy that led Nobel Prize–winner Muhammad Yunus to start the world's best-known microlender, the Grameen Bank. ICICI Bank is taking this kind of thinking and working with over one hundred partner organizations and the government to expand the population they serve while reducing risk, and scaling up microlending to a level no other bank has so far matched. Dr. Mor told me ICICI Bank's microlending program within four years already serves 3 million customers and has $600 million in assets. Their goal is to reach 25 million households and $10 billion in assets. He also said, "Things would be much easier if each borrower's credit history could be made portable across regions and across banks by giving each one a unique biometric identity card that allowed her credit behavior to be tracked. She could then go to an Internet kiosk or a bank branch and use her thumbprint to call up her record, converting her unblemished credit record into immediate access to inexpensive credit." For this to work, Dr. Mor noted, the government or banking regulators would have to mandate the use of such a card. The banks could do the rest.

"This is our market," he said about India's legions of poor. "We have a huge opportunity right here in India. I am tremendously bullish about this country. The 1990s"—India liberalized its economy in 1991—"were less than what they are believed to be. We weren't prepared. It's really now that things are taking off. We are building our business on real value. We are profitable. And we are serving real need."

The Building Boom

In addition to snapping up cars, appliances, and electronics with their newfound credit, Indians have been using mortgages to buy homes and apartments. Demand has sent prices through the roof. Land prices have skyrocketed. Property prices in some cities in India are equal to and in some cases higher than in Manhattan, Los Angeles, or San Francisco. Most Indians, nearly 70 percent, still live in rural areas, but the United Nations Development Program (UNDP) expects urbanization to increase by 40 percent, resulting in a doubling of India's urban population to 600 million people by 2030.[34] At that point, Bombay will have a population of 35 million people, while Delhi and Calcutta will come in at just under 30 million each. Along with this kind of growth in urban populations, there will be a sustained need for housing for decades to come. Meanwhile, the need for state-of-the-art office space to house the information technology and services sectors of India's expanding economy will increase as well.

These industries require buildings with a certain caliber of infrastructure, especially a constant electricity supply to power equipment and air-conditioning. Since urban space in India's major cities is saturated, new office complexes are going up in outlying areas and Special Economic Zones (SEZs), where a mixture of offices, schools, housing, and other amenities are being built.

In India, only 51 percent of the population live in what are considered good dwellings. Forty-four percent live in dwellings considered merely livable, and 5 percent in dilapidated dwellings.[35] India's census defines good, livable, or dilapidated based on "the perception and the response of the respondent."[36] In Bombay, 60 percent of the city's population lives in substandard housing or on the streets, sometimes under an open tarp, sometimes with nothing more than a blanket between them and the sidewalk. If India really is to transform itself into a developed country, it will have to address the housing needs of its poor. However, India's housing boom isn't producing the low-cost or no-cost housing that the majority of Indians so desperately need. Developers and speculators are going for luxury complexes for which they can demand a premium price. There is little incentive to house the poor or even the lower middle class decently, as is evident from the slums that crowd against the walls of luxury properties. While expanding mortgage credit has brought high-priced apartments and bungalows into the reach of a wider market, the market that qualifies for mortgage loans remains comparatively minuscule.

India's land rush makes the recent property boom in the United States pale in comparison. Everyone—from global giants in the real estate construction business to hedge funds looking for outsized opportunities—is getting into the act. In 2005, Farallon Capital Management, a U.S.-based hedge fund, paid the then unbelievable price of $54.5 million for an eleven-acre parcel of land in Bombay. Local developers hadn't stopped laughing when Farallon offered $95.5 million for an adjacent parcel, only to discover that theirs was the second-lowest bid. Land prices went up from 30 to 100 percent in just the eighteen-month period ending last July, while real estate stocks increased 2,000 percent as everyone jumped on the trend. Nearly all the world's big banks have invested in Indian real estate or floated funds investing in Indian real estate, including Morgan Stanley, Merrill Lynch, GE Commercial Finance Real Estate, J. P. Morgan, Warburg Pincus, and Deutsche Asset Management.[37]

This has all been a boon to India's big developers, such as Mantri Developers in Bangalore, Panscheel Developers, along with giants DLF, Raheja, and Hirandani. Everywhere you go in India, apartment blocks are going up. Billboards trumpet the amenities offered by new developments, with vistas of scenery unknown in urban India: vast, clean parks, swimming pools, tennis courts. A full-page ad for Parsvnath Developers Ltd.'s King Citi in Punjab is typical of what these housing complexes promise. King Citi is, well, a "glorious township so regal it's fit for kings." The township will be a self-contained kingdom of comfort and opulence amidst the chaos of India outside its gates. There will be lots of space, "beautifully designed villas, along with wide metaled tree lined roads, landscaped open & greens [*sic*]," plus "school, shopping mall, shopping centre, health facilities, an elaborate club with modern amenities" and, let's not forget, "security."

Where land has been set aside for affordable public housing, unscrupulous developers are not above grabbing it for more lucrative purposes. Bombay's newest and finest shopping mall, the Atria Millennium Mall in Worli, opened quietly last year. The mall, which houses such brands as Pepe jeans, Nike, United Colors of Benetton, Levi's, Aldo, and Sony—not to mention India's first Rolls-Royce showroom and dealership—became mired in controversy when a public-interest litigation (PIL) was filed against it on grounds that it was "built on 1.8 lakh sq ft of land reserved for housing the dishoused" with eighteen "Coastal Regulation Zone (CRZ), DCR, and FSI violations." The Bombay High Court subsequently asked "the State and the BMC [Brihanmumbai Municipal Corporation] to explain the exemptions granted to the developer. The BMC was also directed to explain its policy regarding the Rs 80-crore it took from the developer for housing the dishoused."[38] In other words, the court has asked the municipal corporation to explain how it came to give this land to the developer, and what it did with the money it received from the developer to construct affordable housing (one presumes somewhere else). India's courts and, in some cases, municipal governments are cracking down on illegal construction, but entrenched corruption and the enormous amounts of money in play make this a stubborn problem.

India Takes Off

India's skies are getting as crowded as the country's roads. New airlines seem to spring up every few months. When Air Deccan was launched in 2003, it sent shock waves throughout the limited Indian domestic market by offering no-frills flights at unbelievably low prices. Air Deccan passengers can buy a package of thirty domestic tickets for 50,000 rupees. This works out to 1,666 rupees per ticket or about $37.[39] The low fares put thousands of Indians who had never been able to afford to fly into India's skies. An amazing 40 percent of Air Deccan's passengers were first-time fliers when the airline was launched in 2003.[40] The carrier was credited with boosting total air traffic in India by 10 percent.[41] Seeing the potential, another low-cost carrier, Spicejet, quickly followed.

Vijay Mallya, the flamboyant captain of India's beer brand Kingfisher, launched Kingfisher Airlines in 2005. In contrast to Air Deccan and Spicejet, Kingfisher markets itself on luxury and pleasure. "Fly the good times" is the company's motto. Business-class passengers enjoy fully reclining seats, individual entertainment consoles, and gourmet meals designed to please the famously discriminating taste of the company's founder, Mr. Mallya himself. All passengers benefit from care and feeding by a bevy of young air hostesses in red miniskirts and clunky red shoes. No wonder domestic-passenger air travel in India grew 24.2 percent last year alone. An estimated 100 million new middle-class Indians will become potential air travelers by 2010.

International traffic to India was up 18 percent last year. Richard Branson's Virgin Airlines began flying to Delhi from London three times per week in 2005, and Branson has announced he'd like a major stake in an Indian domestic carrier as well.[42] Indian carrier Jet Airways has expanded its network of routes to include flights to Europe, Southeast Asia, and the Middle East. It has applied to begin service to the United States in 2007. Continental Airlines flies nonstop from

Newark to Delhi, American Airlines nonstop from Chicago to Delhi, and Delta nonstop from JFK to Bombay. Business travel to and from India is increasing as international companies expand their business in India and Indian companies expand their operations abroad. Tourism both to India and by Indian tourists vacationing abroad—spending between $3,000 and $5,000 on their foreign vacations—is also up, and the demand for more international flights far exceeds the number of flights available.

More airlines and more passengers mean more aircraft. India's latest start-up airline, IndiGo, surprised attendees at the 2005 Paris Airshow with an order for a full one-hundred-jet fleet of new Airbus A320s. Kingfisher Airlines also ordered up a raft of new Airbuses. Boeing is forecasting orders from India for commercial aircraft in the $25 to $35 billion range over the next twenty years. Meanwhile, Indian Airlines ordered forty-three aircraft from Europe's Airbus Industries worth approximately $2.5 billion.

Everyone who travels to or within India is painfully conscious of the stress this phenomenal growth is having on the country's airports. Between November 2005 and May 2006, I made three trips to India and took a total of twelve domestic flights. None of my flights—I flew Jet Airways, Kingfisher, and Indian Airlines—was on time. Some flights were delayed several hours. The pet refrain of India's domestic carriers when a flight is delayed is, "Inconvenience regretted." *Inconvenience* is a mild word for being stuck in an airport with extremely limited amenities and few options other than to sit and wait indefinitely.

To begin to address this problem, the government of India has committed to restructuring and modernizing the country's two largest airports at Delhi and Bombay. The job is being done through a private-public partnership in which the Airports Authority of India holds a 26 percent share. In addition, new airports are planned for Bangalore and Hyderabad, with thirty-five additional smaller cities slated to see their airports modernized.[43]

This is all welcome news. However, as has historically been the case in India, this effort, like other badly needed infrastructure upgrades, has been a reactive response to a crisis. Looking at the tremendous numbers on the growth side; there are legitimate fears that by the time these improvements are completed, India's air traffic will have exceeded capacity, and that India will once again be scrambling to cope with an infrastructure crisis. China, in stark contrast, is building out infrastructure well ahead of demand. Experts who track both countries point to China's far better infrastructure as a significant advantage over India. I can't count the number of hours I've spent caught in bumper-to-bumper traffic crawling to an appointment or a dinner date less than ten miles away. Time after time, I have had to cancel appointments or I've had people cancel on me simply because it was not possible to reach the place of rendezvous on time. At a low idle, the car engine cannot power the air-conditioning to a level that can offset the searing heat. There is ample time to study the passengers in surrounding vehicles and catch up on calls or e-mail if the battery hasn't gone dead in your cell phone or BlackBerry. Last year, my cousin, who lives on Bombay's Marine Drive, set out to take her children by car to a theater benefit performance in Bandra, the city's nearest suburb. Two hours later, stuck near their home, they gave up and returned home. The question is whether improvement can happen fast enough to make India competitive, on an infrastructural basis, with China—not to mention Malaysia, Singapore, and other regional commercial centers.

Bling

The lack of infrastructure is not having a dampening effect on spending by India's superrich. According to the World Wealth Report, the population of high-net-worth individuals in India grew by 14.6 percent in 2004.[44] In 1996, three Indians were included on the *Forbes* billionaire list. Exactly one decade later, twenty-three Indians were on the list. Most of these Indian billionaires made their fortunes in India's new technologies' boom, including Azim Premji ($11 billion) of IT outsourcing giant Wipro, Sunil Bharti Mittal ($4.9 billion; no relation to Lakshmi Mittal) of Bharti Televentures, and Tulsi Tanti ($3.7 billion) of wind-energy company Suzlon. Mukesh and Anil Ambani, numbers three and four among the Indians on the list with $7 billion and $5.5 billion respectively, each received a share of Reliance, the company created by their father, Dhirubhai Ambani, and were active in building up the business before their father's death in 2002.[45] The richest is London-based steel baron Lakshmi Mittal ($20 billion).

Several of these superrich Indians are famous for their simple lifestyle, especially those who made their fortune in information technology. Azim Premji takes commercial airline flights and drives a Toyota. Narayana Murthy, of Infosys, is said to wash his own dishes. His partner at Infosys Nandan Nilekani is similarly unpretentious, answering his own e-mail.

Many rich Indians, however, though not in the billionaire set— yet—have no qualms about spending their money on luxury goods and a sumptuous lifestyle. According to India's National Council of Applied Economic Research, 53,000 households in India had annual earnings of one crore (10 million) rupees, or about $250,000, in 2005, a number that was expected to grow to 140,000 households by 2010. The next tranche, households earning 5–10 million rupees ($125,000 to $250,000), will jump to 250,000 households by the end of the decade.[46]

Foreign luxury brands have moved into India to cater to the affluent. Rich Indians used to have to go abroad to indulge their tastes, then pay huge amounts of duty on any purchases at the Indian border. Now they can shop at home. Chanel has a boutique in the gorgeously restored Imperial Hotel in New Delhi. In a store off the lobby of the Oberoi Hotel in Bombay, Chopard sells its diamond jewelry and Piaget its watches. Indians can buy bags by Louis Vuitton or Fendi, shoes by Fratelli Rossetti, clothing by Dolce & Gabbana, Chloé, Stella McCartney, or Valentino. BMW is opening a plant in India to produce its 500- and 700-series cars. Mercedes has been manufacturing and selling cars in India since 2001.

Luxury properties in India involve large expanses of marble floor, potted palms, and hand-woven rugs that are plush under foot. There is either Anglo-Indian antique or antique reproduction furniture with framed prints in the British colonial tradition, even perhaps an original by one of the Daniels, or the now generic "loft look" modern style one sees everywhere in the world, all clean lines and angles, with paintings by contemporary Indian artists. The central air-conditioning is invariably turned to an uncomfortably cool setting. It occurred to me on my last trip to India, when the thermometer regularly hovered above 100 degrees outside, that the temperature inside the five-star hotels was calculated to allow businessmen to comfortably wear a Western suit with their jackets on and their ties knotted.

The most striking thing about luxury establishments in India—whether a hotel, a restaurant, a boutique, or a posh office or home—is the amplitude of the service. There is someone to open the door of your car, to open the door of the building, to offer to fetch you something to drink—a cup of tea, a chilled soda, fresh coconut juice—and to offer something to eat. There is someone who can be sent out to pick up anything you might need. There may be young girls offering you a garland of jasmine flowers. The drinks, even a glass of water, will be presented on a tray with a little doily on it. And all of this will be done with a smile, and you will be addressed as "Ma'am" or "Sir" the entire time.

There is no reticence in India about display, especially in Bombay. Rich women wear outrageously large diamonds, necklaces of perfect South Sea pearls, emeralds, rubies, masses of gold—in the middle of the day, dressed to, say, pick up their children from school or lunch with some friends. With the jewelry, they dress in beautiful silks, finely woven cottons in pale, clean pastels, crisply pressed. Their perfectly polished toenails gleam in sandals with a bit of heel and very thin straps. In a cloud of perfume, they emerge from their car, and breeze into the cool sanctuary of their destination. There need never be any contact with the hoi-polloi outside, and if necessity imposes proximity, well, there are things one simply does not acknowledge.

For centuries, India has been a source of luxury goods for the world: gorgeous textiles, fabulous jewels, intoxicating spices. It is easy to go completely crazy shopping in India. There are so many beautiful things to buy: embroidered silks, inlaid rosewood, hammered silver, opulent earrings. Out of this tradition, India's own luxury brands are taking off. They are riding India's rising economic tide to expand their markets in India and abroad. There are the designers

Rohit Bal, Tarun Tahiliani, and Monisha Jaising, whose outfits sell for thousands of dollars. Tarun Tahiliani takes out double-page ads in Indian fashion and luxury-lifestyle magazines where he lists his locations: Rome, Milan, London, Riyadh, Singapore, Tokyo, Hong Kong, Melbourne, Munich, Vienna, Geneva, Istanbul, Kuwait, Dubai, New York, Moscow, and West Palm Beach. He also has stores in Delhi and Bombay. There are jewelers too numerous to list, and there is *Verve*, the magazine that captures it all.

Verve is a stunningly gorgeous Indian women's magazine that caters to the luxe reader who travels or lives abroad yet revels in India. The magazine was founded just over a decade ago, in 1995. Anuradha Mahindra, editor and publisher of *Verve,* told me she launched the magazine because she and her women friends couldn't find a magazine they wanted to read in India, produced by Indians, that reflected their lives and interests. "When I started," she explained to me over lunch in Bombay last year, "only someone naive or stupid would have undertaken what I did. Who would advertise with us? Who would pay one hundred and fifty rupees [a little over $3] for a magazine like ours?" Anuradha's striking porcelain complexion is set off by long, black hair. The mother of two college-age daughters (though you would never know it from her looks), she told me that she and her friends had made homemaking their priority, yet wanted to do something creative. Working on a magazine was something they could do on their own time, leaving them free to take care of their children. "Now the market has grown up around the magazine," she continued. "But I have to say that, even then, I had a sense of the impending change in India through the women I knew. My magazine was focused on the Indian woman, not the Indian market." Since launching *Verve*, Anuradha Mahindra has started a contemporary men's magazine called *Man's World.*

A former freelance journalist who once worked for J. Walter Thompson and an ad agency in Boston, Mahindra has been committed from the beginning to bringing original writing and high production values to *Verve*. The quality of the paper, the printing, the layout, the photography, the cover design, and the articles inside are all part of a package that is as slick as *Vogue* or *Vanity Fair.*

"The business of getting international content, such as a foreign celebrity, is something that most licensed syndications will reprint from another issue or publication. But if we do it, we'll have one of our own journalists do it, otherwise our readers feel it's too distant. For our Liz Hurley cover story, we could easily have gotten something from the syndicators, but we didn't do that. We did it ourselves," she says proudly.

Verve is all about luxury brands. The magazine's advertisers include Versace, Vacheron Constantin, Chanel, Escada, Van Cleef & Arpels, La Prairie, and a host of Indian designers, jewelers, and interior designers. There are lavish fashion spreads and interviews with celebrities. But the magazine isn't all fluff. There are articles about contemporary cultural trends, individuals who make a difference, art photographs.

Verve has an obsessive following outside India. In London, they sell directly through Harrods and Selfridges. Anuradha shared with me e-mails she has received from readers around the world, as well as from well-known magazines seeking photos that were exclusive to *Verve*. One fan in London pined, "Would love to get my hands on a copy as I'm having India withdrawal symptoms." When I asked her if she was planning to launch any foreign editions, she replied, "Now is the time for a U.S. edition. *Verve* has become a cult magazine for contemporary India, for Indian pop culture. We get contacted by students in Europe and the United States saying they're writing about *Verve*. We'll do Dubai first. We also associated with Satya Paul in Singapore. We do a lot of alliances. We want to provide a one-stop shop for luxury brands via events, workshops."

Satya Paul is another interesting Indian brand. When Sanjay Kapoor, the dashing CEO of Genesis Colors, acquired Satya Paul in 2002, it was a lackluster sari house that was getting left behind by India's consumer boom. It is now one of India's fastest-growing brands, expanding 100 percent per year. There are twenty-five Satya Paul stores in India, with the saris sold at other retail outlets as well. How did Kapoor achieve such a stunning turnaround? I went to meet him in his home in New Delhi to find out.

Kapoor lives on the second floor of a large, pale yellow bungalow in a pleasant residential area of South Delhi. I talked to him on a fine winter morning in his spacious living room. The windows to a small balcony overlooking a garden were wide-open, and the sound of birds filled the room. Given Satya Paul's trademark modernist design sense, its bold graphics and lush colors, I was surprised by the ornately carved traditional Indian furniture. Raised in Singapore and holding an MBA from the University of Rochester, Kapoor was dressed in an elegant, monochromatic, pale green suit and tie.

When I asked him what he did to turn around Satya Paul and make the sari, a most traditional garment, into something so fresh and contemporary, he told me, "We branded Satya Paul with modern art. Mondrian, Klimt, Matisse, Kandinsky. We put calligraphy on the *pallu*," the length of the sari that hangs over the shoulder. "We put Sufi poetry on saris. We even put Central Park on a sari. Color is very important, and the quality of the printing. We have our own printing unit." A phone rang in the adjacent office, and he excused himself to answer it. When he came back, he offered me some tea before explaining more about his strategy.

"All the designers in India were busy dressing film stars. Well, the ordinary Indian woman doesn't live like a film star. She admires her but she doesn't identify with her. She wants to dress up and feel beautiful in the evening, but during the day she needs practical clothes. We dressed Mona Singh, the unknown actress who was cast in the popular television show *Jassi Jaisi Koi Nahin* [There's No One Like Jassi]. Our sales skyrocketed after that. Our designs were in every living room of every middle-class home in India. We did a forty-five percent increase on same-store sales last year."

In addition to tying up with a popular television serial, Sanjay Kapoor has gotten Satya Paul involved with events as diverse as charity fund-raisers, Indian classical-music concerts, and art exhibitions. "What we make is wearable art. The sari is the most elegant garment a woman can wear. It flatters all shapes. It's the most feminine clothing in the world," he enthuses. Still, many young Indian women, who spend most of their time in jeans, don't know how to put on six yards of silk. To make wearing a sari easier for these potential customers, "we invented the trouser sari. It has an elastic waist, and you just pull it on and throw the *pallu* over your shoulder and you're good to go. But ninety-nine percent of our sales are of traditional saris."

Satya Paul has designed airline uniforms and hotel uniforms for Indian companies that want a distinctive look but want their women employees to dress in a sari. The company also does ties and other accessories. His voice full of pride, Kapoor told me, "Eighty percent of our employees are women, especially all the people in the office. I look out in the parking lot and I see all these Mercedes parked out there and I think, 'Wait a minute, I don't pay these girls enough to drive a Mercedes.' But you know there is such a strong feel-good factor today in India. Young kids are proud to be Indian. They're secure in what they are doing. It used to be they might ape an American accent. No more. It's cool to be Indian. And these women, they come from families where they don't have to work but they want to be out there doing something creative and they come in and they work hard. When we are working on a project, everyone is there until ten o'clock at night, everyone."

I wondered how a company that makes saris, even contemporary saris with modern-art prints on them, could expand outside India.

"The sari is such a beautiful garment," he tells me, "and India is very hot, Indian fashion is very big in Europe and the United States, but India is also hot in the Middle East and in Southeast Asia. There are large, affluent Indian communities all over. We decided to go to Singapore and Dubai first, then we'll see, maybe London. But we're also expanding in India. We will open nine new stores here. We're expanding into medium-sized cities. Our experience with *Jassi Jaisi Koi Nahin* has shown us there is a market all over India for our clothes."

Many Indian designers sell out of high-end boutiques in Europe, the Middle East, and the United States. Satya Paul has also been doing that successfully in Britain, France, the United States, Spain, Dubai, and Singapore. With 10 to 15 percent of its revenues coming from these foreign outlets, the company is ready to open its own stores. Satya Paul will be the first Indian designer to do this, marking a milestone in Indian retail. It is a sign of the new level of confidence in India that a designer of saris feels women in Europe and the United States are ready to wear modern versions of one of the most ancient garments of Asia.

Branded Foods Invade India

Every neighborhood and small town in India has its traditional snack purveyors with jealously guarded family recipes. Small vendors sell snacks on the street or in minuscule shops, making a living as best they can. The variety of snacks and sweets available is virtually limitless. Vendors with little wheeled carts sell fresh sugarcane juice, with tall stalks of green cane waiting to be run through the press, releasing their sweet juice into thick, blue-green glasses. Others sell coconut water, hacking off the top of the green coconuts with a little machete and sticking a straw in the top so you can drink the juice out of the shell. People squat in front of vats of hot oil, frying up *bhajias,* puris, samosas, *vadas,* and other savory snacks. Bombay is famous for its *pau bhaji,* a spicy vegetable mixture served with soft buns of white bread that get their name—*pau*—from the Portuguese who introduced such bread to India in the sixteenth century. There is *pani* puri, *bhel* puri, *sev* puri—all variations on snack food Indians associate with street vendors the way New Yorkers do hot dogs and pretzels.

People travel long distances to get a certain sweet or a certain snack from a certain shop. Every Indian knows where the best *pau bhaji* or *boti kabab* or *mithai* seller is in his town. My own family has a special fondness for sweets from Bhagat Penda in Jetpur, a small town in the Kathiawar region of Gujarat state. There is something inimitable about the flavor and texture of these particular soft, milky sweets that others, no matter how good, just can't imitate. It would be tragic if India were to lose all this regional particularity and diversity and become a "fast-food nation" like the United States where every town offers the same chain restaurants, coffeehouses, and supermarkets.

The vast majority of Indian consumers, those in the aspiring lower middle class as well as young people still living at home, are spending their money on much more mundane and more affordable items than designer saris. Snacks, personal care items, clothing, coffeehouse drinks, restaurants, movies—sales in these areas are booming, and India still represents a small percentage of Coca-Cola's Asian business, just 9 percent compared to China's 21 percent.[47] Sales of *namkeens,* traditional Indian snack mixtures, grew 34 percent, and biscuits 18 percent in 2005.[48] More than 75 percent of the snack market in India is unbranded, meaning that it is supplied by millions of small, local providers. Branded snack-food giants such as PepsiCo and Nestlé view this as a huge potential market for their products.[49]

Small stands, open-air markets, and itinerant vendors hawking their wares in piercing nasal cries that reach housewives in their bustling kitchens still abound. Families buy fresh fruits and vegetables every day, though this is beginning to change. In my own family, yogurt was always made at home daily. Sometimes it still is, but often now it is purchased in a plastic container and stored in the refrigerator. The best *lassi,* to my mind, is still made by an expert *lassi* maker and served in a terra-cotta cup that is thrown away after use. The terra-cotta imparts an earthy flavor to the drink that adds a special delicious touch that cannot be imitated. Nowadays, Amul makes a packaged *lassi.* It tastes pretty good, despite the loss of the terra-cotta flavor. In old Delhi, you can still get traditional *lassis,* but you have to find the right back alley twisting through the old neighborhood. It's worth it for the flecks of black cardamom seeds on the frothy surface of the liquid yogurt; for the challenge of tipping the terra-cotta cup to your mouth without getting a rim of white foam on your upper lip.

India's food-retailing market—the market for branded food products—is growing 30 percent annually. It is predicted to become the world's fourth largest by 2020. From a value of $750 million today, food retailing in India is expected to grow to $37 billion by 2015.[50] Retail food companies are jumping to orient Indians' food-buying habits toward large retail stores where packaged foods predominate. Supermarkets and hypermarkets are poised to replace the 12 million *kiranas* that supply most Indians with their packaged food and small consumer goods.[51] Reliance, ITC, Mahindra Shubhlabh, Bharti, Tata's Trent, Godrej Agrovet, and Essar Agrovet are just some of the Indian players in food retailing. Most are looking at how to develop the "cold chain" to bring produce from the field to market without its spoiling en route. Others are looking at how to bring the market to the farmers, providing them with the inputs they will need, such as seeds, fertilizers, and cold-storage units, to supply these ventures.

With the majority of India's people living in rural areas where they have little opportunity to shop, the greatest part of India's consumer potential remains almost completely unexploited. Shiv Sivakumar, chief executive of the large Indian tobacco and processed-food company ITC's International Business Division, told me when I met him in Hyderabad last year, "Even though the per capita income of rural India is low, with a consumer base of seven hundred million individuals, which is more than the population of the United States and the European Union combined, the potential for retailing in rural India is still enormous and remains untapped." One good example of how to tap the retail potential of poor customers is the sachet. Shampoo, laundry detergent, lotions, coffee powder—you name it—all of these can easily be packaged in tiny amounts for sale at tiny prices. For years, consumer-products giants Procter and Gamble and Unilever, as well as other companies, have been selling these single-serving sachets in India and other developing countries, and making a profit.

Wal-Mart Eyes India

Many business leaders and government officials I talked to in India are counting on American-style big retail and agribusiness to do the job. As Wipro's Azim Premji put it, "Retail is opening up. The Kmarts, the Wal-Marts, will get into large-scale procurement and processing for global and Indian markets. That will create a lot of wealth." Large-scale retail and agribusiness will certainly create a lot of wealth. The question is, for whom?

I found most Indians who knew about or were planning to enter the anticipated boom in creating unbroken chains from producer to consumer had no sense at all that (1) there could be any downside, or

(2) there might be different ways to go about this, some win-win and others just win. It is also difficult to follow the logic of how an agribusiness model, with consolidation of land and the certain eviction of large numbers of small-scale farmers, could possibly transform Indian farmers into consumers. The veritable ghost towns of the American Midwest, where so many family farms have been put out of business by giant agribusiness concerns, and people have abandoned their homes and towns in search of low-wage work in larger cities, could hardly be a good model for rural empowerment in India.

Wal-Mart is the United States' biggest retailer, and the retail name most mentioned by Indian businessmen to me. But Wal-Mart has not been universally successful, either in its domestic or its international business. Last year, the company sold off its German and South Korean businesses after massive losses in both countries. Wal-Mart's large-area, huge-discount model didn't work in these two countries, both advanced industrial economies with a low tolerance for economic inequality. In August 2006, partly as a result of these sell-offs, Wal-Mart reported its first quarterly decline in profits in a decade.[52] But international business woes weren't Wal-Mart's only problem. H. Lee Scott Jr., Wal-Mart's CEO, confessed, "We are, quite honestly, disappointed in the sales performance of Wal-Mart U.S."[53]

With Germany and South Korea behind it, Wal-Mart has focused its sights more acutely than ever on India. Wal-Mart's only presence in India to date is a sourcing office in Bangalore. The Indian government has yet to authorize foreign-owned multibrand stores, but Wal-Mart isn't worried about that. Amy Wyatt, international corporate affairs spokesperson for Wal-Mart, was quoted in India's *Economic Times* as declaring, "The divestitures will allow us to focus on our core markets and to search for new opportunities in growing consumer markets such as India."[54] The same article quoted Love Goel, CEO of Growth Ventures, a U.S. investment firm with interests in retail, as calling Wal-Mart's move "brilliant," saying, "The Indian market is much less competitive than Germany and Korea, and its middle class is hungry for modern retailing practices and products sold by Western retailers like Wal-Mart."

India's middle class is clearly enthusiastic about buying retail products and trying new retail experiences, such as shopping malls, but whether they are eager to embrace Wal-Mart's retailing practices is another matter, and whether Indians want to embrace Wal-Mart's employment practices is yet another. Wal-Mart not only drives down prices, it drives down wages. Chances are, Indians have no idea what they are in for, not to mention the many producers, suppliers, distributors, and retailers big and small who will be put out of business when Wal-Mart bulldozes into the country. They don't know about the damage Wal-Mart does in the communities it moves into in the United States, or about the high cost Wal-Mart's sub–living wages inflict on local, state, and federal governments. They may also not know about the working conditions in Wal-Mart's suppliers' low-wage factories, or that the *New York Times* reported that workers in China, Bangladesh, Indonesia, Nicaragua, and Swaziland sued the company in 2005, charging that they were subjected to forced labor and wage violations and were denied the right to associate.[55]

As this book goes to print, the mood against Wal-Mart has become so negative in the United States that the Democratic Party has come out against the company, and that includes both conservatives like Joe Lieberman of Connecticut, now a declared Independent, and liberals like Nancy Pelosi of California.[56] Powerful senior senator Joe Biden of Delaware tore into Wal-Mart last summer, taking it to task for paying substandard wages: "My problem with Wal-Mart is that I don't see any indication that they care about the fate of middle-class people."[57] George Miller, a Democratic congressman from California and the senior Democrat of the House's Education and Workforce Committee, was even more critical, stating in a 2004 report, "Wal-Mart is in the driver's seat in the global race to the bottom, suppressing wage levels, workplace protections, and labor laws." The report details Wal-Mart's negative impact on the American communities in which it does business. It estimates the annual cost to taxpayers for a hypothetical two-hundred-employee Wal-Mart store at $420,750, including government assistance for free and subsidized lunches, housing, medical care, tax credits, and other costs resulting from Wal-Mart's low wages and lack of benefits.[58]

The last thing Indian farmers and potential store employees need is to be put at the mercy of a company like Wal-Mart. While the Indian government holds off admitting Wal-Mart, Carrefour, and other international retail giants, Indian companies are using the window they have to stake a claim to India's untapped rural potential and budget retail sector. They had better hurry. Last November, Wal-Mart and Bharti Enterprises announced a joint venture to set up hundreds of stores across India, a move designed to get around current rules.

A Tale of Tea

Sanjay Bhansal was born on a tea plantation in fabled Darjeeling, India. His father was a plantation manager who acquired a reputation as having a knack for turning around failing plantations. Sanjay, a fit man in his midforties, is now the chairman of the Darjeeling Tea Association and the owner of Ambootia Tea, maker of one of the most exclusive teas in the world. I traveled to Calcutta, where the great wholesale Indian tea auctions still take place, to talk with him about tea.

Bhansal's office is on the site of his tea-packaging facility near the port of Calcutta on the mighty Hugli River. The facility is a low, concrete building. The interior has a relaxed atmosphere, gentle light filtering through the skylights onto pale creams and greens, and hand-painted words in large gold letters on the back wall: PURE, HARMONY, RHYTHMIC, DYNAMIC, SELF-SUSTAINING, NATURE, HOLISTIC.

I talked to Sanjay Bhansal for nearly three hours. Our conversation only ended because I had to leave—he could have gone on talking to me about tea for another three hours. He lives it, breathes it, and drinks gallons of it.

First, he showed me around his warehouse, indicating where the tea was stored when it came down from the plantation high in the foothills of the Himalayas, how it was sorted. Almost as a way of testing my merit, I felt, he gave me a tea tasting. By sheer luck, the tea I liked the most was the one he considered the best.

We then retired to his office. The first of many cups of pale gold Darjeeling was brought, and he began to tell me the story of tea in

India: "The Indian tea industry is the first example of industrial agriculture. The British brought tea plants to India from China, where each grower had his own method of brewing, and tea was a whole culture unto itself." He looked at my cup. "Drink your tea, it will become bitter if you leave it too long," he admonished, gesturing toward the fine bone-china cup and saucer in front of me.

"The British experimented from the beginning, grafting, trying different varieties, different soils. They created a truly organic enterprise, completely vertically integrated. The British tea system in India is an illustration of Adam Smith: land plus labor plus capital plus entrepreneurship." I sipped my tea, which was delicious, as light upon my tongue as a cloud curling down from Kanchenjunga, the massive 28,168-foot-tall mountain that towers above Darjeeling's steep, tea-clad slopes.

"The goal of the plantation owners was to sell tea to the marketer. The goal of the marketer was to create a market for tea. A whole ceremonial was introduced among the European aristocracy around tea. They went wild for it. Much later, the first perk given to workers in England was a morning tea break. Seeing that the workers were reenergized by their tea, an afternoon tea break was introduced. The poor began to drink tea. It was the first time they boiled water before drinking it, reducing disease and mortality."

Another round of Darjeeling arrived. It was served in a different cup with a delicate blue design on porcelain so fine, the tea was held like a shadow within its translucent bowl. Not wanting to let this one get bitter, I reached to sip it right away.

"Careful, it's still too hot. If it burns your tongue, you won't be able to taste anything. Be patient."

I drew my hand back.

"British merchant companies did the marketing and exporting. Brook Bond and Lipton's are the oldest. Harrods of London started as a tea shop. The colonial system thrived. At independence, the British had to divest their ownership of the tea plantations in India. The Marwari traders, well-known to them, were their first choice of buyers for the plantation shares that had to be sold. The result is that the majority of tea plantations are owned by Marwaris now. The

James Finlay plantations were taken over by the Tatas in the 1960s, but most of the plantations are owned by Marwaris. Native ownership is abysmally low, only five percent; *native* meaning Bengalis in Bengal, Tamils in Tamil Nadu, Assamese in Assam." Sanjay Bhansal is a Bengali.

I picked up my cup and sipped the warm tea, gently inhaling the steam that came off the surface of the shimmering liquid.

"It's delicious," I said.

"The aroma of Darjeeling should be in your mouth. It is the fragrance of the tea that sets Darjeeling apart from all the other teas in the world. Its unique character is the result of a rare combination of soil, weather, plant species, agricultural practices, and manufacturing practices. There is no other tea like it in the world."

He waited for me to replace the cup on its saucer so I could continue typing on the laptop he had provided me so that I could capture every word of our conversation.

"The first set of Indian owners continued with the colonial system, perpetuating the huge apparatus of marketing teas for colonial growers—Lipton's and Brook Bond—which they had inherited. Markets and producers were quite separate. This changed with the advent of the fax machine. Tea companies could send a fax and be in instant communication with exporters to markets around the world. The colonial pattern was useful only until communication opened up in the 1970s and 1980s. Then the Russian tea industry collapsed with the fall of the Soviet Union. The Russians had got Indian tea for almost free due to a favorable ruble-rupee exchange. By the late 1980s, the whole game was up. It all collapsed.

"When I got the opportunity to buy Ambootia, I jumped on it. You see, the entrepreneurial character of the industry had died. Inefficiencies had crept in. So what did we do at Ambootia? We became hippies." I must have looked surprised, because he laughed. "I mean about half a dozen out of five hundred tea families in India. We were young, and we saw an opportunity to do something different. There was a new trend in the food sector, organic foods. Darjeeling was easy to grow organically. The quality actually improved with organic methods."

A third cup of tea arrived. The cup was a creamy ivory, rimmed in gold. This time, I just smiled my thanks to the man who set the cup before me and kept typing.

"We were critical of the system that existed. We saw opportunity in the estates, but we had to remove from the structure the colonial freight train. So, we took a first step and removed our production from auction."

"How does the auction system work?" I asked.

"I'll tell you. Basically, there are six layers of middlemen between the plantation and the final retail customer: the broker/auctioneer, an Indian merchant, an international broker, an international trader, a national wholesaler—someone who buys tea by the tons for a specific national market like Austria or France or the United States—a smaller wholesaler who breaks the tea up into unit packages and sells by the kilogram.

"We are the only producer that has an integrated setup: our corporate offices are here, our warehouses are here, our processing is here. We are small fry but we have the very best quality. That allows us to deal with the top tea retailers in the world."

He got up and took a large-format coffee-table book from a shelf and showed it to me. It was a sumptuous book on the history of the elite French tea seller Mariage Frères. The book was personally signed for him by Franck Desains, the company's general manager. He showed me a photograph in the book where Ambootia Darjeeling is prominently displayed in the beautiful Mariage Frères shop in the Marais neighborhood of Paris. A few months later, I visited Mariage Frères. "The new Darjeeling has arrived," trumpeted signs in French. When I asked the salesman what plantation the tea came from, he replied, "Ambootia." "We have never put a price on our tea to Mariage. Whatever they want to pay, that's what we take, and it works out. We value our teas and our tastes; so do they. That's why it works," explained Mr. Bhansal.

"The first certified-organic project on my estate was the Mullootar plantation, then Monteviot, then Ambootia. In 1997, we acquired estates in Assam. In 2004 and 2005, we acquired five more estates. We are in the process of converting them to organic. I'll tell you why I moved up the value chain. Because we are organic, we can transcend the barriers associated with selling a third-world product in terms of the product, packaging, and design. It allows us the audacity to sell directly to Harrods, and to remove those six layers of middlemen. Because we take over sick plantations and revive them and then convert them to premium organic gardens and cut out the middlemen, we go from zero profit to one hundred percent profit.

"At Ambootia we started the revolution of handcrafted teas. We have twenty-eight types of teas which are not the traditional black or green. We were the first people to start making white teas in India, oolong teas in India. And they were successful teas. Our teas are sold not only at Harrods and Mariage Frères but at Whole Foods, at Dean and Deluca. Stash Tea also buys from us. We have our own labels, Ineeka and Tre-leela, sold only in the United States. It's the most expensive tea-bag tea in the U.S. Whole Foods and Target sell it. I am now the only tea estate owner who is not a descendant of one of the original owners, and I sell the most expensive tea in the world."

Mr. Bhansal told me that there are eighty-seven plantations in Darjeeling, covering eighteen thousand hectares, employing directly fifty thousand workers, providing residential facilities to two hundred thousand people. I visited Darjeeling in 1986. I took the storybook toy train up the last stretch of mountain, laughing with the school boys who hitched a ride for a station or two, clinging to the baby blue exterior of the tiny train. We stayed at the anachronistically British Hotel Windermere, where, as I recall, a sit-down lunch, including chicken curry as well as pudding, was served daily and we had to pay extra for the precious wood brought for a fire in our chilly room every evening.

At the Windermere, with its dizzying views of the steep, tea-covered hills plummeting away below well-maintained gardens, it was easy to imagine the life of British colonials, whether plantation owners or seasonal visitors up to the hills to escape the searing heat of summer on the Indian plains. In town, the Mall Road was lined with ornate Edwardian buildings with steep gables. When these buildings were constructed, and for decades after, Darjeeling society was a strictly layered hierarchy of British plantation owners, seasonal British residents or tourists, seasonal wealthy Bengalis, Indian plantation managers brought up from the plains, and Nepali workers. The plantations and the workers remain but the rest of that world has disappeared. Still, life in Darjeeling revolves around tea. The tea industry is the main employer and economic activity in the area. Assam annually produces 400-plus million kilograms of teas. Total world production of tea is 3 billion kilograms. India is the largest producer at 850 million kilograms, consuming about 700 million of that at home.

"My tea taster is one of the best in India. I should also be a good tea taster. Out of the eighty-seven plantations in Darjeeling, I could make out sixty just from sipping the tea. He can make out all eighty-seven."

The premium price Darjeeling commands makes for a lot of adulteration and falsely labeled tea. The region of Darjeeling only produces 10 million kilograms of tea per year, yet an estimated 40 million kilograms of tea are sold around the world as Darjeeling. One of Sanjay Bhansal's missions in life is to protect the integrity of the Darjeeling label. For this, he has turned to the World Trade Organization.

"What we are trying to do," explains Bhansal, "is protect Darjeeling tea in the international market so that the product moves from being a bulk product to becoming a packaged product just like champagne. Champagne has to be bottled in the Champagne region of France, or it can't be called champagne. You promote so you can protect it. We are doing a massive marketing campaign to educate people about Darjeeling."

We pause to sip our tea. Bhansal says with a little smile, "Tea is sip and slow. Coffee is sip and go.

"We are creating our own machinery. The traditional machine is huge in size, extremely energy inefficient—it burns coal or wood— carbon-based fuels, abysmally low productivity. It was designed more than two hundred years ago by the British, not for tea but for bread ovens. It's made of cast iron. And this is supposed to produce the best in the world! We are working on this through the Indian Institutes of Technology, with IIT Kharagpur. The government is funding this. The project is driven by me. It started last year. I have designed a Centre for Excellence, which will be located in Darjeeling. It will deal with agronomics and labor; marketing and distribution will be based in Calcutta.

"Right now, whatever my turnover will be in the next three to five years, I'm going to increase it twenty times. In India now, you really feel the open space where you can venture out into any entrepreneurial activity. My objective is to take the tea business from a service thing into a completely different modern business where entrepreneurship qualities can be enhanced to the highest level. In the next five years, I'm going to go crazy. I'm really seeing the opportunity here where we have one hundred million who have the same earning power as in the U.S. That will grow to two hundred and fifty million. I've never bargained with the guy who sells vegetables and fruit here because that is exploitation, but I had the balls—excuse the expression—to demand unheard-of prices for my teas. I didn't eke out an extra cent; I got an additional dollar."

He asked me if I'd like to taste another one of his teas. I say I would but I've had so much, I don't know if I could properly appreciate it. "Then it's best to stop," he said. I save the document on the laptop and his assistant prepares a CD for me. We go out into the main warehouse area. Night has fallen while we've been talking. The dark blue glow of dusk falls through the row of windows onto a counter, where I see the cups we used for the tea tasting have been washed and set up for another tasting.

"You know," he continued, "it used to be that to be in this business, you had to be a member of one of the guilds. My father was an employee, and I am thriving as an entrepreneur. I consider myself to be an average Indian, but in our industry because entrepreneurship was captive for so long, I am considered a whiz kid."

We reached the entrance door. My driver sat up and turned the key over in the ignition of the car.

"So," concluded Sanjay Bhansal, walking me to my car and opening the door for me, "this is what is happening in India. My father could not have dreamt of what I am planning to do."

CHAPTER FOUR

600,000 Villages

L AST APRIL, AT THE HEIGHT OF THE DRY SEASON, AS REPORTS
of suicides by farmers in Vidarbha, a region in eastern Maharashtra, were hitting the Indian press weekly, I got a call from an old
journalist friend of mine in Bombay, Dilip D'Souza. He invited me to
join him on a trip he was planning to visit villages where farmers were
committing suicide. A couple of weeks later, I was on an overnight
train from Bombay to Nagpur, the nearest major city to the villages
in Vidarbha we wanted to visit.

I had not traveled by train in India since my student days, when
time was more abundant in my life and the only airline was the relatively expensive, and at the time grossly inefficient, state-run Indian
Airlines. I met Dilip at his home in Bandra. We took a commuter rail
train to Dadar station, where we caught our train to Nagpur. Dadar
is a no-nonsense suburban station, grimy and spare. The late-April
air was warm and cloying, even at night. A couple of rats scampered
along the tracks, slipping into a hole along the bottom of the platform as the train rolled in. Dilip, who says air-conditioning makes
him sick, helped me find my berth in a second-class, air-conditioned
sleeper carriage, then proceeded to his own non-air-conditioned carriage. The train was almost completely full when we got on, having
originated at Bombay's main Chhatrapati Shivaji Terminus.

Formerly known as Victoria Terminus, and still called VT by
locals, Chhatrapati Shivaji is a gorgeous example of British imperial
architecture in India, an ornate pile of rounded towers with sculpted

143

gargoyles jutting out from its central cupola. It would have felt different to depart from one of the most fabled train stations in the world rather than plain, suburban Dadar, and I was sorry we didn't have time to trek downtown to get the train there. But the moment I entered the carriage, all the romance of train travel in India, especially on an overnight train, came rushing back. I stowed my luggage and nodded a greeting to the passengers sharing my compartment, a middle-aged woman, an older woman and her husband, and two men. About an hour after we left Dadar, an attendant came through carrying starched white sheets, pillows, and heavy wool blankets. He converted our seats into triple-stacked sleeping berths and made up our beds. I was lulled to sleep by the gentle rocking of the train, the muted percussion of wheels bumping over tie after tie like the diastolic rhythm of a great maternal heart.

When I woke up, I was back in the India I remembered from before the great boom. The attendant returned, stripped our berths, and flipped them up to restore the banquettes to their daytime position. Passengers with tousled hair and rumpled clothes made their way to the bathroom to freshen up. I took my turn at the stainless steel, squat toilet and sink, both of which were much cleaner than the horrid facilities I remembered from years before. A series of personnel from the kitchen circulated through the coaches offering hot tea and greasy breakfast omelets. Most passengers had brought their own food. They broke out *teplas* and rotis, biscuits and fruit. Missing my usual morning coffee, I bought a small thermos of tea, but it was so sweet, I couldn't drink it.

As the engine eased into the stations along its route, it sounded a long, plaintive whistle. Vendors rushed the train with oranges, slices of fresh coconut, roasted peanuts, more tea, cold sodas. Then, the station was left behind. The vast landscape of India rolled past in an endless Technicolor reel of dusty towns, villages huddled near pale green mosques, larger-than-life, blue-suited statues of Dalit (untouchable) leader Dr. Bhimrao Ramji Ambedkar, or saffron flags above a Hindu temple. Emerald fields opened to the pale, endless sky. Dhoti-clad farmers with bright turbans and fantastic mustaches guided patient bullocks through lines of neat furrows. A glorious *gulmohar* (flame of the forest) tree in full crimson flower flashed an explosion of color and was gone. Boys with long staffs shepherded goats through barren gullies. Women walked with ramrod-straight spines under huge loads of firewood or fodder balanced on their heads. There were herds of doe-eyed, humpbacked cows, and troupes of great black-faced langur monkeys careening under the umbrellas of old mango trees heavy with fruit, their tails held aloft like question marks. The train crossed a river in Pulgaon. It was a mere trickle at that time of year, meandering through a wide, sandy bed. Buffaloes sank gratefully into the mud next to white cranes balanced between lily pads. Women pounded clothes clean upon glistening rocks. Behind them, brilliant saris lay drying in rows of insouciant color.

This is the India most Indians know. Seventy percent of India's population lives in rural areas. There are 120 million farming families in India. There are six hundred thousand villages.

I have traveled by train the length and breadth of India by third class on a hard wooden bench, by ordinary second class on a grimy vinyl-upholstered seat, and by air-conditioned second class. Once, on a seventeen-hour journey, I sat in an aisle on my bag, my torso twisted painfully away from my legs by the crush of people. I was riding in the women's compartment on my way to the Pushkar Mela, an annual festival and livestock fair filled with camels and brightly dressed nomads. All around me village women from Rajasthan in full traditional dress sang joyous religious songs that rang through the carriage. Laughing, they cradled babies, scolded toddlers, and recounted bawdy stories.

Traveling by train in India is a nineteenth-century experience. Gliding on tracks laid into vast interiors to bring raw materials to bustling port cities, the train is a souvenir in steel of the conquest of the earth by industrious Western powers. Jet aircraft take passengers to any city in India within a couple of hours. A train journey takes time, whole days and nights, through a country air passengers never see. By the end of the journey, after sharing snacks, watching each other's bags during bathroom breaks, learning each other's life stories, and listening to each other's snores, parting always provokes a peculiar sadness.

In the Land of Cotton

Of all the riches of the East, it was fine, handwoven cloth of cotton and silk that lured the British East India Company to India. The insatiable European appetite for calicoes (named after the Indian port of Calicut whence they came) and muslins, silks and paisleys, drove the men sent from England to procure these luxuries mad with greed. One after another amassed great fortunes or perished in the attempt. To corner the textile trade, the East India Company ruthlessly reduced India's master weavers from independent agents selling their own products to employees of the company, weaving what they were ordered at prices set by the company, take it or leave it. Those who protested had their thumbs cut off so they could never weave again; a barbaric act that condemned them to starvation. The export of cotton to England fueled the industrial revolution and drove the invention of new technologies to harvest, process, spin, and weave cotton into cloth. Mechanization moved weaving out of India to new mills in Lancaster, England, that hummed with cotton that could never grow in frigid Britain. Finished bolts of cloth were sold back to Indians.

Human beings first cultivated cotton in India five thousand years ago. Cotton textile fragments from the ancient Indus Valley civilization show great skill in weaving and printing. Herodotus lauded Indian cotton fabrics in the fifth century BC, and India exported cotton cloth to both ancient Greece and Rome. The cotton species indigenous to India are *G. herbaceum* and *G. arboreum*. These are short-staple varieties. The longer-staple American species of cotton, *G. hirsutum* and *G. barbadense*, are also cultivated now. Hybrids abound. Some two hundred varieties of cotton are grown in India. Short-staple native cotton varieties are well adapted to local conditions and are perfectly suitable for hand-weaving. Power looms demand the greater tensile strength of longer-staple cotton. The suitability of cotton for power looms determines its quality rating. Longer-staple, higher-tensile-strength cotton receives a higher grade, and the farmer receives a higher price.

The nemesis of cotton is the insect *Anthonomous grandis* Boheman, otherwise known as the boll weevil. Winged adults fly into cotton fields, where they mate, and the females lay their eggs in cotton flowers. The larvae grow inside the cotton boll, ruining it. In the 1940s, Indian farmers began using commercial pesticides. Initially these worked wonderfully, but the weevils became resistant. A new generation of pesticides again brought the weevils under control, but in time they became resistant to these as well. Seventy percent of pesticides used in India are used on cotton. Still, the boll weevil's resistance has grown so strong that multiple applications of pesticides, up to ten sprayings a year, cannot control them.

The train arrived in Nagpur at eight thirty in the morning. The temperature was already over a hundred degrees Fahrenheit. Outside the station, we found the driver Dilip had hired. Thankfully, Dilip could tolerate air-conditioning in a car, and I asked the driver to put it on full blast. Nagpur is located in the exact center of India. It has been designated as the future site of India's first air-cargo hub. Boeing is planning to build a new aircraft maintenance center for all of Asia here. More traditionally, Nagpur is famous for being the orange capital of the country. There were billboards for oranges everywhere. We passed a giant concrete orange on a pillar on the side of one of the city's avenues.

Our first stop was for breakfast with journalist Jaideep Hardikar, who has written extensively for a variety of publications on the area's farmer suicides. We went to his modest apartment, where several pet cats rubbed up against our legs as we enjoyed a breakfast of tea and *uppama,* a South Indian breakfast food made from semolina. Jaideep gave us a sense of which districts we might want to check out, and some background on how the farmers' situation had become so desperate.

While India's educated urban elite and large landowners are enjoying the country's economic boom, millions of Indian farming families are struggling. The government has ended some price supports, rains have failed or been erratic, water tables have dropped, and wells have gone dry. These problems are familiar to American farmers, but most get more government support than Indian farmers, and when all else fails, chances are American farmers can get a job off the farm. Indian farmers aren't so lucky. In an effort to survive, farmers borrow money at usurious rates to purchase expensive new hybrid and genetically engineered seeds, synthetic fertilizers, and pesticides. To get the cash they need to repay these debts, they shift production even further from subsistence farming to cash crops. When these fail, they have no way to pay back their debts, and no food either. These factors have conspired to make the future of thousands of Indian farmers so grim, they exert the only power they have left over their fate: they kill themselves.

Since 1997, more than one hundred thousand Indian farmers have committed suicide. This grim number is directly linked to changes in India's agricultural policy, a lack of legitimate credit opportunities that drives farmers to borrow from rapacious moneylenders, and a serious water crisis.[1] The worst-hit states are Andhra Pradesh, Karnataka, Kerala, and Maharashtra. Ironically, these are states where urban centers have flourished during the same period: Hyderabad in Andhra Pradesh, Bangalore in Karnataka, Trivandrum in Kerala, and Bombay in Maharashtra.

We left Jaideep's place refreshed and eager to get out into the country. The city gave way to a semi-industrial exurb. There were dusty, apparently abandoned small-scale factories, little concrete-block shops, and women carrying stacks of twisted branches of firewood on their heads. Out of this parched landscape, seared by the April sun, there suddenly appeared a gigantic water park, a European medieval castle complex with crenellated turrets. Though it was a hot day during India's summer vacation, the park was closed. Just a few kilometers down the road, we saw a huge billboard exclaiming, "Highland Park! Up the Hill, Full of Thrill!" Around the next bend, on a little brown hill, there was yet another amusement park, with a Ferris wheel, a ride that looked like a long dragon with seats along its back, and a couple of water slides. It too was closed and looked semiderelict.

Dilip had a list of farmers who had recently committed suicide published by the Vidarbha Jan Andolan Samiti (VJAS), an organization run by Kishore Tiwari that advocates for the plight of the region's farmers.[2] The list indicates the name of each victim and the district where the village is located. It is compiled from hospital postmortem reports and press reports that are all individually verified by VJAS. We decided to concentrate on a few districts that we could visit on a meandering loop.

On the two-lane highway, lorries jolted along with their gaily painted HORN PLEASE entreaties to honk if passing. SUVs whizzed past without honking, even around blind corners. Three-wheelers overloaded with farm produce or people listed precariously. Every few minutes, a vehicle passing in the opposite direction threatened to hit us head-on, swerving into its own lane at the last moment. Numerous signs exhorted safe driving, and Dilip and I made a game of spying them first and reading them out: "Road signs are signs of life." "Highway is not a way to get high." And on a bridge over a river, the mysterious "Please don't deep down." We left the highway and headed out on single-lane asphalt ribbons that cut across the fields. There was cotton everywhere but it was past harvesttime, and the plants were shriveled and brown. Many of them had the telltale rusty-red leaves of *lalia,* a disease that turns the cotton red and destroys the plant. We stopped to ask directions, told the people we met why we had come, and asked them if they knew of anyone who had committed suicide recently. The villagers readily directed us to victims that weren't on the Vidarbha Jan Andolan Samiti's list.

Outside the small city of Akola, we found ourselves in the village of Dadham, a typical assemblage of ramshackle houses, some made of local materials of wattle and daub topped by tile roofs, and some simple concrete, one-room boxes. None of the lanes in the village were paved, and waste water ran in rivulets wherever gravity pulled it, sometimes along the edge of the lanes but more often snaking around the middle. Semiferal dogs napped in the shade, pigs rooted in the muck, and cows were tethered under scrubby acacia trees. The village leaders came out and ushered us toward the Gram Panchayat office. We got a ready reception from these villagers. The situation of farmers in this area is grim. The arrival of a journalist from Bombay and a foreign writer meant only one thing to these people: surely, we were there to help.

The Gram Panchayat is the village-level governance body. Every village in India has a Panchayat or five-member board that decides local matters and receives government funds allocated to the village. The Gram Panchayat office in Dadham is typical: a single-room, concrete box with open windows protected by iron bars, adorned by a collection of old pictures hung just below the ceiling. There are national and regional heroes: Gandhi, Netaji Subhash Chandra Bose, Rajiv Gandhi, Shivaji, Ambedkar, and, the most recent, Indira Gandhi, assassinated in 1984. Behind Bose's head, a sparrow was busy renovating its nest. There were also two holy figures: Sai Baba and the Buddha.

Dadham, like nearly all the villages we visited, is a village of Dalits or untouchables, the lowest social stratum in India's rigid hierarchy of caste, so low, they are below the four main caste categories of, in descending order: Brahmans or learned priests, Kshatriyas or noble warriors, merchants, and farmers. When we asked villagers what their religion was, they inevitably replied "Buddhist," a religion to which Ambedkar, the great leader of India's untouchables, converted in order to escape India's brutal caste hierarchy. Instead of a Hindu temple or a Muslim mosque, these villages had life-size or larger-than-life-size statues of Ambedkar standing smiling in a robin's-egg-blue Western suit wearing a pair of black-rimmed eyeglasses. A couple of village elders and a half dozen young men hurriedly assembled in the Panchayat office. Out of respect, we all removed our shoes before entering the building. The dusty concrete floor looked as if it hadn't been swept in weeks. We were invited to sit on plastic chairs around a wooden table. The only other furniture was a blackboard and an old metal armoire. The men told us their story.

Premchand Pandurang Kule was twenty-two or twenty-three years old when he killed himself by drinking liquid pesticide. His father was infected with leprosy and had given over his farm of two acres to Premchand. With only that much land, which he planted in cotton, the family could hardly survive. Premchand's father needed medicine and Premchand had no money, so, like several other people in the village and millions of poor people across India, Premchand borrowed two thousand rupees (about $45) from a private moneylender. The moneylender, Bhandu Wakhare, lived in Akola. Several people in the village owed him money, and he came around regularly, always in the company of a couple of strong-arms, to collect on his loans. Wakhare charged 10 percent interest—per week. In the beginning, Premchand could pay him the interest, but soon he fell behind, and as his debt soared, any hope of paying it off was lost.

Wakhare terrified the village, striding in as if he owned the place, bursting into homes, beating people up. "People were very afraid," one of the men told us. "They would run away and hide until he left. He used to take people to his house in Akola and beat them up there too." One day, Premchand witnessed a brutal beating of another villager who owed Wakhare money. He was so scared, he "went out to the jungle and took poison," the men said. He then dragged himself back to the village and died a torturous death. Premchand was married and had a one-year-old son.

When Wakhare discovered his prey had killed himself, he became enraged. He stormed into the village, breaking down doors, bellowing, going into other debtors' houses and verbally abusing their wives. He went out to Premchand's fields, found his wife and mother working there. He beat Premchand's mother so savagely he broke her thigh. He told her when he was done, "If you run away, I will rape your daughter." He stomped back into the village, destroyed the family's chicken coop, and smashed up a motorcycle. Then he left.

Wakhare had gone too far. The villagers were incensed. They forgot their fear and vowed to stop Wakhare from terrifying them. That afternoon, Wakhare returned. He was drunk, and so cocky he'd come without his bodyguards. The men in the village surrounded him and beat him to death with lathis (long batons used all over India even by police to beat people). The villagers called the police at four in the afternoon, but the police didn't come until 9 p.m. The villagers were surprised it took the police so long. In the past when they had called them during Wakhare's rampages, the police hadn't responded at all. The villagers reported they had heard Wakhare saying on his mobile phone, "Shut up. Don't interfere. You're getting your fifty thousand."

When the police finally showed up, they asked who was responsible for Wakhare's murder. No one would say anything. Instead, the villagers told the police about all the bad things Wakhare had done to them. Then, one man stepped forward and said, "I did it"; then another. One after another, each man said, "I did it." The village *patil* or headman said, "Wakhare harassed many people in the village. He also abused these five men." The police promptly took the five into custody along with Premchand's old mother-in-law, accusing them of the murder. In a practice typical in India, the police gathered written witness reports from people outside the village who weren't anywhere near the scene of the crime. Wakhare's father came and verbally abused the villagers, promising revenge.

When the case came up for trial, every man in the village again testified that it was he who had murdered Wakhare. The judge acquitted the five accused and threw out the case. After the trial, the police came to the village and told the men, "What we could not do, you have done." The villagers of Dadham heard that when Wakhare's neighbors in Akola learned he'd been killed, they handed out sweets in the streets.

We visited several other villages. The spectacle of dire poverty was evident everywhere: barefoot children in rags with matted hair, open sewers, broken-down string beds shared by whole families, thin, filthy old quilts, crumbling walls draped with plastic tarps. People were barely hanging on. They begged us to help them. Could we get someone in the family a job? Could we help speed up a government payout? Could we get them a loan?

In the village of Barshi Takli, we entered a broken-down hovel half-open to the elements with a dirt floor and no furniture other than two old cots. Seated on one of them, a mother cried for her twenty-year-old son. "He had completed seventh standard. He was a karate champion at his school," she croaked. She showed us a photograph of her smooth-faced boy, now gone forever. I couldn't help thinking of my own teenage son, and my heart tightened. "We have three and a half acres. We planted them in sugarcane. The rains failed, and the plants dried up," she explained, tears running down her cheeks. We asked her if they had a well for irrigation. "We have a well," she replied, "but it has gone dry." Like everyone else, they'd borrowed money and couldn't pay back their loans. "We rushed him to the hospital and they tried so hard to save him. They tried. The doctor was a good man, but he couldn't save my son," she sobbed, pressing her *dupatta* to her face. I gave this woman some money. I felt so helpless before her grief, her destitution. I knew it would only help her for a couple of weeks, maybe a month, but it was what I could do then and there.

A neighbor arrived. She brought her living but maimed son, Nissar Khan, eighteen years old, to see us. He had lost part of his right arm in a grain thresher. "He was paid twenty thousand rupees compensation by his employer. That was a couple of years ago. Can you help him?" she asked. "Can you get him a job?" We promised to put him in touch with Jaipur Limb, a successful artificial-limb charity in Rajasthan.

In Satargaon, we went to the home of Chhaya Sandesh Shirsat, a pretty nineteen-year-old, newly widowed by her husband's suicide. She sat on the floor and nursed her two-month-old son. She had gone home to give birth, as is traditional in India, and her husband had committed suicide when she was gone. "Did he indicate to you that he was having problems?" we asked. "I tried to ask him but we were just recently married," she replied demurely, waving some flies off the baby's perfect face. "He had some debts but he told me my job was to worry about cooking, that his business was not my business. What could I do?" Her aged parents sat on the floor nearby looking utterly lost. I took in their one-room cottage. In a corner was a shrine to Ambedkar and the Buddha. There were framed family portraits on the wall, along with a poster for Indian tennis champ Sania Mirza and a picture of popular film actress Rani Mukherjee in a pair of hot pants.

It was hard to leave these people with only the promise that we would write about what we had seen. They survive on broken rice they get from the government for two rupees per kilo. It's the same rice better-off farmers feed to their chickens. Sometimes, they eat dal. Otherwise, there is only salt and occasionally some onion to flavor the rice.

One of the suicide victims had tried to supplement the family's failing farm with a small stand selling pan, an Indian delicacy of sweet spices often mixed with betel nut rolled up in a green leaf. When that venture failed, he poured kerosene on himself and set himself on fire six days before we arrived. He was thirty years old. After his death, the family sold off the pan stand for fifteen hundred rupees (about $35). The father told us he had three acres and had borrowed seven thousand rupees to give to his son. The son had also borrowed money from moneylenders.

"What will you do now?" we asked the widow.

"I will work in the fields. I will sell my labor."

"How much will you earn?"

"Twenty-five rupees per day [sixty cents]."

She looked at her two young daughters, thirteen and eleven. They were both real beauties. Her eyes shone with tears she would not shed. She must have been in her thirties, but she was worn-out, and she looked twenty years older.

The victim's father, Mahadeo Kissan Pinjarkar, told us he harvested a total of three quintals—a quintal is one hundred kilograms or 220 pounds—of cotton from his three acres. He said that he was paid fifteen hundred rupees per quintal. He told us that he had spent four hundred rupees per packet of seed and that each packet covered one and one-half acres, so that he had spent a total of eight hundred rupees on seed. He had only been able to pay for one application of pesticide, which cost him five hundred rupees and didn't save his crop. His total profit was thirty-five hundred rupees or $75. Mr. Kissan told us they used to grow *jowar* (sorghum) and vegetables but now they only grew cotton, and they had to buy their food. He said they had a well but it had gone dry. He told us the water table had fallen one hundred feet. He said it cost one lakh or one hundred thousand rupees to dig a deeper well, and they just didn't have the money. A little boy in the family of about five or six years was running around, excited by our most unusual visit. He wore a red polo shirt with a Versace Sport logo on it.

All the farmers we met owed money and all of them grew cotton. All of them had tried to grow the new genetically modified Bt cotton, either Monsanto's and its Indian partner the Maharashtra-based company Mahyco's own patented Bollgard brand or a cheaper Indian brand. There were all kinds of seeds from which the farmer could choose: different hybrids, legitimate genetically modified seeds, illegal knockoffs. The genetically modified seeds carried the gene for *Bacil-*

lus thuringiensis, a bacterium toxic to many insects including the cotton boll weevil. It is commonly referred to as Bt cotton. The effectiveness of Bt cotton in resisting pests is a matter of debate. Most agree it does not eliminate the need for pesticides, though it may reduce it. Critics worry that genetically modified plants may contaminate the soil and spread their genetically altered genes to other plants, leading to uncontrolled mutations. Bt cotton has also been criticized for its toxicity to a wide range of insects, including helpful insects. Monsanto's Bollgard seeds sell for 1,850 rupees a packet, well above the price of ordinary hybrid seeds and above the price for Indian genetically modified seeds. Traditionally, farmers saved a portion of their seed to plant the next year, but genetically modified seeds are patented, and farmers are not allowed to reproduce them.

In August 2006, Monsanto announced it was taking over Delta and Pine Land, the company that perfected the so-called terminator seed. Terminator seeds are genetically programmed to produce sterile seeds in the plant that grows from them, so that a subsequent generation of seeds cannot be saved and planted. The farmer must buy new seeds every year from the company. Commenting on the acquisition, Monsanto CEO Hugh Grant said, "Delta and Pine Land represents an excellent fit for our company as we look to bring value-added traits and high-quality seed to cotton growers around the world."[3]

Many of the farmers we met began their journey into debt with a bank loan or a loan from a moneylender to plant a first crop of Bt cotton. They believed the Bt cotton would give them better yields. Their first crop failed. There wasn't enough water, or the rains came but not at the right time. The plants turned red with *lalia,* against which Bt cotton offers no protection. In debt after losing their first crop of Bt cotton, they took a bigger risk and tried again. A normal cotton crop couldn't save them, so they felt it was better to gamble and hope for a bumper crop. The second crop failed or delivered inferior results. Some tried a third time. Some killed themselves.

It seemed evident based on the handful of farming communities we visited that small-scale dry farmers would never be able to survive growing cash crops. They didn't have money for the fertilizers and the pesticides these crops required. They had no way of irrigating their fields, so if the rains failed or came at the wrong time, they were doomed.

It is almost impossible for small farmers in India to borrow from banks. The size of the loans they need don't interest banks. Banks require them to get a certificate from every other bank in the area proving that they don't have any loans outstanding before a bank will lend to them. The farmers can't really do that. They don't know where all the banks are or have transportation or time to go around and visit them all. Most of them are illiterate. Often, they borrow to pay for a religious festival or a marriage in the family. Banks won't lend money for that. So, they turn to private moneylenders, who charge usurious rates.

We went to talk to Madhu Jadhav, a journalist who works out of the Akola office of *Dainik Bhaskar,* India's second-largest Hindi-language newspaper. The office was in a small apartment on the second floor of a residential building in a quiet neighborhood. He told us that most of the moneylenders are themselves farmers, but bigger, better-off farmers. They take the title to the borrower's land as collateral. The honest ones return it when the loan is paid off. Others, less scrupulous, keep the title and there isn't anything the small farmers can do since there was never any written contract and most of them are illiterate. In this way, big farmers are expanding their landholdings. Jadhav also said that many of the suicide victims are drinkers or gamblers. He said that those who work hard do okay, but that the people in the region "are lazy."

As a counterexample, he pointed out that industrious Kathiawari herders bring their cattle all the way to Vidarbha from Gujarat to eat up the waste stalks left in the fields after harvesting. They milk their cows every day, sell the milk, and make a nice bundle before returning home at the end of the season. "There was a severe rain and hailstorm here recently. The Kathiawaris had little children with them, and people offered them shelter, but they refused, saying, 'If my child dies, okay, but I will not let my cattle die,' and they stayed out there with their cattle." I paid particular attention to this story because my family is Kathiawari but I didn't reveal this.

The pastoral and farming life in India is hard and precarious.

Young people in the villages realize that urban Indians their age are living very different lives. Television has made rural Indians aware of life in the cities, even life in other countries. Jadhav said, "The culture has changed a lot because of television. The new environment is such that young men don't want to farm." Even if farmers were doing well, some of the younger generation probably wouldn't want to take up farming. Given the desperate circumstances of the farmers we visited, it is no wonder that so many young men—nineteen, twenty years old—decided their misery, in contrast to the high-flying, consumer-driven lifestyles they see rich, urban Indians enjoying on television, was simply too depressing to bear.

While passing through the city of Amravati, long a cotton-growing center, we came upon mountains of fluffy white cotton waiting beside a cotton gin. We went inside the compound, past the mounds of cotton, to a small 1920s bungalow with a deep veranda to meet the owner, Zubin Dhotiwala. The bungalow was set amidst a pleasant garden that screened the cotton-processing activity. Mr. Dhotiwala welcomed us into his home and happily shared with us his life in the cotton business. We sat in the drawing room where an immense watercooler made the room tolerably comfortable. The toys scattered around belonged, he told us, to his five-year-old daughter, whom his wife had taken swimming. After what we had seen, it seemed fantastic that there existed somewhere nearby an azure swimming pool of clean, cool, chlorinated water.

The cotton gin has been in the Dhotiwala family for five generations. It was originally run by a steam-powered, heavy iron contraption installed by the British. Mr. Dhotiwala has modernized it since then. He told us the rest of his family is in Bombay now, and they keep telling him to leave the old cotton business and come to the city. "But I am quite happy to do this work. I will not leave it," he asserted.

Dhotiwala is a middleman. He buys raw cotton from the farmers, then gins it to separate out the fibers from the seeds. He sells bales of ginned cotton to agents who then take the cotton down to Bombay or Coimbatore. The seeds are sold for oil. He pays the farmers who bring him their cotton according to the length of the staple and the size of the micronaire as well as how much waste there is mixed in with the lint, as the white fibers are called. "I am paying nineteen hundred to two thousand rupees per quintal depending on the quality. The government is paying seventeen hundred rupees. Earlier, before they reduced the price supports, the government was paying a ridiculous twenty-five hundred to twenty-seven hundred rupees per quintal, and only in the state of Maharashtra. It was not sustainable, but the farmers got used to it, so now they are suffering." He said that the Bt cotton was superior, with improved yield and quality. But he admitted that small dry-farmers could not make it with Bt cotton. "Those farmers who have access to good soil, water, and enough labor are doing well. The small farmers can't make it. Their crops are doomed to fail and this drives them to suicide." He also told us, "Cotton here can't stand up to Gujarati cotton. All these years, the government of Maharashtra's scheme perpetuated inefficiencies. The small farmers here are not educated. There is no way they can compete."

As we talked, bullock carts mounded with cotton passed us as they moved the cotton around the compound. I told him about the conditions we had seen in the villages. He replied, shrugging his shoulders, "They are like pups."

He invited us to meet some farmers he knew who were doing well. "They can tell you a lot." One of them had had an accident with a piece of equipment on his property and was in town at a local hospital awaiting surgery on his leg. Mr. Dhotiwala placed a call. He hung up and told us that, if we wanted, we could go meet the farmers right then.

We piled in our car, a white Tata Indica, and headed to the hospital. It was a private hospital, clean and apparently well equipped. The farmers were on the third floor, gathered in the injured man's room. There were two brothers, Purushotam Laddha and Omprakash Laddha, and a friend of theirs, Juggal Kishore Rathi. These men were physically larger than the poor farmers we'd seen in the impoverished villages. They were educated. The injured man's sons were there, Harsh Laddha, twenty-seven years old, who was taking over the farm, and Vibhor Laddha, twenty-four years old, his younger brother, who worked for ICICI bank as an insurance salesman. They were both educated, well dressed, and spoke good English. Their mother came in and served us tea. She was also elegantly dressed. They had migrated to Maharashtra from Punjab three generations earlier and had obviously done well. They told us they grew cotton, wheat, *toor dal,* sugarcane, safflowers, and sunflowers. They each farmed about six hundred acres, two to three hundred times the amount of land owned by the suicide victims.

They blamed the suicides on drinking and gambling. They thought the small farmers had gotten lazy, dependent on government price supports, so that when these were withdrawn, they couldn't cope. But they also admitted that competition was increasing, and that the trend was toward larger and larger farms. Kishore Rathi said, "The problem is water. There is either not enough rain or the rain falls at the wrong time." Omprakash Laddha was adamant that Bt cotton was not to blame: "We get eight to ten quintals per acre with Bt cotton and only three to four quintals with other cotton." I mentioned the man we'd met who got only one quintal of cotton per acre. They admitted that they had access to irrigation and that this made all the difference. They could deliver the right amount of water to the plants at the right time in the plant's life cycle. They were trying to set up drip irrigation but said banks wouldn't lend money for that. Harsh Laddha said that "where the government has helped with irrigation, production has gone up. They have put in some schemes for rain-harvesting, but the rainfall itself has been so less, it hasn't made a difference." Dhotiwala and Purushotam Laddha argued that farmers had to be careful with irrigation: "In Punjab and Haryana, cheap water and excess use of fertilizer impoverished the soil."

Harsh was confident that farmers would profit more with consolidation. Juggal Rathi agreed: "Segmentation into smaller and smaller farms has decreased production. Consolidation will increase production." These farmers essentially made the same argument about size and efficiency that American agribusiness and other big-business interests make all the time.

However, the vast majority of India's farmers are small landowners who own between one and five acres of land. They have no skills or education they can sell in an urban labor marketplace. When they are forced off their land, they end up in city slums or as migrant laborers. Sociologists Madhav Gadgil and Ramachandra Guha estimated a decade ago that there were hundreds of millions of what they called ecological refugees in India—one-third of the nation's entire population—who had been forced to leave their ancestral farmlands or forested areas. Pushed out due to the construction of dams, the diversion of water, deforestation, the failure of cash crops, or other forms of resource depletion that made it impossible for them to survive in their rural homes, these people ended up as internal refugees on the margins of urban centers of consumption or as migrants ever on the move in search of a little work, a little food.[4] On our way to the airport in Nagpur to catch a flight back to Bombay, Dilip and I met again with Jaideep Hardikar. He told us that Nagpur's slums were growing 10 percent per year, that eight hundred thousand people were living in slums, and that many of these were displaced farmers.

On June 30, 2006, Manmohan Singh visited Vidarbha. The crisis of farmer suicides had become a big national news story, with fresh deaths reported at least weekly. Addressing suffering farmers, the prime minister assured them, "I have come here to know your plight. I know what pain you are going through. I will see what needs to be done to prevent such a crisis in the future."[5] Mr. Singh promised that all interest due on bank loans would be forgiven in the six worst-hit districts, making farmers eligible for new loans. He pledged to allocate funds for immediate emergency relief, and to investigate why irrigation projects had not been implemented. He also said he "was aware of the need to move away from cash crops" and promised help to generate parallel income streams for farmers.[6]

Last November, India's largest farmers' advocacy group, the All-India Kissan Sabha (AIKS), held a rally in New Delhi. Thousands of farmers from various states in India gathered to demand the government respond to the country's agricultural crisis. One of their demands was a census of farmer suicides. The issue has been taken up by different political parties, and was expected to loom large on the agenda of the 2006 winter session of India's parliament.

India's Water Crisis

With its population increasing by 18 million people per year and high economic growth, India already has a severe water crisis that threatens to become much worse. The World Bank is projecting that household water use in urban India will double by 2025.[7] Plans to transform Indian agriculture will no doubt also mean higher water use in rural India. Powerful urban, industrial, and agribusiness interests are locked in a struggle with small farmers and Adivasis over water that has resulted in violent confrontations across the country. Jawaharlal Nehru's mid-twentieth-century vision of modernizing his country included the construction of large dams, which he called the "temples of modern India." Hundreds of thousands of Indian farmers and Adivasis have been displaced by dam projects across the country, including the massive Sardar Sarovar dam on the Narmada River in Gujarat. These forcibly displaced persons have realized little if any of the compensation and relocation assistance promised them. Last year, the popular Bollywood star Aamir Khan made headlines when he controversially protested the lack of sufficient compensation for people displaced by the Sardar Sarovar dam. His films were boycotted by urban Gujaratis, who see dams as necessary to the state's progress, and banned by the state's government, which is wholly committed to urban, industrial, and large-scale agricultural interests.

The damming of the Narmada, especially the construction of the Sardar Sarovar dam, is India's most controversial dam project. Author-activist Arundhati Roy has vociferously protested the construction of the dam and written a book about it, called *The Cost of Living*. Dilip D'Souza has also written a book, *Narmada Dammed*, about the subject. Medha Patkar, widely considered to be the most Gandhian of contemporary Indian social activists, fought the dam for many years and led the Narmada Bachao Andolan (NBA) (Save the Narmada Movement). The NBA succeeded in delaying but not ultimately in stopping the dam, which crept up in height from 88 meters in 1999 to 121.92 meters in 2006, following a series of decisions by

India's Supreme Court authorizing incremental increases. With each increase, a wider area behind the dam was flooded, drowning an ever increasing number of villages, temples, farmlands, and forests. Some 320,000 people have been displaced by the dam. Scores of people died during its construction, hundreds more due to the stress of involuntary relocation. Medha Patkar came to the brink of death several times either through fasting or by refusing to move as the waters rose.

Fierce conflict over the Narmada is hardly the only water controversy in India. The states of Karnataka and Tamil Nadu have engaged in strident fights over water rights to the Cauvery River. The Indian government has a highly ambitious—some would say hubristic, others downright crazy—project to link all the rivers of the country via a system of canals. Known as the "linking rivers" project, it has been challenged by environmental groups as an act of supreme ecological folly that would destroy India's natural riverine system. The city of New Delhi has contracted with Degrémont, a division of French water giant Suez, to convey water from the Upper Ganga canal of the Tehri Dam project in Uttar Pradesh through a new Sonia Vihar water treatment plant to thirsty city-dwellers in South and East Delhi. Farmers who depend on this water for irrigation have vigorously protested the project, maintaining that too little water will be left for them. The Sonia Vihar plant guarantees Suez ten years of unobstructed profits. The government is providing Suez with land, electricity, and the cost of the treatment itself to the tune of two hundred crores rupees or about $45 million to get more water to parched Delhi residents.

The privatization of water is a worldwide trend. The World Bank estimates that water privatization is potentially a $1 trillion business since the vast majority of the world's people do not now buy their water from private sources. In a major report on India's water crisis, "India's Water Economy: Bracing for a Turbulent Future," the World Bank shows a clear bias toward privatization in general and of water in particular, stating, "The state needs to surrender those tasks which it does not need to perform, and to develop the capacity to do the many things which only states can do. Competition needs to be introduced in the provision of basic public water services."[8] Three huge transnational corporations control 40 percent of the world's private

water market: Bechtel, Suez, and Vivendi. Smaller players are jumping in, however, as the lucrative potential of the market in "blue
gold," already valued at $400 billion, takes off.

Population growth, urbanization, and the planned transformation
of India's agricultural economy on an export-oriented agribusiness
model are but some of the factors in India's growing water crisis.
Groundwater provides 80 percent of India's rural domestic water
needs and 50 percent of urban domestic water needs.[9] Water tables are
dropping as aquifers are being depleted faster than they can be
recharged, and many of these are polluted with highly toxic sub-
stances whose removal is simply too expensive for a developing country such as India. Water tables have dropped in some parts of India
by as much as 70 percent. Several of the families of suicide victims I
interviewed in Vidarbha stated that while they did have wells, these
wells had gone dry, and they did not have the money to drill down to
the depth now required to tap water.

Saving Water, Saving Communities

Nirupa Bhangar is a lively yet centered woman in her fifties with
smiling eyes who has been concerned with India's water crisis for
years. An ex–microbiology teacher, turned school administrator, she
worked for the Agha Khan Network from 1987 to 1993. Later, she
worked with Ion Exchange India, a pioneering water treatment company, as an advisor for setting up their Rural Cell. The experience
changed her perspective. She discovered during her work in villages
in rural Gujarat that scores of villagers were afflicted with acute fluorosis, poisoning from too much fluoride in their water. "The water
table had sunk by eighty percent, and the naturally occurring fluoride
was becoming concentrated. There wasn't enough new water coming
in to recharge the underground aquifers. People were so sick, they
couldn't get up without assistance," she told me. Nirupa lives on the
Worli seafront in Bombay, on a high floor with an unobstructed view
of the Arabian Sea. We sat on a tatami mat in her bedroom-cum-
office. I could see out pretty far to sea, far enough to note a distinct

line separating the extremely polluted inky brown water close to shore from the more naturally colored steel blue water farther out.

Nirupa told me that 25 million people in India are at risk of poisoning from fluorosis. "Fluorosis leaches calcium from people's bones. Around Ahmadabad, for example, where people are better off and have more calcium in their diet, they aren't affected as badly as in other areas where people can't afford to eat dairy products," she said. Nirupa talked about the other problems in India's groundwater supply: arsenic and iron. "Things have gotten worse since independence. More and more water is being diverted to the cities, either directly for drinking water, or indirectly via products for urban markets that are water-intensive to produce." Nirupa mentioned the ground water problems that had developed in proximity to Coca-Cola's plants in Kerala and Andhra Pradesh.

Wanting to do something that would be effective in addressing India's rural water crisis, Nirupa traveled to Kutch and around Maharashtra visiting water harvesting and conservation efforts, trying to understand what worked and what didn't. She was particularly inspired by her visit to Ralegaon Siddhi, a village transformed by native son and social activist Anna Hazare. By involving the villagers in the construction of a series of check dams, percolation dams, and other water-harvesting measures, Anna Hazare had raised the water tables and insured sufficient water for drinking and irrigation. Ralegaon Siddhi went from a barren, dysfunctional place in the 1970s where illegal liquor stalls plied their wares and crops fizzled under the relentless sun to a verdant, thriving village that today exports vegetables to the Arabian Gulf.

The core lesson Nirupa took from her investigations was that while rainwater harvesting was the solution, it was essential to involve villagers in any measures taken to help them. They had to feel ownership of the project, or it wouldn't work. "A big problem in India is that water management is handled by civil engineers who are not equipped to do community-based work. When the monsoon hit in 2005, for example, when we had such horrible flooding, many dams, ponds, and other water structures were damaged. Since, in most cases, these had been built by the government with no local involvement, no one in the community bothered to repair them." Nirupa took action "when my *masi*'s [mother's sister's] maid came to me and asked me to help her village with an acute water problem." The villagers trekked to her flat in Bombay for a first meeting. In 2001, she helped start a water-harvesting project in the village. A grassroots NGO in the area, SHARE (Society to Heal, Act, Restore, Educate), undertook project implementation. Now, SHARE, in collaboration with SCESA (Sophia College Ex-Students Association)—of which Nirupa is part of the management committee—is working in sixty villages in Maharashtra. The focus of their work has expanded from water provision to include sanitation and second-cropping. "Where villages have a caste issue or alcoholism or other divisions, we won't start a project until they come together."

One of the typical injustices of caste prejudice in India is Dalits (untouchables) being banned from using the village well by the other villagers. Hindus who hew to traditional notions of caste view any chance contact, including indirectly through food or drink, with Dalits as polluting. Still today in India, a Dalit, particularly in rural areas where traditions die hard, can be killed for accidentally brushing against a caste Hindu. Young couples who dare to fall in love across caste boundaries may be hunted down and killed. In public schools, Dalit children may be allowed into class with caste children, but they often have to sit apart and are made to eat at a distance from the other children. Water shortages disproportionately affect Dalits, since they have last-priority access to vital resources, including water.

Only when villagers have agreed to work together does SCESA-SHARE adopt the village. A local body, a Paani Panchayat (water committee), is selected to represent the village. This can include the *sarpanch,* the head of the village Panchayat. "Sometimes now the *sarpanch* is a woman." It is particularly important to involve the village's women since women are responsible for finding water for household use. Women in India often walk miles every day in search of water, bringing home only what they can carry in pots on their head. In any case, the villagers have to provide free labor. They fully participate in the construction and learn how to maintain the new systems of water catchment they set up. The program has been so successful that people who had left their villages because of survival issues are now trickling back home.

Nafisa Barot is an activist with Utthan, an NGO dedicated to women and water that is active in coastal regions of Gujarat state. What is striking about Nafisa, who comes from a modest village background, is her adherence to the Gandhian principle of deep democracy. She writes, "Gandhi had suggested a way of life that would ensure sustainability and also gender equity and uplift of the underprivileged. The underlying principle of Gandhi's philosophy was people's participation in decision-making, finding local solutions to basic livelihood issues and resolution of conflicts through consensus."[10]

Utthan sponsors check dams, water harvesting, groundwater recharging, the construction of traditional village ponds, and other means of bringing water back to communities that have depleted their natural water supplies to the point of unsustainability. In villages along Gujarat's coast where Utthan is active, the water table has dropped so much, many wells have become contaminated with seawater. Recharging the wells by directing rainfall runoff toward them during the monsoon and other water harvesting tactics dramatically improves the supply of freshwater for affected villages. Water in wells that had become salty becomes sweet again. Nafisa recounts how, time after time, women who began a journey of empowerment by working on a water scheme became confident enough to seek bank loans, set up work collectives, start cooperatives, and demand respect from their families and communities.

M. Dinesh Kumar and Tushaar Shah, two researchers with the International Water Management Institute's South Asia Programme, found levels of fluoride above permissible levels in fourteen Indian states, with up to 65 percent of India's villages exposed to excessive fluoride. They found high levels of salinity in West Bengal and around Delhi, and high iron content in water in the states of Bihar, Rajasthan, Tripura, and West Bengal, as well as coastal Orissa. Arsenic poisoning in West Bengal and Bangladesh, where many people depend on tube wells drilled through naturally occurring arsenic-laden substrata, affects up to 36 million people. Nitrate concentrations, due to fertilizer runoff, are above permissible levels in eleven Indian states. Industrial effluents pollute India's water with heavy metals such as lead, cadmium, zinc, and mercury. Little is being done to clean India's underground aquifers of this gross pollution. "India is too poor to afford some of the technologies that are successfully tried out in the West, especially [the] United States, because they are prohibitively expensive."[11] For a developing country such as India, community-based efforts to recharge aquifers and better manage water are the best hope for addressing the rural water crisis.

The Coming Meltdown

India did not create global warming, but global warming will devastate India. Much of India's population is concentrated along the country's extensive coastline. Tens of millions of people stand to be displaced from coastal areas if sea levels rise as predicted. A landmark report released last fall by the UK's Chancellor of the Exchequer, Sir Nicholas Stern, warns that even the Kyoto Protocol does not go nearly far enough to avert an impending global catastrophe due to climate change. He urges that governments act immediately, spending 1 percent of GDP or 184 billion British pounds, to rein in the production of greenhouse gases. If they do not, he warns, the costs will be greater perhaps than humanity can bear.[12]

The impact of global warming will be felt far more in the global south, including in India, than in the north. The economic toll, not to mention the human toll, is almost too frightening to contemplate. As with many other problems India faces, the sheer magnitude of the damage unmitigated global warming could do paralyzes the mind. But India has within its grasp the technology to find solutions to what may be the most serious crisis humanity has ever faced, and the growing global clout to put pressure on the worse offenders, the United States and China, to act as well.

In 2006, global temperatures climbed within one degree Celsius of the warmest they have been in 1 million years. Temperatures were warmer than at any other time during the twelve-thousand-year-long interglacial period during which civilization as we know it developed.

While warming has been most pronounced in the far north, the Indian Ocean has also become noticeably warmer, as have the Himalayas. The current trend is for more warming, a situation with potentially devastating effects for India's growth story and the future of its people.

Commenting on a report released in the September 26, 2006, issue of the *Proceedings of the National Academy of Sciences,* James Hansen of NASA's Goddard Institute for Space Studies issued this warning: "If further global warming reaches two or three degrees Celsius, we will likely see changes that make Earth a different planet than the one we know. The last time it was that warm was in the middle of the Pliocene, about 3 million years ago, when the sea level was estimated to have been about twenty-five meters (eighty feet) higher than today."[13] In his film and book *An Inconvenient Truth,* Al Gore warns that if the Arctic melts—and there are clear signs that that is exactly what it is doing—60 million people will be displaced from Calcutta and coastal West Bengal and Bangladesh.[14] In July 2005, Bombay was deluged by thirty-seven inches of rain in twenty-four hours, the heaviest downpour any city in India had ever experienced. More than two thousand people died. In the last week of August 2006, the drought-prone district of Barmer, Rajasthan, was inundated with 750 millimeters of rain, five times more than the total annual average. One hundred thirty-nine people and forty-five thousand head of cattle died.

While each extreme weather event can be explained in isolation as exceptional, and history has recorded extreme weather events for centuries, there is no longer any denying these events are increasing in frequency and severity. In 2005, the United Nations World Meteorological Organization reported that 90 percent of all natural disasters occurring between 1992 and 2001 were due to extreme weather events, which killed "622,000 people, affecting 2 billion more, devastating arable land and spreading disease. The total volume of economic losses over the same period is estimated at $450 billion."[15] In a special cover issue on global warming in September 2006, *The Economist* magazine warned, "Arctic sea ice, for instance, is melting unexpectedly fast, at 9 percent a decade. Glaciers are melting surprisingly swiftly. And a range of phenomena, such as hurricane activity, that were previously thought to be unconnected to climate change are being increasingly linked to it."[16]

Temperatures in the Himalaya mountains, the fabled "roof of the world" that includes the highest peaks on earth, have risen in recent years by one degree Celsius. The Himalayas have the highest number of glaciers outside the polar regions. These glaciers are the source of water for 2 billion people. Glacial lakes form a particular hazard: when ice dams suddenly give way, everything is swept away below, as villagers in Nepal have tragically experienced. These incidents have increased by a factor of ten during the past twenty years. As of 2005, twenty-four glacial lakes were in danger of bursting in Bhutan, and twenty-four more in Nepal.[17] As glaciers melt away, the flow of water into the region's major rivers will decline, reducing the flow of water through hydroelectric dams, with a loss of energy the region can ill afford.

Pesticide Poisoning

Pesticide and insecticide use in India is among the heaviest in the world, with 165 pesticides registered. Their use has steadily risen, according to a 2001 report from the Indian Council of Medical Research. DDT, BHC, carbamate, endosulfan, as well as lindane, are produced and used in India and are all present in India's surface and groundwater. Pesticides have provided benefits to India, no doubt. India's tropical climate subjects it to several insect-borne diseases, including malaria, filariasis, dengue, encephalitis, cholera, and typhus spread by human lice. DDT is credited with reducing the annual incidence of malaria from 75 million cases in 1952 to 2–4 million currently. Pesticides were a key component in the Green Revolution, which, with a combination of new hybrid seeds, synthetic fertilizers, irrigation, and pesticides, raised crop yields dramatically during the 1960s and 1970s. However, a steep price has been paid for those yields. Residues of DDT, HCH, and other pesticides have been detected in human and animal tissues, in water, and in air around the world. The campaign to save the American bald eagle led to the 1972 ban on DDT in the United States, significantly reducing but not eliminating its U.S. presence. Levels of DDT and HCH are particularly high in India, as seen in laboratory analyses of samples of blood, fat, and breast milk.

According to the Indian Council of Medical Research report, "Perusal of the residue data on pesticides in samples of fruits, vegetables, cereals, pulses, grains, wheat flour, oils, eggs, meat, fish, poultry, bovine milk, butter and cheese in India indicates their presence in sizeable amounts."[18] The scientists identified HCB, a fungicide, DDT, and HCH in the food they sampled. These chemicals have been linked to cancer and to hormonal disruptions that can harm fertility and have led in wild animal populations, especially among amphibians, to strange hermaphroditic mutations.

Chemical pesticides were an offshoot of the chemical weapons industry and were not developed for commercial use until after World War II. Of all the pesticides posing dangers to human health, lindane is widely acknowledged to be one of the worst. Lindane, a neurotoxin, is an organochlorine in the same family as DDT. High levels can cause convulsions and death. Exposure to lower levels can cause cancer and disrupt the normal hormonal system. Fifty-two countries have completely banned the production and use of lindane. The United States is "using up" 230,000 pounds yearly in seed treatment products and still permits its use to treat head lice. India continues to manufacture lindane.

The Centre for Science and the Environment (CSE) in New Delhi published a report in 2003 citing high levels of pesticide residue in India's food supply, including soft drinks manufactured by Coca-Cola and PepsiCo in India. India's Joint Parliamentary Committee confirmed CSE's findings and recommended that standards be set up for the soft-drink industry. Last year, CSE released a new report, charging that levels were not only still high, they had increased over the 2003 levels. Among the pesticides found in the soft drinks were high levels of lindane.

The reaction from the U.S. government and India-U.S. business groups was swift and aggressive. Undersecretary for International

Trade Franklin Lavin warned, "This kind of action is a setback for the Indian economy," and said, "In a time when India is working hard to attract and retain foreign investment, it would be unfortunate if the discussion were dominated by those who did not want to treat foreign companies fairly."[19] Prabhakar Bothireddy, president of the Indo-American Chamber of Commerce, fretted about sending "the wrong message to investors at a time when there are vast opportunities for businesses in both countries to work together." With rapidly growing economic, military, and strategic ties and the biggest-ever U.S. trade delegation planned for later in 2006, CSE's report targeting American soft-drink giants hit like a bombshell. India's Supreme Court added fuel to the fire when it gave the companies six weeks to reveal their secret recipes in order to find out why such contamination might have occurred. Sensing political blood, opposition parties on the left and the right condemned the companies—potent symbols of Western capitalism and consumer culture—in order to elevate themselves in the eyes of alarmed Indian voters. Several states immediately banned the sale of Coca-Cola's and PepsiCo's soft drinks.

Coca-Cola famously left India in 1977 rather than reveal its secret formula. The company's return in 1993 was a symbol of India's rehabilitation to the global marketplace, and a sign that India was again safe for U.S. business. Though India accounts for only 1 percent of Coca-Cola's global soft-drink sales, the Indian market's potential is perceived to be enormous, and India is part of the company's long-term strategic plan. Coke will work hard to stay in India, but it will never publish its secret recipe.

The real disappointment in the whole debate was that all parties were guilty of taking polarized positions: Coke is an evil sign of Western exploitation versus Coke is a terrific sign of India's joining the advanced Western world. The situation is complicated and requires a more nuanced approach. It is little consolation to exonerate Coca-Cola on the basis that India's sugar and water are the real culprits without opening honest, public debate over how to address the serious problem of pesticide pollution not only in India but around the world. This problem is far beyond the capacity of Western soft-drink companies to solve, but it is also true that India faces severe water and environmental problems that soft-drink manufacturing does nothing to remedy.

Unfortunately, the pesticide controversy comes on top of other woes for Coca-Cola in India. It has been accused of depleting the underground aquifer at its plant in Plachimada, Kerala, lowering the water table to depths local villagers can no longer tap. Village women must make long treks for water, which they carry in vessels back home, while truckload after truckload of bottled soft drinks leave the plant. Coca-Cola has also been accused of dumping sludge, a by-product of soft-drink manufacturing, on farmers' land and along a nearby canal. Local residents have complained about the noxious smell of this substance.

The cola controversy in India stirred many issues. First of all, in a country where so many people lack access to safe drinking water, charges that one of the world's most powerful transnational corporations is converting water—for which it pays nothing and which it is accused of taking from poor local residents—into soft drinks too expensive for these residents to purchase simply doesn't look good, whatever the truth. Second, as CSE's report, like that of the ICMR, pointed out, unsafe pesticide levels are rampant in India's food supply. It would be a miracle if a soft-drink plant tapping groundwater located in an agricultural area in India produced a product that was free of any pesticide pollution. In India, sugar, a key ingredient in Coca-Cola and Pepsi, is also contaminated with pesticide residue. It is hardly inconceivable that the combination of pesticide-contaminated sugar with pesticide-contaminated water could result in pesticide-contaminated soft drinks. According to an article that appeared in the *New York Times* when the controversy broke last year, there is an ongoing debate in India about "how to cleanse sugar of pesticide traces, and a recognition that India's groundwater generally is so badly contaminated that most food products contain some pesticide residue."[20]

Coca-Cola India refuted the results of CSE's analysis, citing an independent laboratory report that showed its soft drinks manufactured in India met EU standards. CSE stood by its results.[21] This is where the matter stood when this book went to print.

Unfortunately for Coca-Cola, U.S. corporations have a long and shameful history the world over of running slipshod over environmental and consumer-safety considerations. Government-imposed standards have been the only way to force many companies to curb pollution or respect the welfare of ordinary citizens and communities. In many cases U.S.-based companies have relocated to countries where the environmental standards, labor laws, and other hard-won, beneficial restraints and regulations of advanced democracies are less rigorous or less efficiently enforced.

Moreover, India has had some high-profile and emotionally charged negative experiences with U.S. corporations.[22] The most sensational of these was the disastrous 1984 accident at a chemical plant in Bhopal. At the time of the accident, this Union Carbide plant was manufacturing pesticide. A leak of toxic gas killed seven thousand people, including many children. Another fifteen thousand died as a result of their exposure. The exact number of victims, including people with chronic illness or permanent physical damage, remains undetermined, with estimates ranging from one hundred thousand to half a million. India unsuccessfully sought extradition of then Union Carbide CEO Warren Anderson. To date, no one has been held responsible.

The Bhopal toxic-gas leak remains one of the worst industrial accidents in history. Union Carbide and Dow Chemical Company, with which it merged in 2001, have denied all responsibility. The site of the leak has never been cleaned up. Amnesty International issued a scathing report in 2004 on the twentieth anniversary of the disaster, charging that the "Bhopal case illustrates how companies evade their human rights responsibilities."[23] As U.S. business interests in India increase, one hopes that a greater sense of responsibility to local communities will prevail.

A Second Green Revolution

The Green Revolution that transformed agriculture in the last century was an American invention. It began in 1944 with a project sponsored by the Rockefeller Foundation in Mexico. Dr. Norman Borlaug, a plant geneticist from Minnesota, was sponsored by the foundation to assist in breeding new plant hybrids that would boost yields of basic food grains. The project was enormously successful: Mexico was transformed from an importer of wheat to an exporter within a couple of decades. In the 1960s, the Rockefeller Foundation helped bring the Green Revolution to India, which was faced with such severe food shortages that there was a fear of major famine. The hybrid seeds developed in Mexico were planted in Punjab, where yields soared. Dr. M. S. Swaminathan went on to shepherd India's own Green Revolution, developing local hybrids and spreading miracle yields throughout South and Southeast Asia. India went from a net grain importer to producing a bumper crop of 131 million tons of grain in 1978, establishing India as one of the world's biggest grain producers.

In addition to new hybrid seeds, the Green Revolution made heavy use of new pesticides, herbicides, synthetic fertilizers, and irrigation techniques. Synthetic fertilizers, based on nitrogen made from natural gas, put the plants on the equivalent of steroids, further boosting production. Rapidly, however, it became clear that organochlorine pesticides were harming more than agricultural pests. The 1962 publication of Rachel Carson's *Silent Spring* drew attention to the dangers of DDT and helped launch the environmental movement.

The cost of synthetic fertilizers has risen in tandem with that of natural gas, increasing the cost of food production. Moreover, pollution from these fertilizers, in the form of nitrates, is a serious problem the world over. In the United States, where nitrogen fertilizers are a key factor in the most productive agriculture in the world, "more public water supplies have been closed due to the violation of drinking water standards for nitrate than from any other contaminant."[24] Without these fertilizers, the high yields of the post–Green Revolution era would not be possible, yet they pose serious risks and may permanently damage our environment, especially our water.[25] Too much water, delivered via irrigation, can be environmentally harmful. Overwatering has negative impacts on soil composition, increasing, especially in conjunction with the use of nitrogen fertilizers, the salinity of the soil and reducing its productivity. Farmers are facing these problems in Punjab, where India's Green Revolution took off.

Dramatically increasing the production of food did not end hunger in India. Though India claims food self-sufficiency, and in terms of sheer quantity of food grains produced the claim is just, more people in India go hungry than in any other single country. At least 232 million people in India do not receive sufficient food. According to a UNICEF report last year, 200 million malnourished children—one-third of all the malnourished children in the world—live in India. Nearly half of India's children, 47 percent, are severely underweight.[26] As Amartya Sen has pointed out, having a sufficient quantity of food is not enough; people have to have access to the food.

Last year, India could not meet its needs in food grains. The country imported 2.2 million tons of wheat, including orders from American giants Cargill, the world's largest grain-trading company, and Archer Daniels Midland. India's strides in increased wheat production—achieving about 70 million tons annually—cannot keep up with the steady growth in population and swelling consumption. The diversion of land by subsistence farmers from food crops to cash crops such as cotton contributed to the problem, as did the reduction of land put to cultivating traditional hardy and nutritious food grains such as *jowar* (sorghum) and *bajra* (millet). The shortfall in wheat production caused prices of wheat flour, the ingredient for India's flatbread that is the staff of life for hundreds of millions, to rise 30 percent last year.[27] This put stress on lower-middle-class households and was a major hardship for India's poor.

A key component of the closer India-U.S. relationship is a new agricultural development initiative that President Bush hailed, during his speech at Delhi's historic Purana Qila fort when he visited India last year, as "a second Green Revolution." The initiative is called the U.S.-India Agricultural Knowledge Initiative. Dr. Norman Borlaug, after winning a Nobel Prize for his work on the first Green Revolution, is participating in the new joint effort. The goals of the agricultural initiative are listed as follows: (1) raise agricultural productivity to promote food security; (2) increase technology transfer, including biotechnology; (3) build a sound policy and regulatory environment; (4) expand trade and investment and promote integration of India into the global economy; (5) ensure a key role for the U.S. and Indian private sectors; and (6) reinvigorate U.S.-India university partnerships.

On first glance, it seems odd to name an agricultural deal a "knowledge initiative." But a core goal of the agreement is to expand patentable intellectual property. According to the Indian Ministry of Agriculture Web site, the private-sector participants are Masani Farm and ITC on the Indian side, and Monsanto, Archer Daniels Midland, and, of all companies, Wal-Mart on the American side. Monsanto and Archer Daniels Midland are already, as we have seen, deeply involved in Indian agriculture. Wal-Mart has every intention of being so the moment the Indian government lets the company in. The *Hindu* newspaper reported last year that "transgenic research," meaning research on genetically modified organisms, "in crops, animals and fisheries would be a substantial part of the collaboration in biotechnology."[28] Reporting for the respected science journal *Nature*'s biotechnology-specialized journal *Nature Biotechnology,* K. S. Jayaraman asserted, "What critics resent most is the presence of Monsanto, the second largest GM seed producer in the world, and Wal-Mart, the world's largest retailer, on the board of the new initiative." The article quotes Indian food-policy analyst Devinder Sharma on the role Indian universities are likely to play with regard to Monsanto and Wal-Mart: "With them on the board, the U.S. multinationals are all set to determine the Indian agricultural research agenda."[29]

The combination of India's rich plant and animal genetic diversity, its potentially large market, and its proven capacity as a research and development center are all powerful attractions for U.S. agribusiness concerns. They can look forward to dramatically expanding the scope of their intellectual property rights holdings, using Indian brainpower to help unlock new applications in biotechnology and transgenic research, using Indian fields to test new transgenic products, and then selling these products to Indian consumers, whether to Indian farmers or to Indian retail customers.

I called up Suman Sahai of Gene Campaign in Delhi to ask her more about her take on the U.S.-India agricultural deal. Gene Campaign is an NGO focused on food and livelihood security of rural and tribal communities, technologies to genetically modify food, indigenous knowledge, sustainable use, genetic resources conservation, and intellectual property rights. Suman has been vocal in criticizing the deal, saying, "India will gain little and give away too much." She told me, "Look, the agricultural deal is payoff for the nuclear deal. I see it very much that way. It's easy to understand why Monsanto and other U.S. agriculture interests need India. There is a huge amount of resistance to GMOs [genetically modified organisms] in Europe, Africa, and Japan. Who are they going to sell this stuff to? An agricultural giant like India is hugely important for them."

In 2006, farmers in Arkansas, Missouri, Mississippi, Louisiana, Texas, and California sued Bayer Crop Science after an unapproved genetically modified strain of rice it had developed entered the food chain and contaminated the U.S. rice crop. The modified rice contains a protein dubbed Liberty Link that allows it to resist herbicides used to kill weeds. After the contamination was discovered, Japan banned imports of U.S. rice and the EU instituted testing requirements to insure that all rice coming from the United States was not contaminated. This was a major blow to U.S. rice producers.[30] No one knows the long-range potential effects of altered plant or animal genes entering the food chain.

I asked Suman why the Indian government would give so much genetic capital away to the United States. Suman would not name names, but she told me that influential policy makers "have direct tie-ups to this." American companies aren't the only ones favored. Swiss biotech giant Syngenta, for example, is working with the Vasantdada Sugar Institute in Pune, Maharashtra, on genetically modified sugarcane. In general, Suman told me, "There has been a huge buy-in at the top level of the Indian government on GMOs.

"This has been packaged very cleverly by linking it to the Green Revolution," she continued. "For Indians, the Green Revolution gave us our sovereignty, it made us self-sufficient, so, to associate this deal with that by calling it 'a second Green Revolution' is very shrewd. But this is nothing like the Green Revolution. All the knowledge generated by the Green Revolution was public knowledge. This will all be private knowledge. This is about intellectual property rights and monopoly corporations extending the reach of what they own."

An Evergreen Revolution for
Sustainable Agricultural Renewal

Norman Borlaug's Indian counterpart, Dr. M. S. Swaminathan, has a different tack from the one being pushed by U.S. agribusiness. An "honorary adviser" to the Indian side of the Knowledge Initiative, Dr. Swaminathan is convinced that only a sustainable "evergreen" revolution can save Indian agriculture, and by extension, Indian society. His foundation, the M. S. Swaminathan Research Foundation or MSSRF "is known for its emphasis on a bottom-up participatory approach, which places people before technology."[31] In his capacity as chairman of India's National Commission on Farmers, Dr. Swaminathan declared at last year's ninety-third Indian Science Congress, "It's not just about increasing yield but also productivity without social or ecological harm."[32]

Basically, Dr. Swaminathan's work aims at a middle road, a direction for Indian agriculture that is neither the U.S. agribusiness model nor a return to purely traditional farming techniques that simply can't meet the needs either of farmers or of India's fast-growing urban population. He is not, for example, categorically opposed to genetically modified plants. But, he believes that India needs and deserves a regulatory body for agricultural biotechnology the public can trust. He is also committed to putting the welfare and food security of farmers above all other considerations as the cornerstone of a national program of food security for all. He would like to see farmers sell only their surplus production, and to make this surplus available in a public distribution system. And he wants to educate farmers, make them literate and technologically savvy so that they have access to the same information and tools as the big agribusiness concerns.

His hairline receding now above his wire-rim glasses, Dr. Swaminathan is keenly aware of what is at stake at this critical moment. He believes that the "technological apartheid" that effectively shuts the poor out of the information technology revolution must be broken, and that access to technology has to be democratic and equitable. He promotes agricultural practices that are sustainable in a natural environment already stressed to the breaking point. Working with the United Nations Development Program (UNDP), his foundation launched the Biovillages initiative in 2000. "Biovillages denotes a village where human development occupies the pride of place. It is thus a term for human-centered development," he explained. He also launched a Community Banking project to advance microcredit schemes and other financial tools useful to the rural poor. Dr. Swaminathan is committed to dealing with "the twin challenges of poverty eradication and natural resource conservation."[33]

In dry areas such as Vidarbha where farmers are dependent on scanty rainfall, Dr. Swaminathan advocates the cultivation of traditional cereal crops in the millet family that are suited to local climate and soil conditions, such as *bajra* and *jowar* that Mahadeo Kissan Pinjarkar and the other surviving family members of farmers I met who had committed suicide used to grow. While the U.S.-India agricultural agreement gives pride of place to "insuring a key role for the private sector," Dr. Swaminathan is adamant that "the growing privatization of food and water security systems is already leading to an unequal social bargain."[34] Dr. Swaminathan is a revered figure in Indian agriculture, and one hopes he will continue to influence Indian agricultural policy. His wholistic vision and intimate knowledge of Indian agriculture have the potential to unleash a revolution of sustainable, equitable agriculture that is critical to India's future.

e-Choupals

Agriculture generates just 24 percent of India's economy yet some 850 million people depend on agriculture to survive. Twenty-five percent of these, 212.5 million people, live below the poverty line, with incomes at or below $1 per day. Low levels of education and precarious health further inhibit their capacity to realize their human potential. Indian agriculture has grown at between only 1.5 and 3.2 percent compared to the galloping national average of 8 percent. To achieve its targeted annual growth rate of 10 percent, the Indian government is keen to boost agricultural growth to 4 percent. However, the policies that the government is supporting to rev up growth quickly via encouraging retail and export-oriented cash crops produced by large-scale farming risk doing serious social and ecological damage to rural India.[35]

While yields have improved dramatically since the days before the Green Revolution, the system is showing signs of stress. India's shortfall of wheat last year was partly the result of stagnant yields, partly due to private companies snapping up wheat the government of India normally buys for reserve stocks. Yields for basic food crops, such as soybeans, remain well below those in Brazil. India has the most land under cultivation of any country on the planet, and a climate that ranges from temperate to tropical. The country has the potential to become one of the top breadbaskets and fruit and vegetable producers of the world. The challenge is how to develop Indian agriculture and build the capabilities of its legions of small farmers to insure their food security, improve their livelihoods, and increase their purchasing power.

Indian agribusiness giant ITC has implemented a revolutionary business-platform strategy for connecting farmers to markets in a way that empowers and enriches the farmer, improves agricultural production and quality, and increases profits and market share for ITC. The strategy uses an information and communications technology or ICT-based platform, leveraging this major driving force of India's economic boom.[36] ITC's is one of the best examples of what I have found to be a philosophy shared widely by Indian businesses, doing well while doing good, or of "increasing shareholder value through serving society."[37]

The strategy consists of setting up kiosks using a personal computer with Internet access. The company calls these e-Choupals. ITC has set up these kiosks in villages within 1.5 kilometers' walk from target farmers, or one for each cluster of five villages. Each e-Choupal is manned by a local village resident trained by ITC called a *sanchalak*. The computer is located in his home. The e-Choupal centers connect to hubs twenty-five to thirty kilometers away from target farmers—the same distance they normally travel to reach markets—which are located in buildings constructed by ITC. These hubs serve as collection points for the farmers' crops as well as pickup points for inputs such as fertilizers and seeds. They are manned by trained purchase-agents-cum-salesmen called *samyojaks*. The hubs, in turn, are connected to a network of companies looking to purchase farm produce or to sell inputs to farmers. ITC itself captures a significant portion of the produce, which it feeds into its growing processed-foods division. The company is also expanding the services it offers at its hubs to include credit, insurance, cooking gas, and other products farmers may want to purchase.

The e-Choupal provides information on market prices for agricultural commodities and knowledge of the best agricultural practices. It does not charge for these services, a conscious strategy designed to solicit wide participation from farmers. The *sanchalak* can also collect soil samples—a visual tutorial on the computer instructs the farmer how to do this—have the sample analyzed by an agricultural extension agent, and then, based on the findings, recommend amendments to improve the soil's productivity. The e-Choupal also provides weather-tracking information so that farmers can best choose when to plant, when to fertilize, and when to apply pesticides to their crops. The farmer, should he choose to sell to ITC, is given a guaranteed price in the village by the *sanchalak*. When he delivers the crop to the hub, the *samyojak* weighs, tests, and judges the quality of the produce, then pays the farmer on the spot at the transparent market price guaranteed earlier. Farmers can also choose to sell at the *mandis* or markets set up all over India where government and independent agents buy crops. But typically he will not know until he has transported his produce what he will be paid. He will also not be paid in full and will likely have to return several times to collect his full payment. ITC is betting that, while the choice remains the farmer's, he will choose to sell to ITC.

I went to ITC's International Business headquarters in Secunderabad (across the river from Hyderabad) to talk to Shiv Sivakumar, CEO of the division and one of the creators of the e-Choupal project.

I was intrigued by the company's commitment to preserving the farmer's ownership of his land and of his life choices. Like so many top business executives I met in India, Mr. Sivakumar is unpretentious and highly articulate about his business and passionate about a vision of improving the lives of the poor in India through better business practices. Medium height, with a no-nonsense air, Mr. Sivakumar was wearing a short-sleeved shirt, open at the neck, and a pair of dark trousers. We talked in his back corner office on a brilliantly sunny day. He told me that the company's commitment to preserving the element of free choice and respecting the farmer's ownership of his land and his business was fundamental to ITC's business philosophy. "By design, our models fuse the belief that we can only do well if we do good, and we only do good when we do well. This is a particular Indian model that offers something unique, something that can do very well in Africa or other parts of Asia, but which can also offer something to North America." Mr. Sivakumar is convinced that preserving the farmer's freedom and agency "drives ITC to be more competitive as we have to offer a more attractive deal to the farmers, and it allows the farmer to keep his dignity."

Not all the corporations rushing to invest in Indian agriculture see things this way. Sunil Bharti Mittal, who made his money in telecom, has jumped on the agriculture bandwagon and is launching an export-oriented agribusiness concern called Bharti Field Fresh. The company has leased five thousand acres in Punjab, and is collaborating with the Rothschild Group to ship fresh fruits and vegetables to supermarkets in the UK. The farmers whose land has been leased can work as laborers on their land if they want to earn additional income. Bharti claims this will improve livelihoods, but there are fears that, once the system is established, cheaper migrant labor will be brought in and the legal owners of the land will in effect be dispossessed. Vice Chairman Rakesh Mittal told the *International Herald Tribune*, "To my mind, this opportunity of agriculture is an opportunity which is larger than telecom, which is larger than IT."[38]

There is a danger that India will lose its food self-sufficiency for good as farmers move "out of staples like wheat to higher-value crops like okra and onions, Alphonso mangoes, spices, shrimp, Darjeeling tea, long-grain basmati rice, cashew nuts, milk, and buffalo meat." What crops are grown will be dictated by the tastes of European and other foreign consumers, not by local markets or national food needs. Agro-giant PepsiCo has designated India as a farm-products hub for Asia, exporting orange juice concentrate, for example, produced in India to other Asian markets.[39]

The transformation of India's agricultural economy to an export-oriented, high-value one leveraging new cold chains to bring fresh produce quickly to urban markets or airports where cargo jets can get it to foreign markets will no doubt transform Indian agriculture and create new wealth. The Dutch bank Rabobank produced a report for India's Ministry of Food Processing Industries in 2005 that projected that "India would double its share of global food and agricultural exports to 3 percent from 1.5 percent in the next decade, with the value of exports soaring to $30 billion by 2015 from $8 billion in 2003."[40] But to what extent India's impoverished farmers will share in this wealth is not clear, and as the prices of basic staples rise in India's domestic market, millions of the country's poor are increasingly at risk of undernourishment or starvation.

Much is made about the wastage of food in India because it lacks a cold chain to rapidly move fresh fruits and vegetables to urban and foreign markets. This argument assumes there are only urban and foreign consumers for India's food. Mr. Sivakumar told me there is no wastage. He maintained, "At a macro level, people keep talking about twenty-five to thirty percent wastage, but very little is wasted. What there is is value erosion. In the marketplace, the price in the morning is one hundred rupees, seventy at midday, and thirty at the end of the day. If everything were to be sold at one hundred rupees, what happens to the buyer at thirty rupees? We have a growing middle class that prefers to spend one hundred rupees if the quality is there, so there is value loss on what is sold at thirty rupees, but there is no wastage as such."

Unless companies can commit to the kind of win-win, bottom-of-the pyramid philosophy of ITC's e-Choupal platform, there is a real risk that India's vast agricultural sector will be looted for the profit of powerful corporations focused on exporting and on producing for the growing demand of India's emerging higher-income market. Independent farmers will be forced to cede their production to corporate owners, reduced to contract labor on the land they once controlled. If that happens, India's twenty-first-century farmers will find themselves in a situation not unlike India's eighteenth-century weavers did when the East India Company took away their agency as independent producers and turned them into piecework laborers turning out products for the European luxury market, in effect instituting a new commercial imperium at the expense, once again, of India's suffering masses.

ITC's Sivakumar thinks India is too diverse and democratic for this kind of exploitative model to work. "In the end, the structure of Indian democracy and the level of heterogeneity will prevent the transformation of Indian agriculture into an American-style industrial farming system. The Indian system is grounded in microfinance and local tastes. Kellogg's has been here for twenty years. They still just do their twenty million dollars. McDonald's had to completely change their products for India. So there is one check in the form of democracy and one check in the form of microfinance. The Indian farmer works under very tough conditions." Microfinance is critical in India because the small-scale Indian farmer works on such tiny margins he is below the radar of traditional lending by big banks. Sivakumar welcomes the churning that is going on and the attention India's agricultural sector is getting from the United States in the form of the Knowledge Initiative because "it has opened up the debate." Tapping his pen on his desk, he said, "We have had no serious debate about what agribusiness model to follow because there is no Indian agribusiness. In the meantime, there is a lot of work we can do together through the agricultural deal. We can learn from the American approach. There is a lot of awareness on the Indian side of what is at stake in terms of IPR, in terms of university research. But there are compromises in any bilateral negotiation. Ultimately, Indians will decide what is best for India."

In the meantime, Mr. Sivakumar is committed to expanding ITC's e-Choupal platform. "We want to be in one hundred thousand villages by 2010." When I met him, the company had just begun a pilot program to bring educational opportunities to villages via the e-Choupal kiosks. He said India's villagers were hungry for education and had no good educational opportunities at hand. ITC is exploring both free adult literacy programs, working with Tata Consultancy's successful TSC program, and high-school-level, tuition-based programs. The potential of platforms such as e-Choupal to connect the underserved rural majority of India's population to commercial, educational, health, and entertainment opportunities is clearly enormous.

Using the City to Save the Country

In 1958, John Bissell, a Connecticut Yankee, left his job as a buyer for Macy's department store and came to India at the invitation of the Ford Foundation to help the still relatively new republic develop its handloom industry. He fell in love with Indian handicrafts and an Indian woman named Bimla. The couple made their home in New Delhi. Both were entrepreneurial: John founded Fabindia, a company dedicated to reviving traditional Indian crafts while creating livelihoods for village Indians. Bimla, or Bim as she's commonly known, founded Playhouse, an innovative preschool that counts many prominent Indians as its alumni.

For many years, John Bissell kept the company small, initially running a single store in Delhi's Greater Kailash neighborhood. Gradually, Fabindia expanded. John passed away after a long illness in 1998. His and Bim's son, William (their daughter Monsoon is a film director who has worked on the movies *Monsoon Wedding* and *Earth*), took over the business. While he has remained passionately committed to his father's vision of the vital role of handicrafts in Indian society and culture, he has steadily been expanding Fabindia. The chain boasted thirty-four stores last year, with thirty more planned. When I went to Fabindia's company headquarters in Delhi's Okhla Industrial Area to meet William Bissell and learn about the company, there was a store owner from Guangdong, China, who was doing so well, she was planning to open a second store. Fabindia has stores in Rome and in Dubai, and they are planning to open one in

New York or Connecticut. The company launched its online business in 2005.

The Okhla Industrial Area is on Delhi's southeastern outskirts, near the Yamuna River, with block after block of faceless, squat, concrete factories and warehouses. From the outside, Fabindia's headquarters looks no different from any other building in the neighborhood. Inside is a cavernous warehouse on several floors. Offices and conference rooms line two sides of the building. The rest serves as a central clearinghouse. Merchandise comes in from all over India. It is then sorted for shipment out to the various stores.

William Bissell is tall, in his early forties. He was wearing a handloom shirt when I met him and remarked immediately that I was not. William attended the Loomis Chaffee school in Windsor, Connecticut, and Wesleyan University. Then he returned to India. Before joining the family business, he worked for the Centre for Science and the Environment and the BBC. He knows as much about handlooms, or more, as anyone else in the country. Walking through his warehouse, he picked up different articles of clothing. There were men's cotton shirts of deep indigo interwoven with small patterns of cream, women's *kameez,* long tunics of a finer, bolder patterned weave in deep oranges and red. Sheer muslin tablecloths in ivory were folded into neat squares. He could identify immediately which village the fabric came from.

There was a family atmosphere at the Fabindia headquarters. Up in William's office, I was invited to lunch with the visiting Chinese buyer and a member of William's design team. The food was homemade, simple and delicious. One level down, store managers from around India were meeting. They were also enjoying the same kind of food. Everyone mingled freely. It struck me that few men were around. Later, when I asked William about this, he told me, "Most of our store managers and senior management are women."

I spent some time with Anjana Batra, who heads the company's training program. Anjana has been with Fabindia for nine years. A pleasant woman in her fifties dressed in a beautiful handloom *salwar kameez*, Anjana gave me a brief tutorial on Fabindia. The first thing I wanted to know about was the food. "All the food," she explained, "comes from a woman who cooks out of her home. Now we give her our organic food products, and she uses those. We've asked her to do some recipes for us." I didn't know about the company's diversifying into organic food. We were sitting in Anjana's corner office. There were old reports, brochures, and company documents stacked in a metal armoire. The office was light, bright, and totally functional. "We started the organic food line about two years ago. We sell grains, nuts, herbs, coffees, and teas now in our stores. Fresh fruits and vegetables are available for delivery in Delhi through our Web site. We've added processed foods, preserves, that kind of thing. We also provide recipes. We're thinking of opening cafés, but if we do that, we'll subcontract it out."

I asked Anjana about Fabindia's phenomenal growth in recent years. "Well," she replied, "a lot of that is William. But we don't advertise. We've always believed in word of mouth. That is how we've grown. You know, our Internet business is completely international. People visit India and discover Fabindia and they want to be able to get our products when they're back home. Indians in the diaspora are another clientele. We get orders from all over the world."

I wondered why the aversion to advertising. Anjana laughed. "This business is about more than business. William's father's vision was to maximize handicrafts. He was fascinated and impressed with the wealth of designs and techniques. He wanted to showcase this for the world. He also believed that people needed to be able to stay in their villages. He felt that if people could be given regular employment, if they could make a living from their traditional crafts or even if old crafts could be revived, they could stay in their communities."

What about the company's name, Fabindia? I told her I found it so catchy, so, well, fabulous. She laughed again and said, "Fabindia is *fabric* plus *India* and it is also 'fabulous India.'"

William stopped by Anjana's office. "So, let me show you how this place works," he invited. We headed through a door away from the office corridor. I was immediately struck by the punishing heat: the warehouse was not air-conditioned and it was at least 110 degrees outside. William seemed unfazed. He showed me a series of floor-to-ceiling cages filled with different merchandise. "Here is where we collect outgoing orders. We only sell through our own outlets. Each one of these cages holds what a particular store has asked for, for their inventory." He took out different shirts, tablecloths, pillow covers. He knew the inventory number of each of these items. I asked him how the ordering and sorting was handled. "We have a tech genius. No, really. He's got us running more efficiently than Wal-Mart. Our system can deal with more bar codes than Wal-Mart's can." I must have looked incredulous because he added, "No, really!"

I asked him about indigenous cotton. I told him about the disturbing things I had seen in Vidarbha and everyone telling me that while indigenous cotton was wonderfully adapted to local dry-farming conditions and soils, its staple length was too short for power looms. His expression grew a little dark. He said, "The villagers we work with source their own yarns. Indigenous cotton is perfectly suitable for handlooms. If we felt we had to step in on the policy level on indigenous cotton, we would. Three to four years ago, we stepped in to address the excise tax on ready-made garments, including handlooms." We made our way back up to his office, which thankfully was air-conditioned.

"We are a group of people concerned about the handloom industry and rural development. Fabindia launched the Craftmark label, like the Woolmark label. It indicates what technique has been used in producing the fabric, like 'woven' or 'block printed.' Development is an interesting thing. Let me show you something." He grabbed a legal pad from his desk and drew me a diagram. "This is where we find good handicrafts." The diagram had two sides, one for rural India and one for urban India. Each one was divided into three areas. On the rural India side, these were one crop, two crops, and three crops. On the urban India side, these were education, governance, and technology. He said that in rural India, the best crafts were found in the one-crop areas. In two-crop areas, the crafts were mediocre. In three-crop areas, there were no crafts. "They don't have time, right?" I asked. "Precisely," he replied. He then listed a number of Indian cities. "You get good crafts where there are none of these advantages, in Lucknow, in Indore, in Siliguri, in Shillong. Bangalore? Cochin? Forget it."

This doesn't mean that William Bissell is against educating India's villagers. He has been instrumental in sponsoring a school in Rajasthan. "If people could get quality education in rural areas, they would stay," he argued. The school was founded in 1992. There are now four hundred students. "Girls pay half the tuition, which is very modest. The school goes up through the tenth standard and will soon go up to twelfth. We are also going to open a second school." He told me they used only local materials to build the school. They do water harvesting, collecting rainwater behind check dams. He gave me a brochure about the school.

Since his whole business is based on cotton handlooms, I asked him about Bt cotton and genetically engineered seeds versus the hundreds of local, traditional varieties. He said, "I'm a pragmatist and a businessman. I think you should do an equation where you put in all the costs when you calculate the benefits. There is a value to genetic diversity. Let's put a value on that. What you're essentially doing is replacing twenty varieties with two that are copyrighted. That's like putting all your survival eggs in one basket.

"I'm into handlooms for practical reasons too," he concluded, smiling. "They keep you cooler. The fabric breathes. I only wear handlooms." I pictured my closet back in New York. I did have some handloom garments from India, but I certainly had a lot of other clothing too. Probably most of it was made from hybrid or Bt cotton. I also had some synthetics, which are made from petroleum. The wool, I wasn't sure about. I haven't purged my closet yet but I have looked at my clothing in a new light.

On my way back into town, I thought about the villages I had seen in the mountains of central France in 1980, where I had done a study of French folk fiddling. I learned a repertory of music from musicians who are all dead now, music they had carried with them intact from the nineteenth century and centuries earlier. I witnessed a way of life that has ceased to exist. Most of those villages are now holiday resorts for Dutch and British families who've bought up the old stone houses for their summer homes. I watched one old farmhouse, with a magnificent thatched roof, slowly crumble to ruin over the next decade. From one year to the next, its unrepaired roof sank a little lower until the whole thing just caved in. The stone walls began to fall down after that.

The world of peasant France, the life of the villages, including the music, the celebrations, and the crafts, all disappeared in little more than a decade. I watched it happen. This same kind of rapid disappearance of traditional Indian villages happened in Gujarat, India, in the 1980s.[41] I wondered, listening to William Bissell, after all that I had learned about India's modernization plans, its plans to industrialize agriculture, how long the life of the villages where William sources his handicrafts could survive. I thought about the once bustling small towns of the American Midwest that have been turned into ghost towns. The 150,000 American family farms going under every year. The millions of farms lost over the past twenty years.

For fifty years Fabindia has played a role in nurturing a wealth of Indian craft traditions. It has provided villagers with a decent livelihood in exchange for their skills, and it has invested in providing an affordable quality education to village children, especially to girls. If William is right, if the company can continue to do that for another twenty years, India, as many of us know and love it, might not only survive, it will be better. If Fabindia can bring an appreciation of handlooms and crafts to millions of city dwellers in India, Europe, China, and the United States, more megacity residents, such as myself, might take a look at what is hanging in their closets and, at least, think about where the clothing comes from, and what went into it.

I asked William about Fabindia's organic foods venture. I told him I'd been disturbed by what I'd learned about pesticide pollution in India.

"The government of India justifies the industrialization of agriculture because they think it will create jobs and that there will be a lot of investment. With the Green Revolution, wheat production went up. There was suddenly so much water for irrigation because of the new water projects, they began to grow rice in Punjab. That was madness. The water table sank. The soil and the water became heavily polluted with nitrates. This time, in a way, we are lucky to be so late in the cycle. The whole Western approach will be revealed. If India can hold out for another twenty years, this latest invasion will be revealed for what it is: a group of powerful corporations looking to maximize profits."

For India to prove William right, it will have to invent its own models, prove they can work in India, then take them to the world.

CHAPTER FIVE

The Cities

WE ARE FAST BECOMING A PLANET OF CITY DWELLERS. Cities attract the young, the talented, and the ambitious. The communications revolution and the expansion of jet travel have linked the world's great cities. The cosmopolitan, educated elite moves effortlessly from Tokyo to Los Angeles to London to Bombay to Singapore. In these cities, they find the same hotel amenities, the same twenty-four-hour television news channels. In nearby upscale shopping arcades, they find familiar international brands of handbags, perfume, clothing, and electronics. At the airport, in the business-class lounge, they are surrounded by people just like themselves who are weaving the fabric of our increasingly globalized world.

Cities also attract the desperate. Millions of the world's poor are being driven off their land and out of their villages by crop failures, the consolidation of agricultural land for industrialized farming, development projects such as dams that drown whole valleys, and violent conflicts. In the cities, they join millions of slum dwellers already waging a daily fight for survival.

In 1950, out of a total world population of 2.5 billion, 731 million people, or 29 percent, lived in cities. By 2030, the planet's population is expected to reach a whopping 8.2 billion, with 4.9 billion people or 60 percent living in cities.[1] Within eighty years, the percentage of people living in cities will have more than doubled, and the ratio of urban to rural residents will have been flipped on its head.

In the planet's cities, affluence and destitution collide. Nowhere is this more true than in India. India counts seven cities with a population over 4 million and thirty-five cities with a population over 1 million. India's cities constitute the second-largest urban system in the world after China's. It is an urban system in crisis. India's cities suffer from decades of neglect, rampant corruption, inadequate infrastructure, and unregulated development. Millions of India's most impoverished citizens have flocked to the nation's cities, where they create, with scant resources, livelihoods and vibrant communities, such as Dharavi in Bombay, a bustling hive of cottage industries and tiny dwellings where families live, work, and play almost literally on top of each other. Unfortunately, many of these communities are slums that lack even basic sanitation, let alone other amenities. The United Nations classifies 40 percent of India's urban population as poor.[2]

Meanwhile, the country's economic boom is attracting hundreds of transnational companies and propelling Indian companies toward ever higher levels of competitiveness and professionalism. These businesses require sleek new office complexes, well-equipped research and development facilities, and modern fabrication plants. Their educated and well-paid employees demand good schools, access to quality medical care, and comfortable housing. Shopping malls, flyovers to take traffic above the urban crush, and gated enclaves where the rich can find respite from urban chaos are proliferating.

Rehabilitating India's Cities

India has embarked on an ambitious project to transform its cities. In December 2005, Prime Minister Manmohan Singh inaugurated the Jawaharlal Nehru National Urban Renewal Mission (JNNURM), committing $28 billion in national funds to a massive makeover of sixty-three Indian cities. India's future will hinge on the success of this unprecedented effort. Without functioning cities, India's dream of becoming a developed country, a peer of China, Europe, or the United States, will come to a grinding halt. The government of India is acutely aware of this. In his speech inaugurating the National Urban Renewal Mission, the prime minister emphasized that in rehabilitating India's cities the focus should be on the needs of the urban poor.[3] It remains to be seen whether India will realize this inclusive vision of transforming the country's cities. But if India can meet this challenge, it will achieve something no other democracy has been able to do: create megacities where the poor are not exiled to far-flung margins, and where residents of all economic means can live decently as fully participating citizens. India's cities have the potential to become role models for burgeoning metropolises elsewhere in the developing world. They may also provide lessons for the industrialized world, where the marginalization of the economically disadvantaged, often along ethnic and racial lines, regularly erupts in violence.

Hyderabad was one of the first Indian cities to renovate its urban center, widening roads, clearing sidewalks of vendors and beggars, and replacing dilapidated old buildings with modern high-rises. Calcutta, Chennai, Bangalore, Ahmadabad, and a host of other Indian cities big and small have embarked on their own projects of modernization and improvement. India's cities understand that they now compete with each other to attract foreign and domestic investment. Taking advantage of the National Urban Renewal Mission, cities are busy submitting improvement plans to the national government for funding.

The Challenges

Decades of neglect and explosive population growth have left India's urban infrastructure in tatters. Car ownership is booming; new roads are being constructed everywhere but not fast enough. Public transportation lags woefully behind the needs of the vast majority of people who cannot afford to buy cars. Traffic jams aren't the only downside of economic expansion: air quality in India's cities is horrendous. I have often wiped my face off after a day out and about in Delhi and had the tissue turn black with particulate. Sore throats, coughs—these come with the territory when visiting urban India. According to the Energy Information Administration of the U.S. Department of Energy, automobiles and untreated industrial smoke contribute to making the air in India's cities "among the world's worst."[4] Bombay is the fifth most polluted city in the world, with 97 percent of its people exposed to air that fails to meet World Health Organization standards.[5]

Just as in the countryside, water is in short supply in India's cities, even in posh residential areas. More and more, residents have their water delivered by tanker truck, even those lucky enough to have indoor plumbing connected to a municipal water supply. There is simply not enough water in the pipelines. When I asked Deepak Parekh, the head of HDFC, Housing Development Finance Corporation, India's largest mortgage lender, about water shortages in Bombay, he told me from a seat in his elegant living room on Bombay's posh Carmichael Road, "We get water delivered by tankers right here. The water commissioner lives across the street. If my wife sees him from our driveway, she'll tease him by saying, 'Today we're coming to your house to do our laundry.' Water shortage is an issue that affects everyone in Bombay, rich and poor."

Any visitor to Bombay is struck by the city's massive slums, which stretch away endlessly from the edge of the airport, the belly of the incoming aircraft nearly grazing the rusted corrugated roofs of a sea of dusty hovels before clearing the chain-link fence at the end of the runway. At night, the homeless crowd every spare patch of pavement. Sidewalks, building thresholds, the bare ground under half-built flyovers, are covered by the sleeping forms of the poor. Mothers shield babies and small children in the protective curve of their bodies, having no other means to shelter them. Those lucky enough to have a charpai, a simple wood-and-string bed, crowd onto it head to toe. There are little huts, shanties, and pavement dwellers next to country clubs, next to luxury apartments, next to five-star hotels.

Despite a housing construction boom, 60 percent of Bombay's 18 million people live in slums or on the streets. That's 10.8 million people. In Dharavi, Bombay's biggest slum, there is one toilet for every fifteen hundred people. According to India's last census, taken in 2001, 40 million people in India's cities lived in slums, and just "49.7 percent of urban households had tap water on their premises and only 57.4 percent had sanitation facilities."[6]

The rich in India live amidst the most unimaginable squalor, seemingly unperturbed. My aunt has a lovely old apartment off Neapean Sea Road in one of the most affluent areas of the city. Her building overlooks a new park built by the Birlas, one of India's business dynasties. The park is on the sea face, where the gentle waves of the Arabian Sea lap against low-lying rocks. The park is open from 5:30 a.m. to 9:30 a.m., and again in the evening. In between, the gate is locked. A walking path around a long oval has distance markers in meters. Running is not permitted, and guards watch people using the park to make sure park rules are respected.

I usually take a morning walk in the park when I stay with my aunt. The park abounds with middle-aged men in polo shirts talking business on their cell phones, new mothers in jogging ensembles, and old ladies in pale cotton saris clutching the arm of a family servant. The park is formally landscaped with neat rows of palm trees and seasonally changing flowers. Around the periphery are elaborately carved stone benches.

The park has no access to the adjacent shore. In fact, you cannot even see the waves breaking next to the park. They are hidden by a sturdy fence of concrete and iron bars, lined with a bamboo barrier. The rocks along the shore are used as public latrines by the people who live in the slums at either end of the park. The people in the neighborhood high-rises could easily afford to pay for the installation of public latrines, but building latrines would mean acknowledging the slums' existence. It would encourage their permanency. The land on which the slums have been built does not belong to the people who are living on it. They are not supposed to be there at all. So, the wealthy pretend that the slums are not there, and that the rocks, just behind the bamboo screen, are not being used as a public toilet. Learning not to see dire poverty all around is a basic life skill of the affluent in India.

My family has lived in Bombay since the 1960s. My father went to college there. I have always felt at home in the city. Still, however often I visit, I know the city well enough to know there is a lot I don't know about it. To get a sense of Bombay from a native son's perspective, I looked up Naresh Fernandes, editor in chief of *TimeOut Mumbai*. I met him at his office behind Bombay's racecourse.

Naresh still looks like the crime-beat reporter he once was, utterly unpretentious with longish hair, open sandals, and rumpled khakis. At a large, round table in a conference room over a cup of coffee, he told me, "My family has always lived in Bombay. Unlike most people here, I am an aboriginal. My grandfather used to farm a plot of land here, despite how the Shiv Sena sees things." His last remark refers to the regionalist political party long headed by the colorful Bal Thackeray, whose caricatured fascism has both terrorized and amused Bombay's citizens. The Shiv Sena views the city as a festering sinkhole of foreign—meaning non-Maharashtrian Hindu—elements. The party is responsible for changing the city's name from Bombay to Mumbai, and for enforcing job quotas both formal and informal for Maharashtrians. The cosmopolitan character of Bombay where people from every corner of India and the world have come to make their home is anathema to the Shiv Sena. Thackeray is in poor health now. His son Uday is ascendant, but it seems unlikely that the Shiv Sena can long control a city that is rapidly becoming more internationalized, and on which India has staked so much of its future. Still, the Shiv Sena is capable of mobilizing mobs of young men to rampage through Bombay's streets when it suits them.

In 1992, while a rookie reporter for the *Times of India,* Naresh covered the Bombay riots that saw ferocious attacks against the city's Muslims following the destruction of the Babri Masjid mosque in Ajodhya by Hindu militants. Justice B. N. SriKrishna, who led a commission that investigated the Bombay riots, stated in his report, "There is no doubt that the Shiv Sena and Shiv Sainiks took the lead in organising attacks on Muslims and their properties under the guidance of several leaders from the level of *shakha pramukh* to that of Sena chief Bal Thackeray."[7] Naresh, whose reporting was included in *When Bombay Burned: Reportage and Comments on the Riots and Blasts from The Times of India,*[8] told me, "I learned then about the power of the press. We went to the morgue and counted bodies. When the police commissioner reported one hundred deaths, we were able to report that we'd seen five hundred. Eventually, the police commissioner got sacked." Frustrated with management changes, he headed to New York to pursue a degree in journalism from Columbia University, after which he worked at the *Wall Street Journal*. When the opportunity of launching a Bombay version of *TimeOut* came his way, he jumped on it.

Naresh has a definite vision for the magazine: "We assume that we have taken up the *TimeOut* original spirit when it was founded in London in the 1960s—the city, policy and culture—and we spin it as it was in the beginning when it was about where hippies could find where the next antiwar demonstration was. We see ourselves as giving not just a snapshot of the city, but we give our take on the city. For example, we're for public transportation, against the privatization of utilities. The powers that be in the city are worried about traffic on Pedder Road. They want to build a flyover that will make life very difficult in a largely residential area. Studies show that only fifty thousand people per day travel Pedder Road by car. That's as many people as get off one train at Churchgate. Our readership is that large middle-class population. The people who want to read about themselves at parties won't find themselves on our pages."

I asked him what he thinks of Bombay's future. "I'm not optimistic about the future of this city at all, even though I love it dearly." As Fernandes sees it, Bombay missed its chance when it failed in its bid to develop equitably the abandoned mill lands, six hundred acres of prime real estate in the middle of the city. Last March, after a bitter contest between the Bombay Environmental Action Group and affiliated organizations and the city's big developers over the fate of these vacant lands, India's Supreme Court, reversing an earlier decision by the Bombay High Court, ruled in favor of the developers. With a green light to put up technology parks, shopping malls, luxury hotels, and apartment blocks, the developers were jubilant. One real estate broker enthused, "We need to show the world we are serious about becoming a global player. By building state-of-the-art facilities, we will be able to prove this."[9] But it was a devastating blow to many engaged Mumbaikars who saw the equitable and environmentally sound development of this land as the city's last chance to redeem itself. The 400 acres these citizen activists had hoped would be available out of the total area for open spaces and low-income housing were reduced by the Supreme Court's decision to 133 acres.

"It was obvious in 1995," Fernandes said, "when the mills had collapsed, that the city's social fabric was fraying because the economic engine had broken down. It was already abundantly clear that development of the six hundred acres in the middle of the city occupied by the empty mills needed to be planned. The Supreme Court decision basically said, 'Bombay: Go to hell!' So, now the city's going down the toilet. The people who have these delusions about the city's future as another Shanghai are deranged."

Naresh's vehement words reflect the intensity of competing visions for a city in flux. Huge fortunes are being made, and the cityscape is being transformed at the expense of some of the poorest people in the world, not to mention the middle class. Naresh continued, "The developers are already eyeing the port land—about eighteen hundred acres. If the port land had been planned together with the mill land, that was the chance to turn this city around, but the mantras of the market have been used as an excuse for unfettered greed. Look," he drove home his point, "if the financial capital of this country's booming economy is sixty percent slums, then we are all damned." Naresh sighed and softly but with bitter irony said, "Under Nehruvianism, we were supposed to care about the poor. Now we don't have to."

Bombay's Vision 2020

By 2020, Bombay will be, with 28.5 million people, the most populous city in the world.[10] That is also the year that Bombay has set for achieving its goal of a total urban makeover. Long known as the city of maya, or illusion, of impossible dreams that come true in Bollywood movies, Bombay is India's New York. Thousands of Indians trek to Bombay every year with nothing more than their hopes and their desperation. Ambitious, educated Indians, Americans, and Europeans, including returning members of India's diaspora, are joining them, albeit in completely different circumstances. Between these two extremes, as property prices go through the roof and basic public amenities such as mass transportation, sanitation, and water are stressed well beyond capacity, the middle class is being squeezed.

Megacities such as Bombay entice and repel by their sheer size. They dare newcomers to take them on. A natural schizophrenia comes with being a resident of a megacity. One is at once anonymous and a member of an elite club. New York was the first city to pass the 10 million population mark and become a megacity. "If I can make it there, I'll make it anywhere," go the lyrics to the famous song "New York, New York." To boast "I'm a New Yorker" says it all. To an Indian, declaring "I'm a Mumbaikar," a resident of Bombay, carries a similar resonance of pride, savvy, and the scars of city battles triumphantly won.[11] Mumbaikars are fiercely proud of their city, even if they may hate its many grave shortcomings. They are capable of going for each other's throat, as happened during vicious rioting in 1992 between the city's Hindus and Muslims. They are just as capable of coming together in spontaneous outbursts of generosity. During the catastrophic flooding in July 2005, and in the aftermath of terror attacks on the city's commuter rail system in 2006, people extended a helping hand, a meal, or a place to spend the night to fellow citizens in need.

Bombay's business leaders envision a Shanghai-style transformation of their city.[12] They want to turn Bombay, already India's financial capital, into a world financial capital rivaling Singapore. This was the thrust of a report prepared in 2003 by McKinsey and Company and a business-led group called Bombay First. The report's title was "Vision 2020." It outlined how Bombay could effect this transformation through constructing new roads, privatizing services, and cleaning up slums. In 2005, the prime minister lent his support to the idea, saying it "was his dream to see Mumbai transformed into a city like Shanghai." He pledged resources from the national government to support this goal.[13]

Last March, the U.S.-India CEO Forum issued a report titled "The U.S.-India Strategic Economic Partnership." The report recommended that the "U.S. partner [with] India in making Mumbai into a Regional Financial Centre."[14] In the section on infrastructure, the report recommends participation by U.S. business and financial institutions such as the World Bank to facilitate private-public partnerships and investment in improving India's infrastructure from a business-needs perspective. Every major U.S. commercial and investment bank now has offices in Bombay. I have been privy to a lot of excited talk among financial types about Bombay becoming an important link in a 24-7 financial trading system in which transactions would seamlessly cascade from New York, to London, to Bombay, to Tokyo, and back to New York. The Bombay envisioned by this crowd has little to do with the Bombay in which most of the city's citizens live.

The Biggest Slum in Asia

Rehabilitating Dharavi is the most ambitious step Bombay is taking to transform itself. One million people are crammed into 535 acres along the Mithi River, squeezed between the neighborhoods of Mahim and Sion. Originally a sleepy fishing village, Dharavi is a thriving community where small-scale industries occupy the same tiny rooms where families live. There are leather tanneries, scrap-metal dealers, potters, and women who toil at home making *papads,* a popular snack food. Narrow lanes twist between brick, one-room houses, built by hand by the people who live in them. Waste water snakes its way through the colony in shallow gutters. Barefoot children jump over them. The stench of Mahim, surely one of the worst-smelling places in the world, is largely due to the untreated sewage and industrial effluent that pours into the Mithi and flows out into Mahim Creek.

The Dharavi Redevelopment Project, the private-sector brainchild of Mukesh Mehta of M. M. Consultants, got a green light in 2006 from the Maharashtra state government. Bids worth $2.5 billion were solicited from construction and urban development companies around the world. Indian giants DLF, Emar, and Hirandani as well as South Korean and Dubai-based companies are all vying for a piece of the action.[15] Developers have to provide a 225-square-foot apartment for each slum household. For each square foot the developer constructs in new housing for the slum dwellers, he will be given 1.33 square feet free to sell or develop as he pleases. The basic plan is to build high-rise apartment buildings to house Dharavi's residents and free up space for schools, parks, and hospitals as well as shopping malls and multiplex theaters. Many of Dharavi's residents are skeptical, especially those who make *papads* and pottery, two of the biggest industries in the slum. Both require outdoor space to dry the finished product, space residents will not get in tiny high-rise flats. To spur economic development and provide enhanced livelihoods for Dharavi's displaced *papad* makers, leatherworkers, and potters, a Special Economic Zone (SEZ) is planned that will include leather showrooms, a pottery institute, gem and jewelry factories, and even information technology businesses, but it is unclear how much resident craftsmen and *papad*-making women will actually benefit from this.[16]

India has gone crazy for Special Economic Zones. Inspired by the success of the Chinese in attracting foreign investment and boosting industrial production in SEZs like Shenzhen and Suzhou Industrial City, India now has twenty-eight such zones. These zones offer companies special tax advantages, provided they generate net export earnings. First launched in 2000, India's SEZs provide "complete business freedom to large multinational companies which are seeking to globalize their production bases."[17] The freedoms SEZs offer to multinationals include freedom from labor unions, as well as guaranteed uninterrupted water and power supplies. SEZ development was capped at 150 sites until 2006 when Kamal Nath, minister of commerce, seeking to raise foreign investment and perhaps do Indian business a huge favor, succeeded in doing away with that ceiling, over protests by Minister of Finance P. Chidambaram. There are now 117 more SEZs given "permission in principle" plus another 200 in the pipeline. The rapid proliferation of SEZs in India has been dramatic enough to attract a warning from the International Monetary Fund about the "perverse economic incentives" of these zones. It seems so many existing businesses have been shifting operations to the new SEZs, where they are relieved of significant tax burdens, that the trend is threatening government tax revenues. The Finance Ministry is claiming losses of $19 billion in revenue by 2010.[18] This is money the government of India simply cannot afford to lose.

It remains to be seen how the creation of a SEZ designed to benefit large multinational corporations will help generate and enhance the livelihoods of Dharavi's micro-enterprise owners and craftsmen. The reconstruction of Dharavi was set as of late last year to begin in January 2007. If India can transform the biggest slum in Asia into a thriving mixed-use oasis with good civic amenities and infrastructure, and replicate that metamorphosis in slums across the country, urban India will become a powerful engine for transforming the entire nation.

An Education Emergency

Not nearly enough of India's young people have the skills or education the new jobs that are being generated in India require. One reason India's information-technology companies are expanding abroad is that they cannot count on getting enough highly skilled workers in India to meet the demands of continued double-digit growth. Qualified candidates regularly receive multiple offers, while many of their less-qualified peers go without a single opportunity. While India's elite educational institutions, including the famous Indian Institutes of Technology and the Indian Institutes of Management, produce superbly qualified graduates, these represent an infinitesimally small number of India's total graduates. Moreover, few Indians complete high school; fewer make it into university at all. Illiteracy remains high. Too many children work, often under conditions no different from slavery. Too many who do attend school receive an education that leaves them unable to read or do simple math.

India has an educational emergency on its hands, and inspired individuals are stepping up to meet the challenge of educating the world's largest school-age population. Last year, Pratham, an NGO active in improving primary education in India, published its first Annual Survey of Education Report (ASER). The results were a damning indictment of the abysmal quality of education available to most Indian children. Of an estimated 140 million children in primary school in India, Pratham finds that 30 million cannot read, 40 million cannot even recognize an alphabet, and 55 million will not complete even four years of school.[19]

Though India's constitution guarantees the right of every child to an education, it is clear that the government cannot cope with the situation. Typical of the most promising efforts, collaborative ventures linking the government with private foundations and other NGOs and the private sector are taking on the challenge of improving the quality and the reach of basic education in India. The Azim Premji Educational Foundation, established by Wipro CEO Azim Premji, is dedicated to improving the quality of elementary education in India, especially in rural, government schools. I visited two schools in Hyderabad where the Foundation is active, and came away filled with hope for India's future.

Rohini Nilekani, the wife of Infosys chairman Nandan Nilekani, has established the Akshara Foundation, which is affiliated with Pratham and focused on "Every Child in School and Learning." She has also spearheaded a program to provide high-quality, low-cost books for children in regional languages. Most of India's people do not speak English. Says Rohini, "One of the things we've not been able to utilize is our indigenous knowledge base because we can't talk to each other." Her foundation has eight hundred thousand books in print, available to fifty thousand children, in thirty-five hundred community libraries.

These are but two of literally hundreds of heroic efforts to address India's education crisis. One of the most innovative ways to extend educational opportunity, especially in rural areas, is via distance learning over wireless Internet connections. India's billions cannot all be brought to urban or international centers of excellence. The obvious alternative is to take those centers to the people. "Education in a connected world after the information revolution has taken on a new meaning in terms of information in real time and information on demand. I don't have to go to Harvard. I can access Harvard online and many of these universities," argues TCS's Ramadorai. "If education is not affordable and on demand, one class of the population is denied an education, another class is given access to a substandard education, and a very small elite to an outstanding education." TCS has a program of extending educational opportunities through wireless kiosks set up in underserved areas of the country. Ramadorai predicts that "education will go through a fundamental paradigm shift," driven in no small part by the imperative to find ways to educate India's children.

As Island of Privilege

On the opposite bank of the Mithi from Dharavi lies the Bandra-Kurla Economic Zone. It is an island of protected privilege created out of reclaimed land, carved away from the Mithi's sinuous course. This is where giants Citibank and IBM have their corporate offices in Bombay. To reach this island, a huge flyover arches away from the main north-south artery connecting the financial nerve center and historic Fort Area of south Bombay to the airport and the suburbs stretching to the north like beads on a long string up the coast of the Arabian Sea. At the apex of the flyover, high above the nauseating stench of Mahim, the shimmering glass oval of the IL&FS building rises in the distance. Then the road swoops down and crosses the inky vein of the river. On the other side lies paradise, an Emerald City of wide avenues, groomed greenery, and office complexes.

The Bandra-Kurla Economic Zone is home to the brand-new campuses of the American School of Mumbai and the Dhirubhai Ambani International School (DAIS). The schools are located next door to each other and share an athletic field.

A few neat shrubs and a couple of trees line the periphery of DAIS, but otherwise the surroundings are bare. Inside the school's high walls, there are more plants, trees, and flowers. The building surrounds a light-filled courtyard. Classrooms are adorned with children's artwork and colorful displays. Though the children wear uniforms, which even public school students do in India, there is nothing regimental about the place.

DAIS was founded in 2003. Of its first fifty-seven graduates, forty-seven gained entrance to top schools in the United States and England, including Stanford, Carnegie Mellon, Northwestern, Brown, Cornell, Wharton and Duke, in the United States; and Oxford, Cambridge, and the London School of Economics in the UK.[20] I wanted to find out how such excellence could be created so fast, and where a school of such exquisite achievement and privilege fit into the changes taking place in India.

Nita Ambani, the wife of Mukesh Ambani, the chairman of Reliance Industries Limited (RIL), is the chairperson of DAIS. She kindly agreed to meet me at the school. When I arrived, she was in an animated meeting with her staff. I could tell that she was deeply engaged in shepherding the school. A few minutes later, she emerged, apologized for making me wait, and ushered me into her office. Modern art canvases were on the wall and some exquisitely embroidered silk cushions on the sofa. There was a large color portrait of the school's namesake, Dhirubhai Ambani, whose vision and values are guiding lights of the school. But Nita Ambani also brings her own experience and spark to the institution. A former schoolteacher, she says she was motivated to create DAIS because of her frustration with the rigidities of India's traditional educational system. Her own children's tears on school mornings convinced her of the need for a better, child-centered approach. DAIS is her special project. She wants to create a world-class Indian school, replicate it on other private campuses, but also apply its formula of excellence to India's public schools.

Nita Ambani draws a great deal from the lessons of her own upbringing. She told me about growing up in a large joint family in Santa Cruz, a suburban area of Bombay not far from Juhu. "I grew up in an atmosphere where you learned to take care of others. We were eleven people in the house, with one bathroom. I tell my children this when they ask for their own bathroom, that, look, we had to queue. You learned patience. You learned to share. My uncle lived with us. He was blind. We had to read to him and take him for walks. My grandfather always stressed compassion. We learned to be caring. I tell Mukesh, it was a fairy-tale childhood."

DAIS is a distinctly Indian school. Nita Ambani told me, "Globalization does not mean westernization. Yoga is compulsory at the school. The children study Indian dance and music." She is also keen that the students understand the history of independent India. "We did a whole program on the freedom fighter. We found a lot of freedom fighters who are still alive, and we invited them to the school. It was part of a program called 'We the People.' We looked at India's struggle for freedom from 1857 up to the constitution."

What I found most striking about DAIS was the spirit of caring Ambani has worked to make integral to the children's educational experience. At DAIS, the students learn about care for the environment by recycling and conserving water. They learn about caring for less fortunate fellow citizens by working in Dharavi. "After their first visit to the slum, they didn't want to go back," Nita Ambani confided in me, "but now it is just a part of their normal school life. It is very important to me," she underlined, "that our kids come to have the spirit of compassion and caring as part of their character. They should never feel like they are doing someone a favor. It should be a part of who they are."

In addition to having the students at DAIS go into the slum to help out, Nita Ambani has worked out a deal with Akanksha, an NGO dedicated to helping slum children in Bombay. DAIS opens its doors to pupils from Akanksha after regular school hours, giving children who live in some of the worst conditions in the world an opportunity to learn in one of the world's best learning environments.

Nita Ambani is extremely aware that it is not enough for India to have just a few centers of excellence such as DAIS if these remain isolated from the rest of the population. Within the school, she says she made it imperative to figure out how to deliver excellence at the lowest possible cost. "Not many parents want to take the support of financial aid if they can help it," she explained. "So, instead of a higher fee structure with scholarships, we opted for a lower fee structure so that all families feel equal. We have a great mix of society here. The classroom is a leveling experience, which contributes to the learning experience." While lowering the overall tuition certainly brings the cost of attending DAIS below the stratosphere of the very rich, without financial aid the mix can only include children from relatively comfortable backgrounds. Having taught poor children, Nita Ambani is acutely aware that no slum children can attend DAIS as regular students.

However, Nita Ambani told me that her goal is for DAIS to be a change leader for Bombay's public schools. She said that the Bombay

Municipal Corporation (BMC) educates eight hundred thousand to 1 million children. "They have an existing infrastructure. If we can take one school and transform it, we can create the model. Then we must scale it up, and scale it up fast. There is no time to be wasted. India is facing an educational emergency, especially in primary education."

Her compassion has clearly been married to the trademark modus operandi of the Ambani family with Reliance: make it the best, make it big, replicate it on a huge scale, push down cost, and expand opportunity. She told me, "This is the model I want to do: excellent standards at affordable cost. It's a difficult balancing act, but we must do it." As we said our good-byes, she couldn't help blurting out, "You know, I love my work so much. I don't want to miss a single day. I feel such a sense of responsibility. How do we realize this dream for India? How do we get every child to read and write? It just never stops eating at you. It propels you. The thoughts never leave you, no matter what you are doing."

Quality Education for India's Poor Children

The Azim Premji Foundation is entirely dedicated to improving primary education in India for the country's poorest children. The foundation works with existing government schools, principally in poor rural villages. Its vision statement is compelling: "Significantly contribute to achieve quality universal education that facilitates a just, equitable and humane society." I traveled to Bangalore to meet with Dileep Ranjekar, chief executive of the foundation, to find out more about the organization. I subsequently visited two schools in Hyderabad where the Azim Premji Foundation is working to see for myself how its strategies play out on the ground.

The foundation's headquarters are in a building designed by Mrs. Premji. Set in a grove of eucalyptus trees behind Wipro's corporate headquarters, the building is a delightful redbrick structure designed to let in maximum light and to minimize the division between the interior and the exterior. In this peaceful, harmonious environment,

Dileep Ranjekar presides over the foundation's efforts to bring revolutionary change on a large scale to India's poorest schools. Ranjekar is a pleasant, middle-aged man with a gray-streaked, closely trimmed beard. He was wearing clothing made from hand-spun cotton khadi when we met.

"We are focused on large-scale change and systemic reform. Our focus is on the quality of elementary education. In India, there are two hundred million children six to fourteen years of age, studying in elementary schools up to eighth standard. There are one million schools and five million teachers. Seventy percent of these children live in rural areas. At the present time, only one-third of India's children complete tenth standard. One-third of the children in fifth standard cannot read and write. But seventy-five percent of our people don't have access to tap water, and fifty-five percent don't have electricity. This is our challenge. In order to do this on the scale required, we work with government schools and state educational departments. Our basic mission is to redefine the *what* and the *how* of education, with the child at the center. We are emphasizing 'child-friendly' schools, learning guarantees, technology initiatives, and educational management reform in order to change the ecosystem."

What was a child-friendly school? I wanted to know. "We are working on this in partnership with UNICEF and the government of Karnataka. This is a holistic intervention. At a child-friendly school, the children should be excited about school and want to attend. All the children without regard for gender or socioeconomic status must be included. The school should be conducive to participatory learning, and it should be clean and hygienic. All the children should complete fifth standard, at least. Under our 'learning guarantee' program the definition of a learning-guarantee school is one where one hundred percent of the children are enrolled in school, ninety percent attend regularly, and at least sixty percent demonstrate expected learning outcomes."

Azim Premji has twice transferred shares worth 3.5 billion rupees or about $80 million to endow the foundation. There are 250 professionals and 1,100 volunteers working for the foundation across India in sixteen different states. Ranjekar said, "Everything is worked out in partnership with the government, and we are not looking for any recognition or brand building. Our kick is when change happens, not to have our name out there. Eventually, the government has to institutionalize initiatives if they are to succeed. We can't be in all of India's schools. Our job is to demonstrate proof of concept, and find out ways and means of changing the mind-set, to create an ecosystem focused on change. The government has to take it from there."

I had heard from many people in India that teacher absenteeism was one of the biggest problems in improving primary education. As government employees, teachers cannot easily be fired. Corruption is a huge problem, with people paying a bribe to get a teacher's position, collecting the salary, and subcontracting with a teenager in the village to show up at the school once in a while. I asked Ranjekar how the foundation got teachers to commit to doing their jobs, especially in rural areas. "That is the focus of our learning guarantee program. It is a voluntary program to begin with. We tell the schools that we will be evaluating all the children in the schools. We will be testing how your children are doing. We will hold that up as a mirror. We will publicize the results to the community. The community needs to take it from there. Parents want good education for their children."

I mentioned how impressed I'd been by the sense of corporate responsibility among the business leaders I'd met in India. Ranjekar was skeptical: "The corporate response is not very encouraging. They can play an important role. They can put pressure on the system by changing their recruitment policy. The fact of the matter is that within five years, India will face a deficit of 350,000 IT professionals. Even so, companies don't want to invest in long-term, indirect commitments. They must admit there is a social component to their business, but most of them talk about is P/E ratios. Corporate leaders have a lack of credibility because there is a lot of hypocrisy. Just give a little something to keep people quiet if you are polluting, then go on polluting. We take an entirely different view. For us, *charity* and *philanthropy* are dirty words. We need systemic change and long-term solutions. We need a professional approach to evolving solutions for public life."

I asked him if Wipro was doing anything outside the foundation, as a company, to demonstrate corporate responsibility. "Absolutely," he replied. "On e-waste," the waste generated by the information technology industry, "for example, Wipro is addressing that."

I was going to Hyderabad the next day. The foundation was working in schools across Andhra Pradesh, including schools in poor areas of Hyderabad. Vijay Gupta put me in touch with Jagadish Babu, who works for the foundation there. Babu arranged for me to visit two schools, and to have a member of the Andhra Pradesh department of education accompany us.

As soon as I landed, I was impressed by the dramatic contrast between Hyderabad and the other Indian cities I knew. Clean, broad avenues lined with shopping malls and luxury apartment complexes, a central lake lined with modern parks, everything lit up in neon at night—Hyderabad, which is fast rivaling Bangalore as India's top IT city, looks more like Bangkok than any other Indian city. As we made our way to the first of the schools we were to visit the next morning, however, and crossed through one of the city's gates into the older part of town, it was like going through some kind of development space warp: suddenly I found myself back in the India of the poor with its dilapidated dwellings, dusty streets, stray goats, and piles of garbage.

The state of Andhra Pradesh has fifty-five thousand primary schools, ten thousand upper primary schools, and twelve thousand high schools. The Azim Premji Foundation is working with five hundred rural schools in the state. If the school can prove it has a legal source of electricity (piracy of electricity in India is rampant) and a room that can be kept clean, then the school is eligible to tap funds from the government of India and the state to get computers. The foundation supplies the educational software.

Babu told me that the first school we were going to visit was in a very poor neighborhood. Monthly family incomes were two thousand rupees per month. That's about $45. The school was set inside a walled enclosure, with a playground in the center. There were flush toilets and a tap for drinking water. There was a clinic where I was told a doctor regularly comes and checks the students' health. "Two students had heart surgery after being checked by the doctor, and one had eye surgery," a teacher told me. All the students receive their immunizations through the clinic. A nutritious meal is served at noontime. Great pots of rice and dal were waiting for the children on the morning I visited. I was impressed by the teachers, all women, who, dressed no better than their students, were of modest means themselves and entirely dedicated. It was near the end of the school term. The tenth-standard students were about to graduate, and some of the girls were hanging on to their teachers, sad to leave these women who had been so important in their lives.

We went upstairs where sandals and rubber flip-flops were piled outside the door of the last room at the end of the open corridor. This was the entrance to the computer lab, which contained ten computers and an air conditioner. Three children sat at each computer. There were children of all ages, but mostly children in the third grade. They were doing different lessons using software developed and provided by the Azim Premji Foundation. I was surprised to see a handmade sign on the wall thanking the American India Foundation. I learned that the computer teacher was subsidized by a grant from AIF. The computers themselves were donated by HP. Thanks to the partnership between corporations, foundations, the state government, and the national government, the children in this school had a computer lab. This kind of three-pronged partnership between government, the private sector, and philanthropy is the key to solving India's problems.

"Five percent of the parents of these children are literate. They can't ever visit the school because they are day laborers, and if they miss a day, they will lose their job. These children have never seen a computer before they come into this room. They like to touch them or even just stand near them. They are fascinated," said Babu.

In the room next door, a hundred children were sitting cross-legged on the floor watching the same computer lesson being done by one child at the head of the class on a keyboard hooked up to a large television set. "There aren't enough computers for all the children to have a turn at once. There are 121 children in the third standard class, 141 in the fifth standard class, so they watch the lesson today. On another day, they will get a turn at the computer," Babu explained. I asked if this was the number of children per classroom per teacher. He said yes.

The representative of the Andhra Pradesh department of education told me, "In Hyderabad, we have a large Muslim population, which is very poor. The government is trying to encourage education. Education is free for girls, and they get free transportation on city buses. When they complete tenth standard, the government deposits money in an account for them. There used to be a lot of nine- or ten-year-old girls sent to the Gulf. Their parents are so poor. Now more are studying in school."

The children were eager to show me what they could do and proud when the computer confirmed a correct response. The teachers told me that they have a before- and after-school program for children whose education has been interrupted or delayed called Bridge to the Future. They can come to school during the off-hours and catch up, with a goal of rejoining their normal class. The teachers showed off PowerPoint presentations the older children had created. Babu told me Andhra Pradesh was one of the first states to introduce computers in India. There is a universal health-insurance program for children. The state had seen a 12 percent improvement in school enrollment and a 50 to 60 percent increase in retention. All teachers have to pass competency tests and attend twenty-one-day refresher courses each year.

"This globalization is making the people want to get more education. There is a lot of impact from this software industry. Everyone wants a better education," said the fellow from the department of education. He said the government of Andhra Pradesh is setting up rural e-service centers where villagers are able to access electronic records of all civic documents, including birth certificates, marriage certificates, tax returns, land titles, caste certificates (important in a country where a percentage of government jobs are reserved for certain castes), and electricity bills. People see information technology in action in their daily lives. This is bound to alert illiterate, rural Indians to the promise of technology and in turn further incite them to demand educational opportunities for their children—which is just what the Azim Premji Foundation wants to happen.

It is difficult to underestimate the impact of India's information technology industry on the country. First, as Narayana Murthy of Infosys pointed out, there is the revolutionary idea of meritocracy, that anyone could make it who got an education and worked hard.

Then, there is the powerful impetus to give back to the country and to scale up educational opportunities so that more of India's future citizens can participate in the country's economic expansion. Finally, there is the transformation of what the Azim Premji Foundation calls the ecosystem, where parents, children, educators, administrators, and finally politicians and business leaders all catch the buzz, where attitudes are transformed. Once enough people involved realize the status quo is not acceptable and that it is in their power to change it, they will force improvement.

The government of India has a program called Sarva Shiksha Abhiyan, whose goal is to insure that all children aged six through fourteen attend school and that all of India's children receive at least eight years of formal schooling. Yet, in 2005, less than half the Indian children who enrolled in first grade finished eighth grade. The dropout rate was 52.79 percent. There are multiple reasons for this. Nineteen percent of primary schools are staffed by a single teacher. Physical facilities are poor. Many lack toilets or running water. Shibani Sachdev, the head of United Way India, told me that over 80 percent of the public schools in the state of Maharashtra, one of India's richest states, lack drinking water. This is in a hot climate. The public schools I have seen have extremely rudimentary facilities. Often, the children sit on the floor because they have no desks or chairs. They work with slates, paper and pencils or pens being far too costly. They share well-worn books. If the school is housed in a concrete building, as many are, it is invariably cheerless. There are no gorgeous plantings, no athletic fields or playground equipment, no artwork hung up in classrooms, and certainly no science labs, art studios, or music rooms. India's public primary schools suffer from high rates of teacher absenteeism, and many children find their educational progress regularly interrupted. In 2005, 42 million children in India between the ages of six and fourteen were not attending school. The persistence of child labor, the millions of internal migrants who take their children with them from job to job, and the widespread discrimination against girls—issues I take up in chapter 6—are also factors that deny many Indian children a primary education.[21]

The image of a sixteen-year-old girl about to graduate from tenth grade, a natural break in India's educational system, whose parents are probably illiterate and whose mother was certainly a mother by her age, clutching her teacher's arm and leaning into her shoulder while they both beam at a PowerPoint presentation she learned to create in a dusty school in a slum because of the faith and dedication of hundreds of motivated individuals who believe in her potential is for me the essence of what is most hopeful about India's future.

Capital Games: Sprucing Up New Delhi

Last year, along every roadway median in Delhi, posters proclaimed, "Chalo Dilli, from Walled City to World City!" *Chalo Dilli* means "Let's go, Delhi." The Commonwealth Games will be held in Delhi in 2010, and India's capital has every intention of being ready to impress international visitors. On the model of what is being required of taxi drivers in Beijing in preparation for the Olympics, Delhi taxi drivers will be required to pass an English-language test upon renewal of their taxi licenses.[22] Not to be beaten by China, Sheila Dikshit, chief minister of Delhi, expressed confidence at a pre–Republic Day ceremony last year that Delhi would host both the Asiad Games in 2014 and the Olympics in 2016. "These international events are a big challenge as Delhi has to make extensive preparation for the Games. But Delhi would definitely become a world-class city in the run-up to the games," she proclaimed.[23]

New Delhi is already the most spacious, greenest urban area in India. No slums are visible in New Delhi, though hidden in some of the by-lanes are small clutches of huts, but plenty of slums surround Delhi. Wherever there is empty ground, some of the five hundred thousand people who pour into the city each year in search of opportunity or mere survival have set up what shelter they can.[24] These *jhuggis,* as they are called, have for decades been the bane of India's better classes and government leaders bent on modernizing the country. Indira Gandhi famously got into trouble when she used the powers she'd granted herself by declaring a state of emergency in 1975 to summarily raze slums. This and other autocratic abuses got her kicked out of office nineteen months later. Every one of the Indian government's five-year plans has included urban planning and low-cost housing, but little has actually been done and the problem grows by the day. In the years since Indira Gandhi's emergency, slums in India's major cities have again and again been cleared, only to pop up either in the same place or somewhere nearby. In 2004, in Delhi, thousands of huts were cleared along the Yamuna River. In 2005, ninety thousand huts in Bombay were demolished to make way for urban development, leaving 350,000 people homeless.[25] Last year, the United Nations reprimanded India for the manner in which it was clearing slums. India made no response.

Laid out by Edwin Lutyens to reflect the grandeur of the British Raj, New Delhi was completed in 1929, after which the British moved their administrative capital there from "Old Delhi," as it is now called, to the north. Here, roughly within the confines of a series of old Mughal walls, are the remnants of different capital cities going back to AD 800, each built up, then conquered and razed to the ground, to be built up, conquered, and razed again by a series of invading armies. The narrow lanes of Chandni Chowk where the cries of vendors compete over three-wheeler horns and blaring Bollywood film songs are in Old Delhi. Wide avenues lined with sprawling white bungalows set amid lush private gardens are in New Delhi. The whole agglomeration is referred to as Delhi. All around Delhi are sprinkled the magnificent architectural remains of past empires: the Red Fort, Kutb Minar, Purana Qila, the ancient tombs in Lodi Gardens, the old city gates, including Kashmiri Gate, and the mosques, including the historic Jama Masjid.

Sadly, untold numbers of architectural remnants of Delhi's layered past are being obliterated by the rush to modernize and build up the city as fast as possible.[26] This is true all over India, where there is virtually no effort to save the architectural heritage of the country apart from the most famous monuments. Stately old *havelis* or merchants' houses, with their interior courtyards and elaborately carved balconies and window friezes, crumble indifferently to ruin or are demolished to make way for undistinguished concrete blocks of apartments. It's all part of India's impatient development.

Delving into the Past to
Sustain the Future

Traditional Indian architecture did not just reflect an ancient ecosystem that united human activity and the natural world in the motifs carved in its stone. Its design emerged out of the environment in which it evolved. Natural solutions had to be found to extremes of heat and cold, to searing winds and torrential rains. Water was a perennial problem. The entire exquisite city of Fatehpur Sikri, located near Agra, the site of the famous Taj Mahal tomb, had to be abandoned in 1585 when it ran out of water.

Karan Grover is an architect who is reaching into India's past to find appropriate technologies that can be applied to invent a better future. Karan's interest in India's rich architectural heritage led him to spend two decades getting Champaner-Pavagadh Archaeological Park in the state of Gujarat, India, named a UNESCO World Heritage Site in 2004. Muhammad Begada, the Muslim king of Gujarat, moved his capital to Champaner from Ahmadabad in 1484. It took twenty-three years to build the city, which included markets, town squares, royal gardens, water structures, and mosques. The city was conquered by Humayun in 1535, Gujarat's capital was moved back to Ahmadabad, and Champaner was deserted. It lay in ruins, overgrown with jungle, when the British came upon it in 1803.

"For years, I led a dual life," Karan told me in the living room of his home in Baroda. The walls were completely covered with paintings, including a portrait of Karan by acclaimed Baroda-school artist Bhupen Khakhar. "I'd work from nine to five in the office, and from five to nine on Champaner. I kept the two completely separate. Then I realized they were interlinked. You cannot avoid culture." It became evident to Karan that the architectural heritage of western India contained in physical form wisdom about how to achieve harmony between the human and the natural worlds. The step wells, he understood, were not only stone monuments, but receptacles for harvesting precious water during the monsoon rains. The *jalis,* carved stone screens, provided tempered sunlight while channeling cooling breezes. The pleasure gardens wove greenery around the buildings.

Karan now incorporates traditional Indian architectural elements into his modern architecture as a way of achieving both aesthetic and environmental harmony. He won the Leadership in Energy and Environmental Design (LEED) Platinum Award from the U.S. Green Building Council for his design of the Confederation of Indian Industry Sohrabji Godrej Green Building Center. He said modestly, "We were surprised to get this for something we've been doing for thirty years." His design resulted in a 50 percent energy savings; a 35 percent reduction in water consumption; and 15 percent increased productivity from the people working in the building. Eighty-eight percent of the building does not require artificial light, and 75 percent of occupants have a daylight view. When he designed the Adivasi Academy at Tejgadh (The Institute of National Excellence in Tribal Studies), he used only brick, no cement. He liberally incorporates *jalis* and courtyards. The CII building he designed in Gurgaon runs parallel to a long garden onto which all the windows face. When I visited the building in April, the temperature was forty-five degrees Celsius (113°F), but in the garden it was bearable. Now he's building the world's largest green building in Calcutta.

Karan's ambition is to design a green city for India. "Everything in the world is connected. Pollution here goes there," he argues. He laments that India has no national conservation policy, and that so many old buildings are being torn down to make way for haphazard modern development. He showed me photographs of the ABB office building he designed in Bangalore where he incorporated wind towers from traditional architecture in Sind. "The hot air enters the tower, and by the time it flows down into the building, it's been cooled down by eleven degrees."

Delhi Metro

Delhi is also the site of India's best urban renewal story, the spanking new mass-transit rail system known as Delhi Metro. Only four cities in India have a metropolitan rail system: Bombay, Calcutta, Chennai, and Delhi. The Mumbai Suburban Rail System, India's largest, sees more than 5.5 million rider trips per day.[27] Its trains are a lifeline connecting distant northern suburbs to the financial hub at the city's southern tip. They are also hopelessly overcrowded, with passengers hanging off the side of compartment doors a common sight. Calcutta has a quaint old system of aboveground trolley cars. It put in an underground metro system in the 1980s, which is still remarkably well run, but service is limited. Chennai's system includes fourteen stations on a 15.5-kilometer elevated line. All major and midsize Indian cities offer bus service, which is how the majority of urban Indians get around. But Delhi Metro is truly the jewel in India's mass transportation crown. The credit goes to one man: E. Sreedharan, "alpha engineer," as he is sometimes called, former head of the Konkan Railway, and manager extraordinaire of Delhi Metro.

Now seventy-three years old, Mr. Sreedharan told me, "They won't let me retire. I have to serve at least three more years." A slight, gray-haired gentleman dressed formally in a suit and tie, E. Sreedharan is modest about his personal role in the success of Delhi Metro. "We are a team. Many people worked very hard to make Delhi Metro a reality." No doubt Mr. Sreedharan assembled a first-class team, but no other person in India, indeed in the world, has been able to pull off the feat he has. The Delhi Metro was built in record time, under budget. It was profitable from day one. A ticket costs as little as six rupees (thirteen cents). The stations and the trains are spotlessly clean. The trains run on time, every six minutes during rush hour. The Delhi Metro, as of this writing, comprises fifty stations and transports 450,000 commuters every day. According to Mr. Sreedharan, Delhi Metro will carry over a million passengers per day within the next three years. To those familiar with legendary Indian inefficiency, broken-down public conveyances, and filthy public spaces, the Delhi Metro is simply a miracle.

In his comfortable New Delhi office furnished in deep burgundy colors and dark wood, Mr. Sreedharan told me, "A combination of many factors contributed to our success." He insisted on having a free hand as a condition of taking the job. He handpicked his team. He sought advice from five different international companies, three from Japan, one from the United States, and one from India. He sent his team abroad to see for themselves how other systems worked. "There was a lot of resistance to the metro when we started. It will be too expensive, bleed the country, objections like that. That has totally changed. Everyone wants more lines now. They all thought that it would be a big drain, financially, but we have, in fact, made a hand-some profit. We were able to repay a loan we got from Japan with 1.3 percent interest."

The accomplishment of which E. Sreedharan is most proud is the change in mind-set that Delhi Metro has had on the citizens of Delhi. "The metro is already changing life in Delhi. Passengers have to be disciplined. They are learning to wait in line. The metro is clean. People don't spit, throw trash, or make graffiti. They have learned respect for a public asset. They realize that Delhi Metro is theirs." Behind him on the wall is a map of Delhi and photos of gleaming trains pulled up to platforms. "Delhi Metro has increased people's wealth and improved their health, and they realize it. Businesses near stations have experienced a thirty to thirty-five percent increase in their business. Property values have gone up fifty to sixty percent along the lines. There is a significant reduction in pollution, down thirty percent along metro lines. And road accidents are down thirty percent as well."

E. Sreedharan started Delhi Metro from scratch in 1998. The ini-tial phase was completed three years ahead of schedule and cost $2.3 billion. I live in New York's East Village. Since the 1920s, the City of New York has been discussing building a new subway line under Sec-ond Avenue. Recently, there was talk again of building the Second Avenue subway line. It was estimated that it would take sixteen years to complete and cost $17 billion. Work has still not begun. Maybe the Metropolitan Transportation Authority of New York should hire E. Sreedharan. That's what other cities in India are doing. Bombay wants three lines. So does Hyderabad. Bangalore has signed up for two lines, Calcutta for an east-west line, and Cochin wants a couple of lines. Delhi Metro has not only catalyzed a change in mentality and brought cheap, reliable, high-quality mass transportation to India's capital, it has inspired other Indian cities to embrace rapid mass transit as a complement to the country's automotive boom.

A Two-Room Apartment for $6,500

J. B. D'Souza, the former head of Bombay's public bus transport system, known by its acronym, B.E.S.T., who is still admired for the way he ran one of the world's biggest urban bus systems, was involved during the early 1970s in creating a plan to create a satellite city to complement Bombay. The brainchild of acclaimed architect Charles Correa, Shirish Patel, and Pravina Mehta, New Bombay would be a self-contained city for the common man. Far from the crush of the original city, the new city would be located across the water from Bombay's skinny southern peninsula.

More than thirty years ago, the decline in quality of life in Bombay was already worrisome to its residents. My aunts and uncles remember Bombay in the 1950s as a clean, pleasant city where you could always get a seat on the commuter trains and where young women traveled unmolested day or night. Two decades later, by the 1970s, that had changed. Mumbaikars watched as their beautiful city began to deteriorate under the combined stress of an unrelenting influx of people and the apparent indifference or impotence of a succession of municipal governments. All the problems that Mumbaikars lament today—overcrowded trains, dirty streets, fetid drains, derelict buildings, strained infrastructure, expanding slums, pavement dwellers—were the subject of concern three decades ago.

Correa, Patel, Mehta, and D'Souza designed New Bombay with the common citizen's needs in mind. They put a high value on public transportation, bicycle lanes, and affordable housing. The plan was never implemented, much to D'Souza's deep disappointment. "New Bombay," he laments, "has left our dreams behind. Nearly all our wonderful ambitions have turned sour. The transportation system? No different than elsewhere in India. Cycle tracks and bus lanes? Abandoned and forgotten."[28] The absence of bicycle lanes in a poor country with severe air pollution is quite striking in Indian urban transportation planning, especially when bicycle lanes have become an integrated part of urban transportation infrastructure in European and American cities. In New York City, for example, there are plans to make bicycle transportation more convenient and safer than it is now as a way to help reduce the use of automobiles in the city.

Despite the setback of New Bombay, J. B. D'Souza never gave up trying to do something for Bombay's working poor. He told me last year about another, more modest project he'd been working on: an affordable housing complex in the northern Bombay suburb of Goregaon. He was going up to the site of the housing complex for a board meeting the next day. I asked if I could come along, and he was gracious enough to say yes. J. B. D'Souza is in his eighties now, but just as sharp and committed to Bombay as ever. From his apartment in Bandra, we took a classic, old, white Ambassador sedan up to Goregaon. On the way, he told me the project had been initiated by activist Mrinal Gore back in the 1970s but that she had asked him to handle it. He went to the chief minister of Maharashtra and asked for some cheap land, which was given in Goregaon for twenty-five rupees per acre. It took twelve years to push the project through local bureaucracy. They planned to sell the flats for 2.5 lakh rupees (about $3,750) but by the time the flats were actually completed, they cost 3 lakhs. "Today," he told me, "they're selling for eight lakhs." Eight lakhs is about $20,000. This is a fraction of their market value. The flats are 280 to 320 square feet. They are divided into two rooms. A flat that size in south Bombay, in a nice area, would sell for $200,000.

On the way, we passed a modern shopping mall called The Hub. It had a multiplex theater and a McDonald's visible from the main road. The road, already four lanes, was being widened. High above our heads where a hill had neatly been sliced through, the gaping insides of small brick huts were visible. Whatever machine cut through the mountain also cut right through these little dwellings. Raw sewage drained down the side of the hill. We turned off the main road and headed toward the housing complex. At an intersection, we passed women and children ferrying loads of gravel for road construction in straw baskets on their heads. Peasants from Rajasthan, the women wore bright, gathered skirts, red half-saris, and stacks of faux-ivory plastic bangles. These costumes seemed so incongruous in far suburban Bombay. On the corner, we passed a bar and restaurant called Paris.

By the time we reached our destination, it was late morning, and hot. Towering in front of us, at the base of a high hill, were tall, visibly fancy residential high-rises. I asked J. B. D'Souza what they were. He told me it was a luxury development by big builder Raheja. Apparently, a brand-new road was being constructed to link the new housing complex directly to Navi Mumbai around the back of the hill.

We arrived at the complex, and while Mr. D'Souza went into his meeting, he had the site engineer, Kishore Joshi, take me around. Mr. Joshi told me the name of the trust that built the complex is Nagari Niwara, which means "shelter for rural people." He said the flats were for people earning between 1.5 to 3 or 4 lakhs per year. There were four thousand flats. I weighed these four thousand subsidized flats, which took decades to build, against the 10 million people living in Bombay's slums. While Nagari Niwara is a noble effort on the part of a few dedicated volunteers, the city is going to have to do much, much better if it is to solve its acute housing crisis. Mr. Joshi told me up to ten people live in a room here, standard occupancy for Bombay.

We visited flats in various stages of completion. They were completely built of concrete. Almost no wood was used. It is too expensive. Because the walls were solid concrete, all the plumbing and electrical conduits had to be set beforehand. The paths between the buildings were roughly paved. Cars and motorcycles were parked around the ground floors. Washing hung out to dry from windows secured with iron bars. Mr. Joshi took me to a newer, posher section in the complex where 450-square-foot, one-bedroom flats were selling for nine lakhs rupees, or about $22,000. He confessed, "So many people have bought the flat to give on a rental basis only. They are not living here. They stay in their slum locality where they have a community. The small flats rent for two thousand to twenty-five hundred rupees per month; the larger ones for three thousand to thirty-five hundred. It is a good income for them."

There is a bus every fifteen to twenty minutes that connects the housing complex to the Goregaon commuter rail station.

We went up to visit the site of a future park in the complex. A few palms had been planted, but mostly it was still wasteland. Below, adjacent to the housing complex, was an open area with the rough tents and open cooking fires of migrant laborers. Mr. Joshi told me they came from northern India, from villages in Punjab. They were working on the Raheja luxury apartments. Joshi said his company, like all the builders, also uses independent labor contractors to get construction workers. "This is a transit area," he said. When I asked him what that meant, he explained that the migrant laborers would only be around long enough to get the project done, then they'd move on to the next one. "Once this is built up, they will be gone," he said, smiling.

New Cities to Renew the Nation

A. G. Menon, director of the School of Habitat Studies in New Delhi, predicts that urban India, which currently accounts for 28 percent of the country's population, will see that share "double within thirty years."[29] This means that India's urban population will increase by 290 million people, or the equivalent of the population of the entire United States, by 2036. India's cities must absorb 10 million new residents per year; that's the equivalent of adding a Paris or a Moscow every year. These new city dwellers are going to need mass transit. They are also going to need housing, sanitation, water, power, schools, hospitals, and parks. This is a very different situation from the United States where migrant laborers from Mexico and Latin America have moved into dying American towns and brought new life to local schools and businesses, abandoned after local family farms went under or local industry moved on.

A. G. Menon believes, like the team of Correa, Mehta, Patel, and D'Souza in the 1970s, that, given the rapid rate of urban growth in India and the abysmal state of India's megacities today, the only solution is to build new cities. The cost of such an undertaking far eclipses the abilities of India's government. The private sector must play a central role, but the scale is more daunting now than ever.

Mukesh Ambani is not intimidated. The chairman of Reliance Industries Limited (RIL)—the biggest private-sector company in the country with a market capitalization of over $35 billion—is planning to construct two large cities, one near Bombay and one near Delhi, from scratch. These cities, as Ambani sees it, will be part of a new economic and social ecosystem linking India's rural agricultural areas to the country's urban agglomerations. The new ecosystem will provide urban multitudes what they need and demand, and rural millions with services and opportunities that will allow them to stick closer to home, relieving some of the influx into existing cities of the rural dispossessed.

I met with Ambani last year in his modest offices near Nariman Point in Bombay to find out what his perspective was on India at this moment of accelerating change. A vibrant, abstract painting in glowing reds and oranges by Raza was in the foyer outside. A large color photographic portrait of his father, Dhirubhai Ambani, like the one I saw at DAIS, hung on one of the walls. When we were seated on comfortable white, upholstered sofas, Ambani shared with me his vision of a resurgent India. At the core of that vision is the imperative to "create purchasing power and turn India's poor into consumers."

Ambani's role model is his father, whose rags-to-riches career is the stuff of modern Indian legend: "My father always said that the way to create value is to create something out of nothing. That's what he did with Reliance." In an era when hereditary houses dominated India's business landscape, Dhirubhai Ambani started as a nobody with nothing. He grew Reliance by taking quantum leaps, moving the company from a garment manufacturer, to a textile company, to a polyester factory, and finally to the owner of India's largest, and the world's third-largest, oil refinery. The refinery was built in record time, three years, and transformed India from an importer into an exporter of refined petroleum products. The company has also branched out into telecommunications. Dhirubhai Ambani's dream was to make it possible for anyone in India to make a phone call for less than the cost of a postcard. That dream was realized last year.

Ambani has inherited both his father's outsized ambition and his commitment to drive down costs to a level affordable to every Indian.

His enterprise knows no bounds: he believes that by changing India, he can change the world. He is focused on nothing less than so radically transforming his country that it will one day—sooner rather than later, if Ambani has anything to do with it—change the planet. To do that, he knows that he must not only invent a new paradigm, he must do it fast and on a huge scale.

Ambani's transformational plan for India rests on three pillars: revolutionize farming and retail; create new cities; insure India's energy security.

Reliance will invest $5 billion by 2011 in creating a distribution system linking farmers with small as well as large-surface mixed retail stores, all using the latest technologies. What he is envisioning is sort of a marriage of the ITC model with the Bharti model, but with a unique Reliance twist and on the inimitable Reliance scale. The plan is to generate $20 billion in agricultural exports every year, plus stock thousands of stores in fifteen hundred towns and cities across India. About seventy distribution centers will relay the flow of produce out and inputs in. On the domestic side, Ambani sees $25 billion in annual sales and the creation of 1 million new jobs.

There could potentially be a lot of upheaval. Ambani is aware of the fears that the thousands of small mom-and-pop *kiranas* will be put out of business, and that many farmers just won't make it. He views this initiative as "the full flowering of our basic philosophy of share and prosper." He has publically called upon the Reliance management team to create a virtuous circle of prosperity by bringing farmers, small shopkeepers, and consumers into a win-win partnership. He also hopes that the changes that will happen in India's rural heartland will create higher incomes, good schools, health-care facilities, and shopping and entertainment opportunities that will keep a substantial number from migrating to the megacities who otherwise would have. Still, with the transformations he foresees, millions of people will move from rural areas toward cities. He knows India's cities are totally overloaded, their infrastructure incapable of handling the population they must bear already. He also knows that cutting through entrenched interests and bureaucracies takes too much time, time that India doesn't have. Ambani has a simple solution: build new cities.

Reliance will spend $11 billion, more than twice what it is investing in overhauling India's agricultural economy, between now and 2010 to construct two major new cities. Taking advantage of the generous terms offered by the government of India for businesses that wish to set up Special Economic Zones, Reliance has acquired 140 square miles of farmland southeast of Bombay at a fraction of the price of land in the city, near where a new airport is being constructed. All necessary infrastructure is being put in, and investors are lining up to be part of the venture. Here too Ambani sees another $25 billion a year of economic activity. Reliance is guaranteed to make a bundle: the return on the investment in land alone will be phenomenal. A similar city is planned near Delhi.

The third pillar of India's transformation will be insuring the country's energy security by expanding its petroleum supply and refining capability while at the same time reducing its dependency on fossil fuels. Reliance is researching jatropha and cellulose as sources of biofuels. This seems a surprising ambition for the owner of an Indian oil refinery. Ambani is also investing $6 billion to expand Reliance's refinery in Jamnagar, Gujarat, to make it the largest in the world.

Chevron is also investing in the expansion, taking a 5 percent stake now with the possibility of increasing that to 29 percent. The American company has decided it makes more business sense to invest in the Reliance refinery in India and get the oil products from there to the United States via tanker ships than to invest in upgrading refining capacity in the United States or Europe, where environmental restrictions make setting up a new refinery more difficult and expensive. Chevron is actively prospecting for oil in Bangladesh. Reliance's Jamnagar refinery is a likely destination to refine that oil if it materializes. The geopolitical implications of this kind of shift in refining capacity toward India are intriguing.

I visited the Reliance refinery several years ago. A highlight of the visit was a ride in an open jeep at night when the place was lit up like a Christmas tree and hummed with the buzz of a thousand high-tension lines. The enormous refinery is surrounded by a campus planted with millions of trees all watered via drip irrigation with the waste water from cooling the plant. Jamnagar is in an arid part of

India. To get the water necessary for the plant's operations, Reliance built a desalination plant. During the dry season, the refinery supplies water to the city of Jamnagar and other neighboring villages.

Because of his experience with desalination, Ambani isn't worried about a water shortage in India. "India is one of the few countries with seawater all around. We've already demonstrated we can do desalination," he said confidently. The construction of a desalination plant to supply water to water-strapped Chennai was approved in 2005 by the city's municipal water authority, with the contract going to Hyderabad-based infrastructure company IVRCL. India's National Institute of Ocean Technology opened the world's first low-temperature desalination plant in the country's Lakshadweep Islands. Tata has won a contract to construct a desalination plant to provide water for a nuclear reactor in Tamil Nadu. As Ambani confirmed, desalination is already on its way to providing water-poor India with a means of meeting growing water needs.

I asked him what the downsides were, if there were any obstacles he saw to pulling off his fantastic vision of India's future. He immediately ticked off a list: "Education, we are not investing in education. Right now the whole thing is being driven by tremendous aspiration, but we need more education. Employment: IT created one million jobs. It inspired the nation. Now we are going into the wholistic knowledge sector in the next twenty years and we are going to create one hundred million jobs. From there, we'll take it up to two hundred million." He paused so I could catch up with my note-taking. "I'll give you an example. For the expansion of the refinery in Jamnagar, we couldn't find the qualified welders we needed, so we are training fifteen thousand welders. Then, there is self-employment. Right now the farmer gets maybe four rupees for what he produces that sells in the marketplace for one hundred and twenty rupees. If we get the rural sector growing, we can create a new model that will enrich the farmers. Contract farming won't work in the long term. You need to give these people purchasing power. We will connect the people growing apples, say, with people who want to buy apples. Right now, they are not connected."

I told him about the people I'd met in Vidarbha where even those who had access to water couldn't pump it into their fields because they had no electricity. Again, he surprised me. "We have to get off the grid." My jaw nearly dropped. I could not imagine an oil executive in the United States saying this. "Forget fossil fuels," he continued. "You take biomass and use it to generate power. Everyone has his own generator. You have to cut the wire. Go wireless. We've done it in India with telecom. Now we will do it with power." This is certainly one way Ambani envisions changing the paradigm for India that could change the whole world.

I asked him what India's number one challenge was.

"Our biggest challenge is the challenge nobody has solved in the world: how to grow equity. Across a five-hundred-meter radius from where I stay, there is a one to one billion income differential. This is not sustainable."

Ambani checked his watch. He looked as if he needed to end the interview but had one last thing he wanted to say: "This generation will be the one to make or mar India. This is our chance. At least we are aware of the problems and what we have to do. I tell my American friends, being a bully doesn't help. Give us some space. My view is that we are rebalancing the world. For too long fifteen percent of the people controlled eighty-five percent of the wealth. Now it's time to give the eighty-five percent of the people their chance. Only twenty percent of mankind has really progressed up to now. If we can take that up to seventy percent, we will have accomplished something. These twenty-five years will determine whether we all sink or swim. This is such an exciting time. We are very lucky to be participating in it."

He checked his watch again. "I have to go help my son with his homework." He smiled apologetically. "I promised him." We got up from the sofas. He was wearing a pair of black slacks and a white safari shirt. I shook his hand and wished him well: one way or another, Mukesh Ambani and Reliance, more than any other single corporate leader or company, are going to change India. And by changing India on the scale they propose, they will have a considerable impact on our planet.

CHAPTER SIX

The Other India

I T TOOK EUROPE AND THE UNITED STATES MORE THAN THREE centuries to go through three successive industrial revolutions: manufacturing, services, and digital. Millions of European peasants left their homes and migrated to cities where they massed in slums and worked for pittances in the new factories. Millions moved farther to the United States, Canada, Australia, and countries in Latin America in search of land and opportunity. Europe's social and political upheaval spawned powerful new political ideologies, bitter contestations over national destinies and the international order, aggressive colonial expansion, bloody revolutions, and terrible wars.

India is going through all three industrial revolutions at once. At the velocity of the information age, the country is being transformed from an ancient agrarian society into a modern manufacturing hub and a global services provider. Some Indians will change from peasant to IT-enabled professional in just a few years. The transformation of India into a consumer society is threatening core values and challenging old identities. People are being propelled away from a world they understand toward a new world they have yet to define.

The resulting strain on India's social fabric is enormous. India is undergoing creative destruction that inevitably leads to social violence ranging from the brutal dislocation of people from their ancestral lands to the bewilderment of parents who feel their children turning away from tradition. The many fault lines of Indian society—caste, gender, religion—threaten India's success. As change accelerates, and as those who suffer the most from the process continue to have the least power over their fate, the prospect of outright revolt by India's poor, and of caste and religious warfare, increases. Millions of India's poor watch the meteoric rise of the privileged classes and wonder if their chance will come.

Aside from limited numbers of laborers that go to the Arabian Gulf, India has no place to send its excess unskilled population in need of jobs and livelihoods. No more tracts of land are waiting for settlement on our planet, assuming Indians wished to migrate as so many European peasants did. India cannot expand the scope of natural resources available for imperial conquest, as Europe did. With limited land and resources, India must find a way to provide a decent life to a population that already stands at 1.2 billion and will not stop increasing until it reaches 1.6 billion.

Given the extreme disparities and the social and cultural dislocations India is experiencing, the astounding thing is that there isn't a full-fledged revolution. Most of the time, people go about their business quite peaceably. Indians regularly join hands across caste and religious lines and help each other out in times of crisis. They did so in the aftermath of the terrible earthquake that devastated Gujarat state in 2001, during the monsoon flooding in Bombay in 2005, and in the wake of the many terrorist attacks that have hit the country in recent years. India's extreme inequality, however, is becoming less and less tenable. My whole life, I have heard members of India's urban, educated elite observe, rather smugly, "Look at the conditions people live in. Anywhere else in the world there'd be a revolution, but not in India." Recently, I've heard people say that unless the lot of the poor improves soon and dramatically, the poor will rise up and slit the throats of the rich. "They have television now, you know. They can see the life they are denied."

Caste

Peter Osnos, the founding publisher of Public Affairs books, was born in Bombay during World War II to Jewish refugee parents from

Eastern Europe. He showed me his Indian birth certificate. On the line after caste was typed "Polish." It was obviously unthinkable to the doctor or administrator at the hospital where Osnos was born to leave the line for caste blank.

India is a severely hierarchical society, in which a caste system orders human beings from inferior to superior rank and allots them specific social roles. India's caste hierarchy bleeds into every aspect of Indian society. Non-Hindus, including Muslims and Christians, though they are outside the caste system, are not exempt from its influence. Some long-established Christian communities in India observe caste differences. Indians are among the most status-sensitive people in the world. Rank is important in India and dictates the minutiae of social interaction.[1] The familiar tone of social interaction in the United States, where students can address teachers and employees their corporate leaders by their first names, is quite shocking in India. High-status Indians enjoy certain privileges and a certain lifestyle, and low-status Indians do without, and many in both groups accept this as the natural order.

The British codified India's complex and almost infinitely subdivided caste system into simplified categories for administrative purposes. Successive governments of independent India further defined caste categories. It is complicated. The Mandal Commission, charged with putting into place an affirmative action program for lower-caste Indians, included three thousand castes under the designation Other Backward Castes in its 1990 recommendations. On government forms, applications for jobs or school admissions, Indians may be asked to state their caste.

Much of the time, a person's caste is evident from his name. Trivedi is a Brahman name. Balmiki is a Dalit name. My own name, Kamdar, is a job designation. As recently as my great-grandfather, my ancestors were courtiers to the princes of Kathiawad, in the state of Gujarat. They were in charge of managing public works: road construction, palace repairs, water tank excavation. *Kam* means "work." The *kamdar* is the person in charge of the work. Our caste is Vaishya, the merchant caste born of Brahma's thighs according to Hindu legend. Brahmans emerged from Brahma's mouth, hence their caste profession of reciting holy verses. Kshatriyas, the warrior caste, arose from Brahma's arms. Sudras, manual laborers and artisans, derived from Brahma's feet. Any Gujarati and most Indians would instantly know my family's caste from my name.

Dalits, formerly called untouchables, or Scheduled Castes, constitute 16 percent of India's population. Scheduled Tribes, indigenous peoples preferably called Adivasis now, represent only 7 percent. Other Backward Castes (OBCs) are the great majority; 52 percent of India's citizens are OBCs. These three lower-caste categories add up to 75 percent of India's population.

Lower castes are guaranteed certain proportions of government jobs and university admission slots. As a result, caste designations have become highly politicized.[2] Indian democracy has been transformed during the past few decades by the emergence of new political parties representing the interests of specific castes. Affirmative action in India has taken the form of quotas or reservations. How many government jobs should be reserved for OBCs? Should there be job quotas in the private sector for Scheduled Castes and Tribes? What percentage of university admission slots should these categories command? These are highly charged political issues in India.

In 1990, when the Mandal Commission proposed raising the 22.5 percent of university admissions and public-sector job slots reserved for lower castes to 27 percent, upper-caste Indians reacted violently. Several students even immolated themselves in protest. Competition for educational and job opportunities in India is fierce, and upper-caste Indians are loath to give up their privileges. Though they constitute less than 15 percent of the population, upper castes dominate the upper echelons of education and society and consume a disproportionate share of the country's resources.

In 2006, the government proposed extending caste reservations to the private sector where job growth is. An emotional and highly charged debate about the issue ensued, with the private sector immediately and forcefully rejecting the idea. Looking to survive in a highly competitive international environment, India's companies want to be free to hire the most qualified candidates they can find, whatever their background. The argument of those who would do away with affirma-

tive action for lower castes entirely is that economic growth and better education for all will, in time, solve the problem. This may be true,
but in the meantime, the continued economic division of India along
caste lines threatens to explode into caste warfare.[3]

India's Prime Minister Manmohan Singh has warned Indian business that if it wishes to avoid mandatory reservations for lower-caste
employees, it had better "invest much more in vocational training and
technical education, particularly for youth from a less privileged background" and insure that employee populations begin to reflect the
caste composition of the general population.[4] India is a democracy.
The majority of voters are lower caste, and they are more and more
conscious of both the injustice of their situation and of their political
power.

Hindu Nationalism

On January 30, 1948, Mahatma Gandhi was assassinated by Nathu-
ram Godse, a Hindu nationalist convinced that the great leader had
betrayed India's Hindus in his commitment to equity in the division
of assets between India and Pakistan following partition. Godse's
crime dealt a severe blow to the cause of radical Hindu nationalism,
forcing it underground for a number of years. Gradually, however, as
the power of the Congress Party eroded and memories of Gandhi
faded, Hindu nationalism became an increasingly powerful political
force in India. In the 1980s, the Hindu right mobilized around the
mission of Ram Janmaboomi, dedicated to razing the Babri Masjid,
a mosque in the city of Ajodhya built in 1528 to honor the memory
of Babur, the founder of the Mogul empire. In the common fashion
of the day, the mosque had been built on the ruins of a Hindu temple.
Hindu militants claimed that this particular temple marked the location of the birth of the Hindu god Rama.

On December 6, 1992, Hindu militants stormed the Babri Masjid
and tore it down. Violence exploded across India as rioting between
Hindus and Muslims swept the country, including in traditionally tol-
erant and diverse Bombay. Bombay's Muslim neighborhoods were

sacked. Muslim citizens were hunted down and killed while fleeing in the streets or cowering in their homes. Hindus were also killed by angry Muslims. However, the Hindu-committed violence was systematic: Hindus had the municipal government of Bal Thackeray and his Shiv Sena party on their side, helping identify Muslim homes and businesses and coordinating with the police to insure the mobs a free hand.

On March 12, 1993, bombs went off in the heart of Bombay's financial and business district indiscriminately killing hundreds of people. The bomb blasts, masterminded by Bombay underworld don Dawood Ibrahim, were a token of revenge by Islamic terrorist groups based in Pakistan for the demolition of the Babri Masjid and subsequent attacks on India's Muslims. Ibrahim remains at large and is believed to be living in Pakistan or Dubai.

With the 1993 Bombay blasts, a link was made between the domestic conflicts between Hindus and Muslims in India and Islamic militants based in Pakistan who were principally focused on the accession of Indian Kashmir to Pakistan. This would have serious consequences for India's citizens. In the many episodes of violence between India's Hindus and Muslims since the Babri Masjid incident in 1992, thousands of people have lost their lives and property.

The worst happened in Gujarat in 2002. Narendra Modi, one of the senior members of the Bharatiya Janata Party (BJP), a Hindu nationalist party, and the chief minister of his state, presided over one of the worst genocides in a democracy in recent times. The massacre was set off when Hindu militants on a train returning from Ajodhya were attacked near the Gujarati town of Godhra. What exactly transpired is subject to furious debate, but over fifty Hindus, including women and children, were burned to death in their railway carriage. After a brief period of calm, a systematic massacre of the state's Muslims began. Modi's government was complicit in genocide, with electoral rolls and other government records used to identify Muslim homes and businesses, exactly as was done in Delhi when Sikhs were targeted for reprisals following the assassination of Prime Minister Indira Gandhi by her Sikh bodyguards.

In both cases, the police generally stood by and did nothing as people were dragged out of their homes and butchered in the most vicious manner. "We have no orders to save you," quipped infamously one policeman to desperate Muslims fleeing a rampaging mob as cited in a thorough and damning investigative report compiled by Human Rights Watch.[5] None of the individuals responsible has been punished, and Modi was subsequently reelected by a landslide by the Hindu majority in his state.

In 2005, based on the report of India's National Human Rights Commission on the Gujarat massacre, Modi's visa to the United States was revoked under Section 212(a)(2)(g) of the Immigration and Nationality Act, which applies to any foreign government official who "directly carried out, at any time, particularly severe violations of religious freedom." Modi is reputed to be applying for a new visa to enter the United States.

Gujarat is a wealthy state. Many successful Gujaratis are in the Indian diaspora, including in the United States. My own family is of Gujarati origin. The BJP, Modi's party, has strong support among conservative Indian-Americans, including Gujaratis. When his visa was revoked, Modi had been invited to the United States to address the Asian American Hotel Owners Association, a group with a large number of Gujarati Americans. Until 2004, while the BJP was in power, the party vigorously courted support from Indian-Americans, even going so far as to name Bhishma K. Agnihotri, an activist with the Overseas Friends of the BJP and an American citizen, as its "ambassador-at-large for NRIs/PIOs" (nonresident Indians/persons of Indian origin).

Hindu militancy is firmly established in the United States. In addition to the Overseas Friends of the BJP, there is a plethora of so-called pro-Hindu groups. Raising money from deep-pocketed Indian-Americans for projects in India is a core activity of these groups. Dubbed "saffron dollars" after the orange color sacred to Hindus, money from the United States is an important source of financial support for the BJP, the RSS, and the VHP in India. An attempt by Hindu militants in the United States affiliated with the VHP to extend the BJP's rewriting of Indian history to textbooks used in California's public schools led to a heated controversy in 2006 in which prominent American historians of India, including Stanley Wolpert of

UCLA and Michael Witzel of Harvard University, felt compelled to participate.[6]

Despite the facile equation Indian = Hindu that many people on the Hindu right wish Americans who don't know India well would make, Indian-Americans are as diverse as Indians themselves. Considerable numbers of Indian Muslims are in the United States, as well as Sikhs, Indian Christians, Zoroastrian Parsis, and Jains (my own family are Jain). Moreover, the majority of Hindus in the United States do not subscribe to the ideology of *hindutva* or to Hindu militancy. The BJP is not in power at the national level in India anymore, but the current UPA coalition is fragile. Many Indians have told me they have no doubt the BJP will return to power someday soon, stronger than ever.

India's Fight against Terrorism

On July 11, 2006, Bombay's commuter rail system was racked by a carefully executed series of powerful bomb blasts. Explosions occurred on different trains at different stations during the evening rush hour when trains were guaranteed to be packed. One hundred sixty-three people were killed outright. This horrible attack on innocent citizens in India's financial capital echoed the blasts of 1993. Prime Minister Singh called for calm.

The most poignant tales of the bombings concerned the homeless children who were victims of the blasts. Railway stations in India are magnets for children on the streets, whether because they've been orphaned for some reason or because they've run away from their families. Often, poor children leave their families because they are starving at home, and most of Bombay's street children come from impoverished states such as Bihar and Assam.

At one suburban station, two boys sitting on the platform were stricken by one of the bombs. The blast severed one of the legs below the knee of a fourteen-year-old named Mohammad. He said his best friend, Malik, was killed, flung away from him through the air by the force of the blast. These two poor Muslim boys were victims of a terrorist bomb planted by local Muslim extremists with help from Muslim terrorists based in Pakistan. The number of street children killed in the 2006 Bombay terrorist attacks will never be known. No families missed them when they failed to come home. They had no identity papers or cell phones with recently dialed numbers, no proof of existence.

The Indian government accused the Pakistan-based militant group Lashkar-e-Taiba, now called Jamaat ud-Dawa, of having a hand in the Bombay bombings and identified "military grade" explosive residues. Lashkar-e-Taiba has been making terrorist incursions against India since at least 1996. Relations between India and Pakistan cooled as India expressed its frustration with the Musharraf government's tolerance of groups that regularly strike Indian civilians on Indian soil. The banned Students Islamic Movement of India was also blamed.

Modi was scheduled to visit Bombay a few days after the attack. He vehemently denied any link between the 2002 massacre in Gujarat and the 2006 train bombings in India. However, evidence suggests that the Gujarat genocide represented for some of India's Muslims a turning point. Before the massacre, India's Muslims remained largely immune to Pakistani-based militants, and to the growing global Islamic terrorist movement represented most notoriously by Al Qaeda. The vast majority still are. However, international Islamic terror networks appear to be making inroads in recruiting Indian Muslims, particularly among the young. This is a potentially ominous development for India, and for the majority of India's Muslims who consider themselves to be Indians first and foremost.

Two bombs were set off in Bombay in 2003, one in front of the Gateway to India across from the posh Taj Mahal Hotel. In that case, according to an article that appeared in the Asia edition of *Time* magazine, "Both Indian and U.S. intelligence officers suspect that last week's blasts were the work of militant Indian Muslims angered by the government's strident Hindu nationalism—particularly by the 2002 pogrom in the western state of Gujarat in which Hindus killed two thousand Muslims while local and national leaders from the Bharatiya Janata Party (BJP) looked on."[7]

Bombs have been going off in India with alarming frequency since 2002. Bombs went off in Sarojini Nagar and Paharganj in Delhi in markets crowded with shoppers getting ready to celebrate Dewali in November 2005. Fifty-five people were killed. On March 7, 2006, in Varanasi, bombs ripped through a Hindu temple and the main railway station, killing at least sixty people. Then came the Bombay train bombings in July of that year. Multiple blasts were set off in Malgaon on September 10, 2006, killing thirty-eight people and injuring 189. The bombs went off in the Rehani Masjid mosque and at two additional sites in Muslim neighborhoods.

Clearly, powerful forces wish to unleash a holy war in India between Hindus and Muslims. There are also international Islamic terrorists who would love to recruit young Indian Muslims to their cause. Despite this spate of vicious provocation, Indians have remained calm. There have been no riots, no massacres. On the contrary, India's citizens, of all faiths, have lined up to donate blood and help survivors in any way possible. India's current government is well aware both of the genuine terrorist threat facing the country and of the danger of demonizing Muslims or otherwise fanning the flames of sectarian violence. Much of the credit for the calm prevailing in the face of such relentless provocation must go to Prime Minister Singh and his resolutely secular UPA government.

Mr. Singh has reiterated on several occasions his rejection of a "clash of civilizations" understanding of geopolitics. He knows that multireligious India, located on the edge of a region seething with Islamic terrorist forces, simply cannot afford to follow that path. The only way for India is to nurture a modus vivendi among diverse religious groups living in mutual trust and respect.

Despite Pakistan's refusal to rein in Jamaat ud-Dawa, India did not launch any attacks against Pakistan or air strikes aimed at Jamaat ud-Dawa. The United States complimented India on its "admirable restraint." Pakistan and India are both armed with nuclear weapons that assure their mutual destruction. This is a powerful dissuader to any military action. Moreover, the United States would not appreciate an Indian attack on Pakistani territory given its own relationship with Pakistan, and India is well aware of that. India finds itself in a situation of irony upon irony in its fight against terrorism. It has formally been designated a partner in the U.S.-led war on terror, yet it is forced to suffer repeated terrorist attacks launched with the blessing of Pakistan, the United States' other regional partner in its war on terror.

Immediately after September 11, 2001, India stepped forward to offer its firm support to the United States. Indians I spoke with were convinced that, finally, the United States was going to see the light with regard to Pakistan, recognize it as a fount of terror, and join with India to put a stop to the nonsense. Of course, that's not the way things worked out.

When the UPA government came to power, it fulfilled one of its campaign promises and repealed the Prevention of Terrorism Act (POTA). Modeled on the United States' Patriot Act, POTA was enacted by the BJP government in 2002 to replace the Terrorist and Disruptive Activities Act of 1987 (TADA), which had expired in 1995. POTA was widely being abused, used more for terrorizing Indian Muslims and settling petty political scores than for thwarting terrorists. Human rights abuses under POTA were proliferating. Experts feared it was doing more to incite fresh terrorism by outraging India's Muslims than to prevent terrorism.

India could do more to reform its antiterrorism policies—there are still people charged with offences under TADA languishing in custody, though it has now been eleven years since the law expired. Indian justice also suffers from colonial-era laws that remain on the books permitting, for example, detention of up to twenty-four months without charge. Serious human rights abuses continue to be inflicted upon the citizens of Jammu and Kashmir both by Indian security forces and by militants, exacerbating the situation in that torn region.[8] Still, the UPA government is to be applauded for taking the courageous and wise step of repealing POTA.

However, repealing POTA has not solved the debate in India of how to deal with terrorism. As of this writing, controversy rages in India over the fate of Mohammad Afzal, an Indian Kashmiri convicted while the BJP was in power of conspiracy in the terrorist attack on India's parliament in December 2001. Sentenced to death by India's Supreme Court in 2004, Afzal's execution, scheduled for October 2006, has been suspended pending a petition for clemency submitted to India's president Abdul Kalam. Afzal's family and supporters claim the case rests on tainted evidence, and that the man was never allowed counsel of his choice for his defense. Ghulam Nabi Azad, the chief minister of Jammu and Kashmir and a member of the Congress Party, as well as the Communist Party and others are against the death penalty for Afzal. Afzal's execution has become a flashpoint for the larger debate on how India should conduct its fight against terrorism, with the BJP accusing the current UPA government of being soft on terror for delaying the grim event, and it has reignited debate over the death penalty in general, which many in India oppose.[9] Last November, India's parliament was adjourned for the day when members of opposition political parties, including the BJP and the Shiv Sena, blocked the aisles and noisily demanded Afzal's execution. There is much at stake for India in the resolution of the Afzal affair, on which so many issues hinge, from human rights to the fate of Kashmir to how India chooses, as a democracy, to deal with terrorism.

With a Muslim population of 150 million, India can set a badly needed example for other democracies of what can be done, in practical terms, to take the moral high ground. Draconian security measures that permit extralegal practices such as indefinite detention and torture do far more to diminish the moral standing of any democracy than they do to harm terrorism. Human rights abuses targeting Muslims alienate people and push them into the arms of terrorists. Violence begets violence. Brute force, the suspension of human rights, and the dismissal of international law feed the beast. In September 2006, a U.S. intelligence report confirmed that the war in Iraq "has invigorated Islamic radicalism and worsened the global terrorist threat."[10] As Chris Hedges reminds us in his book *War Is a Force That Gives Us Meaning*, "The acceptance of all methods to lash out at real and perceived enemies will distort and deform our democracy."[11] This observation is as true for any democracy, including India's, as it is for the United States'.

Of Human Bondage

Of all the dispossessed and destitute in India, the plight of migrant laborers may be the worst of all. Farmers who've lost or abandoned their land, villagers who bond themselves as laborers in exchange for loans they can never pay off, peasants displaced by big development projects such as dams or steel mills—many of these people end up as migrant laborers, possessing nothing more than a plastic tarp and a cooking pot and their hands and muscles and health as long as these last. They are completely disposable, and one sees their little huts and dusty-haired children everywhere in India, right next to the shopping malls and the luxury apartment complexes and the gleaming glass office buildings.

Anita Patil Deshmukh, the director of the Bombay-based NGO PUKAR, told me when we met last year about her efforts to get the Hirandani construction company, involved in many large projects across Bombay, to provide drinking water for laborers on its site. "They work all day in this heat and they have no water. They have to walk more than one kilometer to get water. I just want one thing from Mr. Hirandani: to give his workers water." Anita, a vivacious woman whose dedication to community service brought her to Bombay from Chicago, where she worked as a pediatrician for twenty-five years, got what she wanted. Mr. Hirandani himself returned her call and assured her the situation would be taken care of. Eventually, with the help of a contractor, water was provided. Unfortunately, however, toiling in the heat with no water is a common plight for India's migrant laborers.

Nancy Buehmann, a computer engineer from Colorado who visited Bangalore in 2006 and saw India with the fresh eyes of a first-time visitor, told me, "The first time I went there, they put me up at the Leela, which is the fanciest hotel I have ever seen. It has seven stars. I didn't know you could go as high as seven stars. The second time, I stayed at the Royal Orchid, where I saw a typical Indian landscape: I turned my head one way, and I saw a manicured golf course with the IBM office building looking like one might look anywhere in the United States. Then, I turned my head the other way and I saw these tents—well, that's a strong word for it; not really tents, just tarps maybe—for the construction workers who were working on a new addition for the hotel. There were little children playing in the dirt. Then, I looked back at the perfect green lawn of the golf course.

"One day, we were invited to visit some people at their apartment. In the complex, I saw a boy who was maybe twelve working there, doing construction. I also saw boys tending goats right across the road from Wipro. I guess they don't have the same labor laws we do." Actually, India has laws prohibiting child labor and just enacted new penalties against people who hire children to work. Sadly, these laws are ill-enforced. Many children also have no choice but to work if they want to eat. The UNDP's Human Development Report puts the number of child laborers in India at an astounding 10 percent of the workforce. India has more child laborers than any other country in the world.[12]

Beyond the migrants—men, women, and children—who are visible everywhere in India putting in the new roads or putting up the new high-rises, thousands work in conditions of the worst exploitation making bricks. I have seen brickworks all over rural India. Under the glaring sun, with no shade from even a single tree, families set up tarps on the edge of the property. They work all day long. Little children squat on the bricks laid out to cure in the sun and work all day turning the bricks over so that they will dry evenly. The children's small fingers can get in between the bricks to lift them out. These children and their parents are covered with a layer of reddish dust from the kilns. They have to breathe this dust day in and day out. They are not allowed to leave the property. If one has to leave, the others are kept there to insure that the one who leaves comes back.

I talked to Umi Daniel last year in the Hyderabad office of the British charity Action Aid. He told me about the situation with brickworkers in the booming state of Andhra Pradesh. "Many of the brickworkers come to Andhra from Bolangir in neighboring Orissa state. This is one of the one hundred poorest districts in India. Fifty percent of the land is owned by nine percent of the people. There are regularly documented starvation deaths there. There are an estimated one hundred thousand migrants in Andhra from Orissa." Daniel told me that the peasants in Bolangir borrow money to celebrate an important festival for them, Nuakhai, the new grain festival. They receive fifteen thousand rupees ($334) in exchange for promising a three-person unit to work in the brickworks. The unit has to make 250,000 bricks to repay the loan. They are paid eighty rupees per thousand bricks, or eight paise per brick. Each recruit brings his family. A 250-rupee-per-week food allotment is deducted from their account. The allotment is for up to ten people. That's about fifty-five cents per week per person for food. "The debt cycle is very difficult for these people to break. If one of them becomes sick or dies, they are still responsible for paying back the loan.

"The workers are virtual prisoners. They aren't allowed to leave. Also, the middlemen are very careful to move people to another state where they don't speak the language or know the area; often they don't even know how to get home. Distress migrants from Andhra Pradesh are taken to Delhi, from Karnataka to Orissa, from Rajasthan to Bombay. This prevents any kind of unionizing or protest from the workers. These people are bonded laborers. They are slaves." Daniel talked about the nexus between the migrant handlers, the owners of the brick kilns, the construction companies, and the politicians. He described a pyramid of profiteering resting on the backs of migrant bonded labor, with expensive apartments, hotels, and office complexes at its apex.

One of the casualties of internal distress migration in India is primary education. Children following their parents drop out of their home school and have no educational opportunities at the work sites. There is also pressure for the children to work as well. The American India Foundation (AIF) has made access to education for the children of seasonal migrant workers one of its core efforts. AIF has awarded grants to several NGOs working with these children. One strategy is to set up schools near work sites, for example near sugarcane plantations or near brick kilns. This helps prevent children from being put to work. Another strategy is to provide hostels where children can stay behind when their parents migrate. This allows the children to continue their education uninterrupted in their local school and prevents them being put to work. Yet another strategy is to provide bridge courses for children who have been away from home for a season to ease their transition back into school and prevent them from losing that year of schooling. AIF has also partnered with the governments of several states, including Gujarat, Maharashtra, and Orissa, to scale up these efforts to reach as many affected children as possible. Internal migration of poor families and the disruption of children's education is certainly a factor in India's persistent rates of illiteracy. AIF hopes the children of migrant workers avoid the fate of their parents.

India: AIDS Capital of the World

Sumati married at age fourteen. She bore her first child at age fifteen. When she reached twenty years of age, a second child was born, and she became a widow. Sumati's marriage had been a happy one. Her husband, a truck driver, treated her well. When he died, she discovered he had been sick with complications from HIV/AIDS. She was also infected. To be a widow in India is a cursed status. Widows are burdens, of use to no one. Remarriage is rare. To be the widow of someone who has died of HIV/AIDS is to be doubly cursed. Sumati was shunned by her neighbors. Her aged parents could not take her in.

"After my husband died, my life underwent drastic change. I didn't know what hit me. I was lost and confused, numb, and I moved around like a zombie. But seeing my two hungry children, I was forced to work and make something of my life."[13]

With no support, and no skills, Sumati was forced to do agricultural day labor at thirty or forty rupees per day to try to feed her two small children. When Sumati fell ill with tuberculosis, she was told by a local doctor that she was HIV-positive, and that she needed to have her children tested. She discovered that one of her children, her daughter, was also HIV-positive. Her son tested negative.

Socially ostracized in her small community, too weak to do farm labor, Sumati decided to leave her home and travel to Bangalore. She found work in a factory, and was able to keep going for a while. But, eventually, she fell ill again.

Through a male relative who is also HIV-positive, Sumati found out about Freedom Foundation, an NGO in Karnataka supported by AIF, where she gets free antiretroviral therapy, supplemental food for herself and her children, and has learned skills she can use to make a living. Her parents have joined her in Bangalore. Her son is in boarding school, and doing well. Her daughter's future is less assured.

Sumati's story is unfortunately typical of the experience of women HIV/AIDS victims in India.

According to a 2006 report by UNAIDS, more people were infected with HIV in India than in any other country in the world: 5.7 million. That is the official figure. One of India's most prominent HIV/AIDS specialized physicians, who asked not to be named, told me that she believed the real number to be more like 9 or 10 million. India simply doesn't have the primary health-care network to conduct the kind of testing that could confirm an accurate number.

It is estimated that by 2010, India could have 20–25 million people living with HIV/AIDS. This would, by far, be the greatest number in any single country.[14] HIV/AIDS has the potential to lower India's life expectancy by three to thirteen years.[15] The impact on India's booming economy could be severe, resulting in a reduction of economic growth by almost a full percentage point over the next decade if the spread of AIDS is not effectively countered.[16]

In 2005–6, the government of India budgeted $103 million for HIV/AIDS prevention and treatment. That number was expected to increase to $138 million in 2006–7.[17] That is not nearly enough. For example, the government's free antiretroviral drug program was only able to reach 15,000 of the 100,000 people targeted in 2005.[18] As of January 2006, this number had increased to 34,634, according to Dr. Suniti Solomon, who directs YRG Care, which provides health care for more than 4,500 persons living with HIV/AIDS.[19] This is woefully inadequate. India launched its AIDS Control Programme in 1987 and established NACO, the National AIDS Control Organization, in 1992, but these underfunded and limited initiatives have not prevented the epidemic from spreading.

The biggest national effort to combat HIV/AIDS is that of the Gates Foundation, which has committed $200 million to stem the spread of HIV/AIDS in India. The Gates Foundation's initiative, called Avahan, spends 300 percent more on HIV/AIDS awareness, prevention, and treatment than the Indian government does. The Clinton Foundation has partnered with India's NACO to help it roll out a national care and treatment program for people living with HIV/AIDS. The American India Foundation has made HIV/AIDS in India one of its priority funding areas and has partnered with the Gates Foundation to galvanize the Indian-American community to get involved.

While AIDS is present in every Indian state and region, it is concentrated in Tamil Nadu, Maharashtra, Karnataka, and Andhra Pradesh. In these relatively prosperous states, the main vector of transmission is sexual. The northeastern states of Manipur and Nagaland also have relatively high numbers of HIV cases, but the main vector of infection in this region is intravenous drug use.

There are many fine localized efforts such as Dr. Solomon's at YRG Care. Anjali Gopalan started the NAZ Care Home in New Delhi in 1994 for women and orphaned children living with HIV/AIDS. While prevention is obviously important to the fight against the spread of HIV/AIDS, there is a critical need for care for those who have already been diagnosed. Gender inequality plays an enormous role in HIV transmission in India. An astounding 39 percent of HIV-positive Indians are women. Married women are particularly vulnerable, as they have little ability to protect themselves. Rural women, who are more likely to be illiterate and ill-informed—most have never heard of HIV or AIDS—are particularly vulnerable. The stereotype in India is that the only women infected with HIV are sex workers, when in fact less than 1 percent of infected women are sex workers. Nevertheless, the government of India has focused awareness efforts on sex workers and other perceived high-risk groups such as gay men and truck drivers.[20]

Migration by men for work means long periods away from home. When they come home for a visit, they can unknowingly infect their wives. India's sexual conservatism has inhibited efforts at expanding AIDS awareness. Women may not know how the disease is spread or what they can do to protect themselves. Many discover they, and even their children, are HIV-positive only after their husbands have died of the disease. Tragically, the usual reaction of their relatives is to throw them out of the house, particularly if the child or children are girls. In India's extreme patriarchal system, girls are viewed as financial liabilities. The existence of care homes such as the one provided by NAZ literally can be a lifesaver for infected women and children orphaned by HIV/AIDS who would otherwise find themselves on the street.

The New York– and New Delhi–based NGO Breakthrough has used innovative, mass media techniques to get the word out about women's vulnerability to HIV in India. Reaching out through television ads, radio plays, bookmarks available in India's Crossword's bookstore chain, and even SMS, Breakthrough uses catchy taglines, music by award-winning artists, and famous actors to involve audiences, especially the youth population, where HIV infection rates are increasing the fastest. In 2005–6, Breakthrough ran a campaign with the message "What kind of man are you?" The campaign asked men if they were man enough to protect their wives from HIV by using condoms at home.

Advertising guru Prasoon Joshi of McCann-Erickson donated his talents to help craft the campaign. Mallika Dutt, Breakthrough's founder and director, told me, "We have limited resources—$150,000 compared to the millions other campaigns receive—but we don't skimp on production values and we have built amazing pro bono partnerships with the media and entertainment industry in India. We get what we need donated. Our television ads and music videos are very professionally produced because, if they're not, they'll be tuned out and our message won't get across." She added wryly, "We've taken so much shit from the left for working with the commercial side, for working with men. But the bottom line is that unless it's salable, it just doesn't matter what it says." Breakthrough's music video to raise awareness about violence against women won the Link music video award. Perhaps the best illustration of how Breakthrough has succeeded in establishing a presence was the appearance on *Kaun Banega Crorepati* (Who Wants to Be a Millionaire) of a question on Breakthrough and HIV/AIDS.

Increasingly, private business is getting into the HIV/AIDS awareness act. The potential costs to employers for treating sick employees with expensive drug cocktails, not to mention absenteeism or even the loss of highly trained workers, is motivation enough for the private sector to get involved.[21] Nita Ambani told me that Reliance is actively doing HIV/AIDS awareness at its truck stops. Most of the new infections are occurring among people age fifteen to thirty-five, the exact population tranche most attractive to marketers. It is also the age bracket of the newly educated and trained employees driving India's economic miracle. CII, Confederation of Indian Industry, the powerful Indian business group, launched the Indian Business Trust for HIV and AIDS in 2001. Five thousand public and private sector businesses participate in the trust. Larsen & Toubro, one of the largest engineering firms in India, has been running an HIV-prevention program for employees since the epidemic first emerged in the 1980s.

India also needs to get rid of outdated colonial-era antisodomy laws that criminalize homosexual conduct. A movement led by prominent Indians and Indian-Americans, including revered economist Amartya Sen and acclaimed novelist Vikram Seth, is demanding that India repeal Section 377 of the Indian Penal Code, a law that dates from 1861 that criminalizes consensual sex acts between persons of the same sex. The law has, most disturbingly, been invoked to halt the distribution of condoms, inhibiting India's desperately needed fight against the spread of HIV/AIDS.

Under PEPFAR (President's Emergency Plan for AIDS Relief), the United States provided $26 million in bilateral aid to India in 2006. The World Bank contributed $84 million to Phase I of NACO's National AIDS Control Project and $191 million for Phase II. The Heroes Project, cochaired by actor Richard Gere and Indian socialite Parameshwar Godrej in partnership with the Kaiser Family Foundation and with a grant from the Gates Foundation's Avahan initiative, is leveraging celebrity power and the media to increase awareness about HIV/AIDS.

Whether the collective efforts of government, nonprofit foundations and NGOs, volunteer doctors, and private business can stem the tide of HIV/AIDS is an open question. Every epidemic has its tipping point. Some fear the response to India's HIV epidemic has been too little too late. Only time will tell. What is clear is that gender inequality, a lack of commitment to primary health care by the government of India, illiteracy and ignorance, penury that forces men to migrate away from their families in search of livelihoods, and the cost of treatment have all accelerated the virus's progress. If India can harness its increasing economic prosperity to address these debilitating issues, it will go a long way toward stopping an epidemic that has the potential to deal a serious blow to a country just beginning to realize its promise.

The Second Sex

The rampant HIV/AIDS epidemic is only one symptom of India's serious gender discrimination problem. Women are seen as burdens to families in traditional Indian society. I have had a male family member tell me that I am not a member of the Kamdar family I was born into (he is an exception, thank goodness). Only male offspring can claim this connection. Females are destined to be married off, at which point they belong to someone else's family. "Raising flowers for someone else's garden" or "watering your neighbor's garden" are common expressions. If India is to make good on its promise to create a knowledge-based society, it cannot afford to throw away the potential contribution of so many of its female citizens.

Often large dowries have to be raised when girls get married, dowries that can push families deep into debt. Especially in North India, parents boast that they never enter their daughter's house after her marriage; that, if they come to the door, they will not even accept a glass of water. These confessions of extreme respect for tradition are greeted with respectful admiration as often as with bemusement. Indian patriarchy dictates that only sons can be counted on to provide support for aging parents in a society with no social security system. In such a society, girls are liabilities, not assets, except to the extent they bring prestige by marrying into what is often referred to as a "respectable family."

Killing girl babies is an old story in India. In some areas of the country this is a specialized profession. More commonly, the baby's mother is charged with getting rid of the unwanted baby girl. She may suffocate her or strangle her. Female infanticide is generally practiced by people so poor they feel they cannot afford to raise a girl, who will take from them and never give anything back. Female feticide, the practice of selectively aborting female fetuses, is the modern version of this scourge. With the advent of ultrasound technology, pregnant women can now determine the sex of the child they are carrying before it is born. If that child is a girl, the mother may be pressured to abort it. One of the most perverse effects of India's rising prosperity is the increase in sex-selective abortion, which is practiced far more commonly by the rich or the aspiring middle class than by the poor. Indians want to improve their economic prospects. They see one sure way of doing so: avoid having a girl child and the expense of a big dowry. Sex-selective abortion in India is illegal, as is ultrasound for the purposes of determining the sex of a fetus. Doctors have recently been jailed for these practices. But the problem remains rampant. The proof: there are between 50 and 60 million "missing" women and girls in India.[22]

The sex ratio of females to males, while largely normal across India, has become so skewed in some areas of the country there are serious concerns about the social impact. Prosperous regions such as Haryana, Gujarat, and especially Punjab have the highest incidence of sex ratios favoring boys. In India, the ratio of girls aged less than seven years to boys is down to 927 to every 1,000. In Punjab, it is down to 793, and even lower in some districts. This has given rise to truly alarming practices. Women are now being trafficked from poorer regions to low-female population areas as wives. Sometimes, they are married to one man, sometimes to several siblings. In Punjab, a new trend is for these women—called Draupadis after the character of that name in the *Mahabharata* who was married to the five Pandara brothers—to be a "wife" to all the brothers in the family. The violence and degradation to which women become subjected under these circumstances is laid out in a report by Patricia Liedl for the United Nations Population Fund called "Silent Spring: The Tragedy of India's Never-Born Girls."[23] Truly insidious is the practice of male sex selective sperm sorting followed by artificial insemination. This technique is virtually untraceable.

Girls in India are the last to be educated. Indian female literacy stands at only 54 percent against male literacy of 76 percent (2001 Census). When girls are allowed to go to school, they must still shoulder household chores, causing many to drop out. In many public schools in India, there are no toilets, an uncomfortable situation for girls in a mixed-sex environment. Schools are often located far from home. It is not safe for young girls to walk alone, and so many stay back from school. When families are strapped for funds, as so many are, they will educate their sons rather than waste the money on daughters, who will soon enough leave home.

A society with skewed sex ratios, millions on the move as they migrate from place to place in search of livelihoods, and a gross devaluation of women is naturally a society prone to violence against women in all its forms. Forced prostitution and the trafficking of women and girls for the sex trade are serious problems in India. According to the United States Department of Labor, "India is a source, destination, and transit country for trafficking of children for the purposes of commercial sexual exploitation and other forms of exploitive labor."[24] Women are trafficked into India from neighboring Nepal and Bangladesh, and out of India as far away as the Middle East. Many are children. Save the Children India reports, "Every day about two hundred girls and women in India enter prostitution and eighty percent of them against their will. At the current rate of growth, by 2025 one out of every five Indian girl children will be a child prostitute."[25] Clearly, something will have to give before then.

One of the perverse side effects of the HIV/AIDS epidemic is the increase in marketability of young children for the sex industry. The younger the child, the less chance, it is believed, of contracting HIV/AIDS. According to Nicholas D. Kristof, writing in the *New York Times,* "India alone may have half a million children in its brothels, more than any other country in the world. Visit the brothel district in almost any city in India, and you can meet fourteen-year-old girls who have been kidnapped off the street, or drugged, or offered jobs as maids, and then sold into a world that they often escape only by dying of AIDS."[26]

Educating girls is widely acknowledged as the best measure to alleviate poverty and raise a country's living standards. Empowering women by providing them with basic education and a way to earn a living raises their confidence and their chances at good nutrition and health. Improving women's lives is also the best way to improve children's lives.

India will only realize its goal of becoming a developed country if it uplifts and empowers its marginalized and dispossessed populations, builds trust between diverse religious, caste, and ethnic groups, and ends brutal discrimination against women and girls.

Solving India's Health Crisis,
Saving the World

India spends only 1.3 percent of its budget on health care.[27] In rural India, there are two thousand people for each doctor, and 70 million Indians cannot afford to see a doctor or buy medicine. More farmers become indebted due to health-care emergencies than crop failures.[28] The result of these dismal statistics is not only the toll on millions of Indians' health but an environment where disease flourishes.

My aunt, Usha Kamdar, is the chief dietitian at Sion Hospital in Bombay, a large public hospital. It provides critically needed health-care services to Bombay's poor and to poor people from around India who can get there. I visited victims of the devastating 2001 earthquake in Gujarat who had been transported to Sion for surgeries and the treatment of multiple fractures. The facilities at Sion are rudimentary. Patients lie on metal cots lined up side by side in large wards. Family members stay on pallets on the floor, some no more than a folded old blanket, next to their ill or injured loved one. The families help nurse the patients and bring food for them. There are many services the hospital cannot afford to offer poor patients, such as X-rays or certain medications. If patients can't pay, they can't get these services. Charitable organizations come into the hospital and make the rounds of the wards, finding out what different patients need and offering to pay for it. My aunt says that, ultimately, no one is denied care.

I did not visit any of the operating rooms or post-op areas, but in the general wards the sanitary conditions were bleak. But even so, people who make it to Sion are lucky. Because it is a large hospital in India's largest city, it offers a full range of services and its doctors and staff are competent.

While all major cities and many midsize cities have outstanding private clinics and hospitals that can rival the world's best, both the quality and availability of public health care in India declines the moment one leaves the larger cities. I remember briefly entering a public hospital in Baroda in the mid-1980s and being absolutely shocked by the conditions: a wood table doubled as an examination table, there was dust everywhere (the windows had no panes, only iron bars), and it looked as if the only equipment the doctor had was the stethoscope around his neck. At the Pushkar Mela near Ajmer, my first husband came down with a high fever. Our friends asked around and found a small clinic. The doctor, whose credentials were not in evidence, offered to give him a B-vitamin shot, waving an enormous steel syringe that he dipped into a cup of dubious water to clean, grinning as he squirted a high stream of water from it. "Do I have to get a shot?" asked my husband in his delirium. "No, honey," I replied, steering him over the open gutter out front, "you don't have to get a shot." Rajasthani peasants in fabulous crimson turbans and magnificent handlebar mustaches trooped through this doctor's office getting cure-all B-vitamin shots. The HIV/AIDS epidemic was just beginning to be noticed in the West in those days. It was not something I even thought about at the time. I shudder to think now of that doctor with his syringe and his glass of water to clean it and the line of peasants waiting for shots.

In addition to the HIV/AIDS epidemic in India, tuberculosis is spreading, often in individuals whose immune systems are weakened by HIV/AIDS. Polio, once nearly eradicated, has had a recent upturn in India. An outbreak of the disease that began in Uttar Pradesh in 2006 spread rapidly to neighboring states, and then on to neighboring countries, with outbreaks reported in Nepal and Bangladesh. Jay Wenger, project manager of the National Polio Surveillance Project, a joint effort of the United Nations and the government of India, said, "The entire area of western Uttar Pradesh is acting as a reservoir for the wild polio virus, and the disease has spread outside the country."[29] Also in 2006, three separate outbreaks of avian flu were reported in India. Tens of thousands of birds were slaughtered. Individuals exhibiting flulike symptoms were quarantined, and none tested positive for the H5N1 virus. Still, the U.S. embassy in New Delhi issued a warning to Americans "to monitor news reports, and to avoid any areas with active outbreaks of avian influenza in India."[30] India is a potential hotbed of the planet's most lethal pandemics. It is also rapidly becoming the capital of noncommunicable epidemics, with rates of diabetes and heart disease well above global averages. As

Indians have become more prosperous, they are eating more starches, fats, and sugars and exercising less, all factors in diabetes and heart disease.

But India is also where there is perhaps the most hope of finding ways to deal with these and other scourges on a scale that could actually serve the world's billions. High-cost regimens will only help a few of those afflicted. If India can find low-cost, convenient therapies, for example oral insulin therapies where patients don't have to inject themselves, the lives of millions of people will improve.

Top-quality health care is available in India—for a price. Apollo Hospitals and Escorts Hospitals, to name just two of the most prominent chains, provide state-of-the-art medical care and surgery, especially heart surgery. Many of their resident doctors were trained in the United States or are diplomates of the American Medical Association. While the care provided at these facilities is much too costly for most Indians, it is a bargain compared to what equivalent care costs in the United States. Medical tourism has flourished as a result, with five hundred thousand Americans expected to travel abroad for medical care at a savings of 30 to 80 percent over what they would have to pay at home. Given the high numbers of uninsured Americans, this trend is likely to increase as time goes by, providing a valuable service to thousands of Americans who might otherwise have to forgo needed medical care.[31]

Unless revenue from medical outsourcing is used to drive down costs for less well-off patients, it will not address the urgent healthcare needs of India's poor. Medical care is one more area where India's extremes of wealth and poverty lead to savage inequalities in life chances. There are many efforts to bridge the gap between the high-quality care that exists in the country and the ability of most of India's citizens to access it. Founding clinics where care is provided at low or no cost is a time-honored philanthropy in India, one that has brought relief and hope to millions. However, India is facing a veritable healthcare emergency. A clinic here, a hospital there, no matter how excellent, will not address this emergency on the scale required.

One of the most amazing efforts to improve health care in India is Dr. Devi Shetty's Narayana Hrudayalaya Institute of Medical Sciences and Hospital. I came to know about Dr. Shetty's extraordinary work through Kiran Mazumdar Shaw, the dynamic head of Biocon, India's leading biotech pharmaceutical company. There is an interesting symbiosis between Biocon and Narayana Hrudalaya. It is representative, I believe, of what is most exciting in India's renaissance. When corporate social responsibility is taken seriously, is focused on a critical challenge for India, uses the latest technologies and best practices, and works as a partner with the government, costs are driven down while the quality of service goes up. This is the only way India will deliver solutions on the scale and at the speed required to address its many problems.

An interesting person, Kiran Mazumdar Shaw started off wanting to get into the beer business. She went to Australia, where she became a master brewer, returned to India, and as a twenty-five-year-old woman was firmly shut out of the all-male alcoholic beverages preserve. "Vijay Mallya," the head of United Breweries of Kingfisher fame and India's beer baron, "is like a brother to me, but it was tough," she told me. With beer brewing off-limits, she started a biotechnology firm, from scratch, literally in her garage, with seed capital of $2,000. The rest, as they say, is history. Biocon is now a billion-dollar-plus company, and India's leading biotechnology firm.

A Gujarati by heritage, Kiran Mazumdar Shaw is married to a Scotsman. Scotland has its consular office in Bangalore inside the Biocon corporate office. She is an ardent aficionado of beer, recently publishing a lavish coffee-table book called *Ale and Arty*, dedicated to her father, a longtime master brewer at Mallya's United Breweries. Perhaps because of her unusual background and because she had to fight so hard to get where she is today, Kiran Mazumdar Shaw has a radical approach to doing business, an approach that captures this moment of opportunity for India.

First of all, she is completely bullish about India's future. "Absolutely, we can create this 'made in India' story. You are going to see that this will be the trend, India as leader. I can really see that we are in a very different time zone. I've been in this business for twenty-five years, and I've never seen a moment like this. My business has always been global, but what is happening now is India is becoming the market. This is very exciting. India can become the laboratory to the world. That's been clear for a while. We have bright minds and a cost advantage. But now, it's all about the market potential. 'You ain't seen nothin' yet' because so far you're only talking about urban markets. You haven't seen rural yet."

Mazumdar Shaw sees India as having several unique advantages. There is the cost advantage, the scientific research acumen, but there is also potential to connect India's underserved rural population with the whole world through urban centers of excellence such as Bangalore. She sees Bangalore as a unique magnet for an extraordinary concentration of talent. She also sees it as a portal where rural India, with its huge unmet needs and untapped potential, meets global markets and capital. And she is convinced that the Indian way of doing business is much more focused on social responsibility than the American way, which, ultimately, makes it a better way of doing business.

"In the United States, it's just a mercenary world where all they care about is money," she complained. "U.S. biotech companies have a very hard time. It's a high-risk business. If you succeed, it's a bonanza, but if you fail, it's a disaster. The venture capitalists are ruthless. They want to see substantial data. I tell U.S. companies to use India to get their data. They spend so much money on lawyers and presentations." Mazumdar Shaw sees a definite advantage for India in this kind of environment. "We're addressing the medical needs of the world. When you can bring a drug to market for a much lower cost, you can get it out to many more people. We have a new cancer drug that comes from Cuba. This was an opportunity for me because India doesn't have a problem with Cuba. Cuba had this interesting drug but they didn't have enough patients to test it. I could see its potential. I knew I could scale it up and provide this drug to India. The competing drug available in the U.S. has significant side effects.

"For the first time, Indian patients will have access to a superior drug at an affordable price." This captures the essence of the dream India is turning into a reality.

Mazumdar Shaw insisted I cancel my next appointment and go instead down the road—which happens to be Hosur Road, where Biocon and Infosys have their corporate headquarters—and meet

Dr. Devi Shetty. "What he is doing is really what this is all about," she told me.

Of all the amazing people and companies I met in India, Dr. Devi Shetty and Narayana Hrudayalaya Heart Hospital are, without a doubt, the most amazing of all. The hospital is huge. Outside the building is a multireligious shrine where Hindus, Muslims, Christians, and Sikhs can pray. The hospital's name in Sanskrit means "God's compassionate home."

Hundreds of people were waiting in the immaculate lobby on the ground floor, but I got the sense that this was due to the volume of people coming in for treatment rather than sluggish service. Everything evidently functioned with great efficiency. I was struck by the modest demeanor of most of the people, as well as by how patiently they sat, and how quiet and orderly everything was. On the wall were framed posters with inspirational slogans: "Never doubt that a small number of committed people can change the world. Indeed, it is the only thing that can." "Most of the things worth doing in the world had been declared impossible before they were done." When I entered Dr. Shetty's office upstairs, a Muslim couple were talking with him. He spoke with them as if he had all the time in the world. When they finished, the woman, wearing a black hijab, bent down to touch his feet in the time-honored Hindu gesture of respect and veneration. The hospital has a large pediatric cardiac unit, and I wondered if they had come for their child.

Dr. Shetty was wearing full medical garb, a drab green tunic and slacks, protective covers over his shoes, face mask down around his neck. He founded Narayana Hrudayalaya in 2001. It has five hundred beds, ten fully commissioned operating theaters, two cardiac catheterization laboratories, and its own blood bank. The pediatric cardiac ward has forty beds. When I went up to see it, children of all ages were in the post-op recovery room. Some were tiny infants. The person escorting me said that sometimes women whose fetuses were found to have heart problems came to give birth at the hospital so the baby could immediately be taken for open-heart surgery.

After greeting me, Dr. Shetty got right to the point. "We are trying to dissociate health care from affluence. People may continue to be poor, but they will have access to high-tech health care with dignity. Outside of the United States, India has the most FDA-approved drug sites, we produce the most doctors and nurses. We can reduce salaries to twenty percent of cost. As individuals, the poor are weak, but as a group they are strong. You put five rupees in one hand, it does nothing. You put it in two hundred million hands, it can do a lot."

Dr. Shetty's strategy is to use cutting-edge technology both to insure high quality and to drive down costs wherever possible. He uses telemedicine and distance diagnosis to connect people in rural areas to doctors and diagnosticians at the hospital. "There are five countries in the world with satellites," he told me, "one of them is India." This service is offered for free. "Technology gives the rich what they always had. It gives the poor what they never had," he said. The hospital uses digital X-rays, which are far cheaper than conventional X-rays because they require no film. Narayana Hrudayalaya has set up heart clinics all over rural Karnataka. I visited the telemedicine center, where EKGs were coming in from various clinics. Doctors were reviewing them for any abnormalities. Each rural clinic has a technician trained to administer the EKGs and in basic diagnostics. If the doctors back at the hospital see a situation that requires serious intervention, then the patient is called to the hospital. Dr. Shetty wants to replicate this all over India.

In the elevator, I met a little boy and his mother. She had brought him from Nigeria to Bangalore for open-heart surgery. Patients come to the hospital from twenty-two different countries. The rich pay full fee. The poor pay in accordance with their means. The hospital provides microfinance. The very poor pay nothing. Narayana Hrudayalaya Hospital has a lower infection rate than U.S. hospitals, and a death rate from open-heart surgery of less than 5 percent. Still, the costs are minuscule compared to comparable care in the United States. A full package of heart surgery plus post-op hospitalization costs $2,400. Patients who want a private room and have the means to pay for it pay $3,100 to $4,300. Patients with limited resources pay $1,400. The hospital absorbs the remaining cost. A trust pays for patients who have no money at all. No one is turned away.

Dr. Shetty tells me that only 8 percent of the people on the planet have access to heart surgery. His mission is to increase that number. His hospital is only six years old. By 2005, the hospital had already completed 11,228 open-heart surgeries. Biocon is providing the hospital with extremely low-cost generic drugs. Kiran Mazumdar Shaw told me, "We make a profit on them. On a unit basis, the profit is negligible. We make the profit on volume." Dr. Shetty is extending his network via satellite links to Kuala Lumpur, Mauritius, and a medical school in Germany. He plans to set up centers in Pakistan, Bangladesh, Tanzania, Yemen, and Zambia. In India, he has launched Heart Care on Wheels, a mobile echocardiography unit with color Doppler, laptop computers, and a computerized treadmill. The unit treats up to five hundred persons per day in the state of Karnataka.

Dr. Shetty and Kiran Mazumdar Shaw have teamed up to create Arogya Raksha Yojana, a trust dedicated to creating an ultra-low-cost health insurance plan to bring health-care facilities to the very poor in rural areas. Leveraging telemedicine and remote diagnostics and generic drugs from Biocon and other companies at 30 percent below market cost, Arogya Raksha is targeting the poorest of the poor. Hygiene awareness, including water and sanitation, is an integral part of the program. People pay premiums—120 rupees, less than $12 per year for a family of four. Their premiums go, in part, to cover the cost of building a clinic, which is the initial contact point and comprises a pharmacy, a consultation room, a diagnostic laboratory, and an administrative office. This is not a charitable scheme. Arogya Raksha Yojana is determined to be self-sustaining and replicable.

The other India, the India of poverty and disease, of the basest exploitation of the weak by the strong, is all too often swept off television screens and out of people's consciousness by the euphoria of India's rapid rise. It is the tremendous dedication of individuals such as Dr. Devi Shetty that inspires hope that India will embrace the opportunity that each of its seemingly intractable problems presents, and close the gap between that portion of the country that is thriving and the larger portion that is left out and left behind.

CHAPTER SEVEN

Power

O N MAY 15, 1998, THE NEWLY ELECTED BJP INDIAN
prime minister Atal Behari Vajpayee flew to Pokhran in the
Rajasthani desert to scatter flowers on the site where days earlier
India had successfully set off a series of nuclear explosions. Across the
country, there was music and dancing in the streets. People in India
and Indians around the world handed out sweets and clapped each
other on the back, positively giddy at having proved that India could,
by itself and in defiance of the world, break into the exclusive nuclear
club. I remember my own shock as post-Pokhran jubilation swept up
members of my family, Jains dedicated to nonviolence. There was
even talk of taking soil from the blast site, now made sacred by the
fabulous explosion of nationalist pride, and having Hindu holy men
distribute it around the country. This idea was mercifully dropped
when someone pointed out the stuff was dangerously radioactive.
Dubbed Pokhran-II, these were the first nuclear tests India had conducted since 1974. Pakistan immediately followed suit, and a new
nuclear arms race was on in South Asia.[1]

Justifying the 1998 nuclear tests, former external affairs minister
Jaswant Singh famously quipped that India's is "a dangerous neighborhood." Since 1998, India, along with archrival Pakistan, has been
expanding its military capabilities and working on developing a
longer-range missile delivery system capable of carrying nuclear
bombs.

India is one of the world's biggest purchasers of arms. In fact, according to the Stockholm International Peace Research Institute (SIPRI), India ranked second only after China in the value of total arms received between 2001 and 2005: $9.2 billion to China's $13.3 billion.[2] A U.S. Congressional Research Service report released to members of Congress last fall placed India first among conventional arms buyers in the developing world. India's $5.4 billion dwarfed the $3.4 billion number-two buyer Saudi Arabia spent and the mere $2.8 billion spent by China.[3]

A Dangerous Neighborhood

South Asia is a highly unstable region—nearly every country around India is racked by internal conflict, be it intermittent civil war in Sri Lanka, a powerful Maoist insurgency in Nepal, growing Islamic militancy in economically lagging Bangladesh, or Pakistan. West Asia, also known as the Middle East, is perennially wracked by deadly conflict. It is the primary birthplace of global Islamic terrorism, and is now the theater of a badly bungled war.

India's relationship with Pakistan is by far its most contentious. The year 2007 is the sixtieth anniversary of the partition of India, which created Pakistan. Between two hundred thousand and 1 million people died in a paroxysm of unleashed rage during the partition, when Hindus and Sikhs set upon Muslims, and Muslims upon Hindus and Sikhs, as each group fled to its designated side of the new border. Partition is a gaping wound in the national psyches of both countries that refuses to heal. India and Pakistan have been locked in an unending cycle of conflict since 1947,[4] engaging in four wars and countless border skirmishes. The two nations last came dangerously close to all-out war, including the risk of a nuclear exchange, in 2002. The spark for these wars is almost always the unresolved question of Kashmir, a region in the Himalaya mountains claimed by both countries, and bisected by a UN-designated line of control. India and Pakistan remain at the top of the list of potential flashpoints for nuclear war.

India has centuries-old connections to the countries of Central and Western Asia, especially Afghanistan and Iran. India has been a major donor country to Afghanistan following the overthrow of the Taliban, providing food aid in the form of wheat. Indian workers are engaged in reconstruction activities, and India has sent a small contingent of special forces to protect them from attacks by the Taliban. Indian movies and music are extremely popular in Afghanistan wherever a resurgent Taliban has not again banned their enjoyment. India has good relations with Iran, and is pursuing constructing a pipeline to bring Iranian natural gas to India.

More than 4 million Indian nationals work in the Arabian Gulf region. Many of these workers are little more than indentured laborers with few rights and no guaranteed minimum wage or benefits. They are often mistreated, a source of friction in India's relations with countries in the Gulf, but few have better options. Each year they send $5 billion in wages back to India. This is an important source of foreign exchange for India, and brings much needed money to the families and communities of India's expatriot workers. Their presence in the Gulf affects India's strategic view of the oil-rich region.

Joining the Nuclear Club

India's nuclear tests had been decades in the preparation, but India, which never signed the Nuclear Nonproliferation Treaty (NPT), had held off testing because of close scrutiny from the United States. The Pokhran tests were a bold and defiant move. As then Indian national security adviser Brajesh Mishra explained drily, "One either changes the policy to suit the environment or changes the environment to suit the policy. The nuclear tests helped us change the environment." That they did. The action, which took the United States by surprise, angered then president Clinton.[5]

With the tests, India not only caught the world's attention, it earned its respect. India had long chafed at the "nuclear apartheid," as it called it, that kept nuclear technologies out of the hands of all but a few powerful, developed countries. China was a nuclear power. Why, asked India, shouldn't it be allowed this same advantage? By defying the existing nuclear powers and pulling off the successful testing of nuclear devices, India struck a blow for the independence of its strategic action, and for all the developing countries that had been stopped from entering the nuclear club.

This was precisely what unnerved the United States. From the U.S. point of view, India's nuclear tests flouted the international nuclear regime and long-standing U.S. policy on nonproliferation. Deeply concerned that India's nuclear tests and the tests by Pakistan that rapidly followed would set off a nuclear arms race on the Asian subcontinent, not to mention inspire a slew of nuclear wannabes to emulate India's example, the United States rushed to punish India by imposing sanctions. These were largely ineffective. In the late 1990s, the information technology industry was booming, and American companies needed Indian brainpower to fuel continued expansion and deal with the looming Y2-K crisis. India's economy remained fairly isolated from the world, which also protected it from the 1997 Asian financial crisis.

India's nuclear tests did not deter President Clinton from pursuing closer relations with India. His historic trip to India in 2000 was the first visit by a U.S. president in twenty-two years. Clinton's impassioned address to a special joint session of India's parliament on March 22, 2000, received a standing ovation, with members of parliament scrambling to congratulate him personally afterward. Prime minister Atal Behari Vajpayee declared that the United States and India were "natural allies," setting the tone for a new era in India-U.S. relations. President Clinton told the Indian audience Americans "welcome India's leadership in the region and in the world" and encouraged the two countries "to turn a common vision into common achievements so that partners in spirit can be partners in fact."[6] With President Clinton's speech, the Cold War period of U.S.-India estrangement officially ended. The stage was set for an unprecedented partnership between India and the United States.

A New Strategic Partnership

President George W. Bush came into office in 2001 with a well-defined view of India's importance to the long-term advancement of U.S. interests and the preservation of American power. That view was reinforced by the attacks of September 11, 2001. In a world where China was fast emerging as the next superpower and Islamic terror groups had focused their rage on America and other democracies, the Bush administration approached creating a strong partnership with India as both a strategic and an economic imperative.

Whereas the Clinton administration had stressed nuclear nonproliferation, an end to nuclear testing, and encouraged both India and the United States to join the Comprehensive Test Ban Treaty (CTBT), the new Bush administration had a different notion of the role nuclear weapons should play in America's security calculus. In 1999, a Republican-controlled Senate defeated ratification of the CTBT. The effort was led by the conservative then chairman of the Senate Foreign Relations Committee Jesse Helms and then Senate majority leader Trent Lott. George W. Bush, in the months leading up to the 2000 presidential elections, repeatedly stated his opposition to the CTBT as well. The failure of the Senate to ratify the CTBT was a blow to President Clinton, who had argued passionately for ratification and championed the cause of nuclear nonproliferation and disarmament.

After a bitterly contested election, the incoming Bush administration laid out its new vision for America in the world in *The National Security Strategy of the United States of America*. It is a document awesome in its ambition to preserve the sole superpower status of the United States, and it lays out the new role India is to play in this endeavor:

> The United States has undertaken a transformation in its bilateral relationship with India based on a conviction that U.S. interests require a strong relationship with India. We are the two largest democracies, committed to political freedom protected by repre-

sentative government. India is moving toward greater economic freedom as well. We have a common interest in the free flow of commerce, including through the vital sea lanes of the Indian Ocean. Finally, we share an interest in fighting terrorism and in creating a strategically stable Asia.

Both the "vital sea lanes of the Indian Ocean" and "a strategically stable Asia" refer clearly, if indirectly, to the growing power of China, as well as to the terrorists operating out of Pakistan and Afghanistan.

The new relationship envisioned by the Bush administration is hardly one between equals. There are huge differences of scale in military power and economic might between India and the United States. The United States is the planet's military titan, spending half of the world's entire military expenditure. No other country can project its power anywhere in the world, in multiple locations at once. The United States welcomed a strategic partnership with a country located in proximity to the shipping lanes of the Indian Ocean, within refueling distance of the Arabian Gulf, next door to Afghanistan and Central Asian oil, and on China's border.

After dithering over lifting the sanctions and despite a letter recommending just that from Senator Joseph Biden, chairman of the Senate Foreign Relations Committee, the incoming Bush administration finally lifted the sanctions imposed by the Clinton administration on India and Pakistan, but did so as the result of a bipartisan effort following 9/11. The Bush team made a realist argument that recognized the de facto situation of India having the bomb and pledged "to start with a view of India as a growing world power with which we have common strategic interests." The new administration vowed to forge "a strong partnership with India" to "shape a dynamic future."

India, for its part, chose to hitch its star to the American juggernaut, garnering what tactical, technological, and weapons advantages it could from an alliance with the superpower. Its partnership with the United States is at once a confirmation of its rising stature and a means to accelerate the realization of its great-power ambitions.

Relations between the government of India and the new Republi-

can administration became so publicly warm, Indians took to referring to the closeness between the two sides as *"BJP Bush, bhai bhai"*
meaning "BJP and Bush, best buddies" (literally "as close as brothers"). India's economic reform was humming along. U.S. companies
were expanding their business with India. Joint military maneuvers
were held. The Bush administration even succeeded in getting India to
give rhetorical support for the U.S. withdrawal from the ABM treaty,
which India quickly retracted, to no effect.[7] Everything was looking
up in U.S.-India relations.

India Shining

The United States was thus taken completely by surprise when the BJP
was defeated in national elections in 2004. The Hindu nationalists
were replaced by a thirteen-party coalition led by the country's historically powerful Congress Party. Dubbed the United Progressive
Alliance (UPA), the coalition was supported by India's communist
parties, though they did not officially join the government. Indian and
American business feared the leftist coalition would reverse India's
economic opening and throw cold water on its budding partnership
with the United States. Bombay's stock market crashed on the news,
losing more than 564 points.

The BJP had run a slick campaign. Billboards trumpeted its slogan,
"India Shining," over images of smooth new highways. Clean-cut,
educated Indians lauded the progress the country was making, thanks
to the BJP. The party's star ally, Chandrababu Naidu, chief minister
of Andhra Pradesh, had assiduously courted American business
investment. He had transformed his capital, Hyderabad, into a high-
tech center replete with abundant neon, shopping centers, and some
of the fabled new roads. "Have you been to Hyderabad?" a senior
American diplomat at the U.S. embassy in New Delhi asked me
shortly before the elections. "It's like Gurgaon, Delhi's booming modern suburb, without the cows," he enthused. "It's the other face of
India." When I asked him if there was any downside to India's rapid-
development story, he replied immediately, "None."

Unfortunately for the BJP, a significant number of less well-off Indians, who did not use the new roads, or buy the glittering new products, or invest in the stock market, and for whom life was getting harder rather than easier, did not share this rosy view. Moreover, the BJP, committed to a political philosophy called *hindutva,* had presided over a series of bloody confrontations between Hindus and Muslims as the party endeavored to transform India from a secular multireligious country into a Hindu state.

Much to the relief of business, the change of governments did not cause the feared shutdown of India's path toward greater economic liberalization. A sentiment I heard expressed by Indian businessmen at the time was that, as one senior executive put it, "the process is too far along to be reversed. It's got its own momentum now. There's no going back." The new coalition government did not miss a beat in pushing forward with closer relations with the United States. It installed in New Delhi what Indians still refer to as "the dream team" of free-market-oriented economists, including Prime Minister Manmohan Singh, who, as minister of finance, had overseen India's dramatic economic opening thirteen years earlier. Singh was quick to pledge his country's continued commitment to liberalizing its economy, its solidarity with the United States in the fight against terrorism, and its wish to help spread democracy. The Bombay stock market shot back up.

A Nuclear Deal for India

Indian attitudes toward the United States have changed dramatically since I lived in India in the mid-1980s. Back then, an amazing number of Indians, including university professors and government officials, assumed that my then young first husband, an artist from San Francisco, was a CIA agent. They couldn't believe his Fulbright Fellowship served a purpose other than as a cover for spying. This deep suspicion has metamorphosed into a pragmatic if not an enthusiastic embrace of the United States.

India's leaders see a strong partnership with the United States as strategically useful and economically essential. They have actively been courting U.S. investment, pushing for access to U.S. markets, and lobbying for advanced-technology transfers, including so-called dual-use technologies with potential military applications. Indian business leaders, once afraid of competing with American and other global giants, have fully adapted to the competitive international environment. Flush with cash from rapid growth, they are aggressively expanding abroad, including in the United States. Indian business views access to new technologies and the chance to partner with U.S. companies on cutting-edge research and applications as a major opportunity. This view was one of the driving forces behind the Indian government's effort to secure a deal for sharing dual-use technologies, including nuclear technologies, with the United States.

Over the last several years, India and the United States have brokered deals, signed agreements, formed working groups, and submitted reports forging ties across a range of sectors including defense, agriculture, biotechnology, nanotechnology, energy, the environment, trade, and investment. The culmination of this relationship was a civil nuclear cooperation deal signed by Prime Minister Singh and President Bush when Bush visited India in March of last year.

Reaction to the deal in the United States and in India was mixed. Americans concerned about nuclear proliferation said the nuclear deal with India set the stage for a new global arms race, sending a message to countries like Iran to hurry up and go nuclear as fast as they could: India did, and look at it now. Congressman Edward Markey was perhaps the most vociferous in his criticism of the deal, saying it was a "nuclear domino that falls against 187 other nations" and that it empowered "the hawks in every rogue nation to put their nuclear weapons plans on steroids now that they can no longer be isolated as nonsigners of an agreement that has been shredded."[8] George Perkovich, a scholar at the Carnegie Endowment for International Peace and the author of *India's Nuclear Bomb: The Impact on Global Proliferation,*[9] questioned the premises of the Bush administration's rationale: that a foreign-policy priority is the need to counterbalance China, that strengthening U.S.-India relations is a way to achieve this, and that both are worth throwing out a rules-based nonproliferation regime.[10] Others supported the deal in principle, seeing it as a potential opportunity to strengthen U.S.-India relations, but wished to see more demanded of the Indians in terms of oversight of their military nuclear program. Despite the fact that the deal was designed to have no impact on India's nuclear weapons' program, former congressman and respected Georgia Democrat Sam Nunn declared that, were he still in office, he would be "looking at conditions that could be attached."[11] Perhaps the strongest opposition to the deal came from Republican senators Kyl, Ensign, and Sessions.

The administration argued that the deal actually reduced the risk of nuclear proliferation by bringing India, currently outside the NPT, into some compliance and oversight. It further maintained that the deal was necessary for India to develop its civilian nuclear energy capacity, critical both to meeting the country's exploding energy needs and to reducing greenhouse emissions. There was also strong support for the deal from the Democrat-dominated House India caucus. Finally, the deal would be a bonanza for American business, which stood to reap billions of dollars in contracts prohibited with India under the current nonproliferation regime. The money argument, as we shall see, ended up being the most persuasive.

On the Indian side, virulent opposition to the deal came from India's nuclear scientists, who feared that it was a ploy to rob them of a near breakthrough in the use of thorium that could make India's nuclear program uranium-independent. Uranium is the standard fuel of nuclear reactors. India has little uranium, but one of the world's largest reserves of thorium, and it has assiduously been working to develop indigenous technologies to run its nuclear reactors with thorium. Last year, on August 14, the eve of India's Independence Day anniversary, fourteen of India's top nuclear scientists sent a letter to Prime Minister Singh warning him against conditions attached to the deal that could impair India's "future ability to develop and pursue nuclear technologies for the benefit of the nation."[12] Opposition political parties, especially the BJP, which has always positioned itself as hawkish on defense matters, also seized the opportunity to critique the deal on the grounds that India was giving too much away to the Americans.

The deal capped off what was dubbed the NSSP or Next Steps in the Strategic Partnership between the two countries announced on July 18, 2005, when Prime Minister Manmohan Singh visited Washington, D.C. Under the NSSP, the United States pledged to share with India advanced, sensitive technologies in missile defense, civilian space, high technology, and civilian nuclear. Last year's nuclear deal followed the completion of this quartet of sectors. The core idea of the NSSP is to use India as a research and development partner in the arena of strategic defense. India will lend its proven brainpower in complex technical and scientific areas to technologies critical to preserving the strategic dominance of the United States and, in the process, gain access to and mastery of these technologies.

When Secretary of State Condoleezza Rice visited India in 2005, she stated, "It is the policy of the United States to help India become a major world power in the twenty-first century." Of course major world power is not the same thing as superpower. Clearly, the Bush administration is grooming India for major world power status so that it may better help the United States preserve its status as the global superpower.

One of the main arguments put forward by the Bush administration for approval of the nuclear deal was that India would be able to place orders for new nuclear reactors, giving a boost to U.S. trade and to the administration's campaign to rehabilitate nuclear energy in the United States. But every single senior Indian with whom I spoke in New Delhi in 2006 assured me that, once the United States gave its blessing to the deal and brought the Nuclear Suppliers Group around, "we will buy what we need from Russia and France. They are much cheaper, and they have the experience." French president Jacques Chirac visited India just before Bush did last year. Chirac assured India that France was standing by to help it develop its civilian nuclear capability as soon as the Americans gave the green light. Russia's Vladimir Putin went one step further, awarding India a contract for nuclear fuel over U.S. opposition.

To make its case, the Bush administration argued that India was a responsible nuclear power that had never engaged in any proliferation activities. There is no doubt India has conducted itself as a responsible nuclear power in this regard, unlike Pakistan, where Pakistani senior nuclear scientist A. Q. Khan ran a veritable nuclear-bomb supermarket for rogue states, passing on secrets to Libya, Iran, and North Korea before he was shut down by the United States. Still, the day after the U.S. House of Representatives voted to approve the U.S.-India nuclear deal, the administration revealed it was sanctioning two Indian companies for missile-related transfers to Iran. This stunning revelation came as Israel attacked, with the blessing of the United States, Hezbollah strongholds—armed by Iran—in Lebanon. According to a news report carried by Reuters, the administration had been aware of the missile transfers by the two Indian companies to Iran for months but had withheld the information and held off on sanctions until the nuclear deal with India was approved by Congress. "Clearly they were waiting for the House to vote on the nuclear agreement," observed an aide.[13] This action underlined the extreme importance the Bush administration placed on a successful outcome for the nuclear deal with India.

The Bush administration has made its partnership with India a key to realizing its ambitions, including missile defense and the militarization of space (the so-called Star Wars project), enhancing the United States' military technological superiority past all possible challenge, rehabilitating nuclear power as a central part of U.S. energy policy, and opening the door to billions of dollars in sales to India by U.S. defense contractors. In particular, the administration was keen to clear the way for the sale of F-18 fighter jets to India. The administration has actively promoted the interests of powerful corporations that see India as a source of highly skilled labor at prices vastly lower than what they have to pay similarly qualified people in the United States, and as a market of potentially gigantic proportions. When Bush took office, India's BJP government hurried to offer its full support for Star Wars–style missile defense, making India one of the very few countries in the world that support a program that has yet to prove it can work, and that many consider a complete boondoggle.

From the beginning, the administration has aggressively moved to transform the relationship between India and the United States via a top-down strategy. The nuclear deal was crafted in utmost secrecy at the highest levels of the administration and then announced to a stunned Congress that initially balked at approving an agreement requiring changes in U.S. law on the sensitive issue of nuclear nonproliferation. The Indian government handled the deal in much the same manner, and it too ran into vehement opposition from surprised constituencies. In both countries, powerful business interests and well-developed military-security establishments wield considerable influence over government policy.

Citizen Skeptics

When I was in India during President Bush's visit last year, there were massive anti-Bush demonstrations across the country. On the second day of the visit, Delhi was paralyzed by demonstrations. I could not get back to my hotel after a morning outing in a car and had to make my way up the broad avenues of New Delhi, near Connaught Circus, an area usually more thronged with tourists than demonstrators, on foot. I saw people from all over India—farmers, workers, housewives, students—carrying placards blaming President Bush for the war in Iraq. An effigy of President Bush rendered as Ravana, the multiheaded evil demon in the *Ramayana,* complete with fangs dripping blood, was carried aloft by one group. There is strong opposition in India, as in much of the world, against the war in Iraq, especially among the country's Muslims. In the weeks following President Bush's visit, I saw anti-Bush posters plastered all over Muslim neighborhoods in Calcutta and Bombay. Many featured heartbreaking images of dead Iraqi women and children, killed by aerial bombings by U.S. forces. Images of the humiliation of Iraqi prisoners at Abu Ghraib were everywhere.

India and the United States are democracies with fractious and divided political landscapes whose citizens hold competing and sometimes contradictory positions on policy matters vital to each nation's future. India's current government, at the helm of a wide-ranging coalition that includes parties stridently opposed both to further liberalizing the economy and to a closer relationship with the United States, is particularly vulnerable to dissension. The India-U.S.

relationship looms larger on the Indian domestic political stage than it does with American voters.

There are plenty of signs that citizens of both countries are disaffected, if not outright angry, with their governments. In India, some of this sentiment has been focused on the close relationship with the United States. Critics of the nuclear deal accuse the prime minister of "mortgaging India's strategic needs to overbearing American lawmakers."[14] In addition to tensions between Hindus and Muslims, the rapid push for liberalization and industrial development, often associated with American corporations and business practices, has had devastating consequences for many of India's poor—including slum dwellers, peasants, Tribals, and members of the lower castes. Many Indians believe India has been restrained by the United States from going after Pakistan and the groups that strike India from that country. On the core issues of national security, economic liberalization and development, and terrorism, the current Indian government's closeness to the United States is seen by many Indians as a liability.

An opinion survey conducted last summer indicated that only 34 percent of Indians questioned viewed Prime Minister Singh as "propoor." Fifty-six percent expressed unhappiness with price increases.[15] The UPA government argues that growth is the only way for millions of Indians to make their way out of poverty, that jobs are being created in manufacturing. But this process takes time, and India's poor cannot wait.

The Bush administration, for its part, placed enormous importance on approval of the India-U.S. nuclear deal, a clear foreign-policy achievement that would stand out from the spectacular foreign-policy failures of President Bush's administration. According to a CNN poll conducted in late August 2006, only one-third of the American people supported the war in Iraq. Sixty-one percent opposed it. Fifty-seven percent of Americans said they disagreed with the president on the issues they care about, the same percent as disapproved of him overall. These sentiments were reflected in the resounding defeat of Republican candidates during the 2006 midterm elections that restored control of both houses of Congress to the Democrats.

India and the issue of nuclear nonproliferation are completely overshadowed in U.S. public opinion by the war in Iraq, terrorism, and the price of oil. Eroding support for the Bush presidency did not result in defeat for the India-U.S. nuclear deal, which was approved by a resounding bipartisan vote of 85 to 12, and a series of amendments opposed by India were defeated. However, the outsourcing of jobs to India and the granting of large numbers of H-1B visas to Indian workers, an issue in the 2004 presidential election, have the potential to reemerge as contentious issues as information technology companies in the United States continue to lay off large numbers of American workers. If American voters realized the extent to which U.S. auto giants GM and Ford—both of which have slashed payrolls in the United States—are ramping up production in India, they would not be pleased.

India's Multipolar World

The new strategic partnership between the United States and India, booming trade between the two countries, and the increased visibility and political clout of the successful Indian-American community can give Americans the idea that India is exclusively focused on the United States. Nothing could be further from the complex reality of today's geopolitics.

India is a leader among developing nations. One of the architects of the Nonaligned Movement (NAM), India still hews to NAM's goals of empowering the nations of the global South, on their own terms, and to democratizing international institutions monopolized by a handful of rich and powerful nations. This has been made abundantly clear by India's role representing the G-20 group of developing nations participating in World Trade Organization (WTO) talks during the so-called Doha round of negotiations. Begun in Doha, Qatar, in 2001, the Doha round's purpose is to eliminate unfair subsidies and restructure global trade rules in order to give the economies of developing countries a boost.

The talks collapsed in 2006, when India blamed the United States for refusing to reduce subsidies for key agricultural products, such as cotton, while demanding unfettered access to India's markets. In the face of U.S. intransigence, India's minister of commerce Kamal Nath asserted that "it was important for developing countries to remain united to ensure that no unfair rules were thrown at them."[16] Without a successful outcome on the Doha round of talks, the future of the WTO as the world's only multilateral trading framework was thrown into doubt.

The world has changed a lot since the United Nations was founded in 1945. The ongoing dominance of the UN by the five permanent members of the Security Council—the United States, Russia, China, France, and England—particularly rankles India. At the NAM meeting in Havana, Cuba, in September 2006, Indian prime minister Manmohan Singh told the assembled members, "Reforming the UN and revitalizing the UN General Assembly is a pressing imperative. The developing world must find its due representation among the permanent members of the UN Security Council. We must join hands with other like-minded countries to promote democratization of the processes of global governance, ushering in a new global polity, based on the rule of law, reason, and equity." Mr. Singh warned that NAM members "again confront the danger of a world being split along an artificially created cultural and religious divide."[17]

India, Brazil, China, Mexico, South Africa, and Congo attended the G-8 Outreach Summit in Geneva in July 2006. India used its participation to encourage partnerships between developed and developing countries, especially on education, fighting infectious diseases, and global energy security, and to forge new partnerships with other developing countries. While in Geneva, Mr. Singh discussed bio-diesel and ethanol with Brazilian leader Lula Da Silva. Brazil has emerged as the global leader in the production of these alternative fuels. India and Brazil again took up the issue of energy security when they met in Brasília two months later for the first plenary meeting of the India, Brazil, South Africa Summit (IBSA).

"The idea of IBSA is without precedence," emphasized Mr. Singh. IBSA is not only intended to benefit India, Brazil, and South Africa, but to serve as a catalyst for change across the developing world. "The

IBSA Facility for Alleviation of Poverty and Hunger is a pioneering initiative for South-South cooperation. It is unique for three major developing countries to come together and establish replicable and scalable projects in other developing countries,"[18] underlined Mr. Singh.

India is pursuing increased trade and cooperation with Japan, South Korea, Singapore, Australia, and the countries of Southeast Asia. It is a designated full-dialogue partner of ASEAN, the Association of Southeast Asian Nations. India's "looking East" policy explicitly focuses on the commercial and strategic importance of expanding India's ties with this region, including with Myanmar—against which the United States and the European Union maintain economic sanctions and regularly criticize its human rights record. India signed an agreement with Myanmar for oil and gas exploration in 2005. As with Iran, India's interest in securing additional sources of badly needed energy will trump other factors as it engages with oil- and natural gas–rich countries.

Following a transitional period after the fall of the Soviet Union, India is rebuilding its relations with Russia. A year earlier, the two countries signed a Comprehensive Economic Cooperation Agreement (CECA), projecting an increase in bilateral trade to $10 billion by 2010. Russia remains an important military partner—the country is still India's top arms supplier—and has pledged to help India develop its civil nuclear capability. India's Oil and Natural Gas Corporation (ONGC) has launched a consortium with Russia's state oil company Rosneft to develop new fields in Sakhalin, the Caspian Sea, and Siberia.[19] Russia and the United States are increasingly competing for Indian defense procurement and nuclear technology. In the context of deteriorating relations between Russia and the United States, India's resurgent relations with Russia have the potential to strain U.S.-India relations.

The European Union and India have a long history: India was one of the first countries to recognize the European Union's predecessor, the European Economic Community (EEC), in 1963. The European Union is India's largest trading partner, and trade between India and the European Union is growing at 20 percent per year. Though France and Germany are working to grow their relationships with India, and France has long been an important source of arms sales to the country, the largest portion of India's EU trade is with the United Kingdom. India and the United Kingdom have a special relationship, marked by four centuries of intense interaction. Immigration from India and Pakistan to the United Kingdom has created a thriving British Asian population.

The Deal with China

India is not likely to play junior research partner to America's military and corporate research apparatus. India is far too wary of compromising its vibrant, independent indigenous research capability. India has forged strong relationships with the European Union, Russia, China, and a host of other countries, and it is actively pursuing strategic partnerships, trade deals, and arms purchases from many other sources. India's energy needs are propelling it in directions that the United States can simply neither control nor inhibit, much as it may wish to, including strong relationships with Iran and Myanmar.

In November 2006, Chinese premier Hu Jintao visited New Delhi. The two countries pledged to boost bilateral trade to $40 billion by 2010 and were reported to be on the verge of a civil nuclear deal. India, long a sanctuary for exiled Tibetans, placed enough importance on the visit that it kept Tibetan protesters out of sight while President Hu was in the country. India's interest in a deal with the Chinese was reported to be twofold: one, traditionally nonaligned India did not wish to be seen to be tilting too much toward the United States, and a similar deal with China contributed to redressing this impression; two, India needs China, as a member of the Nuclear Suppliers Group (NSG), to approve the U.S.-India nuclear deal. Not to be outmaneuvered in its neighborhood by the United States, China was reported to be on the verge of offering a similar deal to Pakistan.[20] In both cases, China effectively checkmated the United States' move to build India up as an allied counterweight to growing Chinese clout in the region, and reasserted its intentions to remain very much engaged in South Asia.

The implications for the entire nuclear nonproliferation regime are sobering. As Stephen Cohen, a South Asia specialist at the Brookings

Institution observed, "This is a sign of chaos. There is no game-plan."[21] The United States, having initiated this latest round of nuclear brinkmanship—if within the arena of civil nuclear development—bears a responsibility to help come up with a new set of rules to replace the old nonproliferation regime which is clearly now obsolete. It must also acknowledge that any material or military assistance it extends to India can be supplemented or even matched by China—not to mention nuclear powers Russia and France who are also eyeing India's market potential—and that India is anxious to live equably with its huge northern neighbor.

India's Ambition

Already the world's fourth-largest economy when measured by Purchasing Power Parity (PPP), and destined by 2034 to become the planet's most populous nation, India has great-power ambitions. India is by far the major power in South Asia. It is an acknowledged nuclear power, with tested close-range and intermediate-range missiles. Last year, India tested a long-range missile capable of carrying a nuclear warhead. India has a professional standing army of approximately 1 million men, an air force whose pilots were reported to outperform their American counterparts during joint military exercises in 2004,[22] and a navy that sent help to Indonesia following the disastrous tsunami later that year.

Coupled with these hard-power assets is India's soft-power advantage. As a democracy and an open society, as well as a leader of the developing world, India has great moral authority. India's leadership role in pushing for the democratization of the institutions of world order, whether it be a reconfigured United Nations Security Council or trade talks under the auspices of the World Trade Organization, and its commitment to a multipolar world, add to India's standing among nations. The allure of Indian high and popular culture is expanding as the center of gravity of the global economy, as capital and ideas shift toward Asia. As India rises as a new global competitor and megamarket, its ability to assert its ambition will as well.

Yet India could be undone if it fails to address the plight of its poor and if it allows itself to be seduced by the promises of brute power. The disproportion of India's expenditure on armaments versus on any one of the urgent problems the country faces already shocks. If India does not find ways of addressing these problems, a vast military arsenal will do it little good.

India's is still the dangerous neighborhood about which Jaswant Singh warned nearly a decade ago, and it is in part because of India's own militarism. The nuclear tests by Pakistan that immediately followed India's in 1998 did not reduce the ante, they upped it. In defiance of the new nuclear deterrent—and perhaps precisely because it guaranteed necessary restraint on India's part—Pakistan engaged shortly thereafter in cross-border incursions that culminated in 2002 in the Kargill war.

South Asia remains the most likely flashpoint for a nuclear exchange on the planet. The human cost of such an event is too horrifying to contemplate.

CONCLUSION

As Goes India, So Goes the World

MAHATMA GANDHI WAS A GREAT BELIEVER IN THE power of the people. The strength of Indian society for Gandhi was found in its most humble members. His utopian vision of India was of a nation of self-sufficient villages of equitable citizens governed by India's native political body, the village Panchayat. Surprisingly, as India rushes to embrace a consumer culture, Gandhi's notions of a politics of inclusion and of deepening democracy to include the full participation of the poor is gaining rather than losing currency. "What you are seeing now in India is a new sensitivity to spread the wealth," T. C. Ramadorai told me, "not just in the *über*-class but in the middle class that is expanding into rural areas."

Gandhi believed that the logic of technology advanced for its own sake led inevitably to destruction. He shared this view with German philosopher Martin Heidegger and American physicist Robert Oppenheimer, the inventor of the atomic bomb. As Oppenheimer learned, too late, once the genie is out of the bottle, there is no putting it back. Once a technology has been invented, chances are it will be used.

Gandhi's spinning wheel graced the center of the Congress nationalist flag. Indians continue to embrace it as a symbol of their country's struggle for independence. Most soundly reject, however, its message about technology. Technology, Gandhi warned, tends to create desires that satisfy its own dictates rather than human needs. Gandhi's response to this was literally to strip himself and his life of everything that was not the product of the most basic technology possible.

My Indian grandfather was a strict Gandhian, having been caught up in the swadeshi movement for India's independence in his youth. We all called him Bapuji, the same affectionate yet respectful name used by Gandhi's close followers for the Mahatma. It means something like "respected papa." No matter how much money he made or his children made, my Bapuji, like Gandhi, always wore khadi dhoti, a drape of hand-loom cotton cloth Indian men wear to create a form of loose trousers. I loved to sit in his bedroom in the flat in Juhu on the old iron bedstead, the Voice of America or the BBC on the radio in the background, and listen to my grandfather's words of wisdom. So many times Bapuji told me, his American granddaughter, "You must rule technology. Don't let technology rule you. You should never use any machine you cannot take apart and put back together yourself."

Given the evident impracticality of renouncing the use of almost every kind of machinery if this principle were truly applied, Gandhi's views on technology have been trivialized. In fact, they are profound and live on in the concept of appropriate technology.

"People tend to fetishize technology," Reuben Abraham told me. "They fail to recognize that technology is a means to an end and not the end itself. Electricity by itself does nothing. It's what you do with the electricity that matters." Reuben is setting up a joint initiative for sustainable development between Cornell University and the Indian School of Business in Hyderabad. He asked me, "How do you have this kind of growth without destroying the environment? If India and China develop like the United States has, we're all in trouble. Sustainability has to be embedded in business processes. You can't do business first, over here, and then think about sustainability, over there. That's not going to cut it."

Visionary Indian business leaders, as we have seen, are forging a new model of inclusive, sustainable capitalism that is perhaps our best hope for a future menaced by global warming and stark inequalities. Their efforts are rooted in the hard realities of India today. "Why will India leap forward?" Dr. Shetty asked me. "I'll tell you. We are good at creating institutions. Money alone won't do anything. This is the right moment for India."

As Rohini Nilekani, Nandan Nilekani's wife, a woman strongly committed to social change and saving India's environment, told me, "Many of us try to dissect this animal called poverty. It has many avatars. In India, three hundred million people are living with less than they need to eat. Anything can happen," she warned, "so, we have to ask ourselves, 'How are we to manage decision-making in this country?' We are working in the trenches to deepen democracy."

These efforts are also inspired by a cultural renaissance that is searching to redefine what it means to be Indian in the twenty-first century. "The aspirational urge is enormous, the desire to find a place in the sun, but we need a notion of self-respect that is not derived only from rising economic clout," Pavan Varma, the author of *Being Indian* and the head of the Indian Council for Cultural Relations, told me. "Our culture was not created yesterday. We have to dip into our culture, and take it to a global level." The green architect Karan Grover put it this way, "Ultimately, what I want to say is that we have the resources, we have the stories, to take us to another place."

India is a complicated, fractious, often cacophonous democracy where viewpoints and visions clash and compete. Yet, I have found an astounding consensus around the notions of inclusion and sustainability, grounded in India's unique cultural heritage.

But there is another India: The India that embraced the explosion of a nuclear device as a triumph of achievement and a good nose-thumbing at those who would exclude this great nation from the club of nuclear powers; the India that outspends every other developing country on military procurements while hundreds of millions of its people go hungry. India's missiles are named after conquerors such as the Prithvi, after the twelfth-century ruler Prithvi Raj Chauhan. India's missiles are also named after the elements: Agni, meaning *fire,* and Akash, meaning *sky.* Agni is also the name of the Hindu god of fire. The Trishul missile is named after the weapon wielded by the god Siva. This is the India of the lines quoted by Robert Oppenheimer from the *Bhagavad Gita* at the terrible realization of what had been unleashed by the bomb: "Now I am become Death, the destroyer of worlds." India has vowed that its military program, including nuclear weapons, is for defensive purposes only, but there is no doubt that an arms race is on in South Asia and that the region is one of the world's most perilous.

The waters and forests of ancient India were alive with *apsaras,* water and wood nymphs, whose dances and songs enchanted with their loveliness. The *apsaras'* sinuous forms adorn the columns of temples all over India. Twining their smooth limbs toward the heavens, they represent the sap of life itself. In India's Hindu cosmogony, rivers are goddesses: the Ganga, the Sabarmati, the Narmada, the Saraswati now flowing underground. Women in India have led the most strident efforts to save the country's environment from the wanton destruction of unchecked exploitation. The women in the Chipko movement wrapped themselves around trees in a loving embrace in order to save them from the timber man's saw. India's celebrity environmental activists are all women: Medha Patkar, who fought the damming of the Narmada; Sunita Narain of the Centre for Science and the Environment, who won the 2005 Stockholm Water Prize; Arundhati Roy, who has ceaselessly written and spoken out for a number of causes; Vandana Shiva, who describes herself as an ecofeminist and who fights for sustainable agriculture.

From the World Bank to UN agencies to leading NGOs there is agreement on one thing: essential to ending poverty, ignorance, environmental destruction, and disease in India, including stemming the country's galloping HIV/AIDS epidemic, is the empowerment of women. This is easily said, less easily done, and rarely thought through in all its implications.

A little over a year ago, I gave a talk in New Delhi to a group of senior Indian policy and military analysts on India's soft-power advantage. There were many retired generals in the room. Aside from a research assistant, I was the only woman present. One gentleman wanted a clarification: "Soft power, then, does not mean soft country." No, I replied, it does not. Imperialism has always been about emasculation. Though it was Gandhi's radical nonviolence that showed the impotence of brute force and brought an end to imperial rule, India in the decades that followed has fought to assert its potency as a hard power, culminating with its possession of nuclear weapons.

India has within its grasp all the elements it needs to imagine a different trajectory. Because it is still a developing country, it can choose to develop differently. India does not have to blindly follow the American agribusiness model and become another fast-food nation. It does not have to allow a military-industrial complex to dictate national priorities. It can—it must—forge its own path, lest a world hell-bent on consumption for its own sake and the dangerous vanities of military one-upmanship lead us all into oblivion.

The United States must also do its share, if not for India then for ourselves, because our survival depends on India's success. In the interconnected world in which we live, we are all ultimately vulnerable to pandemic disease, to global warming, to the collapse of the old world order and the uncertainties of what will replace it. Americans can start by forcing our government to join the rest of the world in facing squarely the urgent problem of global warming and by admitting our own disproportionate contribution to a situation with potentially devastating consequences for mankind. Indian environmental writer Ramachandra Guha asks the question in the title of his new book *How Much Should a Person Consume?* It is a timely and profoundly moral question to ask.

Americans can also begin to question the bloated mess that our military-industrial complex—as President Dwight D. Eisenhower warned nearly half a century ago—has become, dictating policy priorities that have cost us dearly in blood and in silver. If we are concerned about China brokering a nuclear deal with Pakistan, we have only ourselves to blame for opening that door and no moral high ground to claim.

Last year, U.S. contractors, already the world's leaders in arms sales, doubled sales of weapons to foreign governments, from $10.6 billion to $21 billion. A significant portion of the increase came from arms sales to Pakistan, including a $5 billion order for F-16 fighter jets. With approval of the India-U.S. nuclear deal, India has become one of the most lucrative potential markets for U.S. weapons contractors, who are burning jet fuel trekking to the subcontinent to show off their products.[1] With the United States and China racing to cement deals and sell arms and nuclear technology to both India and Pakistan, South Asia is on its way to holding on to the championship title for decades to come as one of the most dangerous places on Earth.

I believe that the United States cannot beat China in the long term on sheer economic or military might: a race to do so will destroy our environment and our society. We can beat China—or rather woo it—if we reorder our priorities and return to our roots as a government of, by, and for the people, able to assert moral authority in the arena of world affairs with a clear conscience.

India and the United States, undoubtedly two of the world's great democracies, have a real opportunity to recall each other to the moral bedrock of our respective founding moments; to turn away from rampant militarism and save our environment. We can contribute to the creation of a new global order dedicated to the pursuit of life, liberty, and happiness; to ensuring justice and fullness of life to every man and woman. To continue with business as usual is suicide, a choice—as Jared Diamond has reminded us—more than one civilization has made along history's winding way. But this time, the whole world is at stake. We must not allow imagination to fail us now.

If we are to survive as a planet, we need India to summon up from its deep cultural past—as so many of the remarkable individuals profiled on these pages are doing—a new ethos. This will be India's renaissance; its shaking off once and for all the yoke of subjugation to the West, and its triumphant reemergence as a truly great power.

Then, if we are lucky, India's journey of self-invention will reinvent the world.

Afterword

India's Dilemma

The time has come for the better-off sections of our society to
understand the need to make our growth process more inclusive—to eschew conspicuous consumption, to save more and
waste less, to care for those who are less privileged, to be role
models of probity, moderation, and charity.

—Manmohan Singh, Prime Minister of India
Ten Point Social Charter, May 25, 2007

India celebrated sixty years of independence as a vibrant democracy
on August 15, 2007. Many were skeptical in 1947 that democracy
could work in such a poor and populous nation. Many still see India's
democracy as a major obstacle to bringing the country more quickly
to heel behind an accelerated program of focused market liberalization, infrastructure improvement, and industrial development favorable to foreign investment.

Why can't India be more like China? Why can't the government
just push through what needs to be done? Widespread corruption and
poor governance are certainly major impediments to India's progress,
but, warts and all, democracy insists on surviving in India. One of the
most diverse populations on the planet, the citizens of India have
never been afraid to speak their minds. They simply will not follow
passively the dictates of government.

A plethora of political parties and the necessity of cobbling together a coalition government mean that dissenting views have much more power to be heard in India than in, for example, the United States. And every Indian politician knows that it is the poor in India who vote. But India's leaders also know that economic growth is essential to improving the life chances of all of the country's citizens, and that it is hard to transform a developing country into a developed one without unleashing forces of creative destruction that disproportionately hurt the poor.

The faster India's economy grows, the more India is caught on the horns of a dilemma. How can it keep the engine of extraordinary economic growth humming along at top speed without further eroding the already tenuous existence of the poor, dangerously undermining social cohesion, and finishing off what is left of India's natural environment?

The Persistence of the Poor

Despite the rosy numbers, the spikes in foreign investment, and the expansion of leading Indian companies abroad, the sad fact is that most of India's citizens remain extremely poor. This is after sixty years of independence and sixteen years of economic liberalization and exceptionally high growth. The week before India celebrated its sixtieth anniversary, the government of India released a thoroughly dispiriting report revealing that 86 percent of Indians who work in the informal sector, whose jobs, in other words, are not taxed or officially tracked by the government, earn less than fifty cents per day. Since the majority of working Indians fall into this category, this report revealed that half of India's population is not living on just less than two dollars per day, or even just less than one dollar per day: 600 million Indians are living on a pitiful fifty cents per day.

At the same time, India's poor are increasingly treated to the spectacle of conspicuous consumption by an Indian elite intoxicated with new purchasing possibilities and the lifting of the old Gandhian stigma against the overt display of wealth. Hence the prime minister's admonishment in the Ten Point Social Charter he presented in the spring of 2007 to India's business elite to live a little more modestly out of respect for the plight of their millions of lesser well-off fellow citizens. The business press mocked him but listeners with longer historical memories heard echoes of Gandhi and Nehru, India's founding fathers, whose promises to the people of India at independence have still not been fulfilled.

India's poor are having a harder and harder time of it. The 2007 annual report of the Asian Development Bank warned that economic liberalization is causing the gap between rich and poor in Asia to widen, not narrow. In India, inflation has teamed up with high growth. Prices generally are rising at a rate of 7 percent, while the prices of basic foods are rising at an annual rate of 10 percent, faster than India's annual rate of economic growth. Naturally, it is the poor who are hit the hardest.

Development projects such as dams, mines, and Special Economic Zones (SEZs) in "green field" areas have forced the dislocation of millions of peasant farmers and Adivasis, traditionally forest dwellers, with only a small portion ever receiving promised resettlement or compensation packages. Most of these end up as internal migrants in the very poor informal sector profiled in the government's report. It is a recipe for widespread social and political unrest, of which India's growing Maoist rebel movement is but one symptom.

Beyond poverty, India still faces all the daunting challenges outlined in this book a year ago, with one encouraging exception: The HIV/AIDS epidemic appears to have been overestimated. A study released in 2007 indicated that the population of people in India infected with the disease may actually be between 2 and 3 million people, half of what it had earlier been estimated to be. The new report was based on house-to-house surveys rather than on data from maternal blood-testing. If its results are accurate, this is terrific news for India.

On the other hand, the water crisis has worsened. The energy crunch continues to produce regular electricity cuts, which affect the poor and the middle class far more than the rich who simply switch on their diesel generators. Record floods again laid waste to vast areas of India this past monsoon season, leaving wrecked fields, destroyed villages, death, and disease. The government of India has not invested what it needs to in disaster preparedness for this annual tragedy. The impact of the 2007 monsoon was made worse by the overconstruction of earth embankments, which gave way, New Orleans–style, before an onslaught of water and sludge. The plight of India's long-suffering farmers remains dire, with suicides pegged at more than one hundred thousand in the past decade.

India was again forced to import record amounts of wheat to meet demand in 2007 and 2008. In fact, panic-buying by India was blamed for sending the price of wheat on commodity exchanges in 2007 to record-breaking levels and raising food prices around the world.

The Cost of Business as Usual

The inspiring vision of so many of the Indians I interviewed for this book is fading with each passing day that India embraces a consumption-based, business-as-usual approach to its development. Willy-nilly urban development with little attempt at energy efficiency or the realities of most urban citizens' lives continues as if India faced no energy or pollution problems, and all Indians were destined to get from point A to point B in a private automobile. This is all the more striking as cities in the developed world make serious strides toward "greening" their infrastructure with everything from stricter building codes on energy efficiency, curbs on vehicular traffic, and the construction of a pedestrian- and bicycle-friendly urban environment.

I live in New York City. Like many New Yorkers I know, I do not own a car, nor do I aspire to. Most Parisians I know don't either. But New Yorkers and Parisians have something urban Indians don't: sidewalks, crosswalks, excellent public transportation, bicycle lanes, and schools, post offices, parks, and shops within easy proximity. With the exception of citizens of New Delhi who have a stellar Metro system, only the very privileged residents of expensive, gated, private developments in India enjoy these basic urban amenities.

It doesn't have to be this way. The extraordinary individuals profiled in this book state again and again that India has within its grasp all the elements to imagine a different future than going through the various painful stages of industrialization and militarism the West did in the twentieth century. Thousands of dedicated individuals and grassroots movements and groups are working every day in India to chart a different course. But the incentives to continue conducting business as usual are hard to resist, especially in a country where so many are experiencing the seductions of a modern consumer culture for the first time.

Much of India's business leadership, emboldened by a new ability to compete head-to-head with the leading multinationals of Europe, North America, and East Asia, and benefiting directly from lucrative deals with major foreign corporations, have joined their American counterparts in pushing for a Reagan-era model of aggressive, business-friendly "trickle-down" capitalism. The two countries' leading business lobby groups, the Confederation of Indian Industry (CII) and the U.S.-India Business Council (USIBC), have spent millions of dollars lobbying on Capitol Hill to push approval of the U.S.-India Civil Nuclear Agreement because of the billions of dollars their members will reap if the deal goes through.

Their next project: a free-trade agreement between the two countries. One can only imagine the devastating impact on India's poor if their fate is anything like Mexico's peasants in the aftermath of the North America Free Trade Agreement. And, unless it is managed carefully, the "giant sucking sound," as onetime presidential candidate Ross Perot so prosaically put it, of jobs leaving the United States will be coming from India, not Mexico, and they will be highly skilled jobs as well as jobs in manufacturing.

For Indian and American big business, it's all about the money. The government of India is planning to ramp up its defense capabilities in a bid to forge great power status on a credible standing with that of France, Russia, and the United Kingdom—if not China or the United States. Over the next five years alone, India is expected to spend up to $60 billion on conventional weapons procurement. (Despite modest raises in social spending, it will spend a comparative pittance on health, education, alternative energy, and the environment.) American companies want a big piece of this incredibly juicy pie, and they are afraid that, without the gift of the civil nuclear deal to India, they will be shut out by the other defense-hungry sharks chasing India's defense dollars: Russia, France, Israel, and even Sweden.

Indian companies also see big business opportunities in their country's planned defense procurements. The government of India is requiring that a significant portion of the new weapons' contracts include investment in India, and that Indian industry get a leg up on developing its own capability as one of the world's big arms manufacturers. They are eager to increase ties to powerful American corporations, as the tie-up between Sunil Mittal's group and Wal-Mart demonstrates. The deal is "win-win" for Indian and American business.

The other lucrative component of the nuclear deal is in the energy sector, with intense competition between the United States, Russia, and France anticipated for the construction of India's new nuclear reactors and substantial opportunities for Indian companies to get into the act as well. This even though nuclear power is expected to provide a very small amount of India's (or the United States') total energy needs for the next half century. The nuclear energy industry has managed to rehabilitate itself through exploiting fears of global warming and repackaging nuclear power as the "clean, safe" energy that will miraculously save us from climate change. Meanwhile, a nuclear reactor had to be shut down in Tennessee in the summer of 2007 because the temperature of the river water used to cool it was too warm to be effective; a reactor in Japan was seriously damaged by an earthquake; and a reactor in Sweden suffered a terrifying near-meltdown. But, no worries, nuclear reactors are "pollution-free."

The U.S.-India Partnership Under Fire

All the lobbying in Washington has done nothing to stifle objections to the deal in India. Partly petty party politics—the BJP has objected on national sovereignty grounds when it was the party that initiated the deal in the first place and under whose watch India became a nuclear power in 1998—partly a lingering national insecurity that provokes an exaggerated sense of threat to national sovereignty from any foreign quarter, objections to the deal in India have been vociferous. Most alarmingly for Prime Minister Singh and his Congress Party, India's communist parties, on whose support Congress depends to hold the current government in power, have ripped the agreement, calling for, at the least, a delay in forging ahead. They have dug in their heels, and the government may yet face a crisis of confidence that could precipitate early elections.

The Left's main objection: a fear that India's growing strategic and economic partnership with the United States is compromising India's foreign-policy independence and opening the country up to unmitigated exploitation by powerful U.S.—and Indian and other foreign—corporate interests. India's Left simply does not view the United States as a benign actor. Given the pressure by foreign investors to scuttle India's labor laws, though they apply to a very small portion of the country's workforce, as well as a host of other Indian laws pertaining to land rights and other areas, India's Left potentially has a lot to lose from a closer U.S. embrace. This would be no loss from the point of view of U.S. business, which fears that a "Venezuela effect" in India could rip this lucrative market, whose potential has barely been tapped, from its grasp.

By sheer size of population, economy, and growing military might, India is bound to fulfill the basic criteria for the entrée it seeks into the awesome realm of the "great powers." But, as top French India expert Christophe Jaffrelot has asked: "Power to do what?" A huge army equipped with medium-range missiles, nuclear submarines, F-18 fighter jets, and up-to-the-minute surveillance systems will do India little good if it loses sight of what has truly made India a great nation.

India is taking a page from the United States' own playbook, and the United States is all too willing to act as coach and equipment supplier. But the race for military supremacy is a race to oblivion in the long run and to economic ruin in the shorter run. One need only look at the current state of U.S. indebtedness in the wake of the Iraq war, the multiplying evidence that the United States has failed to sufficiently maintain and improve its basic physical infrastructure, or the sad evidence of a failure to invest in the basic human needs of quality health care and education for all its citizens. A platform for strong future national competitiveness is not thus constructed.

At the end of the day, it bears remembering that India is a nuclear power with two nuclear neighbors in a region fraught with instability, much of it resulting from grotesque social and economic inequalities and serious environmental degradation that no amount of weaponry is going to solve.

A Growing Backlash

Sixty years after independence, and despite the best assurances of the Indian government, India is in danger of turning its back on the poor and on the incredible legacy of the nation's most influential founding father, Mahatma Gandhi. Under intense pressure from business interests, India is throwing away its rich agricultural, peasant, nomad, and Adivasi heritage in favor of a toxic and dangerously outmoded nineteenth-century and twentieth-century model of industrial development, monopoly agriculture, and chaotic urban growth.

Is it possible to "grow equity," as India's top billionaire Mukesh Ambani challenged early in these pages over a year ago? Mr. Ambani's personal wealth has exploded in the year since I wrote this book. He is now one of the richest men on Earth, worth in excess of $60 billion. Despite the prime minister's pleas, he is not at all shy about flaunting what he's got. In 2007, the press around the world carried stories about the planned construction of a sixty-story personal residence for the six members of Mr. Ambani's family, complete with four levels to park his extensive automobile collection and a helicopter landing pad. The new home will tower over the city of Bombay, where 60 percent of the residents are homeless or live in slums. According to news reports, the Ambani residence will employ a staff of six hundred. Construction is expected to be finished by fall 2008. It is hard to imagine India's economy could ever grow enough wealth for all the residents of Bombay to live as lavishly as Mr. Ambani does.

One economist told me that there is a tried and true way to grow equity: "It's called income redistribution through taxation and government spending," he said. The government of India has made some commitment to do this, more than the business community would like but much less than India's poor masses need and very little when compared to India's military spending. While some of India's business leaders are taking practical steps to toe a Triple Bottom Line, others are using their newly deep pockets to put into practice business models that produce high returns for investors but do so at an unacceptable social and environmental cost. Mesmerized by the lure of foreign direct investment and the imperative of industrial development, the government seems incapable of putting a stop to many of these practices. Unfortunately, its actions simply don't match its laudable rhetoric.

What the government cannot curb, Indian citizens are increasingly taking upon themselves to stop, sometimes with violent means. A backlash against development with every concession for corporate investors and no protections for the thousands of Indians who are forced off their land or out of their jobs is growing, and growing ever more violent. The Maoist Naxalite rebels continue to gain ground. In the Nandigram area of West Bengal, farmers and villagers protested violently against the establishment of a Special Economic Zone for a vast, 34,000-acre chemical plant development that threatened to dispossess them of the only way they had of making a living, their land. In March 2007, the conflict came to a head and scores of people were killed. Ironically, it was the communist government of the state that orchestrated the violent suppression of the protests. Ultimately, the government was forced to move the project elsewhere.

In September 2007, violent protests at the site of several new Reliance Fresh supermarkets set up on the Wal-Mart, big-box model led the newly elected state government of Uttar Pradesh to order the stores closed until their impact on the livelihoods of local vegetable sellers and small shop owners could be assessed. Tens of thousands of vegetable sellers and mom-and-pop stores have been instantly relieved of their source of income by these megastores, which promise to "eliminate the middleman" in order to pay farmers higher prices and offer consumers lower prices (and pocket huge profits on the margin in between). The protests have not been limited to Uttar Pradesh, and threaten to engulf the whole country. A zeal to eliminate inefficiencies in the market in India can have devastating social consequences when the "inefficiencies" consist of millions of people eking out a living with nowhere else to turn for employment. And the promised lower prices are only lower for middle-class consumers who will shop in the new, air-conditioned stores.

Moreover, these stores demand industrial agricultural practices that include monoculture; heavy synthetic fertilizer and pesticide applications; and increasingly in India, genetically modified crops. Food irradiation, already present, is poised to become widespread in India as well. Indian mangoes were allowed to be imported into the United States in 2007 on the condition that they arrive only in commercial shipments (guaranteeing the market to big growers) and have been subjected to nuclear irradiation in a facility approved by the U.S. government prior to shipment.

This puts India's food chain on the opposite trajectory of that in the United States where organic food is the fastest-growing food market segment, farmers' markets are booming, and the local food and slow-food movements are rapidly increasing in popularity. In the United States, citizens are fed up with industrial agriculture but it is difficult to stand up to powerful agribusiness lobbies and undo the damage that has been done to the land, water, and wildlife—not to mention human communities and the population of experienced farmers—and restore a sane food-producing ecosystem. India does not have to go down this same path. It can—it must—embrace farmer-centered, sustainable agriculture. The human and environmental cost of not doing so will be too much for India to bear.

Even the middle class is having a hard time in high-growth India. My aunt and uncle are finding life in Gurgaon increasingly wearing. They are fortunate enough to be able to decamp to North America during the hot season when temperatures regularly top 100 degrees Fahrenheit and the power goes out for hours every stifling day, shutting down the air conditioners, the television, and the computer. Though they are in no danger of starving, they have felt the impact of rising prices on the family budget.

The dizzying bullishness I encountered in India in 2005 and 2006 when I did the bulk of the research for this book still exists. Indians continue to have high hopes for the future of their country. They still believe it is finally on the path to recognized greatness. But there is now more than a tinge of anxiety as well, a tangible sense of fear lapping at the edges of the giddy buoyancy. With each power outage, each devastating flood, each lost morning in a traffic jam, each bloody revolt by a Maoist rebel, or visible distress of a displaced peasant, the fear increases.

Most Indians have accepted that India will never catch up with China, and is, in fact, falling further and further behind its giant neighbor. As in the rest of the world, the current credit crisis in the United States is cause for alarm in India. A prolonged U.S. recession could undo much of India's promised growth, increasingly tied to the U.S. economy. A voice, sometimes a whisper, sometimes a shrill bark, warns that the Western party of consumption for its own sake, the "turbo-charged" capitalism, as George Soros called it, that has captured so many institutions of national and global governance, and a global economy held hostage by the dictates of an enormous military-industrial complex, will someday face its morning after.

Another World Is Possible

Will India fulfill the promise of this moment and make good on the pledge Jawaharlal Nehru made to the people of India in his famous speech at the hour of his country's independence to free all Indians from "poverty and disease and inequality of opportunity"? Will India have the political courage and the intellectual daring to imagine a postindustrial, twenty-first-century national destiny grounded in its own ancient traditions and the truly revolutionary message of nonviolence that secured its freedom?

The sheer vitality of India's people, the magic of its rich culture both ancient and contemporary are wellsprings of creativity and resilience which inspire and sustain millions of people in India and around the world every day. There is a sufficient level of chaotic exuberance in every facet of this magnificent country that India will always escape easy generalizations, even, it is my sincerest hope, about the direst tendencies of the current moment. India's political and cultural soft power remain enormous assets that will see the country far toward achieving it goals. The world continues to be just as enchanted with all things Indian as Indians themselves, who revel in the dynamic creative possibilities of their nation as it rushes forward. Still, when rhetoric and reality drift too far apart, even the mightiest soft power can lose its potency, and the credibility of even the greatest nation can be lost.

In the end, India's most precious asset of all is its democracy. No matter how high India's growth rate spikes or how many new Indian billionaires make the Forbes list, India's primarily poor voters will turn the current government out if it fails to make meaningful progress toward meeting their basic needs. The head of a powerful lobbying group in Washington, D.C., told me recently, "Business is leading this whole thing now with India. We just need to make sure the governments bring the people along." I hope the coming elections in India and in the United States prove this man has the equation of democratic governance turned on its head.

Will a new U.S. administration have the courage to radically refocus the relationship between the United States and India around the major challenges of our time? It will if American citizens, including Indian-American citizens, demand that it does. Imagine the power of a bilateral relationship between two of the world's great democracies focused on promoting sustainable agriculture that preserves family farms and plant diversity; on tackling global warming by dramatically reducing greenhouse gases, bringing down America's disproportionate consumption of world resources, and making concrete plans to help citizens and businesses cope with what climate change is likely to inflict; on designing low-cost, environmentally friendly, and energy-efficient housing and transportation; on investing in preventative medicine and using technology to bring down health care costs to make excellent health care a universal right and not a limited privilege; on making quality education accessible to all so that every child can realize his or her full life potential.

Imagine a U.S.-India Civil Nuclear Agreement that focuses on universal nuclear disarmament—including of the United States—something India has advocated for many years, and on finding alternative energy sources sufficient to allow us to forego both fossil fuels and fissile fuels.

Another world is possible. As many of the people interviewed in this book amply show, we the people need only translate what has already been imagined into reality.

India is moving forward faster and faster, no doubt. We all are. The question is toward what destiny.

New York City
September 10, 2007

Acknowledgments

India is in my blood. It is also lodged in my heart. I wrote this book because I believe that India matters as never before to the future of a world in crisis.

India is inexhaustible, an endlessly fascinating wonder of a country. It is seductive, even transcendent in the beauty of its rich culture, fairy-tale monuments, and stunning landscape. India is also a place of exquisite social cruelty, great suffering, and truly frightening problems. An exemplar of the postmodern condition, India exists simultaneously in every moment of human history, and under every great religious, philosophical, and scientific rational narrative ever enunciated.

It is not possible to capture the totality of India in a single book, especially when the country is changing at a pace of historic velocity. Inevitably, many fine individuals and important efforts have not found a place in these pages. Still, on my journey into twenty-first-century India, I met ordinary people coping with extraordinary times, and people of exceptional vision and drive who are committed to transforming India, and in so doing the world, within their lifetime. My hope is that their stories will convey much more than the facts that I relate, and that, in the end, something of the incredible human-ity of India will move the reader to see India and our world in a new light.

The response from people I contacted for help with researching this book was simply tremendous. There is such excitement about India's amazing rise, such deep concern over the serious challenges India faces, that time and time again complete strangers opened their hearts, their homes, and their address books to me without hesitation.

If I have inadvertently left anyone out in the acknowledgments that follow, I sincerely apologize, and am no less grateful.

Christophe Jaffrelot at the Center for International Relations Studies in Paris urged me to take an idea I shared with him for a book on India Global to Rajesh Sharma at Actes Sud. Rajesh was extremely encouraging—and remained so throughout—and the project began.

I want to thank in particular my agent, Sterling Lord, for believing in this book and in me from the beginning, and for all of his support. My editor at Scribner, Alexis Gargagliano, worked almost as hard as I did to see this to a speedy completion, spurring me to tap new reservoirs of energy, and forcing me to dig deeper and write better at every step. For the incredible support and hard work of Susan Moldow, Kate Bittman, and the entire team at Scribner: thank you. I also want to thank my research assistants for all their hard work: Garima Singh, Tom Ogorzalek, Meron Tesfamichael, and Patricia Swart, who shared her good insights into Indian film and entertainment and generously connected me to Toonz in Trivandrum. And I want to thank the people who read the book in manuscript: Marc Aronson, Alyssa Ayres, Jonah Blank, Marina Budhos, and Michele Wucker. While I take full responsibility for any errors or deficiencies that remain, the honest, practical feedback from these fine writers and excellent friends made this a much better book.

In addition to the many people who generously shared their stories with me, I want to thank Judi Kilachand of the Asia Society, who introduced me to scores of people in India who became key to the book. Sreenath Sreenivasan was an enthusiastic supporter who also introduced me to several people I profiled or quoted. At the American India Foundation, Pradeep Kashyap, Anjali Sharma, and Rema Nanda were unreservedly helpful. Sridar Iyengar of TIE unhesitatingly connected me to many people whose help became essential. Mallika Dutt, Nirupam Bajpai, and Nusrat Durrani were extremely helpful. Richard Celeste gave me a core list of influentials early on that guided my research. Ron Hira generously shared his views. Stanley Wolpert urged me to write the book when the idea was just beginning to take form.

In India, I want to thank my family, especially my uncle and aunt

Dilip and Dipti Kamdar. I felt so welcome coming out of international arrivals at the Delhi airport after a long trip, seeing my uncle's smile, and knowing a delicious meal and a comfortable bed waited at home. In Bombay, my aunt Rama Parekh, my cousin Reshma Parekh, my aunt Usha Kamdar, and my uncle and aunt Himmat and Padma Khara all provided loving hospitality and support. Friends who put me up, fed me, and encouraged me include Mala and Tejbir Singh, Rasik and Panna Hemani. My friend Minu Tharoor's family in Calcutta, the Mukherjis, gave me a very warm welcome indeed, and her brother Shekhar showed me the great work he was doing in one of Calcutta's slums, introduced me to Sanjay Bhansal, and put me in touch with Ina Puri in Delhi, who introduced me to Shankar Rao, who took care of my stay in Hyderabad. Thanks are due to Rakesh Chopra and Gulshan Luthra. R. K. Mishra opened many doors.

Special thanks is due in Paris to Christophe Guilmoto and Ines Zupanov, who finally gave me a key to their apartment after I stopped in so often on my way in and out of India, and to Gilles Courtois and Jean-Damien Thiollier, and Ingrid Gestin-Therwath. In London, thanks are due to Hitesh and Trupti Mehta, and to Ila and Chetan Mehta. In India, I must specially thank for their friendship, guidance, or good ideas Kanti Bajpai, Dilip Cherian, J. B. D'Souza, Dilip D'Souza, Anita Patil Deshmukh, Meenakshi Ganguly, Karan Grover, Ramchandra Guha, Abid Hussain, Pralay Kanungo, Gurmeet Kanwal, Naazneen Karmali, Pratap Bhanu Mehta, Ajay Mehra, Roger Pereira, Sri Renganathan, Nilima Rovsen, Varun Sahni, Mallika Sarabhai, Samir Saran, Satvik Varma, Pavan Varma, Harjiv Singh, Jyotsna Singh, Rita Soni, and Jyotsna Uppal.

Finally, my parents cheered me on as always, while my own family made do with a series of frequent and long absences, and then with a mightily distracted mother and wife. I thank them from the bottom of my heart for their love, patience, and forbearance.

Notes

Introduction: Life on Planet India

1. "America's Image Slips," *Pew Global Attitudes Project Report,* Pew Research Center, June 13, 2006, http://pewresearch.org/reports/?ReportID=27.
2. A. Shankkar, "Moolah Rage," *India Today,* January 9, 2006.
3. Diane E. Lewis, "Indian Tech Firms Seek U.S. Talent in Offshoring Twist," *Boston Globe,* May 30, 2006, http://www.boston.com/news/world/asia/articles/2006/05/30/india_tech_firms_seek_us_talent_in_offshoring_twist/.
4. Alan S. Blinder, "Offshoring: The Next Industrial Revolution?" *Foreign Affairs,* March/April 2006, 114; and Ron Hira and Anil Hira, *Outsourcing America: What's Behind Our National Crisis and How We Can Reclaim American Jobs* (New York: AMACOM Books, 2005), 44–48.
5. Blinder, "Offshoring," 114.
6. Kouteya Sinha, "UN Report Slams India for Farmer Suicides," *Times of India,* September 24, 2006, http://timesofindia.indiatimes.com/articleshow/2021582.cms.
7. Peter Wonacott, "In India, HIV Threatens Economy: Epidemic Could Trim the Country's Growth Over Coming Decade," *Wall Street Journal,* July 21, 2006.
8. Somini Sengupta, "In India, Maoist Guerillas Widen 'People's War'," *New York Times,* April 13, 2006, http://www.nytimes.com/2006/04/13/world/asia/13maoists.html?ex=1302580800&en=b397a84735c2f9cb&ei=5088&partner=rssnyt&emc=rss.
9. Jawaharlal Nehru, Speech on the Granting of Indian Independence, August 14, 1947.
10. Y. C. Deveshwar, "Vision, Values and Vitality Powering ITC's Transformation" (speech by the chairman, 95th Annual General Meeting, July 21, 2006), http://www.itcportal.com/chairman_speaks/chairman_2006.html.

Chapter One: Indians and Americans

1. See Sudharshan Kapur, *Raising Up a Prophet: The African-American Encounter with Gandhi* (Boston: Beacon Press, 1992). I want to thank Marc Aronson for referring me to this book and for giving me valuable insight into

the history of Indians and African-Americans. His book, tentatively titled *Race: The History of an Idea; a Prejudice; a Central Strand in Western Civilization; and in My Own Life* was at this writing forthcoming with Ginee Seo Books, Simon & Schuster, 2007.

2. Ibid., 3.

3. For a full history of these and other early struggles of Indian immigrants to the United States, see Ronald Takaki, *Strangers from a Different Shore: A History of Asian Americans* (Boston: Back Bay Books, 1998).

4. Barbara Kiviat, "Chasing Desi Dollars," *Time,* July 6, 2005, http://www.time.com/time/insidebiz/article/0,9171,1079504,00.html.

5. See the American Association of Physicians of Indian Origin Web site, http://www.aapiusa.org/index.aspx.

6. See the AAHOA Web site, http://www.aahoa.com.

7. Michael Lewis, *The New New Thing: A Silicon Valley Story* (New York: W. W. Norton, 2000), 116.

8. Raj Jayadev, "Silicon Valley Indian Entrepreneurs: Where Are You When the South Asian Community Needs You?" Pacific News Service, November 23, 2001, http://news.pacificnews.org/news/view_article.html?article_id=086aa5ac9c7a387d5c2fde13c60d03cb.

9. As posted on TIE, The Indus Entrepreneurs official Web site, http://www.tie.org/Home/AboutTie/FAQs/index_html/view_document.

10. Interview with Darshana V. Nadkarni, *India Currents,* August 26, 2006, http://indiacurrents.com/news/view_article.html?article_id=cf2ad5b8ba37ba14336ee664988da0ec.

11. Ibid.

12. Justin Hibbard, "Catching Up with Vinod Khosla," *BusinessWeek,* May 31, 2005, http://www.tie.org/view_news?id_news=132.

13. Douglas Waller, "India Plays the Game," *Time,* March 12, 2006.

14. Ingrid Therwath, "Working for India or Against Islam? Islamophobia in Indian American Lobbies" (unpublished paper, September 19, 2005).

15. See USINPAC's Web site, http://www.usinpac.com.

16. Robert M. Hathaway, "Washington's New Strategic Partnership," *Seminar* 538 (2004), http://www.india-seminar.com/2004/538/538%20robert%20m.%20hathaway.htm.

17. Ibid.

18. Quoted by Alan Cooperman, "India, Israel Interests Team Up," *Washington Post,* July 19, 2003.

19. See the "Ethnic Partners, Indian / South Asian" Web page, http://www.engagingamerica.org/ajc/ethnPartner/index.asp?partnerID=33.

20. www.usinpac.com/issue_details.asp?News_ID=3.

21. Ted McKenna, "Indian-American Group Promotes Nuclear Trade," *PRWeek,* July 27, 2006.

22. http://www.usindiafriendship.net/congress1/housecaucus/caucusonindia.htm.

23. Aziz Haniffa, "Criticism Aplenty of India Caucus," *India Abroad,* May 6, 2005, A6.

24. Aziz Haniffa, "U.S. Senate India Caucus," March 31, 2004, http://www.usindiafriendship.net/congress1/senatecaucus/senatecaucus.htm.

25. Michael Forsythe and Venna Trehan, Bloomberg News, "Friends in High Places," *International Herald Tribune,* July 17, 2006.
26. Farah Stockman, "Trade Plan Would Allow Nuclear Sales to India; Critics Call Deal Bad Foreign Policy," *Boston Globe,* July 3, 2006.
27. Ibid.
28. Forsythe and Trehan, "Friends in High Places."
29. "Does Your Company Have an India Strategy?" http://www.export.gov/indiamission/.
30. "The Rich, the Poor and the Growing Gap between Them," *Economist,* June 15, 2006, http://www.economist.com/world/displaystory.cfm?story_id=7055911.
31. Ibid.
32. Steven Greenhouse and David Leonhardt, "Real Wages Fail to Match a Rise in Productivity," *New York Times,* August 28, 2006, http://www.nytimes.com/2006/08/28/business/28wages.html?ex=1156910400&en=0d0f342076 33d3fc&ei=5070.
33. Testimony of Ronil Hira, Ph.D., P.E., to the Committee on Small Business on the Offshoring of High-Skilled Jobs, October 20, 2003, http://www.ieeeusa.org/policy/POLICY/2003/102003.html.
34. Ed Frauenheim, "Salary concerns renew H-1B visa opposition," CNET News.com, October 6, 2005, http://news.com.com/Waging+battle+on+foreign+labor/2009-1022_3-5888772.html.
35. Blinder, "Offshoring"; and Ron Hira and Anil Hira, *Outsourcing America: What's Behind Our National Crisis and How We Can Reclaim American Jobs* (New York: AMACOM Books, 2005), 44–48.
36. India Brand Equity Foundation (IBEF) official Web site economic overview available at http://www.ibef.org/economy/services.aspx.
37. Two widely read recent books outline these trends in depth: Tom Friedman, *The World Is Flat* (New York: Farrar, Straus and Giroux, 2005) and Clyde Prestowitz, *Three Billion New Capitalists: The Great Shift of Wealth and Power to the East* (New York: Basic Books, 2005).
38. "Subcontinental Drift: More Westerners Are Beefing Up Their Résumés with a Stint in India," *BusinessWeek,* January 16, 2006, http://www.businessweek.com/magazine/content/06_03/b3967085.htm.
39. "The Foreigners Amongst Us," *TimeOut Mumbai,* March 11–24 , 2005, 20.

Chapter Two: India Imagines the Future

1. "Entertainment and Media," report by PricewaterhouseCoopers for India Brand Equity Foundation (IBEF, New Delhi), 7.
2. Ibid.
3. Numbers are for 2002, from Earthtrends study by World Resources Institute, 2003, http://earthtrends.wri.org/pdf_library/country_profiles/pop_cou_356.pdf.
4. An excellent source for more on the connection between television and politics in India is Arvind Rajagopal, *Politics after Television: Hindu Nationalism and the Reshaping of the Public in India* (Cambridge: Cambridge University Press, 2001).

5. For more, see Melissa Butcher, *Transnational Television, Cultural Identity and Change: When STAR Came to India* (New Delhi: Sage Publications, 2003).

6. For a brilliant analysis of the role of advertising in modernizing India, see William Mazzarella, *Shoveling Smoke: Advertising and Globalization in Contemporary India* (Durham and London: Duke University Press, 2003).

7. "The Indian Entertainment and Media Industry: Unraveling the Potential," report by FICCI and PricewaterhouseCoopers, March 2006, 12, http://www.pwc.com/extweb/pwcpublications.nsf/docid/BE7E56C3FF8E90A6CA257185006A3275/$file/Frames.pdf.

8. T. N. Ninan, "The Changing Indian Media Scene," *Seminar* 561 (May 2006): 15.

9. "Entertainment and Media," 26.

10. Rajdeep Sardesai, "Pushing the Boundaries," *Seminar* 561 (May 2006): 15.

11. "Entertainment and Media," 26.

12. Geoffrey A. Fowler, "Disney to Acquire India TV Channel Geared to Children," *Wall Street Journal,* July 27, 2006.

13. Melissa Marr, "Kids, Let's Exploit a Show," *Wall Street Journal,* May 19, 2006, B1.

14. Indiantelevision.com interview with Walt Disney Company (India) CEO Rajat Jain, August 30, 2005, www.indiantelevision.com/interviews/y2k5/executive/rajat_jain.htm.

15. Fowler, "Disney to Acquire."

16. Juliet B. Schor, *Born to Buy* (New York: Scribner, 2004), 9.

17. "USAID Brings *Sesame Street* to India," USAID press release, August 26, 2005. See also "Turner to Get Indian Kids Ready to POGO," Time Warner press release, November 24, 2003.

18. *Galli Galli Sim Sim (Sesame Street India),* USAID press release, March 8, 2006, http://www.usaid.gov./in/newsroom/press_releases/fs_galli.htm.

19. "Sesame Workshop and Turner Agree to Co-Produce *Sesame Street* in India," Sesame Workshop press release, January 17, 2004, http://www.sesameworkshop.org/aboutus/inside_press.php?contentId=13411483.

20. Indiantelevision.com interview with *Sesame Street India*'s Shaswati Banerjee, July 27, 2006, http://www.indiantelevision.com/interviews/y2k6/executive/sashwati_b.htm.

21. World Bank, "India at a Glance," June 21, 2006, http://devdata.worldbank.org/AAG/ind_aag.pdf.

22. Ryan Dilley, "Is Elmo Bush's Secret Weapon?" *BBC News Magazine,* September 3, 2003, http://news.bbc.co.uk/1/hi/magazine/3200699.stm.

23. Deborah Sontag, "I Want My Hyphenated-Identity MTV," *New York Times,* June 19, 2005.

24. "Mumbai Slum Dwellers' Sewage Project Goes Nationwide," *Bulletin of the World Health Organization* (2002): 684, http://www.who.int/bulletin/archives/80(8)News.pdf.

25. Alan Deutschman, "Attack of the Baby Pixars," *Fast Company* 101 (December 2005): 61.

26. Ibid.

27. "Animation and Gaming Industry Offers India Potential Growth,"

NASSCOM study, 2006, http://www.nasscom.in/Nasscom/templates/Normal Page.aspx?id=2004.

28. Ronnie Screwvala, "Chairman's Statement," UTVnet.com, http://www.prdomain.com/companies/N/NASSCOM/newsreleases/200611229795.htmj.

29. Aarti Razdon, "Indian Animation Industry—an Analysis," exchange4 media.com, 2004, http://www.exchange4media.com/e4m/izone1/izone_focus.asp?izonefocus_id=4.

30. Sukanya Verma, "*Hanuman* Is Good Fun," rediff.com, movies, October 21, 2005, http://in.rediff.com/movies/2005/oct/21hanuman.htm.

31. Madanmohan Rao, "Marketing to Youth? Get Mobile!" http://www.techsparks.com/Marketing-to-youth-get-mobile.html.

32. Cellular Operators Association of India statistics, http://www.coai.in/archives_statistics_2006_q2.htm. See also Asia Pacific Research Group report, 2006, http://www.aprg.com/; and "Connect Asia India Mobile Communications Report: Outlook to 2007," http://www.mindbranch.com/products/R330–0026.html.

33. "MobileYouth06," World Wireless Forum report, http://www.w2forum.com/i/mobileYouth06_part_one.

34. Figures from Pyramid Research BRICs Mobile Adoption Study, 2005, www.pyr.com.

35. "Information Economy Report 2005," UNCTAD, http://www.unctad.org/en/docs/sdteedc20051_en.pdf.

36. "Internet Usage in Asia," www.internetworldstats.com.

37. "Reliance Infocomm joins hands with LG Electronics to accelerate Internet penetration in India," Reliance Infocomm media release, July 23, 2006, http://www.relianceinfo.com/webapp/Infocomm/jsp/media/PressRelease.jsp?id=120.

38. "Women Lead Rural India's Internet Rush," BBC News online, July 7, 2006, http://news.bbc.co.uk/2/hi/south_asia/3871529.stm.

39. "India Online 2006," Juxt Consult report, cited in Sevanti Ninan, "Interactive Interplay," *Hindu,* July 16, 2006, http://www.hindu.com/mag/2006/07/16/stories/2006071600210300.htm.

40. Mark Glasser, "Indian Cities on Verge of Restricting Access to Cyber Cafes," *USC Annenberg Online Journalism Review,* December 4, 2003, www.ojr.org/ojr/glaser/1070576918.php.

41. "Israelis Fined for Wedding Kiss," BBC News, http://news.bbc.co.uk/1/hi/world/south_asia/4268058.stm.

42. Suresh Nambath, "Freedom at Stake . . . ," *Hindu,* November 27, 2005, http://www.hindu.com/mag/2005/11/27/stories/2005112700360100.htm.

43. "Is Rediff.com's Share Price Justified?" www.india.seekingalpha.com/article/14258. "India Online 2006," Juxt Consult report, cited in "Survey: Yahoo Top Portal, Shaadi and BM Tie in Matrimony," http://www.contentsutra.com/juxtconsult-user-preference-survey-yahoo-top-portal-shaadi-and-bm-tie-in-matrimony.

44. Study of Indian-American immigrants conducted in 2004 and 2005 by Paul Adams and Emily Skop, "Internet Use and Attitudes Toward Cultural Preser-

vation Among Asian Indians in the U.S.," University of Texas at Austin, Department of Geography and the Environment, www.utexas.edu/depts/grg/adams/356T/indianinternetsurvey.ppt.

45. For an excellent study of the anxieties of Indian-Americans around the question of race in the United States, see Vijay Prasad, *The Karma of Brown Folk* (Minneapolis: University of Minnesota Press, 2000).

46. Sarah McBride and Geoffrey A. Fowler, "Studios See Big Rise in Estimates of Losses to Movie Piracy," *Wall Street Journal,* May 3, 2006, B1.

47. Shriya Bubna, "*Pirates of Caribbean* Gets a Taste of Piracy," *Business Standard,* July 24, 2006, http://www.business-standard.com/common/storypage.php?autono=99137&leftnm=8&subLeft=0&chkFlg=.

48. Nate Anderson, "Movie Studios Expand Online Distribution, Still Forbid DVD Burning," *Ars Technica,* July 11, 2006, http://arstechnica.com/news.ars/post/20060711–7235.html.

49. Erika Morphy, "Hollywood Embraces Internet Movie Distribution," *Tech News World,* April 3, 2006, www.technewsworld.com/story/media-convergence/49729.html.

50. "Virgin Expands Entertainment Initiatives with the Formation of 'Virgin Comics' and 'Virgin Animation,'" Virgin Comics press release, January 6, 2006.

51. "Global Entertainment and Media Outlook, 2006–2010" (and 2005 edition), PricewaterhouseCoopers report, http://www.pwc.com/extweb/industry.nsf/docid/E7376CAA22C376408525662700504BD4; and Shekhar Kapur, quoted in "The Indian Entertainment Industry: The Next Success Story," November 24, 2003, http://www.weforum.org/en/knowledge/KN_SESS_SUMM_10232?url=/en/knowledge/KN_SESS_SUMM_10232.

Chapter Three: Retailing India

1. Anupam Goswami, "Conspicuous Consumers," *Business India,* April 9, 2006, 119.

2. Malini Bhupta, "Mall Mania," *India Today,* November 7, 2005, 11.

3. Ibid., 1.

4. *Inside Outside,* April 2006, 123.

5. Stephen Roach, "Here Comes the Indian Consumer," *Wall Street Journal,* November 9, 2005.

6. Stephen Roach, "In Search of Big Spenders," *Newsweek International,* September 3, 2006, http://www.msnbc.msn.com/id/1463748/site/newsweek/print/1/displaymode/1098/.

7. Peter Wonacott, "Wallets Crack Open in India," *Wall Street Journal,* January 3, 2006.

8. Ibid. Source: Federation of Indian Chamber of Commerce and Industry.

9. Wonacott, "Wallets Crack Open."

10. "Motorola Establishes India as Center for High-Growth Markets," on company Web site, http://www.motorola.com/content.jsp?globalObjectId=6988.

11. Sushmita Choudhury, "India Mobile," *India Today,* August 22, 2005, p. 29.

12. "Mobile Manufacturing: India Goes China's Way," India Brand Equity Foundation, http://ibef.org/download/mobiles.pdf.

13. "India's Laptop Sales Leap," United Press International, in PhysOrg.com, http://www.physorg.com/printnews.php?newsid=10165.
14. Siddharth Srivastava, "PC Market Heats Up in India," *Asia Times,* June 21, 2006, http://www.atimes.com/atimes/South_Asia/HF21Df02.html.
15. "India's Laptop Sales Leap."
16. Saritha Rai, "Dell to Double Indian Work Force and Seek Site for Factory," *International Herald Tribune,* March 21, 2006, http://www.iht.com/articles/2006/03/20/business/jobs.php.
17. "Annual PC Sales Grow 37%; Touch 2.3 Million Units," MAIT's Industry Performance Review, conducted by Indian Market Research Bureau, June 29, 2006. Full report available at http://www.imrbint.com/media/second-half.html.
18. Sumner Lemon, "Lenovo Gets Ready for Big India Push," IDG News Service, September 30, 2005, http://www.infoworld.com/article/05/09/30/HNlenovoindiapush_1.html.
19. Elizabeth Corcoran, "Booting Up India," *Forbes.com,* June 19, 2006, http://www.forbes.com/business/global/2006/0619/020.html.
20. Keith Bradsher, "The Ascent of Wind Power," *New York Times,* September 28, 2006, http://www.nytimes.com/2006/09/28/business/worldbusiness/28wind.html.
21. Naazneen Karmali, "Wind Man," *Forbes,* June 6, 2006, http://www.forbes.com/business/global/2006/0605/042.html.
22. Abdul Kalam, "Address at the Inauguration of the South Asian Conference of Renewable Energy," New Delhi, April 18, 2006, http://mnes.nic.in/president/splangnewPDF%2520Format758.pdf.
23. Karmali, "Wind Man."
24. Srivastava, "PC Market Heats Up in India." Much of the preceding is drawn from this article, which provides a wealth of detail about India's fast-expanding PC market.
25. "Ford Sales to Double in 2006; CNG Ikon by September," *Hindustan Times,* August 14, 2006, http://www.hindustantimes.com/news/181_1764341,0002.htm.
26. "GM Sales Jump 37 p.c.," http://www.hindu.com/2006/08/04/stories/2006080403961810.htm; and "General Motors to Invest $300 M in Maharashtra Car Plant" *Hindu,* August 4, 2006, http://www.hindu.com/2006/08/04/stories/2006080410301900.htm.
27. "Mahindra Ties Up with Renault—Joint Venture to Make Logan Cars in India," *Hindustan Business Line,* February 2, 2005.
28. Ravi Krishnan, "Car Capacity to Overtake UK, Canada," *Financial Express,* August 12, 2006, http://www.financialexpress.com/latest_full_story.php?content_id=137134.
29. R. Sridharan, "Still in the Driver's Seat," *India Today,* October 10, 2005, 14.
30. Report prepared by IBM Institute for Business Value and cited by the India Brand Equity Fund (IBEF) in "Consumer Markets," http://www.ibef.org/economy/consumermarket.aspx.
31. Roach, "Here Comes the Indian Consumer."
32. Kala Rao, "Reflection on Credit Risk," *Banker,* July 3, 2006, http://www.thebanker.com/news/fullstory.php/aid/4090/Reflections_on_credit_risk.html.

33. Sarbajeet Sen, "Banks Gear Up to Curb Education Loan Defaulters—Notations on Mark Sheets, Bar Coding Passports Likely," *Business Line,* December 4, 2005, http://www.thehindubusinessline.com/2005/12/05/stories/2005120502660100.htm.

34. "Building up India: Outlook for India's Real Estate Markets," report prepared by Deutsche Bank Research, May 8, 2006, http://www.dbresearch.com.

35. Ibid.

36. "Concepts and Definitions," Census of India, http://www.censusindia.net/2001housing/metadata.pdf#search=%22good%20livable%20dilapidated%20dwellings%20india%20definition%22.

37. Yasir A. Pitalwalla, "Indian Real Estate: Boom or Bust?" CNNMoney.com, July 5, 2006, http://money.cnn.com/magazines/fortune/fortune_archive/2006/07/10/8380919/index.htm.

38. "Atria Mall: Court Wants Answers from State, BMC," *Daily News & Analysis,* July 18, 2006, http://cities.expressindia.com/fullstory.php?newsid=193416.

39. "Air Deccan Offers Lower Fares," *Hindu,* January 23, 2005, http://www.hinduonnet.com/2005/01/23/stories/2005012303410300.htm.

40. "Air Deccan Launches Daily Flight Service to Kochi," *Hindu,* September 27, 2005, http://www.hindu.com/2005/09/27/stories/2005092717640300.htm.

41. "Air Deccan to Fly to Kochi Soon," *Hindu,* September 15, 2005, http://www.hindu.com/2005/09/15/stories/2005091503901900.htm.

42. Zubair Ahmed, "Branson in India-Wide Flights Bid," BBC News/South Asia, March 31, 2005, http://news.bbc.co.uk/2/low/south_asia/4397133.stm.

43. Praful Patel, "Aviation Sector—An Overview," Press Information Bureau, Government of India, August 1, 2006.

44. "World Wealth Report 2005," prepared by Merrill Lynch and Capgemini: Consulting Technology Outsourcing report available online http://www.ml.com/media/48237.pdf.

45. "At the Top: The List of Indians in the Richest List Is on the Rise," *Business India,* April 9, 2006, 42–46.

46. Sunil Jain, "53,000 Crorepatis by Next Year," Rediff.com, July 17, 2004, http://www.rediff.com/money/2004/jul/17rich.htm.

47. Beverage Market Corporation: Coca-Cola Company 2005 Report, http://www.beveragemarketing.com/multiplebeverageasiagr.htm.

48. "A Nation of Snackers: Branded Snacks Now the Fastest Growing FMCG Category in India," ACNielsen Trends & Insights Regional Market Report, June 2005, http://www2.acnielsen.com/news/20050600_in.shtml.

49. Ratna Bhushan, "Frito-Lay to Serve Desi Snacks," *Hindu Business Line,* November 2, 2002, http://www.thehindubusinessline.com/2002/11/08/stories/2002110802780100.htm.

50. Sushmita Choudhury, "An Appetizing Future," *India Today,* May 15, 2006, 25.

51. John Larkin and Eric Bellamy, "Reliance to Invest $750 Million in Indian Retailing," *Wall Street Journal,* January 24, 2006, http://online.wsj.com/article_print/SB113805841617554065.html.

52. Michael Barbaro, "Wal-Mart Profit Falls 26%, Its First Drop in Ten Years," *New York Times,* August 16, 2006.
53. Ibid.
54. "Wal-Mart Deepens India Focus," *Economic Times,* August 14, 2006, http://economictimes.indiatimes.com/articleshow/1891029.cms.
55. Stephen Greenhouse, "Suit Says Wal-Mart Is Lax on Labor Abuse Overseas," *New York Times,* September 14, 2005.
56. Adam Nagourney and Michael Barbaro, "Eye on Elections, Democrats Run as the Wal-Mart Foe," *New York Times,* August 17, 2006, http://www.nytimes.com/2006/08/17/washington/17dems.html?ex=1157860800&en=f81347ea7c40f3bc&ei=5070.
57. Ibid.
58. "New Report Details Wal-Mart's Labor Abuse and Hidden Costs," press release, Congressman George Miller, Committee on Education & the Workforce, U.S. House of Representatives, February 16, 2004, http://edworkforce.house.gov/democrats/releases/rel21604.html.

Chapter Four: 600,000 Villages

1. "Seeds of Suicides: India's Desperate Farmers," *Frontline/World,* PBS, July 26, 2005, http://www.pbs.org/frontlineworld/rough/2005/07/seeds_of_suicid.html.
2. http://andolan.blogspot.com.
3. "Monsanto Company to Acquire Delta and Pine Land Company for $1.5 Billion in Cash," *PR Newswire,* August 15, 2006, http://www.monsanto.com/monsanto/layout/media/06/08-15-06.asp.
4. Madhav Gadgil and Ramachandra Guha, *Ecology and Equity* (London: Routledge, 1995), 4.
5. Vivek Deshpande, "I Know the Pain You Are Going Through," *Indian Express,* July 1, 2006, http://www.indianexpress.com/story/7638.html.
6. Somini Sengupta, "On India's Farms, a Plague of Suicides," *New York Times,* September 19, 2006, http://www.nytimes.com/2006/09/19/world/asia/19india.html?_r=1&n=Top%2fReference%2fTimes%20Topics%2fPeople%2fS%2fSengupta%2c%20Somini&oref=slogin.
7. Alex Kuffner, "Water Crisis Deepens India's Rural-Urban Rift," *Providence Journal,* August 20, 2006.
8. Pratap Ravindran, "India's Water Economy—World Bank Prescription Does Not Hold Water," *Hindu Business Online,* November 10, 2005, http://www.thehindubusinessline.com/2005/10/11/stories/2005101100691000.htm.
9. M. Dinesh Kumar and Tushaar Shah, "Groundwater Pollution and Contamination in India: The Emerging Challenge," IWMI, South Asia Regional Programme.
10. Nafisa Barot, *Cross-Cutting Issues: A Gandhian Approach* (paper presented at the International Dialogue on "Water for Food and Environment," Hanoi, Vietnam. Unpublished paper in author's possession).
11. Ibid., 3.
12. Gaby Hinsliff, "£3.68 Trillion: The Price of Failing to Act on Climate Change:

Landmark Report Reveals Apocalyptic Cost of Global Warming," *Observer,* October 29, 2006, http://observer.guardian.co.uk/print/0,,329613556-102285,00.html.

13. "Global Temperature Highest in Millennia," Associated Press, in *Washington Post,* September 25, 2006, http://www.washingtonpost.com/wp-dyn/content/article/2006/09/25/AR2006092500786_pf.html.

14. Al Gore, *An Inconvenient Truth: The Planetary Emergency of Global Warming and What We Can Do About It* (Emmaus, Pa.: Rodale, 2006), 206.

15. "Weather, Climate, Water and Sustainable Development," message from Mr. M. Jarraud, secretary-general, World Meteorological Organization, http://www.wmo.ch/web/Press/wmd-mes2005_E.doc.

16. "The Heat Is On: A Special Report on Climate Change, *Economist,* September 9–15, 2006, 6.

17. Robin McKie, "Millions Face Glacier Catastrophe: Global Warming Hits Himalayas," Sunday Observer, *Guardian,* November 20, 2005, http://observer.guardian.co.uk/international/story/0,6903,1646656,00.html.

18. "Pesticides Pollution: Trends and Perspectives," *ICMR Bulletin,* 31, no. 9 (September 2001), http://www.icmr.nic.in/bulletin.htm.

19. Jitendra Joshi, "US Warns India of Investment Fallout from Coke-Pepsi Row," Yahoo!News, August 13, 2006, http://uk.news.yahoo.com/13082006/323/warns-india-investment-fallout-coke-pepsi-row.html.

20. Amelia Gentleman, "Pesticide Charge in India Hurts Pepsi and Coke," *New York Times,* August 22, 2006, http://www.nytimes.com/2006/08/22/business/22cnd-coke.html?ex=1158120000&en=766036efc9086255&ei=5070.

21. Shilpa Kannan, "Pepsi and Coke under Fire," BBC Online, August 2, 2006, http://news.bbc.co.uk/2/hi/south_asia/523978.stm.

22. For years Enron was mired in a much contested construction of a power plant near Dabhol, Maharashtra, that became somewhat of a boondoggle. Stakeholders GE and Bechtel filed claims against the government of India. Saritha Rai, "India: Dhabol Claims," World Business Briefing: Asia, *New York Times,* September 23, 2003, http://query.nytimes.com/gst/fullpage.html?res=9B02E3D61F3AF930A1575AC0A9659C8B63.

23. "Clouds of Injustice: Bhopal Disaster 20 Years On," Amnesty International, 2004, http://web.amnesty.org/pages/ec-bhopal-eng.

24. Devender K. Bumbla, "Agriculture Practices and Nitrate Pollution of Water," West Virginia University Extension Service, http://www.caf.wvu.edu/~forage/nitratepollution/nitrate.htm.

25. "Natural Gas: Domestic Nitrogen Fertilizer Production Depends on Natural Gas," United States General Accounting Office, September 2003, http://www.gao.gov/new.items/d031148.pdf.

26. "The Picture in India," UNICEF, http://www.unicef.org/india/nutrition.html.

27. Sarita Rai, "India to Import Wheat after a 6-Year Hiatus," *International Herald Tribune,* June 30, 2006.

28. Gargi Parsai, "Wal-Mart, Monsanto on Indo-U.S. Agriculture Initiative Board," *Hindu,* February 10, 2006, http://www.hindu.com/2006/02/10/stories/2006021007771200.htm.

29. K. S. Jayaraman, "UW-Indian Agbiotech Deal under Scrutiny," *Nature*

Biotechnology, May 1, 2006, http://www.nature.com/news/2006/060501/full/nbt0506–481.html.

30. "US Rice Farmers Sue Bayer Crop Science over GM Rice," Reuters, August 28, 2006, http://today.reuters.com/News/CrisesArticle.aspx?storyId=N8S 372113.

31. From the MSSRF Web site at http://mssfr.org/about_us/about_us.htm.

32. "Swaminathan Moots Evergreen Revolution," *Deccan Herald,* January 5, 2006.

33. Asha Krishnakumar, "A Human-Centric Concept," *Frontline,* 17, no. 5 (March 4–17, 2000), http://www.hinduonnet.com/fline/fl1705/17051170.htm.

34. "Swami for 2nd Green Revolution in Drylands," *Financial Express* (Mumbai), July 16, 2006, http://www.financialexpress.com/fe_full_story.php?content_id=134182.

35. See the excellent study by Jeffrey Whitsoe, "India's Second Green Revolution? The Sociopolitical Implications of Corporate-led Agricultural Growth," *India in Transition: Economics and Politics of Change,* ed., Deresh Kapua, Center for the Advanced Study of India, University of Pennsylvania, Fall 2006.

36. Ravi Anupindi and S. Sivakumar, "ITC's e-Choupal: A Platform Strategy for Rural Transformation" (paper presented at Business Solutions for Alleviating Poverty [BSAP] Conference, Social Enterprise Institute, Harvard Business School, December 1–3, 2005. Given to me by S. Sivakumar).

37. Ibid., 2.

38. Anand Giridharadas, "Growing in India: Food for the World," *International Herald Tribune,* May 31, 2006.

39. Ibid.

40. Ibid.

41. This was one of the themes of my book *Motiba's Tattoos: A Granddaughter's Journey from America into Her Indian Family's Past* (New York: Plume, 2001).

Chapter Five: The Cities

1. Population Division of the Department of Economic and Social Affairs of the United Nations Secretariat, 2004, http://www.unpopulation.org.

2. Ehtasham Khan, "UN Flays India for Slum Demolition," Rediff.com, March 30, 2005, http://in.rediff.com/cms/print.jsp?docpath=//news/2005/mar/30un.html.

3. A copy of the prime minister's speech is available on the Web site of the Jawaharlal Nehru National Urban Renewal Mission at http://pmindia.nic.in/speech/content.asp?id=235.

4. "India: Environmental Issues," Country Analysis Briefs, Energy Information Administration, U.S. Department of Energy, http://www.eia.doe.gov/emeu/cabs/indiaenv.html.

5. Tara Sahgal, "Urban Emergency," *TimeOut Mumbai,* August 26, 2005, 25.

6. Jo Johnson, "A 'Maximum City' at Its Limits: Why Mumbai's Best Hope Lies in Building Anew," *Financial Express,* August 26, 2006.

7. R. Padmanabhan, "The Shiv Sena Indicted," *Frontline* 15, no. 17 (August 15–28, 1998), http://www.hinduonnet.com/fline/fl1517/15170200.htm.

8. Dileep Padgaonkar, ed., *When Bombay Burned* (UBSCD, January 1993).

9. Anupama Katakam, "All for the Builder," *Frontline* 23, no. 6 (March 25–April 7, 2006), http://www.hinduonnet.com/fline/fl2306/stories/20060 407003003800.htm.

10. "Bombay Faces Population Boom," BBC News, December 30, 2000, http://news.bbc.co.uk/2/hi/south_asia/1093424.stm.

11. The best portrait of Bombay in all its lovable and detestable extremes is Suketu Mehta's *Maximum City: Bombay Lost and Found* (New York: Knopf, 2005).

12. Sumit Bhattacharya, "Mumbai 2020: Dream or Nightmare?" Rediff.com, January 17, 2005.

13. *Financial Express,* October 7, 2004, cited in Nikhil Anand, "Disconnecting Experience: Making World-Class Roads in Mumbai" (paper presented at the Breslauer Symposium: The Right to the City and the Politics of Space, University of California, Berkeley, April 14, 2006).

14. "US-India Strategic Economic Partnership," US-India CEO Forum, March 2006. The report is available on the government of India's Planning Commission's Web site at http://planningcommission.nic.in/reports/genrep/USIndia .pdf#search=%22mumbai%20financial%20capital%20us%20india%20ceos %22.

15. Kavitha Iyer, "Dubai, Korea Firms Eye New Dharavi Pie," Expressindia.com, June 18, 2006, http://cities.expressindia.com/fullstory.php?newsid=188563.

16. Smita Deshmukh, "Dharavi Slum Is Now Realty Gold Mine," *Daily News & Analysis,* January 30, 2006, http://www.dnaindia.com/dnaPrint.asp?News ID=1010214&CatID=1.

17. From section "Uniqueness of SEZ in India" on the CIDCO (City and Industrial Development Corporation of Maharashtra Ltd.) Web site, http:// cidcoindia.com/sez.htm.

18. Jo Johnson, "India Warned on Tax Breaks for Industry," *Financial Times,* September 2–3, 2006, 5.

19. See the Pratham Web site, www.pratham.org.

20. Nandini Raghavendra and Gouri Shah, "Make Your Road to Harvard Easier," *Economic Times* online, April 19, 2005, http://economictimes .indiatimes.com/articleshow/msid-1081428,prtpage-1.cms.

21. "Global Campaign for Education: More Teachers Needed," UNICEF India, http://www.unicef.org/india/education_1551.htm.

22. India Tourism newsletter, June 2006, http://evalu8.org/staticpage?page= review&siteid=10207.

23. "Delhi to Become World-Class City in Run Up to Commonwealth Games: CM," Tribune News Service, January 25, 2006, www.tribuneindia.com/ 2006/20060126/delhi.htm#3.

24. For an account of these arrivals in Delhi and the other fast-growing megacities of the developing world, see Mike Davis, *Planet of Slums* (New York: Verso, 2006).

25. Randeep Ramesh, "Poor Squeezed Out by Mumbai's Dream Plan," *Guardian,* March 1, 2005. A report by Miloon Kothari, UN special rapporteur on adequate housing, in the UN *Chronicle;* online edition is available at http:// www.un.org/Pubs/chronicle/2006/issue1/0106p44.html.

26. William Dalrymple, *The Last Mughal: The Eclipse of a Dynasty, Delhi 1857* (London: Bloomsbury, 2006). For a wonderful memoir of a year in Delhi intercut with a fantastic voyage into Delhi's history, see Dalrymple's *City of Djinns: A Year in Delhi* (London: HarperCollins, 1994; London: Penguin, 2003).

27. Sanjay K. Singh, "Review of Urban Transportation in India," *Journal of Public Transportation* 8, no. 1 (2005): 85.

28. J. B. D'Souza, "New Bombay," *TimeOut Mumbai*, July 29-August 11, 2005, 24.

29. Johnson, "A 'Maximum City'."

Chapter Six: The Other India

1. For a brilliant analysis of Indian society, including the issue of status, see Pavan K. Varma, *Being Indian: The Truth about Why the 21st Century Will Be India's* (New Delhi and New York: Penguin, 2004).

2. Christophe Jaffrelot, "The Impact of Affirmative Action in India: More Political than Socioeconomic," *India Review* 5, no. 2 (April 2006): 173–89.

3. Praful Bidwai, "Bringing the Caste-aways on Board," *Asia Times,* June 2, 2006, http://www.atimes.com/atimes/South_Asia/HF02Df01.html.

4. Sudha Ramachandran, "The Die Is Caste for Corporate India," *Asia Times,* April 29, 2006, http://www.atimes.com/atimes/South_Asia/HD29Df04.html.

5. "'We Have No Orders to Save You': State Participation and Complicity in Communal Violence in Gujarat, India," *Human Rights Watch* 14, no. 3 (April 2002).

6. Daniel Golden, "New Battleground in Textbook Wars: Religion in History," *Wall Street Journal,* January 25, 2006, http://online.wsj.com/public/article/SB113815619665855532-q_QXocYrPdQxU5EI7lCdSziI1xw_2006 0203.html?mod=blogs; and Sudarshan Padmanaban, "Debate on Indian History: Revising Textbooks in California," *Economic and Political Weekly,* May 6, 2006, http://www.epw.org.in/showArticles.php?root=2006&leaf=05&filename=10046&filetype=html.

7. Alex Perry, "Bloody Monday: As Bombay suffers the latest in a string of deadly bomb blasts, suspicions focus on domestic Muslim terrorists enraged by Hindu nationalism," *Time Asia,* September 1, 2001, http://www.time.com/time/asia/magazine/printout/0,13675,501030908-480330,00.html.

8. "India: Impunity Fuels Conflict in Jammu and Kashmir; Abuses by Indian Army and Militants Continue, With Perpetrators Unpunished." *Human Rights Watch,* September12, 2006, http://hrw.org/english/docs/2006/09/08/india14159.htm.

9. Somini Sengupta, "Death Sentence in Terror Attack Puts India on Trial," *New York Times,* October 10, 2006. http://travel2.nytimes.com/2006/10/10/world/asia/10india/html?fta=y.

10. Philip Sherson and Mark Mazzetti, "Study of Iraq War and Terror Stirs Strong Political Response," *New York Times,* September 25, 2006, http://www.nytimes.com/2006/09/25/world/middleeast/25terror.html.

11. Chris Hedges, *War Is a Force That Gives Us Meaning* (New York: Anchor Books, 2002), 9.

12. Estimates of the number of child laborers vary widely, from 14 million to 100 million, chiefly because this is so difficult to measure. See Vipin Bihari, "The Scourge of Child Labour in India," Finnish Institute of Occupational Health, http://www.ttl.fi/Internet/English/Information/Electronic+journals/Asian-Pacific +Newsletter/2000-02/04.htm. See also UNDP's India report at http://www .undp.org.in/report/POSITION/CCA.htm.

13. I have changed Sumati's name to protect her privacy. Her story was provided to me by Rema Nanda, director, Public Health-HIV/AIDS Program, New York, American India Foundation, from unpublished reports of examples where AIF-supported programs are affecting lives. I am very grateful to Rema for sharing this account with me.

14. United States National Intelligence Council, "The Next Wave of HIV/AIDS: Nigeria, Ethiopia, Russia, India, and China," 2002.

15. Nicholas Eberstat, "The Future of AIDS," *Foreign Affairs*, 2002.

16. Amelia Gentleman, "India: Report Says AIDS Could Slow Economy," *New York Times*, July 21, 2006.

17. "HIV/AIDS in India," *HIV/AIDS Policy Fact Sheet*, Henry I. Kaiser Foundation, September 2006.

18. Dr. Sanjay Pujari, in "TREAT Asia Site Profile: Ruby Hall Clinic, Pune, India," Therapeutics Research Education AIDS Training, *TREAT Asia Report* 4, no. 1 (February 2006).

19. Talk given at American India Foundation headquarters, New York City, July 20, 2006.

20. Smita Jain, "Bringing the Virus Home," *Hindu*, November 27, 2005.

21. Jonathan Allen, "Indian Firms Waking Up to HIV Threat," Reuters, July 14, 2006, http://today.reuters.com/news/articlenews.aspx?type=healthNews& storyID=2006-07-14T121203Z_01_DEL89591_RTRUKOC_0_US-INDIA-HIV.xml.

22. Swami Agnivesh, Rama Mani, and Angelika Koster-Lossack, "Missing: 50 Million Indian Girls," *International Herald Tribune*, November 25, 2005, www.iht.com/articles/2005/11/24/opinion/edswami.php. French demographer Christophe Guilmoto disputes this, putting the number at a still disturbing 40 million.

23. Patricia Liedl, "Silent Spring: The Tragedy of India's Never-Born Girls," United Nations Population Fund Web site, http://www.unfpa.org/news/ news.cfm?ID=690.

24. U.S. Department of Labor, Bureau of International Labor Affairs, "India: Incidence and Nature of Child Labor," http://www.dol.gov/ilab/media/ reports/iclp/tda2004/india.htm.

25. "Anti-Trafficking—Save Our Sisters Movement (SOS)," Save the Children India, http://www.savethechildrenindia.com/antitrafficking.htm.

26. Nicholas D. Kristof, "Slavery in Our Time," *New York Times*, January 22, 2006, http://select.nytimes.com/2006/01/22/opinion/22kristof.html.

27. "Improving Women's Health in India," a summary of the World Bank publication, http://www.worldbank.org/html/extdr/hnp/population/iwhindia.htm.

28. From "Arogya Raksha Yojana: Insuring Affordable Healthcare," a publication of the Arogya Raksha Yojana Trust, Bangalore, India.

29. Amitabh Avasthi, "Polio Making Rapid Comeback, Poses Epidemic Risk, Scientists Say," *National Geographic News*, September 12, 2006, http://news .nationalgeographic.com/news/2006/09/060912-polio.html.

30. "Avian Influenza," updated May 18, 2006, Embassy of the United States, New Delhi, Web site, http://newdelhi.usembassy.gov/acsinfluenze.html.

31. Krysten Crawford, "Medical Tourism Agencies Take Operations Overseas," *CNN Money*, August 3, 2006, http://money.cnn.com/2006/08/02/magazines/ business2/medicaltourism.biz2/index.htm.

Chapter Seven: Power

1. For an outstanding essay on the 1998 tests, see Amitav Ghosh's *Countdown* (Delhi: Ravi Dayal, 1999).

2. Stockholm International Peace Research Institute, *SIPRI Yearbook 2006: Armaments, Disarmaments and International Security* (London: Oxford University Press, 2006), 477–80.

3. Thom Shankar, "Russia Led Arms Sales to Developing World in '05," *New York Times*, October 29, 2006, http://www.nytimes.com/2006/10/29/world/ europe/29weapons.html?th&emc=th.

4. See Sumit Ganguly, *Conflict Unending: India-Pakistan Relations Since 1947* (New York: Columbia University Press, 2002).

5. For a firsthand account of this period, see Strobe Talbott, *Engaging India: Diplomacy, Democracy, and the Bomb* (Washington, D.C.: The Brookings Institution, 2004).

6. President Bill Clinton, Remarks by the U.S. President Bill Clinton to the Joint Session of Indian Parliament, March 22, 2000, New Delhi, India, http:// www.indianembassy.org/indusrel/clinton_india/clinton_parliament_march_ 22_2000.htm.

7. I owe much insight into the early history of the George W. Bush administration and India to Jonah Blank, professional staff member, Committee on Foreign Relations, U.S. Senate.

8. Aziz Haniffa, "U.S. Congressman vows to scuttle nuclear deal," Rediff.com, March 3, 2006, http://www.rediff.com/news/2006/mar/03bush10.htm.

9. George Perkovich, *India's Nuclear Bomb: The Impact on Global Proliferation* (Berkeley: University of California Press, 1999).

10. George Perkovich, "Faulty Promises: The U.S.-India Nuclear Deal," Carnegie Endowment for International Peace, September 2005, www.carnegie endowment.org/files/PO21.Perkovich.pdf.

11. Glenn Kessler, "Nunn Urges Congress to Set Conditions on U.S.-Indian Nuclear Pact," *Washington Post*, March 21, 2006, A09.

12. T. V. Padma, "Indian Scientists Oppose U.S. Changes to Nuclear Deal," SciDev.net, August 15, 2006, http://www.scidev.net/News/index.cfm?fuse action=readNews&itemid=3049&language=1.

13. Carol Giacomo, "U.S. Sanctions Two India Firms for Transfers to Iran," Reuters, Washingtonpost.com, July 27, 2006, http://www.washingtonpost .com/wp-dyn/content/article/2006/07/27/AR200672701152_pf.html.

14. Somini Sengupta; Hari Kumar contributing reporting, "A Test of Friendship

for India's Leader," *New York Times,* July 24, 2006, http://select.nytimes
.com/search/restricted/article?res=F40D10F83F5B0C778EDDAE0894DE40
4482.

15. Ibid.

16. "India Blames U.S. for Failure of WTO Talks," *Hindu,* July 26, 2006,
http://www.hindu.com/2006/07/26/stories/2006072607061200.htm.

17. Manmohan Singh, statement by the prime minister at the XIV NAM Summit,
Havana, Cuba, September 15, 2006, press release, embassy of India,
http://www.indianembassy.org/newsite/press_release/2006/Sept/5.asp.

18. Manmohan Singh, "Prime Minister's Speech at the Plenary IBSA Meeting,"
Brasília, September 13, 2006, http://www.indianembassy.org/newsite/press_
release/2006/Sept/4.asp.

19. Won-Jae Park, "India Steps Up in the Competition for Russian Oil," *Energy
Bulletin,* February 4, 2005, http://www.energybulletin.net/4246.html.

20. Jehangir S. Pocha, "China and India on Verge of Nuclear Deal," *Boston
Globe,* November 20, 2006, http://www.boston.com/news/world/asia/
articles/2006/11/20/china_and_india_on_verge_of_nuclear_deal/; and Mark
Sappenfield and David Montero, "China Woos India and Pakistan with
Nuclear Know-How," *Christian Science Monitor,* November 21, 2006,
http://www.csmonitor.com/2006/1121/-012-2-woap.html.

21. Sappenfield and Montero, "China Woos India and Pakistan with Nuclear
Know-How."

22. Chidhanand Rajghatta, "Aging IAF Shoots Down USAF Top Guns," *Times
of India,* June 18, 2004, http://timesofindia.indiatimes.com/article
show/745557.cms.

Conclusion: As Goes India, So Goes the World

1. Leslie Wayne, "Foreign Sales by U.S. Arms Makers Doubled in a Year, *New
York Times,* November 11, 2006, http://www.nytimes.com/2006/11/11/
business/11military.html?ex=1320901200&en=89a9de2e9f22613b&ei=508
8&partner=rssnyt&emc=rss. I would also like to thank my longtime col-
league at the World Policy Institute, Bill Hartung, quoted in this article, for
his insights on U.S. weapons sales.

Selected Bibliography

Bakshi, Rajni. *Bapu Kuti: Journeys in Rediscovery of Gandhi*. New Delhi: Penguin Books, 1998.

Bhagat, Chetan. *One Night @ The Call Center*. New Delhi: Rupa, 2005.

Breckenridge, Carol, Sheldon Pollack, Homi K. Bhabha, Dipesh Chakrabarty, eds. *Cosmopolitanism*. Durham: Duke University Press, 2002.

Butcher, Melissa. *Transnational Television, Cultural Identity and Change: When STAR Came to India*. New Delhi: Sage Publications, 2003.

Calasso, Roberto. *Ka: Stories of the Mind and Gods of India*. New York: Alfred A. Knopf, 1998.

Cohen, Stephen Philip. *India : Emerging Power*. Washington, D.C.: Brookings Institution Press, 2001.

Diamond, Jared. *Collapse: How Societies Choose to Fail or Succeed*. New York: Viking, 2005.

Frankel, Francine, Zoya Hassan, Rajeev Bhargava, Balveer Arora, eds. *Transforming India: Social and Political Dynamics of Democracy*. New Delhi: Oxford University Press, 2000.

Fraser, Arvonne S. and Irene Tinker, eds. *Developing Power: How Women Transformed International Development*. New York: The Feminist Press, 2004.

Friedman, Thomas L. *The World Is Flat: A Brief History of the Twenty-First Century*. New York: Farrar, Straus and Giroux, 2005.

Gadgil, Madhav and Ramachandra Guha. *This Fissured Land: An Ecological History of India*. Berkeley: University of California Press, 1992.

Gandhi, M. K. *Hind Swaraj and Other Writings*. Anthony J. Parel, ed. New York: Cambridge University Press, 1997.

Ganguly, Sumit. *Conflict Unending: India-Pakistan Tensions Since 1947*. New York: Columbia University Press, 2001.

George, Abraham M. *India Untouched: The Forgotton Face of Rural Poverty*. Cranston, RI: The Writers' Collective, 2005.

Gore, Albert. *An Inconvenient Truth: The Planetary Emergency of Global Warming and What We Can Do About It*. New York: Rodale Books, 2006.

Guha, Ramachandra. *The Ramachandra Guha Omnibus*. New Delhi: Oxford University Press, 2005.

Hedges, Chris. *War is a Force that Gives Us Meaning*. New York: Anchor Books, 2002.

Hira, Ron and Anil Hira. *Outsourcing America: What's Behind our National Crisis and How We Can Reclaim American Jobs*. New York: AMACOM Books, 2005.

Jaffrelot, Christophe. *The Hindu Nationalist Movement in India*. New York: Columbia University Press, 1998.

Jayakar, Pupul. *The Earth Mother: Legends, Ritual Arts, and Goddesses of India*. New York: Harper and Row, 1990.

Kabir. *The Weaver's Songs*. Vinay Dharwadker, trans. New Delhi: Penguin Books, 2003.

Kakar, Sudhir. *The Colors of Violence: Cultural Identities, Religion, and Conflict*. Chicago: University of Chicago Press, 1996.

Kapur, Sudharshan. *Raising Up a Prophet: The African-American Encounter with Gandhi*. Boston: Beacon Press, 1992.

Khilnani, Sunil. *The Idea of India*. New York: Farrar, Straus and Giroux, 1997.

Kohli, Atul. *Democracy and Discontent: India's Growing Crisis of Governability*. Cambridge: Cambridge University Press, 1990.

Kolbert, Elizabeth. *Field Notes from a Catastrophe: Man, Nature, and Climate Change*. New York: Bloomsbury, 2006.

Krepon, Michael, ed. *Nuclear Risk Reduction in South Asia*. New York: Palgrave Macmillan, 2004.

Lewis, Michael. *The New, New Thing: A Silicon Valley Story*. New York: W. W. Norton, 2000.

Mazzarella, William. *Shoveling Smoke: Advertising and Globalization in Contemporary India*. Durham: Duke University Press, 2003.

McLuhan, Marshall. *Understanding Media: The Extensions of Man*. Cambridge, Ma.: MIT Press, 1994.

Mehta, Suketu. *Maximum City: Bombay Lost and Found*. New York: Alfred A. Knopf, 2004.

Mishra, Pankaj. *The Temptations of the West: How to be Modern in India, Pakistan, Tibet, and Beyond*. New York: Farrar, Straus and Giroux, 2006.

Mitchell, Stephen. *Bhagavad Gita: A New Translation*. New York: Three Rivers Press, 2000.

Mohan, C. Raja. *Crossing the Rubicon: The Shaping of India's New Foreign Policy*. New Delhi: Viking, 2003.

Nye, Joseph S., Jr. *Soft Power: The Means to Success in World Politics*. New York: Public Affairs, 2004.

Pearce, Fred. *When Rivers Run Dry: Water—The Defining Crisis of the Twenty-First Century*. Boston: Beacon Press, 2006.

Perkovich, George. *India's Nuclear Bomb: The Impact on Global Proliferation*. Berkeley: University of California Press, 1999.

Prahalad, C. K. *The Fortune at the Bottom of the Pyramid: Eradicating Poverty through Profits*. Upper Saddle River, N.J.: Pearson Education; Wharton School Publishing, 2005.

Prashad, Vijay. *The Karma of Brown Folk*. Minneapolis: University of Minnesota Press, 2000.

Prestowitz, Clyde. *Three Billion New Capitalists: The Great Shift of Wealth and Power to the East*. New York: Basic Books, 2005.

Rajagopal, Arvind. *Politics after Television: Hindu Nationalism and the Reshaping of the Public in India*. New York: Cambridge University Press, 2001.

Roy, Arundhati. *The Cost of Living*. New York: Modern Library, 1999.

———. *Power Politics*. Cambridge, Ma.: South End Press, 2001.

Rushdie, Salman. *Imaginary Homelands: Essays and Criticism 1981–1991*. London: Granta Books, 1991.

Schor, Juliet B. *Born to Buy*. New York: Scribner, 2004.

Seabrook, Jeremy. *In the Cities of the South: Scenes from a Developing World*. London: Verso, 1996.

Sen, Amartya. *Development as Freedom*. New York: Alfred A. Knopf, 1999.

———. *Identity and Violence: The Illusion of Destiny*. New York: W. W. Norton, 2006.

———. *Poverty and Famines: An Essay on Entitlement and Deprivation*. New York: Oxford University Press, 1983.

Sen, Amartya and Jean Drèze. *India: Development and Participation*. New York: Oxford University Press, 2002.

———. *India: Economic Development and Social Opportunity*. New York: Oxford University Press, 1999.

Shiva, Vandana. *India Divided: Diversity and Democracy under Attack*. New York: Seven Stories Press, 2005.

Singh, Jaswant. *Defending India*. New Delhi: Macmillan India, 1999.

Stiglitz, Joseph E. *Making Globalization Work*. New York: W. W. Norton, 2006.

Takaki, Ronald. *Strangers from a Different Shore: A History of Asian Americans*. Boston: Back Bay Books, 1998.

Talbott, Strobe. *Engaging India: Diplomacy, Democracy, and the Bomb*. Washington, D.C.: Brookings Institution Press, 2004.

Tharoor, Shashi. *India: From Midnight to the Millennium*. New York: Arcade, 1997.

Uchitelle, Louis. *The Disposable American: Layoffs and Their Consequences*. New York: Alfred A. Knopf, 2006.

Vandarajan, Siddharth, ed. *Gujarat: The Making of a Tragedy*. New Delhi: Penguin Books, 2002.

Varma, Pavan. K. *Being Indian*. New Delhi: Penguin Books, 2004.

Wolpert, Stanley. *A New History of India*. New York: Oxford University Press, 2003.

Yagnik, Achyut and Suchitra Sheth. *The Shaping of Modern Gujarat: Plurality, Hindutva and Beyond*. New Delhi: Penguin Books, 2005.

Index

About the Author

Mira Kamdar, an Associate Fellow of the Asia Society, has commented on India for such outlets as the BBC, CNN, NPR, *International Herald Tribune,* and *Los Angeles Times.* The award-winning author of a memoir about her Indian family, *Motiba's Tattoos,* she lives in New York with her husband and two children.